SCHOOL OF ORIENTAL AND AFRICAN STUDIES

THE BUDDHIST FORUM

VOLUME IV

THE BUDDHIST FORUM

VOLUME IV

Seminar Papers 1994-1996

edited by
Tadeusz Skorupski
Senior Lecturer in Buddhist Studies
School of Oriental and African Studies
University of London

HERITAGE

HERITAGE PUBLISHERS
New Delhi India

SCHOOL OF ORIENTAL AND AFRICAN STUDIES
UNIVERSITY OF LONDON
1996

Published by the School of Oriental and African Studies
(University of London), Thornhaugh Street, Russell Square,
London WC1H 0XG

Published in India by Heritage Publishers,
4C Ansari Road, Daryaganj, New Delhi 1100032

British Library Cataloguing in Publication Data
The Buddhist forum. Vol. IV
1. Buddhism
1. University of London. *School of Oriental and African Studies*
294.3

81-7026-198-8

Printed at Neeraj Print Services. Laxmi Nagar. Delhi-92

Contents

Contents

Preface

Ever since their introduction in 1987, the Buddhist Forum seminars continue to offer an interesting and stimulating variety of papers on Buddhist topics. The seminars are regularly convened once a month during term time and they attract a regular and handsome group of people from SOAS and outside. During the past years we have been fortunate to have discussed an excellent number of papers presented by SOAS staff members and invited speakers from other universities and institutions in this countiy, and visiting scholars from other countries in Europe and overseas. The majority of the papers presented at the Buddhist Forum have been published in the past three volumes. The present volume, like the previous ones, offers an attractive selection of papers some of which deal with contemporary issues and some cover topics appertaining to the mainstream classical research.

The universities and academic institutions in this country do not always have comfortable financial resources to sustain and fully develop their academic and other relevant potentials. The publications of academic books, journals and seminar papers are a good example how difficult it is to secure funds so that they can be published on a regular basis. Bearing all such things in mind, the School of Oriental and African Studies deserves words of gratitude for continuing to publish the Buddhist Forum papers.

While preparing this volume for publication I have received help with typing and some editorial work from my students Joss Winn and Joanna Mazur. I wish to record here my gratitude for their assistance. I would also like to thank the Publications Committee for accepting this volume for publication, and to Martin Daly for his professional advice in various matters relating to publishing, and for seeing this volume through its publication stages.

Tadeusz Skorupski
14 January, 1996.

Abbreviations

Pāli titles are abbreviated as in H. Smith, *A Critical Pāli Dictionary*, Epilegomena to Vol. I, Copenhagen, 1948, and in O. von Hinüber & O. H. Pind, *A Critical Pāli Dictionary*, Vol. III, Copenhagen, 1992–.

AO	*Archiv Orientalni*
BEFEO	*Bulletin de l'Ecole Française d'Extrême-Orient*
BMFEA	*Bulletin of the Museum of the Far Eastern Antiquities*
BMQ	*The British Museum Quarterly*
BR	*Brackwell Review*
BS(BK)	*Buddhist Studies (Bukkyō Kenkyū)*
CAJ	*Central Asiatic Journal*
CUP	Cambridge University Press
EB	*Eastern Buddhist*
EFEO	l'École Française d'Extrême-Orient
HR	*History of Religions*
IIJ	*Indo-Iranian Journal*
JA	*Journal Asiatique*
JAAS	*Journal of Asian and African Studies*
JIABS	*Journal of the International Association of Buddhist Studies*
JIBS	*Journal of Indian and Buddhist Studies*
JLS	*Journal of Law and Society*
JPTS	*Journal of the Pali Text Society*
JTP	*Journal of Transpersonal Psychology*
OUP	Oxford University Press
PEFEO	Publications de l'École Française d'Extrême-Orient
PEW	*Philosophy East & West*
PR	*Partisan Review*
PS	*Process Studies*
PTS	Pali Text Society

RHR	*Revue de l'histoire des Religions*
SBB	Sacred Books of the Buddhists
SBE	Sacred Books of the East
SIS	*Sino-Indian Studies*
SO	*Studia Orientalia*
WZKS	*Wiener Zeitschrift für die Kunde Süd- und Ostasiens*
ZVS	*Zeitschrift fur vergleichende Sprachforschung*

The Fate of Buddhist Political Thought in China: The Rajah Dons a Disguise

T.H. Barrett

In political matters the Buddha was, it must be admitted, a bit of a bolshie; for whatever the spiritual significance of his renunciation of palace life, his life story can also be read as a comment on the value of hereditary monarchy as well. Either as a result of their founder's personal rejection of kingship, or because of Buddhism's early development in parts of ancient India where monarchical government was not itself an established institution, the Buddha's later followers for some time seem to have taken a similarly dim view of autocracy. But over the long centuries of the religion's coexistence with Asian autocrats this aspect of Buddhism has, I would suggest, become less self-evident, and as a result has been surprisingly little researched. In 1974 Hubert Durt published in Japan's *Journal of Indian and Buddhist Studies* an article which deserves to be better known on the use of the counting-stick in Buddhism, apparently as a relic of distant times when Buddhist communities decided their affairs on a straight vote. But as far as I am aware, though a connection between Buddhism and democracy had indeed been vaunted yet earlier in research based on a (somewhat problematic) reading of South Asian materials, very little further work has been done in quite this vein, at least on those early Buddhist materials preserved in East Asia.

It therefore came as a considerable shock to me recently when I was able to devote a couple of hours to chasing up references to 'local magistrates' (in Chinese, *hsien-kuan*) in the Chinese Buddhist Canon. Though I cannot claim as yet to have carried out a full survey, it seems quite clear that in Buddhist materials translated into Chinese, from the earliest times onwards, local magistrates are viewed in an extremely negative light. They are indeed most frequently grouped with bandits as a potential threat to property or worse, and the prospect of unjust imprisonment by them appears to have been considered such a high risk that many Buddhist texts or practices (such as invocations to Bodhisattvas and so forth) are recommended as having the effect of a 'Get Out of Jail Free' card. The reason for my shock may perhaps not be so obvious to an Indologist, but in a Chinese historiographic tradition written (as has long been recognised) almost exclusively by bureaucrats for bureaucrats, the sinologist does not expect to find even a trace of anti-bureaucratic feeling, except in government reports of the beliefs of peasant rebels, which are usually cast in a highly unsympathetic light.

True, negative remarks about magistrates do not feature strongly (if at all) in the *sūtras* most commonly read in China, and one may perhaps surmise that this totally unexpected subaltern point of view on monarchical government barred certain *sūtras* from acceptability with influential patrons. But the materials still exist, and were evidently not subjected to censorship, as for example it has been claimed some texts were for reasons of Confucian prudery when translated from Indian languages. This has encouraged me to bring forward some further evidence which suggests that another Buddhist political belief relating to central rather than to local government was perhaps seen as more threatening, but that materials demonstrating exactly how that threat was countered also still exist in the Chinese Buddhist Canon. But rather than start with the contemporary canon, we should perhaps first take a look at the contemporary Chinese Buddhist monastery.

The title *yüeh-chung* as used in Chinese Buddhism today signifies a monastic office of moderate importance. Holmes Welch, in his classic description of modern Chinese monasticism, finds the closest analogous term in Western monasticism to be 'succentor', an office junior to the more important administrative post of 'precentor'.[1] In former times, however, *yüeh-chung* was one of the terms used in the hierarchy of offices imposed over the years on Buddhism by a succession of Chinese dynasties anxious to provide a level of state control which, as the Chinese pilgrim I-ching (635-713) found to his evident surprise, was quite different from the much less structured arrangements which prevailed in South Asia even at the lowest level of the individual monastery.[2] But if we consult dictionaries,[3] standard historical surveys,[4] even monographs on the Chinese Buddhist hierarchy,[5] we are repeatedly told that the term *yüeh-chung,* literally meaning 'pleasing the masses', is simply an alternative translation of the Sanskrit *karmadāna.*

---

1. Holmes Welch, *The Practice of Chinese Buddhism,* Cambridge, Mass.: Harvard University Press, 1967, 422-3; some of the duties of this office are described *e.g.* on 44.
2. I-ching, ed. Wang Pang-wei, *Ta-T'ang Hsi-yü ch'iu-fa kao-seng chuan chiao-chu*, Peking, Chung-hua shu-chü, 1988, 113, and n. 20, page 124.
3. Most recently, for example, the *Fo-kuang ta-tz'u-tien,* Kao-hsiung, Fo-kuang ch'u-pan-she, 1988, II, 4110.
4. Kenneth K. S. Ch'en, *Buddhism in China,* Princeton, Princeton University Press, 1964, 254.
5. Hsieh Ch'ung-kuang and Pai Wen-ku, *Chung-kuo seng-kuan chih-tu shih* , Hsi-ning, Ch'ing-hai jen-min ch'u-pan-she, 1990, 15.

This latter term was certainly well known to the Chinese, since it too was used (in abbreviated transliteration) for one of the other posts in the hierarchy - one now equivalent to Welch's 'precentor'.[6] What is more, the Chinese seem to have known (to their satisfaction, if not to that of the contemporary Indologist) precisely what *karmdāna* meant, since they also translate the term, either as 'manager of affairs' or 'assigner of tasks'.[7] But the authority for stating that *yüeh-chung* translates *karmadāna,* which it patently does not, derives, as far as I have been able to discover, solely from an assertion on this point by the Buddhist historian Tsan-ning (919-1001) in his institutional history of Chinese Buddhism, the *Seng-shih lüeh.*[8] It should be pointed out that Tsan-ning, for all his erudition, was never known as a master of Indian languages;[9] the alleged equivalence between *yüeh-chung* and *karmadāna* can only be put down to simple error.

But what Sanskrit, if any, does this term meaning 'crowd-pleaser' translate? The only Indian administrative office known to me which was ever deemed to have such a meaning is that described by A. L. Basham:

> "He was called 'the Great Chosen One' (Mahāsammata), and he received the title of *rājā* because he pleased the people. The derivation of the word *rājā* from the verb *rañjayati* ('he pleases') is certainly a false one, but it was widely maintained and is found even in non-Buddhist sources."[10]

Basham is, of course, summarizing from a well-known passage in the *Dīgha-nikāya* on the myth of the 'Great Elect', the primal ruler figure in the Buddhist conception of the contractual origins of kingship.[11] More recent writing on this topic has echoed Basham's summary in stressing the ubiquity of the myth and its attendant etymologising, both in Buddhist sources,[12] and also beyond.[13] Less

6. See the references given above in note 1.
7. See for example the explanation given by I-ching, cited in note 2 above.
8. Tsan-ning, *Ta-Sung Seng-shih lüeh,* B, 242b, in *Taishō Canon,* vol. 54, no. 2126.
9. See Albert Dalia, "The 'Political Career' of the Buddhist Historian Tsan-ning", in David W. Chappell, ed, *Buddhist and Taoist Practice in Medieval Chinese Society* Honolulu, University of Hawaii Press, 1987, 146-180, for a brief biography in English.
10. A. L. Basham, *The Wonder That Was India,* 3rd, revised ed., London, Sidgwick and Jackson, 1967, 83.
11. *Cf.* T. W. and C. A. F. Rhys Davids, trans., *Dialogues of the Buddha,* Part III, London, Humphrey Milford, 1921, 88. The *Mahāvastu*, also cited by Basham at this point, has a slightly different etymology.
12. See John S. Strong, *The Legend of King Asoka,* Princeton, Princeton University Press, 1983, 44-5 and notes.
13. Note the materials brought forward by Richard Gombrich, on page 174 of "The Buddha's Book of Genesis?", *IIJ,* 35, 1992, 159-178, and also page 176, note 9, for another dimension of recent interest in this passage.

has been said about Chinese materials, though Western scholarship has been aware for some time that this myth and the etymology here associated with it were also known in China. Samuel Beal summarizes one such passage as early as 1875, perhaps without fully understanding its purport; his source is in any case too late a translation to bear upon the origins of the term *yüeh-chung.*[14] In 1908 Edouard Huber published a translation of a further passage not alluding to Mahāsammata but explaining the word 'king' as meaning one who 'spreads his benefits in the universe' (evidently a toning down of the Indian etymology to suit Chinese sensibilities),[15] but his confidence in the ascription of the Chinese translation of his text to the famous early fifth century translator Kumarajīva has not been vindicated by more recent research, which again would suggest that it comes too late to enter into discussion here.[16]

More recently, however, Konrad Meisig has dealt with the *Dīgha-nikāya* passage in three Chinese parallel versions,[17] in the course of an attempted reconstruction of the original state of this material—an attempt which has, however, not been universally accepted.[18] While one of his Chinese texts is again far too late to concern us,[19] a *Madhyamāgama* parallel passage does seem to antedate the appearance of the term *yüeh-chung* some time shortly before A.D. 401,[20] since the Chinese translation dates to A.D. 400 even in the finished form in which we now have it.[21] As it stands, however, the direct etymological

14. Samuel Beal, *The Romantic Legend of Sâkya Buddha,* London, Trübner & Co., 1875, 17, based on *Fo pen-hsing chi ching,* 5, 672a in *Taishō Canon,* vol. 3, no. 190. This same text, incidentally, 690c-691a, has Mahāsammata descend from the heavens, producing a hybrid of contractual and divine concepts of the origin of kingship like that found in Tibet: *cf.* R. A. Stein, *Tibetan Civilization,* Stanford, Stanford University Press, 1972, 48.
15. E. Huber, *Açvaghosa Sûtrâlamkâra,* Paris, E. Leroux, 1908, 421, and *cf.* index entry, 470, quoting *Ta Chuang-yen lun ching,* 15, 340a, in *Taishō Canon,* vol. 4, no. 201.
16. *Cf.* Entai Tomomatsu, "Sūtrālamkāra et Kalpanāmanditikā", *JA,* 1931, 135-74; 1931, 245-337.
17. K. Meisig, *Das Sûtra von der vier Ständen: Das Aggañña-Sutta im Licht sein chinesischen Parallelen,* Wiesbaden, Otto Harrasowitz, 1988, 144-5, lays out the parallels; his comments may be found on page 25.
18. See the remarks of Richard Gombrich on this study contained in the article cited above, note 13; both references courtesy of Professor K. R. Norman.
19. This is because it dates from the Sung period. It is by no means the only later text in Chinese to mention either the origins of kingship, the etymology for king, or both at once. In fact, Mahāsammata was eventually to enter Chinese discourse on kingship via the alien dynasties of conquest: see Herbert Franke, *From Tribal Chieftain to Universal Emperor and God,* Münich, Verlag der Bayerischen Akademie der Wissenschaften, 1978, 55, 64, 68 n. 137. This study is concerned with the possibility of an admittedly strangely distorted but much earlier impact of the myth.
20. Thus Hsieh and Pai, *Chung-kuo seng-kuan,* 14-15, quoting *Kao-seng chuan,* 6, 363b, in *Taishō Canon,* vol. 50.
21. Erik Zürcher, *The Buddhist Conquest of China,* Leiden, E. J. Brill, 1959, 204.

association between kingship and pleasure-giving is obscured in the Chinese by the presence (interpolation?) of other remarks, even if it is detectably present.[22] This is more than can be said for the earliest version of Basham's passage translated, the *Ta-lou-hui ching*, dating to about A.D. 300, which gives no etymology for the title *rajah* in any form.[23]

Clarity, however, was not long in coming. The entire *Dirghāgama* (plus another account of Mahāsammata in the Dharmaguptaka *Vinaya*)[24] was rendered into Chinese by a translation team by A.D. 411.[25] Of the two accounts of Mahāsammata in the former collection, one, already noted by Meisig, quite clearly reproduces the false etymology, even if the term *yüeh-chung* does not occur:

> "At that time that one man (Mahāsammata) further with wonderful words consoled the mass of the people (*chung-min*). When the mass of the people heard this they all rejoiced greatly, and all together proclaimed him, saying 'Wonderful, O Great King! Wonderful, O Great King!' At this the world then had the title of king."[26]

Of the members of the translation team responsible for this passage, Buddhayasas, teacher of Kumarajīva, had only arrived in China in A.D. 408,[27] but his partner Chu Fo-nien had already been hard at work through the late fourth century.[28] Given the strong interest in the *Āgamas* during this period, which had (as we have seen) already witnessed the translation of the *Madhyamāgama* (and indeed the *Ekottarāgama*) into finished, revised versions by A.D. 400, it would not be surprising if the content of this portion of the *Dīrghāgama* was already known and discussed, and perhaps even translated in draft, well before A.D. 401, even if a finished translation did not appear until over a decade later.

---

22. The passage in question is in the *Taishō Canon*, vol. 1, p.676a, col.19-22, as Meisig's listing of parallels shows.
23. *Ta-lou-hui ching,* 6, 308c, in *Taishō Canon,* vol. 1, no.23. The translators involved did attract later false attributions of translations to their names, but this is one of their genuine products, attested in the earliest sources: *cf.* Erik Zürcher, *The Buddhist Conquest of China*, 70, and Tokiwa Daijō, *GoKan yori Sō, Sei ni itaru yakkyō sōroku,* Tokyo, Tōhō bunka gakuin Tōkyō kenkyūjo, 1938, 879.
24. The famous *Ssu-fen lü,* 31, 779a in *Taishō Canon,* vol. 22, no. 1428; note, however, that this text does speak of the 'Great Elect' being raised up by the masses *chung*.
25. Tokiwa, *Yakkyō sōroku,* 879.
26. *Ch'ang O-han,* 6, 38b-c, in *Taishō Canon,* vol. 1, no. 1; *cf.* also 22, 148c in the same text.
27. See Richard Robinson, *Early Mādhyamika in India and China,* Madison, Wisconsin, Wisconsin University Press, 1968, 72, which cites the older man's Chinese biography for the friendship between the two, and Zürcher, *Buddhist Conquest*, 408, n. 71.
28. Zürcher, *Buddhist Conquest,* 202.

But maybe such an assumption is both slightly problematic, and completely unnecessary. Meisig's meticulous glossary of the materials he is interested in shows at any rate that the word *yüeh* is never associated with kingship in his texts: where the pleasure etymology is introduced, entirely different synonyms are always used. But if, following Gombrich, we read the whole myth as a joke, and the etymology as "surely yet another joke",[29] then was it not equally surely (in the light of the ubiquity of references to it) a joke on everyone's lips, likely to cross linguistic boundaries without depending on the formal assistance of translation teams?[30] If Tsan-ning did not get the joke, then that was either because he did not live in a time and place subject to such strong Central Asian Buddhist influence as Ch'ang-an in A.D. 400, or else (and this is not impossible) because it was simply impolitic for him to understand it.[31]

There remains, of course, the matter of motive in turning the joke back on to the Buddhists by distorting its meaning so utterly. Why press this term into service in constructing a monastic hierarchy? Here we can only resort to speculation, but it has been noted by most historians that Yao Hsing, the local potentate who was Kumarajīva's patron and the sponsor of much of the translation activity of this period, was nothing if not an autocrat, hardly likely to welcome the contractual model of kingship presented in these texts.[32] He himself carried the title *t'ien-wang*, literally equivalent to *devarāja,* though the term has been explained as harking back to early Chinese usage associated with a more loosely knit polity, and it may carry Inner Asian overtones too, suggesting a link between rulership and the sky god.[33] The learned monks under his patronage were however in contact with their colleagues living under the Chin dynasty in the South, where the famous Hui-yüan (334-417) was just at this

---

29. Again, see note 13, above. It is in fact hard to know how to describe such etymologies in English: "joke" makes them sound too casual, and "false etymology" (which I originally wrote above) underplays the deliberateness of their use. The nearest analogy would seem to be the substitution of the word "herstory" for "history": neither a straightforward joke, nor a careless error, but a deliberate modification to make a certain point.

30. Note that this argument for informal translation based on the ubiquity of the myth and the etymology holds good even if by A. D. 400 generations of commentators had been taking them all far too seriously.

31. The study cited in note 9 above would certainly support such an interpretation.

32. For Yao Hsing's insistence that Kumarajīva should take part in eugenic experiments, see Ch'en, *Buddhism in China,* 83. It should perhaps be mentioned that though Yao's dynasty used the Chinese language, the ruling family was of non-Chinese descent.

33. The sinological interpretation of this title, common during this chaotic period of non-Chinese rule in the north, is espoused by Tanigawa Michio, for example in (*Iwanami kōza*) *Sekai Rekishi,* Tokyo, Iwanami shoten, 1970, vol. 5, 205; on the sky god, see e.g. W. Eberhard, *Conquerors and Rulers,* Leiden, E. J. Brill, 1952, 92-3.

point articulating his reasons for defending the autonomy of the *saṅgha* against the threat of state control.[34] Might it not be that Yao Hsing was prepared to see contractual leadership as part of Buddhism, on the understanding that it applied only within the Buddhist domain of the *saṅgha* itself? Such sleight of hand may even have been encouraged by the fact that the word *chung*, 'masses', while clearly referring in translations of the Mahāsammata story to the primeval population of the earth, was often used as a translation for *saṅgha*.[35]

It is hardly likely that any materials might ever come to hand either to confirm or deny such a hypothesis, but we cannot rule out the possibility that at this extraordinary epoch when the relationships between Buddhist and East Asian political traditions were subject to vigorous debate, the initiative of one particularly unpleasant ruler ensured the survival of the Indian etymology for *rajah* in a completely unlikely Chinese context. As we know, the notion of democracy in any sense tends to find powerful enemies in China (even if, ironically enough, Yao Hsing was in contemporary ethnic terms more Tibetan than Chinese); perhaps it is now time for this 'political prisoner' detained in monastic confinement to be recognised.

---

34. Notably the essay translated by Leon Hurvitz, "'Render unto Caesar' in Early Chinese Buddhism", *SIS,* 5.3/4 1957, 80-114. The contacts between Hui-yüan and Kumarajīva and his circle are covered in Robinson, *Early Mādhyamika*, Chapter IV.

35. For instance in the Chinese version of the *Udānavarga* translated by Chu Fo-nien as the *Ch'u-yao ching,* 701c in *Taishō Canon,* vol. 4, no. 212, to take an example from materials contemporary with those under discussion. It occurs to me on rereading this paper that the term upon which the Chinese "crowdpleaser" might be based could therefore be *sangha rāja*, but I am not so far aware of any use of this title known to the Chinese at such an early date, and so hesitate to modify the conclusions given above.

Existence, Enlightenment, and Suicide: The Dilemma of Nanavira Thera

Stephen Batchelor

"The Buddha's Teaching is quite alien to the European tradition, and a European who adopts it is a rebel." Nanavira Thera (1964).[1]

In the early 1960's Somerset Maugham encouraged his nephew Robin to expand his horizons and go to Ceylon: "Find that rich Englishman who is living in a jungle hut there as a Buddhist monk,"[2] he suggested. An aged and somewhat embittered man living alone in a luxurious villa on the Riviera, Maugham's interest in a Westerner who had renounced a life of comfort to live as a hermit in Asia reflected an earlier fascination with the American Larry Darrell, the fictional hero of his novel *The Razor's Edge.*

Traumatised by his experiences of active service in the First World War, the young Larry Darrell returns home to an affluent and privileged society now rendered hollow and futile. The subsequent events of the novel unfold through the urbane and jaded eyes of Maugham himself, a narrator who assumes a haughty indifference to Larry's existential plight while drawn to him by an anguished curiosity.

Late one night in a café Larry tells Maugham how the shock of seeing a dead fellow airman, a few years older than himself, had brought him to his impasse. The sight, he recalls, "filled me with shame."[3] Maugham is puzzled by this. He too had seen corpses in the war but had been dismayed by "how trifling they looked. There was no dignity in them. Marionettes that the showman had thrown into the discard."[4]

Having renounced a career and marriage, Larry goes to Paris, where he lives austerely and immerses himself in literature and philosophy. When asked by his uncomprehending fiancée why he refuses to come home to Chicago, he answers,

1. Anonymous [Samanera Bodhesako], ed., *Clearing the Path: Writings of Nanavira Thera (1960-1965),* Colombo, Path Press, 1987, 390.
2. *The People,* 26.9.65.
3. S. Maugham, *The Razor's Edge.* London, Mandarin, 1990, 272.
4. *ibid.*

"I couldn't go back now. I'm on the threshold. I see vast lands of the spirit stretching out before me, beckoning, and I'm eager to travel them."[5]

After an unsatisfying spell in a Christian monastery Larry finds work as a deckhand on a liner, jumps ship in Bombay and ends up at an *ashram* in a remote area of South India at the feet of an Indian *swami.* Here, during a retreat in a nearby forest, he sits beneath a tree at dawn and experiences enlightenment. "I had a sense," he tells Maugham,

> "that a knowledge more than human possessed me, so that everything that had been confused was clear and everything that had perplexed me was explained. I was so happy that it was pain and I struggled to release myself from it, for I felt that if it lasted a moment longer I should die."[6]

The final glimpse we have of Larry is as he prepares to board ship for America, where he plans to vanish among the crowds of New York as a cab-driver. "My taxi," he explains, "[will] be merely the instrument of my labour. ... an equivalent to the staff and begging-bowl of the wandering mendicant."[7]

Maugham's story works insofar that it reflects an actual phenomenon: Western engagement with Eastern traditions in the wake of the First World War. Larry's anonymous return to America likewise bears a prophetic ring. But the novel fails in the author's inability to imagine spiritual experience as anything other than a prolonged mystical orgasm. The sincerity and urgency of Larry's quest is trivialised, and his final resolve fails to carry conviction.

The handful of Westerners who actually travelled to Asia in the first half of the 20th century in search of another wisdom had to leave behind not only the security of their traditions but also the non-commital Romanticism of Somerset Maugham. For the first time in nearly two thousand years, they were preparing to embrace something else. And this step was of another order than either the intellectual enthusiasms of a Schopenhauer or the muddled fantasies of a Blavatsky.

So, at his uncle's behest, Robin Maugham, an investigative journalist, novelist, travel writer and defiantly outspoken homosexual, set off on what he would later describe as his "Search for Nirvana." Six weeks later, around New Year 1965, he arrived in Ceylon. At the Island Hermitage, founded in Dodanduwa in 1911 by the German Nyanatiloka, the doyen of Western Buddhist monks, he was directed to the town of Matara in the extreme south. From Matara Maugham was driven by jeep to the village of Bundala, where the farmers led him to a path that disappeared into the forest. "It was very hot," he

---

5. *ibid.*, 73-4.
6. *ibid.*, 298.
7. *ibid.*, 307.

recalled, "I could feel the sweat dripping down me. The path became narrower and darker as it led further into the dense jungle." He came to a clearing in which stood a small hut. As he approached, "a tall figure in a saffron robe glided out on to the verandah."

> "The gaunt man stared at me in silence. He was tall and lean with a short beard and sunken blue eyes. His face was very pale. He stood there, motionless, gazing at me.
> 'Would you care to come in?' he asked.
> His voice was clear with a pleasantly cultured intonation about it; it was calm and cool yet full of authority. He might have been inviting me in for a glass of sherry in his rooms at Cambridge."[8]

Harold Edward Musson was born in Aldershot barracks in 1920. From the age of seven to nine he had lived in Burma, where his father commanded a battalion. He remembered asking someone, "Who was the Buddha?" and being told, "The Buddha was a man who sat under a tree and was enlightened."[9] From that moment he decided that this was what he wanted to do. He was educated at Wellington College and went up to Magdalene College, Cambridge, in 1938, where he read mathematics and then modern languages. It was during this time that he "slowly began to realise that ... I would certainly end my days as a Buddhist monk."[10] He nonetheless volunteered for the army in 1940 and became an officer in Field Security, first in Algiers and later in Italy. His task was to interrogate prisoners of war. In 1945 he was hospitalised in Sorrento and became absorbed in a book on Buddhism called, *La Dottrina del Risveglio* ("The Doctrine of Awakening") by the Italian Julius Evola.

Julius Cesare Andrea Evola was born to a devout Catholic family in Rome in 1898. Having served in a mountain artillery regiment during the First World War, he found himself (like his fictional counterpart Larry Darrell) incapable of returning to normal life. He was overcome with "feelings of the inconsistency and vanity of the aims that usually engage human activities."[11] In response, he became an abstract painter involved in the Dadaist movement and a friend of the founding figure, the Rumanian Tristan Tzara. But by 1921 he became disillusioned with the Dadaist project of "overthrowing all logical, ethical and aesthetic categories by means of producing paradoxical and disconcerting images in order to achieve absolute liberation."[12] He finally rejected the arts as

---

8. R. Maugham, *Search For Nirvana,* London, W.H.Allen, 1975, 186.
9. *ibid.,* 189.
10. *ibid.*
11. J. Evola, *Le Chemin du Cinabre* Milan, Arche-Arktos, 1982, 12.
12. *ibid.,* 13.

inadequate to the task of resolving his spiritual unrest and after 1922 produced no further poems or paintings.

A further response to his inner crisis was to experiment with drugs through which he attained "states of consciousness partially detached from the physical senses, ... frequently approaching close to the sphere of visionary hallucinations and perhaps also madness."[13] But such experiences only aggravated his dilemma by intensifying his sense of personal disintegration and confusion to the point where he decided, at the age of twenty-three, to commit suicide.

He was only dissuaded from carrying this out by coming across a passage from the *Middle Length Sayings* (*Majjhima Nikaya* I, 1) in the Pali Canon where the Buddha spoke of those things with which the disciple committed to awakening must avoid identifying. Having listed the body, feelings, the elements and so on, he concludes:

> "Whoever regards extinction as extinction, who thinks of extinction, who reflects about extinction, who thinks: 'Extinction is mine', and rejoices in extinction, such a person, I declare, does not know extinction."[14]

For Evola this was "like a sudden illumination. I realised that this desire to end it all, to dissolve myself, was a bond - 'ignorance' as opposed to true freedom."[15]

During the early 1920's Evola's interests turned to the study of philosophy and Eastern religion. During this time he came into contact with Arturo Reghini, a high-ranking Mason and mathematician who believed himself to be a member of the Scuola Italica, an esoteric order that claimed to have survived the fall of ancient Rome. Through Reghini Evola was introduced to René Guénon, whose concept of 'Tradition' came to serve as "the basic theme that would finally integrate the system of my ideas."[16]

Evola distinguishes two aspects of this concept. Firstly, it refers to "a primordial tradition of which all particular, historical, pre-modern traditions have been emanations." Secondly, and more importantly, Tradition

> "has nothing to do with conformity or routine; it is the fundamental structure of a kind of civilisation that is organic, differentiated and hierarchic in which all its domains and human activities have an orientation from above and towards what is above."[17]

---

13. *ibid.*
14. *ibid.*
15. *ibid.*, 14.
16. *ibid.*, 86.
17. *ibid.*

Such civilisations of the past had as their natural centre an elite or a leader who embodied "an authority as unconditional as it was legitimate and impersonal."[18]

It comes as no great surprise, therefore, that Evola strongly identified with the Right and supported the rise of Fascism in both Italy and Germany. Following Reghini he denounced the Church as the religion of a spiritual proletariat and attacked it ferociously in his book *Pagan Imperialism* (1927). Around the same time he published such titles as *Man as Potency* and *Revolt Against the Modern World*, revealing his indebtedness to Nietzsche and Spengler. He did not, however, join the Fascist party and looked down upon Mussolini with aristocratic disdain. (Towards the end of his life he declared that he had never belonged to any political party or voted in an election.)

After Hitler came to power, Evola was feted by high-ranking Nazis, his books were translated into German and he was invited to the country to explain his ideas to select aristocratic and military circles. But, as with many of his German admirers, he kept aloof from what he considered the nationalist, populist and fanatic elements of National Socialism. He claims in his autobiography that because of his position as a foreigner from a friendly nation, he was free to present ideas which had they been voiced by a German would have risked imprisonment in a concentration camp. Nonetheless, when Mussolini was overthrown in 1943, Evola was invited to Vienna by a branch of the SS to translate proscribed texts of Masonic and other secret societies.

In the same year *The Doctrine of Awakening*, Evola's study of Buddhism, was published in Italy. He regarded the writing of this book as repayment of the 'debt' he owed to the doctrine of the Buddha for saving him from suicide. The declared aim of the book was to "illuminate the true nature of original Buddhism, which had been weakened to the point of unrecognisability in most of its subsequent forms."[19] The essential spirit of Buddhist doctrine was, for Evola, "determined by a will for the unconditioned, affirmed in its most radical form, and by investigation into that which leads to mastery over life as much as death."[20]

As its sub-title *A Study on the Buddhist Ascesis* suggests, Evola's aim was to emphasise the primacy of spiritual discipline and practice as the core of Tradition as represented by Buddhism. He condemns the loss of such ascesis in Europe and deplores the pejorative sense the term has assumed. Even Nietzsche, he notes with surprise, shared this anti-ascetic prejudice. Today, he argues, the ascetic path appears with the greatest clarity in Buddhism.

18. *ibid.*
19. *ibid.*, 138.
20. *ibid.*

Evola bases his arguments on the Italian translations of the Pali Canon by Neumann and de Lorenzo published between 1916 and 1927. Like many of his generation, the Pali texts represented the only true and original source of the Buddha's teaching. He was nonetheless critical of a large body of accepted opinion that had grown up around them.

Renunciation, for example, does not, for Evola, arise from a sense of despair with the world; he maintains that the four encounters of Prince Siddhartha should be "taken with great reserve" for true *aryan* renunciation

> "is based on 'knowledge' and is accompanied by a gesture of disdain and a feeling of transcendental dignity; it is qualified by the superior man's will for the unconditioned, by the will ... of a man of quite a special 'race of the spirit'."'[21]

The bearing of such a person is "essentially aristocratic," "anti-mystical," "anti-evolutionist," upright and "manly." This race of the spirit is united with the "blood ... of the white races who created the greatest civilisations both of the East and the West"[22] in particular males of warrior stock. The aryan tradition has been largely lost in the West through the "influence on European faiths of concepts of Semitic and Asiatic-Mediterranean origin." Yet in the East, too, Buddhism has degenerated into Mahāyāna universalism that wrongly considers *all* beings to have the potentiality to become a Buddha. As for Buddhism being "a doctrine of universal compassion encouraging humanitarianism and democratic equality," this is merely one of many "Western misconceptions."[23]

Evola considers the world of his time to be perverse and dysfunctional. "If normal conditions were to return," he sighs, "few civilisations would seem as odd as the present one."[24] He deplores the craving for material things, which causes man entirely to overlook mastery over his own mind. Nonetheless,

> "one who is still an 'aryan' spirit in a large European or American city, with its skyscrapers and asphalt, with its politics and sport, with its crowds who dance and shout, with its exponents of secular culture and of soulless science and so on—amongst all this he may feel himself more alone and detached and nomad than he would have done in the time of the Buddha."[25]

Evola believed that the original Buddhism disclosed through his study revealed the essence of the aryan tradition that had become lost and corrupted in the

21. J. Evola, *The Doctrine of Awakening: A Study on the Buddhist Ascesis*, London, Luzac, 1951, 95.
22. *ibid.*, 17.
23. *ibid.*, 43.
24. *ibid.*, 135.
25. *ibid.*, 129.

West. For him aryan means more than "noble" or "sublime," as it was frequently rendered in translations of Buddhist texts. "They are all later meanings of the word," he explains, "and do not convey the fullness of the original nor the spiritual, aristocratic and racial significance which, nevertheless, is preserved in Buddhism."[26] Other "innate attributes of the aryan soul" that are described in Buddhist texts are an absence of "any sign of departure from consciousness, of sentimentalism or devout effusion, or of semi-intimate conversation with a God."[27] Only among some of the German mystics, such as Eckhart, Tauler and Silesius, does he find examples of this spirit in the Western tradition, "where Christianity has been rectified by a transfusion of aryan blood."[28]

Not only does Buddhism display an aryan spirit but, for Evola, it also endorses the superiority of the warrior caste. Brushing aside the Buddha's well-known denunciation of the caste system, Evola notes that "it was generally held that the *bodhisatta* ... are never born into a peasant or servile caste but into a warrior or brahman caste."[29] He cites several examples where the Buddha makes analogies between "the qualities of an ascetic and the virtues of a warrior."[30] Of all the Mahāyāna schools the only one he admired was that of Zen, on account of its having been adopted in Japan as the doctrine of the Samurai class.

What appeal could this book have had for an officer of the Allied forces advancing through Italy as part of a campaign to overthrow a regime based on notions of aryan supremacy? Yet Captain Musson immediately set about translating *The Doctrine of Awakening* into English, a task he completed three years later. In his brief foreword he offers no apology for the author's extreme views, but simply asserts that Evola had "recaptured the spirit of Buddhism in its original form." The book cleared away "some of the woolly ideas that have gathered around ... Prince Siddhartha and the doctrine he disclosed." But its "real significance" was to be found in "its encouragement of a practical application of the doctrine it discusses."[31]

If one ignores Evola's suprematist and militaristic views, *The Doctrine of Awakening* offers a clear and often thoughtful account of early Buddhist doctrine. Evola proudly recalls that the English edition "received the official approbation of the Pali [Text] Society," through their "recognition of the value

---

26. *ibid.*, 16.
27. *ibid.*, 14.
28. *ibid.*, 17.
29. *ibid.*, 20.
30. *ibid.*
31. *ibid.*, ix.

of my study."[32] It is nonetheless curious that in 1951, so shortly after the war, the book would be published in London by a reputable Orientalist publisher (Luzac) without any reference to the author's extreme right-wing views.

By the time *The Doctrine of Awakening* appeared in print, Musson had followed the book's advice and was already a *bhikkhu* in Ceylon. "I think the war hastened my decision," he later told Robin Maugham in the course of their conversation. "Though it was inevitable, I think, in any case. But the war forced maturity on me."[33] Since Harold Musson, like Larry Darrell (and probably Julius Evola), had a private income, he did not have to seek work upon leaving the army. He settled in London. With time and money on his hands, he leisurely worked on his translation of Evola and "tried to get as much pleasure out of life as I could."[34] Then one evening, in a bar, he ran into Osbert Moore, an old army friend who had shared his enthusiasm for *The Doctrine of Awakening* while in Italy. They began comparing notes. "Gradually we came to the conclusion that the lives we were leading at present were utterly pointless. We shared the belief that the whole of this existence as we saw it was a farce."[35] By the time the bar closed, they had resolved to go to Ceylon and become *bhikkhus*.

They left England in November 1948 and were ordained as novices in an open glade at the Island Hermitage by Nyanatiloka, then an old man of seventy-one, on April 24, 1949. Moore was given the name Nanamoli, and Musson Nanavira. In 1950 they both received *bhikkhu* ordination in Colombo.

For the next year Nanavira devoted himself "fairly continuously" to the practice of meditative absorption (*jhāna*, *samādhi*), the attainment of which, he later declared, had been his motive in coming to Ceylon. A few months before Maugham's visit he had explained to a Singhalese friend that it was

> "the desire for some definite non-mystical form of practice that first turned my thoughts to the East. Western thinking ... seemed to me to oscillate between the extremes of mysticism and rationalism, both of which were distasteful to me, and the yoga practices—in a general sense—of India offered themselves as a possible solution."[36]

This is what he had seen as the "real significance" of Evola's book and, as he confirmed sixteen years later, the point on which "Eastern thought is at its

---

32. J. Evola, *Le Chemin du Cinabre,* Milan, Arche-Arktos, 1982, 142.
33. R. Maugham, *Search For Nirvana,* London, W.H. Allen, 1975, 190.
34. *ibid.,* 189.
35. *ibid.,* 190.
36. Anonymous [Samanera Bodhesako], ed., *Clearing the Path: Writings of Nanavira Thera (1960-1965)* Colombo, 1987, 368.

greatest distance from Western."[37] But after a year's practice he contracted typhoid, which left him with chronic indigestion so severe that at times he would "roll about on [his] bed with the pain."[38] It also prevented him from attaining anything more than the "low-level results of [the] practice."[39]

Unable to pursue the *jhānas* he turned his linguistic skills to the study of Pali, which he soon mastered, and set about reading the Buddha's discourses and their Singhalese commentaries. His analytical bent led him to assume that "it was possible to include all that the [Buddha] said in a single system—preferrably portrayed diagrammatically on one very large sheet of paper."[40] But the more he read, the more he realised that this approach was "sterile" and incapable of leading to understanding. And the more he probed the discourses, the more he came to doubt the validity of the commentaries, which, "in those innocent days," he had accepted as authoritative. His friend Nanamoli, meanwhile, had likewise mastered Pali and was preparing to translate the greatest Commentary of them all, Buddhaghosa's *Visuddimagga*.

Over the following months and years Nanavira became increasingly independent in his views, both challenging the accepted orthodoxy and refining his own understanding. Temperamentally, he acknowledged a tendency to stand apart from others. "I am quite unable," he wrote in 1963, "to identify myself with any organised body or cause (even if it is a body of opposition or a lost cause). I am a born blackleg."[41] Having renounced a life of comfort in England and all the values it stood for, he now rejected the prevailing orthodoxy of Singhalese Buddhism. But he did not turn against the Buddha's word: "It was, and is, my attitude towards the [Buddha's discourses] that, if I find anything in them that is against my own view, *they* are *right*, and I am *wrong*."[42] He came to view only two of the three "Baskets" (*Piṭaka*) of the Canon as authentic: those containing the discourses and the monastic rule. "No other Pali books whatsoever," he insisted, "should be taken as authoritative; and ignorance of them (and particularly of the traditional Commentaries) may be counted a positive advantage, as leaving less to be unlearned."[43]

This radical tendency towards isolation led him in 1954 to leave the Island Hermitage for the physical solitude of his hut in the jungle. "Aren't you lonely?" inquired Maugham. "After a bit," he replied, "you find you simply

---

37. *ibid.*, 367.
38. R. Maugham, *Search For Nirvana*, 198.
39. Anonymous [Samanera Bodhesako], ed., *Clearing the Path: Writings of Nanavira Thera (1960-1965)*, 440.
40. *ibid.*, 485.
41. *ibid.*, 310.
42. *ibid* ., 305.
43. *ibid.*, 5.

don't *want* other people. You've got your centre of gravity within yourself ... You become self-contained."[44] Two years earlier he had confessed: "I am one of those people who think of other people as 'they,' not as 'we.'"[45] Despite persistent ill-health, his study and practice of mindfulness continued with increasing intensity.

Then, on the evening of June 27, 1959, something happened that radically changed the course of his life. He recorded the event in Pali in a private journal:

> "HOMAGE TO THE AUSPICIOUS ONE, WORTHY, FULLY AWAKENED.
>
> At one time the monk Nanavira was staying in a forest hut near Bundala village. It was during that time, as he was walking up and down in the first watch of the night, that the monk Nanavira made his mind quite pure of constraining things, and kept thinking and pondering and reflexively observing the Dhamma as he had heard and learnt it, the clear and stainless Eye of the Dhamma arose in him: 'Whatever has the nature of arising, all that has the nature of ceasing.'
>
> Having been a teaching-follower for a month, he became one attained to right view."[46]

Thus he claimed to have 'entered the stream,' (*sotāpatti*) glimpsed the unconditioned *nirvāṇa*, and become, thereby, an *ārya*.

The Buddha used the term '*ārya* 'to refer to those who had achieved a direct experiential insight into the nature of the four truths (suffering, its origins, its cessation and the way to its cessation). For such people these truths are no longer beliefs or theories, but realities. When someone comes to know them as such, he or she is said to have 'entered the stream' which culminates, within a maximum of seven further lifetimes either as a human or a god, in *arahat*-hood, i.e. the final attainment of Nirvana. While the Buddha used this term in a purely spiritual sense, he maintained a distinction between an *ārya* and an 'ordinary person' (*puthujjana*), *i.e.* one who had not yet had the experience of stream-entry. The experience, however, is available to anyone, irrespective of their social position, sex or racial origins. By offering this radical redefinition of 'nobility', the Buddha introduced into caste-bound India a spiritual tradition able to transcend the limits of the indigenous culture. Yet in the final analysis, concluded Nanavira, "the Buddha's Teaching is for a privileged class—those

---

44. R. Maugham, *Search For Nirvana,* 194.
45. Anonymous [Samanera Bodhesako], ed., *Clearing the Path: Writings of Nanavira Thera (1960-1965),* 223.
46. *ibid.,* 495.

who are fortunate enough to have the intelligence to grasp it..., and they are most certainly not the majority!"[47]

Up to this point Nanavira had maintained a continuous correspondence with his friend Nanamoli (Moore). Now he stopped it, because "there was no longer anything for me to discuss *with* him, since the former relationship of parity between us regarding the Dhamma had suddenly come to an end."[48] And it was never to be resumed, for eight months later, on March 8, 1960, Nanamoli Thera died suddenly of a heart attack in a remote village while on a walking tour. He left behind some of the finest English translations from Pali of key Theravada texts. Added to this loss had been the death three years earlier of Nanavira's first preceptor, Nyanatiloka, on May 28, 1957.

In the year following his stream-entry (1960) Nanavira began writing a series of "notes." By the summer of 1961 he had finished two such notes, one on *paṭiccasamuppāda* (conditionality) and one on *paramattha sacca* (higher truth). In July of the same year, a German Buddhist nun called Vajira (Hannelore Wolf), who had been in Ceylon since 1955 and since 1959 had been living as a hermit, called on Nanavira for advice. He subsequently sent her a copy of the two notes he had just finished typing. These had a tremendous impact on her. "Your notes on *vinnana-namarupa*," (consciousness-name/form) she wrote, "have led me away from the abyss into which I have been staring for more than twelve years." And added: "I do not know ... by what miraculous skill you have guided me to a safe place where at last I can breathe freely."[49] The correspondence and one further day-long meeting resulted in Vajira likewise 'entering the stream' in late January 1962. Vajira underwent an ecstatic but turbulent transformation from an ordinary person (*puthujjana*) to an *ārya*, the validity of which Nanavira did "not see any reason to doubt."[50] Vajira, from her side, now regarded Nanavira as an *arahat*. But the rapidity and intensity of the change provoked a kind of nervous breakdown and the Ceylonese authorities deported her to Germany on February 22, 1962. On her return she ceased to have any contact with her former Buddhist friends in Hamburg. This, commented Nanavira, was "a good sign, not a bad one—when one has got what one wants, one stops making a fuss about it and sits down quietly."[51]

Four months after Vajira's departure, Nanavira's chronic indigestion (*amoebiasis*) was further aggravated by satyriasis—a devastatingly inappropriate

47. *ibid.*, 396-7.
48. *ibid.*, 386.
49. *ibid.*, 529.
50. *ibid.*, 386.
51. *ibid.*

malady for a celibate hermit. Satyriasis—"the overpowering need on the part of a man to seduce a never-ending succession of women" (Britannica)—is the male equivalent to nymphomania in women. "Under the pressure of this affliction," he noted on December 11, "I am oscillating between two poles. If I indulge the sensual images that offer themselves, my thought turns towards the state of a layman; if I resist them, my thought turns towards suicide. Wife or knife, one might say."[52] In fact, the previous month he had already made an unsuccessful attempt to end his life. Although he realised that the erotic stimulation could be overcome by meditative absorption, such practice was prevented by his chronic indigestion. By November 1963, he had "given up all hope of making any further progress for myself in this life"[53] and had also resolved not to disrobe. It was simply a question of how long he could "stand the strain."[54]

While for the ordinary person (*puthujjana*) suicide is ethically equivalent to murder, for an *ārya* it is acceptable under circumstances that prevent further spiritual practice; for the *ārya* is no longer bound to the craving that drives the endless cycle of death and rebirth, his or her liberation being guaranteed within a finite period of time. Nanavira cites instances from the Canon of *ārya bhikkhus* at the time of the Buddha who had taken their lives and become *arahants* in the process. He does not seem to have been driven by the conventional motives for suicide: resentment, remorse, despair, grief. He writes openly of his dilemma to friends with droll understatement and black humour:

> "All the melancholy farewell letters are written (they have to be amended and brought up to date from time to time, as the weeks pass and my throat is still uncut); the note for the coroner is prepared (carefully refraining from any witty remarks that might spoil the solemn moment at the inquest when the note is read out aloud); and the mind is peaceful and concentrated."[55]

His friends responded with a mixture of concern, bewilderment and alarm. "People want their Dhamma on easier terms," he reflected, "and they dislike it when they are shown that they must pay a heavier price—and they are frightened, too, when they see something they don't understand: they regard it as morbid and their concern (unconscious, no doubt) is to bring things back to healthy, reassuring, normality."[56]

---

52. *ibid.*, 216.
53. *ibid.*, 241.
54. *ibid.*, 276.
55. *ibid.*, 238.
56. *ibid.*, 376.

Most of 1963 was taken up with preparing his notes for publication, something he would have considered "an intolerable disturbance"[57] had his health not prevented him from practice. Despite such disclaimers, one has the strong impression that he wished to communicate his vision of the Dhamma to a wider public. (Maugham records him as saying: "I'm hoping to find an English publisher for [them].")[58] Through the help of the Ceylonese Judge Lionel Samaratunga a limited edition of 250 cyclostyled copies of *Notes on Dhamma (1960-1963)* was produced towards the end of the year and distributed to leading Buddhist figures of the time and various libraries and institutions. The response was largely one of polite incomprehension.

When Robin Maugham entered the tiny hut at the beginning of 1965, Nanavira had largely completed the revisions to his *Notes on Dhamma*. "I looked round the room with its faded blue walls," Maugham recalls. "There was a table made from a packing-case with an oil-lamp on it, a chair, a chest and a bookcase. There were two straw brooms and two umbrellas—and his plank bed and the straw mat I was sitting on."[59] But he was quite unaware of Nanavira's work. The questions he asked as he squatted uncomfortably on the floor were typical of those a sympathetic but uninformed European would still make today. Maugham's principal interest was to understand Nanavira's character. To this end he asked at length about his relations with his family, the reasons why he became a monk, if he felt lonely and whether he missed the West.

Maugham left the first meeting with a positive impression. "I liked his diffident smile and I admired his courage," he reflected. "But I still wondered if he was completely sincere."[60] During the second meeting his doubts were put to rest. Nanavira explained how his mother had come out to Ceylon and tried to persuade her only child to return home. When he refused she suffered a heart-attack. As soon as she recovered she went back to England and died. "His voice was quite impassive as he spoke," explained Maugham. "I find it hard to describe the tone of his voice. Yet if I don't I shall miss the whole point of the man I'd travelled so far to see. There was no harshness in his tone. There was no coldness. There was understanding and gentleness. And it was only these two qualities that made his next remark bearable."

> "My mother's death didn't worry me", he said. "Even now, during this life, every moment we are born and die. But we continue. We take some other shape or form in another life."

---

57. *ibid.*, 253.
58. R. Maugham, *Search For Nirvana*, 198.
59. *ibid.*, 197-8.
60. *ibid.*, 192.

Nanavira fell silent. He was visibly tired. Then he added: "The whole point of Buddhism is to bring an end to this farcical existence. The whole point of our present existence is to reach Nirvana - complete understanding of natural phenomena—thereby ending the chain of re-birth."[61]

In Nanavira's account of the meeting, however, it is Robin Maugham's sincerity that is put into question. "The visitors I spoke of in my postcard," he wrote in a letter two days later,

> "came and talked and took photographs and notes for several hours on the afternoon of the eighth. The older one is Robin Maugham, a nephew of the celebrated Somerset Maugham. He is a novelist (third-rate, I suspect) and a writer of travel books. Although they both seemed interested in the Dhamma, I rather think that their principal reason for visiting me was to obtain material for their writings. I had a slightly uncomfortable feeling of being exploited; but, unfortunately, once I start talking, I like going on, without proper regard for the repercussions later on. So probably, in about a year's time, there will be a new travel book with a chapter (complete with photographs) devoted to yours truly, and the romantic life he is leading in the jungle."[62]

Contrary to his own version, Maugham was not alone. Thus the dramatic encounter between two tormented souls—the man of the world and the hermit—is compromised by the presence of a third man—probably Maugham's secretary and assistant. Nanavira's prediction about the outcome of the visit proved entirely accurate except in the timing. Maugham's sensational account of the meeting was published in the *People* newspaper of September 26, 1965, but it took ten years before the travel book (*Search for Nirvana*, 1975) appeared. This book devotes most of its pages to Maugham's search for *nirvāna* in the arms of dusky-skinned youths, but a chapter (complete with photographs) is given to his meeting with Nanavira.

At root, though, Maugham seems sincere. As they were parting, he had the strong impression that Nanavira still wanted to tell him something "of such importance that it would change my whole life." But the monk abruptly averted his "mellow gaze" and simply said goodbye. Maugham and his companion walked away towards the path that led from the jungle glade to the village. Then he turned back: "His lean gaunt figure in a saffron robe was standing motionless on the verandah. Perhaps he knew a truth that would make the existence of

---

61. *ibid.*, 200.
62. Anonymous [Samanera Bodhesako], ed., *Clearing the Path: Writings of Nanavira Thera (1960-1965)*, 403.

millions of men a happier thing. Perhaps he knew the answer. Perhaps he had found the secret of life. But I would never know."[63]

The revision of his *Notes* completed, Nanavira returned to his simple routine of meditation, correspondence and daily chores. His chronic indigestion continued to be aggravated by satyriasis. Six months (Maugham, presumably for dramatic effect, says two weeks) after their meeting, on the afternoon of July 7, 1965, Nanavira ended his life by putting his head into a cellophane bag containing drops of chloroform. Only a month earlier his letters had been exploring the meaning of humour.

The memory of the English monk from Aldershot continued to haunt Robin Maugham. In 1968 he published *The Second Window*, an autobiographical novel about a journalist who becomes entangled in a child sex-abuse scandal in Kenya. As a digression from the main theme, the protagonist visits Ceylon to track down a certain Leslie Edwin Fletcher who is rumoured to be living there as a Buddhist hermit. While clearly based on Maugham's encounter with Nanavira, the fictionalised version turns him into a gloomy, confused and pathetic figure. A radio-play (*A Question of Retreat*) followed in a similar vein.

Shortly afterwards, in 1972, Julius Evola published his autobiography. Towards the end of the war Evola had been injured by a bomb in Vienna and for the remainder of his life was partially paralysed. He returned to Italy and became a focal figure for the far right, receiving in his apartment a steady trickle of those who still admired the values he espoused. Although he died in 1974, he has been resurrected recently as a hero of resurgent neo-fascist groups in Italy.

Recalling *The Doctrine of Awakening*, he wrote in his autobiography: "The person who translated the work [into English], a certain Mutton (*sic*), found in it an incitant to leave Europe and withdraw to the Orient in the hope of finding there a centre where one still cultivated the disciplines that I recommended; unfortunately, I have had no further news of him."[64] Evola also confessed that he himself was not a Buddhist and his study was intended to balance his earlier work on the Hindu *tantras*. He saw Buddhism as the "'dry' and intellectual path of pure detachment" as opposed to that of the *tantras* which taught "affirmation, engagement, the utilisation and transformation of immanent forces liberated through the awakening of the Shakti, i.e. the root power of all vital energy, particularly that of sex."[65] The only other work of Evola's to have been translated into English was *The Metaphysics of Sex* (London, 1983).

---

63. R. Maugham, *Search For Nirvana,* 202.
64. J. Evola, *Le Chemin du Cinabre,* 142.
65. *ibid.,* 143.

In 1987 a book was published by Path Press, Colombo, with the title *Clearing the Path: Writings of Nanavira Thera (1960 - 1965).* This hard-cover book of nearly six hundred pages contains the text of Nanavira's revised *Notes on Dhamma (1960 - 1965)* together with 149 letters of varying lengths written by Nanavira to nine correspondents, which serve (as the author himself stated) as a commentary on the *Notes*. The texts are scrupulously edited, extensively annotated and cross-referenced by means of a comprehensive index. The compilation, editing and publication of this book was a labour of love performed (anonymously) by Ven. Bodhesako (Robert Smith), an American *samaṇa* from Chicago, who died suddenly of gangrene of the intestines in Nepal in 1989, shortly after completing the work. With his death Path Press ceased to function and the book can now only be obtained from a Buddhist distributor (Wisdom Books) in London.

Clearing the Path is presented by Bodhesako as a "work book. Its purpose is to help the user to acquire a point of view that is different from his customary frame of reference, and also more satisfactory."[66] As such it is to be used as a tool for inner change. This supports Nanavira's own contention in his preface to the *Notes* that "the reader is presumed to be subjectively engaged with an anxious problem, the problem of his existence, which is also the problem of his suffering." He adds:

> "There is therefore nothing in these pages to interest the professional scholar, for whom the question of personal existence does not arise; for the scholar's whole concern is to eliminate or ignore the individual point of view in an effort to establish the objective truth - a would-be impersonal synthesis of public facts."[67]

He later remarked that the *Notes* "were not written to pander to people's tastes" and were made "as unattractive, academically speaking, as possible."[68] He declared that he would be satisfied if only one person were ever to benefit from them.

In their final version, *Notes on Dhamma* consist of the two essays on *paṭiccasamuppāda* (conditionality) and *paramattha sacca* (higher truth) and twenty shorter notes on a range of key Pali terms, such as *atta* (self), *citta* (mind), *rupa* (form) etc. They are all written in a dense, exact style in numbered sections, most of the key terms remaining in *Pali*. Nanavira composed them as an explicit critique of the orthodox Theravada position "with the purpose of

---

66. Anonymous [Samanera Bodhesako], ed., *Clearing the Path: Writings of Nanavira Thera (1960-1965),* Colombo, 1987, vii.
67. *ibid.*, 5.
68. *ibid.*, 321-3.

clearing away a mass of dead matter which is choking the [Buddha's discourses]."[69]

In keeping with Nanavira's wishes, the *Notes* have not been indexed. This, he felt, would turn the book into a "work of reference." Whereas "it is actually intended to be read and digested as a single whole, with each separate note simply presenting a different facet of the same central theme."[70] Elsewhere he describes his *Notes* as being like "so many beads inter-connected with numbers of threads, in a kind of three-dimensional network."[71]

This holomorphic character of the *Notes* is reflected most explicitly in the fourth and final section entitled 'Fundamental Structure', which consists of two parts, 'Static Aspect' and 'Dynamic Aspect.' In his usual ironic manner, Nanavira describes this section as "really a remarkably elegant piece of work, almost entirely original, and also quite possibly correct. I am obliged to say this myself, since it is improbable that anybody else will. It is most unlikely that anyone will make anything of it."[72] This is certainly true for the present writer.

'Fundamental Structure' attempts to describe by means of terse philosophical language and symbolic diagrams the "inherent structure governing the selectivity of consciousness"[73] which is common to both the enlightened and unenlightened person alike. Nanavira compares this fundamental structure to a chessboard on which both "passionate chess," *i.e.* a game following the rules but complicated by the influence of passion, and its opposite, "dispassionate chess," can both be played. But he admits that these ideas are "only indirectly connected to the Buddha's Teaching proper."[74] He sees them as a possible corrective to certain tendencies in abstract, scientific thinking to distance oneself from a sense of concrete existential location. For someone who does not suffer from this problem, however, he acknowledges that it will serve no purpose to study "Fundamental Structure."

Nanavira recognises a yawning gulf between the world-view of the average Western person and the Teaching of the Buddha. For those uninclined to the somewhat dry and technical approach of "Fundamental Structure" he recommends prior study of Existentialist philosophy, as found in the writings of Kierkegaard, Sartre, Camus and, in particular, Martin Heidegger's *Being and Time*. For these thinkers had also discarded the detached, rationalist approach to philosophy and emphasised immediate questions of personal existence. He also

69. *ibid.*, 339.
70. *ibid.*, 254.
71. *ibid.*, 337.
72. *ibid.*, 240.
73. *ibid.*, 302.
74. *ibid.*, 261.

speaks highly of James Joyce's *Ulysses,* the early novels of Aldous Huxley, and the writings of Franz Kafka, all of which had a strong influence on him as a young man. Nanavira nonetheless warned against confusing Existentialism with Buddhism. For "one who has understood the Buddha's Teaching no longer asks these questions; he is *ārya* 'noble,' and no more a *puthujjana,* and he is beyond the range of the existential philosophies." The Dhamma does not offer answers; it shows "the way leading to the final cessation of all questions about self and the world."[75]

Nanavira also found the very positivism he so deplored in the West infecting the writings of some of the most respected Sri Lankan authorities on Buddhism. K.N. Jayatilleke, O.H. de A. Wijesekera and G.P. Malalasekera are all taken to task on this point. Despite their being professed Buddhists, Nanavira compares the former two unfavourably with the Christian thinker Kierkegaard. He criticises Jayatilleke, for example, for presenting the Four Noble Truths as though they were propositions of fact, thus obscuring their character as imperatives for action. He compares them to the bottle in *Alice in Wonderland* labelled "Drink Me!" From this perspective (also that of the *Dhamma-cakkappavattana Sutta*),

> "the Four Noble Truths are the ultimate tasks for a man's performance— Suffering commands 'Know me absolutely!', Arising commands 'Abandon Me!', Cessation commands 'Realize me!', and the Path commands 'Develop me!"[76].

Startling images of this kind abound throughout Nanavira's letters, which reveal him both as a rigorous analytical thinker and also as a literary stylist of a high order. By reflecting, in addition, the radical seriousness and renunciation he adopted towards the personal realisation of the Buddha's Teaching, Nanavira's writings stand out as one of the most original and important contributions to Buddhist literature this century.

But why then, if this is true, does Nanavira Thera remain such an obscure figure? The short answer is because he singularly fails to fit the popular stereotype of what a contemporary Buddhist should be.

It is frequently assumed in the West that Buddhists are mystically inclined, liberal, ecologically sensitive, democratic, pacifist, tolerant, life-affirming, compassionate and spiritual. After reading *Clearing the Path,* however, such are not the qualities one would readily ascribe to Nanavira Thera. Since the image he presents is at odds with this stereotype, he is liable to appear to many Western

75. *ibid.,* 12.
76. *ibid.,* 259.

(and modern Asian) Buddhists as instinctively unattractive. What validity then does the stereotype have? Could it be that it is no more than a romantic re-invention of Buddhism, which presents a model of 'spirituality' that embodies those values the 'materialistic' West feels it has lost? Is the real reason for Nanavira's unattractiveness the challenge he presents to the assumptions on which the stereotype is based? Or, alternatively, is the stereotype valid and Nanavira Thera deluded and misguided?

As the first step in unravelling Nanavira's motives, it is helpful to consider his relation to the book that inspired him to become a *bhikkhu* and its author Julius Evola. In only one of his published letters (21 February 1964) does he mention (in passing) Evola's *The Doctrine of Awakening.* He adds in parenthesis: "which, however, I cannot now recommend to you without considerable reserves."[77] But nowhere does he state what those reserves are.

While there is no evidence in Nanavira's writings that he subscribed to Evola's political or racist views, there are a number of threads that forge a link between the spiritual outlook of the two men. One of these threads would be Nanavira's privileged military background and somewhat aristocratic bearing, which would have been endorsed by Evola's ideas on the superiority of the warrior caste and the aristocratic nature of Buddhism. While nothing in the content of his writings suggests any conscious promotion of such values, his capacity for self-discipline and his wry, detached tone of voice reflect a person who assumed authority as a right rather than a privilege.

Perhaps the strongest thread is the fact that Harold Musson's foreword to *The Doctrine of Awakening* could, with minor adjustments, have served as a foreword fifteen years later to Nanavira Thera's *Notes on Dhamma.* For the aim of the two works is essentially the same. To summarise Musson's foreword, these are: (1) "to recapture the spirit of Buddhism in its essential form;" (2) "to clear away some of the woolly ideas" (the preface to *Notes on Dhamma* says "dead matter") which have gathered around the Buddha's Teaching; and (3), and most importantly: the "encouragement of a practical application of the doctrine."[78]

While Nanavira makes no reference to, and could well have been unfamiliar with, Evola's Guénonist conception of Tradition, he certainly is a traditionalist, though in a narrower sense than Guénon. He says at one point that there is nothing he dislikes more than someone who declares that the aim of all religions is the same. While Guénon, who spent the last twenty years of his life as a convert to Islam in Cairo, eventually came to include Buddhism as part of the

---

77. *ibid.*, 357.
78. J. Evola, *The Doctrine of Awakening: A Study of the Buddhist Ascesis*, London, Luzac, 1951, ix.

revelation that lies at the heart of all religions, Nanavira came to regard any view that did not accord with his reading of the early Buddhist Canon as deficient. He is dismissive of theistic belief and religion in general and Christianity in particular.

Nanavira likewise shares Evola's contempt for the modern world. He is scathing about evolutionary and relativist conceptions of ethics and regards the Buddha's ethical code as an absolute and invariable truth. He also has little sympathy for the Western devotion to democracy, which he describes as "a general inadequacy in modern European thought—the growing view that the majority must be right, that truth is to be decided by appeal to the ballot-box."[79] For Nanavira the majority are simply a majority in delusion and therefore unlikely to arrive at the kinds of conclusions which would be reached by an enlightened minority of *āryas.* He would disagree with Evola, though, in the value of pursuing *any* course of political action. For Nanavira it is not the modern world that is flawed, but existence as such.

A real but rarely acknowledged problem lies in the Buddhist conception of a "superior" person, one who has gained privileged insight into the nature of existence. This view is held in common by all Buddhist schools and is pivotal to the oft-repeated argument that Buddhism, unlike other traditions, offers a practical way of personal transformation through spiritual practice. As Evola was aware, this doctrine plays into the hands of the political right. This principle was the basis for the government of old Tibet, which believed that the best way to run a country was by an enlightened elite, particularly an elite motivated by boundless compassion for all beings.

As soon as one seriously introduces Buddhist values into the arena of politics, one will encounter difficulties in reconciling them not only with capitalism and consumerism, but also with liberal democracy. While it may be fashionable to draw on Buddhist doctrines such as interconnectedness to support a Green political ideology, for example, one needs to be aware that the body of doctrine that enshrines such a notion could also be used to support a Green totalitarianism, a society governed by an enlightened minority who would compassionately dictate what would be best for the survival of the planet.

Not that any of these questions would have been of concern to Nanavira. For in many ways Nanavira represents the kind of Theravada Buddhist monk that Mahāyāna Buddhists would criticise as self-centred and uncaring. (It comes as no surprise that he vehemently asserts that the "Mahāyāna is *not* the Buddha's teaching.")[80] Only once in his writings does he mention the traditional

79. Anonymous [Samanera Bodhesako], ed., *Clearing the Path: Writings of Nanavira Thera (1960-1965),* 397.

80. *ibid.,* 296.

Theravāda meditation of loving-kindness (*mettābhāvanā*), only to say that he has never formally practised it. His tendency to physical isolation could arguably reflect a philosophical tendency to solipsism; in one letter he describes the appearance of another person as merely "a certain modification of my experience that requires elaborate description."[81] And elsewhere he writes: "I am far more strongly moved by episodes in books than by those in real life, which usually leave me cold."[82] He is quite unequivocal about *nirvāna* being the cessation of existence in any form. "There *is* a way out," he insists, "there is a way to put a stop to existence, if only we have the courage to let go of our cherished humanity."[83]

Nor should Nanavira's experience be judged negatively according to Mahāyāna Buddhist standards. A so-called Hīnayāna *ārya* is considered even in the Mahayana traditions as part of the Buddhist Saṅgha, and, as such, an object of respect and refuge. Nanavira may not have been motivated by great compassion, but he did claim to have experienced directly the unconditioned reality of *nirvāna,* which is the central truth of all Buddhist traditions.

Is a right-wing misogynist with uncontrollable lusts and a penchant for suicide thereby automatically disqualified from experiencing *nirvāna*? Nanavira points to passages in the Pali Canon where the stream entrant is shown to be capable of anger, jealousy, deceit and drunkenness, transgressing the lesser monastic rules, even disrobing on account of sensual desire, and, as a layman, breaking the five precepts. "Unless you bring the [practitioner] down to earth," he writes, "the Buddha's Teaching can never be a reality for you. So long as you are content to put the *sotāpanna* (stream entrant) on a pedestal well out of reach, it can never possibly occur to you that it is your duty to become *sotāpanna* yourself ... here and now in this very life."[84]

For Nanavira, Buddhism offers a radical and uncompromising praxis as a response to the deepest questions of human existence. As such it avoids the extremes of rationalism and romanticism. A scholar of Buddhism, he comments, can only feel safe as long as his subject "is not one day going to get up and look him between the eyes. ... (Quite the last thing that a professor of Buddhism would dream of doing is to profess Buddhism—*that* is left to mere amateurs like myself.)"[85] He is likewise aware of how his solitary life in the Ceylonese jungle is liable to be interpreted romantically: "The British public wants romance," he complains, "and I am *not* a romantic figure, and have no desire to be portrayed

81. *ibid.*, 270.
82. *ibid.*, 292.
83. *ibid.*, 444.
84. *ibid.*, 282.
85. *ibid.*, 452.

as one."[86] As in the Buddha's famous parable of the raft, Buddhism is a means to an end and *not* an end in itself. For Nanavira even the terms 'Buddhism' and 'Buddhist' carry "a slightly displeasing air about them—they are too much like labels one sticks on the outside of packages regardless of what the packages contain."[87]

Towards the end of his life Nanavira was convinced that the Dhamma was "very far from being understood in the West."[88] For whether aware of it or not, Europeans were still fundamentally preoccupied with the question of God, the very idea of a "moral but Godless universe"[89] being utterly alien. Yet behind the belief in God lies the even more deeply entrenched sense that the universe has a meaning or purpose. He approvingly quotes Nietzsche:

> "*Has existence then a significance at all?*—the question that will require a couple of centuries even to be heard in all its profundity."[90]

Nietzsche's question disturbs in the same way as Nanavira's suicide. For such statements challenge those collectively held, Christian-based views about the nature of life which still dominate our instinctive ethical sense of good and evil. For Buddhism to penetrate deeply into the European psyche it will have to reach such pre-articulate strata of experience. Otherwise it is liable to become merely a consoling set of beliefs and views still founded on a Theistic ethos. Enlightenment is not a transcendent mystical rapture but an ethical experience that reveals the nature of the existential dilemma and the way to its resolution.

Nanavira firmly challenges the idea that the Buddha's Teaching is in any way life-affirming. He condemns the fairly common practice at his time among Buddhists to call upon the good authority of notable non-Buddhists to attest to the Buddha's good character. He finds it particularly galling that a certain Sri Lankan professor would recruit Albert Schweizer to this purpose. For "Schweizer's philosophy is 'Reverence for Life', whereas the Buddha has said that just as even the smallest piece of excrement has a foul smell so even the smallest piece of existence is not to be commended."[91]

This scatological view of existence is for many Western people very difficult to swallow. Yet Nanavira feels justified in making such statements not merely on the basis of Canonical authority, but on the authority of his own enlightenment, his stream entry. And it is this authority that he likewise calls upon to justify his final act of suicide.

---

86. *ibid.*, 466.
87. *ibid.*, 255.
88. *ibid.*, 442.
89. *ibid.*, 307.
90. *ibid.*, 243.
91. *ibid.*, 256.

The debate over the validity of Nanavira's claim to be a stream entrant had already begun in Sri Lanka before he died. It is an offence deserving expulsion from the order for a *bhikkhu* to declare himself to have a spiritual attainment that he in fact does not have. Even if he does have the attainment, he is forbidden to tell of it to anyone except a fellow *bhikkhu.* Nanavira's claim to stream entry was recorded in a letter in a sealed envelope that was only to be opened by the senior *bhikkhu* of the Island Hermitage in the event of his death. For some reason (perhaps a rumour of suicide?), the letter was opened in 1964 and the contents became known. To defuse the matter, Nanavira spoke openly about it for the first time to a fellow *bhikkhu* in Colombo, thus letting "this rather awkward cat ... out of the bag."[92]

How does one decide whether another person really is a stream entrant or whether they are deluding themselves? According to the *sutta*s, only an *ārya* can recognise another *ārya.* It would follow, therefore, that only a bona fide *ārya* would have the authority to deny Nanavira's claim. But then the same questions would arise with regard to *that* person, which would require the authority of yet another bona fide *ārya*, and so on ad infinitum.

Subjectively, however, the attainment of stream entry can be validated by a discernible and definitive psychological change. For upon attaining stream entry three 'fetters' (*samyojana*) disappear for good: (1) views that a self abides either in or apart from the psycho-physical aggregates (*sakkāya-diṭṭhi*); (2) doubts about the validity of the Buddha, the Dhamma, the Saṅgha, the Training, Conditionality and other key doctrines (*vicikicchā*); and (3) attachment to the efficacity of mere rules and rituals (*sīlabbata-parāmāsa*). For Nanavira to have made the claim he did implies that he actually experienced the disappearance of these tendencies from his own mind. But only he (or another clairvoyant *ārya*) would have been able to know this. Although his writings bear no trace of these attitudes, that alone would be insufficient evidence to conclude anything about the degree of the author's attainment; for it could reflect merely a commitment to doctrinal orthodoxy.

One also cannot rule out the possibility that Nanavira Thera was suffering from a delusion, that he was driven to suicide by unconscious fears and desires over which he had no awareness or control. The clearest statement of his own views on the matter appears in a letter of 16 May, 1963. "Do not think," he writes,

> "that I regard suicide as praiseworthy—that there can easily be an element of weakness in it, I am the first to admit... but I certainly regard it as preferable to a number of other possibilities. (I would a hundred times

92. *ibid.*, 381.

rather have it said of the *Notes* that the author killed himself as a *bhikkhu* than that he disrobed; for *bhikkhus* have become *arahants* in the act of suicide, but it is not recorded that anyone became *arahant* in the act of disrobing.)"[93]

It might help overcome the unease about the stigma of suicide if one described Nanavira's act as one of 'enlightened euthanasia.'

The greatest irony of this story is how a passage from a *sutta* saved an Italian fascist from committing suicide, in gratitude for which he wrote a book that impelled an English army officer to become a *bhikkhu*, who eventually committed suicide with the conviction that it was fully justified by the *suttas*.

The value of Nanavira Thera's life lies not so much in the answers it gives but in the questions it raises about what it means for a European to be a practising Buddhist. His writings clear away many woolly ideas about the Buddha's Teaching (at least as found in the Pali Canon) and force one to address uncomfortable questions that are usually ignored. Are either Evola's fascist or Nanavira's life-denying interpretations of the Buddha's Teaching any more or less tenable than the liberal-democratic and life-affirming readings of the tradition that abound in the West today? Even if Nanavira's work only forces us to recognise the sub-conscious and culturally biased assumptions we project onto Buddhism, then it will have provided an important service. This does not mean that we would then have to adopt his (or, heaven forbid, Evola's) views rather than our own, but simply that we would have stepped free of one more 'thicket of views', thus enabling a clearer vision of how to proceed along a path whose ultimate destination we cannot know.

Whatever reservations one may have about Nanavira Thera, one has to acknowledge that he was the first European to have left such a vivid and rigorous account of a life dedicated to realising the truths disclosed by the Dhamma. Of course, it is impossible to say whether other Western Buddhists have not accomplished the same or more. But their published writings tend not to discuss these matters. Nanavira's uniqueness lies in his having embraced the Dhamma with wholehearted confidence, having sought to clear away with reason much of the confusion surrounding its orthodox interpretation, having practised it relentlessly, having recorded his experience of it in detail, and ultimately having sacrificed his life for it.

Postscript

Since completing this essay (an earlier version of which was originally intended as a chapter in my book, *The Awakening of the West: The Encounter of*

93. *ibid.*, 279.

Buddhism and Western Culture [London, Thorsons/ Berkeley, Parallax, 1994]) further writings by and concerning Nanavira Thera have come to my attention.

By far the most significant of these is an unpublished volume of 638 typewritten pages entitled *Early Writings (1950 - 1960),* likewise compiled by Samanera Bodhesako. The bulk of this volume (426 pages) consists of Nanavira's extensive correspondence with Nanamoli Thera from 1954-1959. Unfortunately, only fragments of Nanamoli's side of the correspondence have been found. These letters shed considerable light on the relations between the two men and provide a wealth of material on the formation of Nanavira's thought prior to his 'stream entry.' The remainder of the volume includes two early essays (Nibbana and Anatta and Sketch for a Proof of Rebirth) as well as notes from a Commonplace Book and Marginalia from books owned by Nanavira.

I hope at some later date to be able to incorporate this additional material into a more detailed and critical study of Nanavira, Nanamoli and their times.

The Origins of Insight Meditation

Lance Cousins

It is easy to get the impression from reading the literature that the principal form of meditation current today in Theravāda Buddhism is a particular type of insight meditation (*vipassanā*)—one which is keenly recommended by adherents. Meditation practice of this kind has in relatively recent years spread from Burma to other Southern Buddhist countries and even outside the traditional environment of this form of Buddhism. Today centres and teachers for the practice of insight meditation are to be found in England, Germany, India, U.S.A., and many other countries. Almost all of these derive ultimately from Burma, although they are not all of the same branch of Burmese meditation. This method is advocated with great, if not excessive, enthusiasm—perhaps a single quotation (from the well-known German monk Ñāṇaponika Mahāthera) will suffice:[1]

> "This ancient Way of Mindfulness is as practicable today as it was 2,500 years ago. It is as applicable in the lands of the West as in the East; in the midst of life's turmoil as well as in the peace of the monk's cell.
> Right Mindfulness is, in fact, the indispensable basis of Right Living and Right Thinking—everywhere, at any time, for everyone."

In this article I look first at the present-day practice of this type of meditation and its competitors, then touch briefly on the historical roots of these schools in recent centuries so far as they are known, afterwards turning to the specific features of this kind of *bhāvanā* and to the literary sources of this approach, as they are given in the Theravādin commentarial literature of the first millennium A.D. Looking then to the sources of the commentaries themselves, I find the principal origin of this type of material in a later canonical work, the *Paṭisambhidā-magga* and seek to situate its historical context in the period of the formation of the Vibhajjavādin and Sarvāstivādin schools. Finally I look briefly at the earlier origins of the wisdom tradition in Buddhism and comment on the

1. Nyanaponika Thera, *The Heart of Buddhist Meditation,* third ed., London, 1962 [1953], 7.

work of those scholars who consider it to be a later development, posterior to the time of the Buddha himself.

Schools of meditation practice today

Leaving aside forms of Buddhist meditation which have their roots in Northern or Eastern Buddhism, almost all commercially published accounts of meditation by Buddhist (and non-Buddhist) practitioners are derived from some branch of Burmese insight meditation, and usually from one of two branches of that.[2] Most other writing is either based on that or on the fifth century *Visuddhimagga* of Buddhaghosa or on a mixture of the two.[3] Even Kornfield's *Living Buddhist*

2. Some examples are: M. Byles, *Journey into Burmese Silence*, London, 1962; J.E. Coleman, *The Quiet Mind*, New York, 1971; V.R. (Sobhana Dhammasudhi) Dhiravamsa, *The Real Way to Awakening*, London, 1969; V.R. (Vichitr Tissadatto) Dhiravamsa, *Insight Meditation*, London, 2508; V.R. Dhiravamsa, *The Dynamic Way of Meditation, The Release and Cure of Pain and Suffering through Vipassanā Meditative Techniques*, Wellingborough, Northants, 1982; V.R. Dhiravamsa, *The Way of Non-attachment*, Wellingborough, Northants, 1975; V.R. Dhiravamsa, *The Middle Path of Life, Being Talks on the Practice of Insight Meditation*, London, 1974; V.R. Dhiravamsa, *A New Approach to Buddhism*, London, 1972; J. Goldstein, *The Experience of Insight: A Simple and Direct Guide to Buddhist Meditation*, 2nd ed., New York, 1983 [1976]; J. Goldstein & J Kornfield, *Seeking the Heart of Wisdom, The Path of Insight Meditation*, Boston & London, 1987; Henepola Gunaratana, Mahāthera, *Mindfulness in Plain English*, reprinted ed., Taipei, 1991; J. Hamilton-Merritt, *A Meditator's Diary, A Western Woman's Unique Experiences in Thailand Monasteries*, 1979 [1976]; A. & J. James, *A Meditation Retreat*, Box, Wiltshire, 1986; A. & J. James, *Modern Buddhism*, Box, Wiltshire, 1987; A. James, *The Unfolding of Wisdom, The Buddha's Path to Enlightenment*, Bradford on Avon, 1993; Chua Jantrupon, *Vipassanā Bhāvanā (Theory, Practice and Result)*, 2nd ed., tr. by F. Tullius, Chonburi, 1988; W.L. King, *A Thousand Lives Away*, Cambridge, Massachusetts, 1965; Mahāsi, Sayadaw, *Satipaṭṭhāna Vipassanā*, Bangkok, 1975; Achan Sobin S. Namto, *Moment to Moment Mindfulness, A Pictorial Manual for Meditators*, Fawnskin, California, 1989; Thich Nhãt Han, *The Miracle of Mindfulness, A Manual on Meditation*, rev. ed., tr. by Mobi Ho, Boston, 1987; Thich Nhãt Han, *The Sun My Heart: From Mindfulness to Insight Contemplation*, Berkeley, Calif., c. 1988; E.H. Shattock, *An Experiment in Mindfulness*, London, 1970 [1958]; D.K. Swearer, *Secrets of the Lotus, An Introduction to Buddhist Meditation—Contemporary Classical Interpretations of the Zen and Theravāda Traditions*, New York & London, 1971; J. Walters, *Mind Unshaken*, London, 1961. Other accounts include: G.D. Bond, "The Insight Meditation Movement in Contemporary Theravada Buddhism," *JISRC*, 2.4, 1987, 23–76; R. Gombrich, "From Monastery to Meditation Centre: Lay Meditation in Modern Sri Lanka," in *Buddhist Studies — Ancient and Modern*, eds., P. Denwood and T. Piatigorsky, 20–34, London, 1983; J. Maquet, "Expressive Space and Theravada Values: A Meditation Monastery in Sri Lanka," *Ethos*, 3.1, 1975, 1–23; J. Maquet, "Meditation in Contemporary Sri Lanka: Idea and Practice," *JTP*, 7.2, 1975, 182–96.
3. To mention some of the more influential—largely based on the *Visuddhimagga* are: Edward Conze, *Buddhist Meditation*, London, 1956; Paravahera Vajirañāṇa, Mahāthera, *Buddhist Meditation in Theory and Practice, A General Exposition According to the Pāli Canon of the Theravāda School*, Colombo, 1962; partly based

Masters[4] is heavily and misleadingly biased towards the insight meditation tradition in its selection, although this book does give some coverage of Thai approaches and its final chapter provides a good overview. Of course there is a considerable body of pamphlet literature, distributed by individual monasteries and meditation centres. This is much more varied, but many such works are difficult to obtain except by personal visits.

Before pursuing the history of this tradition it is perhaps useful to look briefly at the other kinds of meditation current at the present time. In Sri Lanka today, there are a number of forest centres which do not practise exclusively insight meditation, although there are certainly influences there from Burma. Most of these probably come from an earlier stage in the development of the Burmese insight tradition. In particular some of these centres teach *kasiṇabhāvanā* i.e. meditation on colours and the qualities of the four elements.[5] It is possible, however, that this tradition is a relatively recent development, partly based upon the texts. Widespread among individual monks are two practices: the development of loving-kindness (to oneself and usually to all sentient beings) and mindfulness of in-and-out breathing.[6] The first of these is strictly a form of *samatha* or calm meditation, although it is not unusual for it to be practised in conjunction with insight meditation or as a balancing adjunct to other methods. Equally it may be (and often is) adopted as the main form of meditation. As to the second, many different techniques for working with the breath are in fact current, but breathing mindfulness differs crucially from the other methods in that it can be used to develop insight or calm or both together. All these kinds of practice, as found in the island today, seem to be partly individual creations from the literature and partly something transmitted through the network of individual connections within the Buddhist *saṅgha*. It is of course impossible to assess how old the meditative traditions of that network may be, but it certainly includes ideas and practices coming from both Burma and Indo-China.

---

on experience of insight meditation and partly on the *Visuddhimagga* are: G.D. Bond, *The Buddhist Revival in Sri Lanka, Religious Tradition, Reinterpretation and Response*, Columbia, S.C., 1988; W.L. King, *Theravāda Meditation: The Buddhist Transformation of Yoga*, University Park & London, 1980; Nyanaponika Thera, *The Heart of Buddhist Meditation*, third ed., London, 1962 [1953]. The principal exceptions (among larger works) to this rule are: Bhikkhu Khantipalo, *Calm and Insight, A Buddhist Manual for Meditators*, London, 1981; Phra Mahā Singhathon Narāsabho, *Buddhism, A Guide to a Happy Life*, Bangkok, 1971. Hammalawa Saddhātissa, *The Buddha's Way*, London & New York, 1971/1972 is also rather more wide-ranging than most in its sources.

4. J. Kornfield, *Living Buddhist Masters*, Santa Cruz, 1977.
5. I have twice stayed for a few weeks at one such centre (Kalugala). Others are described in M.B. Carrithers, *The Forest Monks of Sri Lanka: An Anthropological and Historical Study*, Delhi, 1983.
6. This statement is based upon personal observation.

In Burma many schools of insight meditation are current, but in addition to that there is a great deal of concentration-orientated meditation.[7] Most of the latter seems to be associated either with esotericism of some kind or with the development of psychic powers and is often especially linked to developing mental contact with some kind of non-human being.[8] This kind of thing is found in Thailand, but what is also found there is a tradition (or rather a number of traditions) which seek to develop concentration to a high level as the basis for the subsequent achievement of insight and the higher levels of the Buddhist path. I shall contrast this approach as calm meditation, although it should be noted that there are Burmese insight schools which place more emphasis on concentration than others, while there are Thai schools which introduce the insight aspect at a somewhat earlier stage than others. (I shall exclude from consideration here Thai schools of insight meditation as these seem to have been introduced from Burma either in the post-war period or earlier in the twentieth century.)

Among the Thai schools the most well-known to European practitioners is certainly the *samādhi* tradition of North-East Thailand. This approach, also referred to as the Forest Tradition, is particularly, but not exclusively, current in the Thammayut *nikāya*. It often involves the attempt to develop some degree of *samādhi* but does bring in some insight at an early stage. It can also be characterized by its use of meditation on the thirty two parts of the body and by use of the *mantra Buddho* together with mindfulness of breathing. This tradition is both conservative and reformist but not usually modernist or ultimatist.[9] It can

7. G. Houtman writes: "Today at least two dozen distinct nationally renowned insight methodologies operate many hundreds of centres, in which many thousands of independent teachers teach, and to which hundreds of thousands of independent practitioners commit themselves for temporary retreats." (Draft Introduction to Gustaaf Houtman, *Contemplating Insight*, forthcoming, page 5). No doubt there are more which operate only in small groups or even on a one-to-one basis with a single teacher.

8. G. Houtman, "Traditions of Buddhist Practice in Burma," Ph.D, SOAS, University of London, 1990.

9. It should be noted, however, that it has its roots in the Thammayut reform of King Mongkut (king 1851–1868, but ordained as a monk from 1824), a reform which was certainly actively modernist in the second quarter of the nineteenth century. For the reform of King Mongkut and the Forest Tradition, see: F. Bizot, *Le Bouddhisme des Thaïs*, Bangkok, 1993, chapter 3; S.J. Tambiah, *World Conqueror and World Renouncer, A Study of Buddhism and Polity in Thailand Against a Historical Background*, Cambridge, 1976; S.J. Tambiah, *The Buddhist Saints of the Forest and the Cult of Amulets, A Study in Charisma, Hagiography, Sectarianism and Millennial Buddhism*, Cambridge, 1984, chapters 6 and 9–11; J.L. Taylor, *Forest Monks and the Nation-State, An Anthropological and Historical Study in Northeastern Thailand*, Singapore, 1993. Many pamphlets for free distribution from this tradition circulate. See Kornfield, *op. cit.*, chapters 9 (and 4). English versions of some are available on the InterNet from the DharmaNet archives, currently available

be contrasted with the highly modernist approach of the followers of Buddhadāsa Bhikkhu with their distinct tendency towards ultimatism.[10] A more traditionalist approach is that of Wat Paknam involving concentration on various centres in the body, particularly one just above the navel, and the *mantra sammā arahaṃ.*[11] An offshoot of this is the Dhammakāya movement with the same kind of meditation practice, but with a strongly modernizing tendency.[12] Here however the modernization lies rather in presentation than in ideas; so it is perhaps better characterized as revivalist. It is sometimes referred to as fundamentalist, but this is rather misleading.

The last two of these must have their roots in the kind of Southern Buddhist esotericism so ably described in the writings of François Bizot.[13] In fact Bizot

---

via anonymous FTP from the node sunsite.unc.edu in the sub-directory /pub/academic/religious studies/Buddhism/DEFA/ Theravada.

10. By 'ultimatist' I mean the perennial tendency within most forms of Buddhism to emphasize the highest levels of wisdom or enlightenment and discard more elementary levels. For a full bibliography on Buddhadāsa, see: Louis Gabaude, *Une herméneutique bouddhique contemporaine de Thaïlande: Buddhadāsa Bhikkhu*, Paris, 1988; *cf.* also Peter A. Jackson, *Buddhadasa: a Buddhist Thinker for the Modern World*, Bangkok, 1988 and Buddhadāsa, Bhikkhu, *Toward the Truth*, Philadelphia, Pa., 1971.
11. A visitor's account from 1954 in Richard Randall, *Life as a Siamese Monk*, Bradford on Avon, 1990. Some English pamphlets: T. Magness, *Sammā Samādhi, Being an Exposition of the Method of Samatha-vipassanā as Discovered and Attained by All Buddhas*, Bangkok, c. 1960; T. Magness, *Sammā Samādhi (Part Two), Being an Exposition of Attainments Derived From Samatha-vipassanā*, Bangkok, c. 1961; T. Magness, *The Life and Teachings of the Ven. Chao Khun Mongkol-thepmuni*, Bangkok, c. 1970 ?; Phra Wai Cattālayo, *Brightness of Dhamma*, Bangkok, 1986; The Venerable Pra (*sic*) Bhavana-kosolthera, (Veera Ganuttamo), *Basic Meditation Practice by Vijja Dhammakaya Approach*, Bangkok, 1984.
12. Ven. Mettānando, Bhikkhu, "The Dhammakāya Movement—An Aspect from Within," in *IABS Tenth International Conference in Paris*, edited by Ananda W.P. Guruge, 35–36, 1991(a much shortened version of the conference paper). Various English language pamphlets are available from Wat Dhammakāya.
13. F. Bizot, *Le Figuier à Cinq Branches, Recherche sur le bouddhisme khmer*, Paris, 1976; F. Bizot, "La Grotte de la Naissance. Recherches sur le bouddhisme khmer, II," *BEFEO*, LXVII, 1980, 221–273; F. Bizot, *Le Don de Soi-même, Recherches sur le bouddhisme khmer III*, Paris, 1981; F. Bizot, "Notes sur les *yantra* bouddhiques d'Indochine," in *Tantric and Taoist Studies in honour of R.A. Stein*, ed., M. Strickmann, Vol. I, 155–191, Brussels, 1981; F. Bizot, *Les traditions de la pabbajjā en Asie du Sud-Est, Recherches sur le bouddhisme khmer, IV*, Göttingen, 1988; F. Bizot, *Rāmaker, L'Amour symbolique de Rām et Setā, Recherches sur le bouddhisme Khmer, V*, Paris, 1989; F. Bizot, "La consécration des statues et le culte des morts," in *Recherches nouvelles sur le Cambodge*, ed., F Bizot, Paris, 1994, 101–39; F. Bizot, *Le bouddhisme des Thaïs*, Bangkok, 1993; F. Bizot and O. von Hinüber, *La guirlande de Joyaux*, Paris, 1994 and see also: O. de Bernon and F. Bizot, *Le Rāmaker du vieux Chak*, Paris, 1995; Catherine Becchetti, *Le mystère dans les lettres*, Bangkok, 1991; C. Becchetti, "Une ancienne tradition de manuscrits au

has described a number of types of meditation practice of a loosely tantric kind which he has met with in Cambodia (and Northern Thailand ?). Some at least of these traditions have clearly survived the period of Communist rule.[14] It seems that they have had some currency at a popular level through most of mainland South-East Asia, but tend to be disliked in the higher levels of the hierarchy and by some of the western-educated upper classes.[15]

Historical roots

There has been some discussion among scholars as to exactly how old the meditation tradition is. In fact we should distinguish carefully here what we mean by meditation and who exactly we are referring to. First of all it is necessary to distinguish between monks and lay people. It is often claimed that meditation among lay people in Ceylon is a relatively new phenomenon of the post-war period. Certainly a middle class movement, attending meditation centres catering for the laity is indeed a recent development. Relatively few village people seem to take up meditation before they reach a more advanced age. It may however be a mistake to assume that this is merely formalistic or ineffective.

In South-East Asia lay practice in youth is again claimed to be a recent phenomenon, although certainly considerably older than in Ceylon. I have doubts about this, however, as the strong tradition of spending a period in the *saṅgha* must have led to a certain number of individuals continuing to meditate after disrobing. Of course, there is no doubt that the majority of meditators would have been monks before relatively recent times. In any case lay meditation seems to have been a normative part of the various forms of esotericism.

For monks, it is clear that there has always been some tradition of meditation, at least in South-East Asia. In Ceylon it is usually held that relatively few monks meditate. This seems to me to be a slight overstatement of the case. Nevertheless for Ceylon the impression one has is that the meditation tradition was largely moribund at some point in the past and has been in part reintroduced from elsewhere. The same claim that few monks meditate is also made for Burma and Thailand. Here I find it flatly unbelievable. My own experience is that meditation is widely practised and well-known, although certainly not universal. The claim is based upon anthropological data which I find partially suspect. Sometimes one feels that it is a bit like sending a questionnaire to vicars asking

---

Cambodge," in *Recherches nouvelles sur le Cambodge*, ed., F Bizot, Paris, 1994, 47–62.

14. F. Bizot, *Le Chemin de Laṅkā*, Paris, 1992, 72.
15. On this tradition, see L.S. Cousins, "Esoteric Southern Buddhism," in title to be announced, ed., Susan Hamilton, 1996.

them if they are mystics—probably even those with a considerable spiritual experience and commitment would be likely to answer 'no'. In fact a much more sophisticated sociological analysis than is usually undertaken seems required, taking into account such things as regional differences, what is meant by meditation and the overall pattern of the different stages of a monk's life.

Above all, it is essential to attempt to ask questions in terms which are actually meaningful to the meditation tradition. This is where what we actually mean by 'meditation' becomes crucial. In general English usage of the word 'meditation' seems to refer to methods or techniques of repetitive exercise for developing some kind of mental state or understanding. This is very far from covering the full range of meaning of Buddhist *bhāvanā*. Indeed this term refers very precisely to the bringing into being of the *bodhipakkhiyadhammas* in general or the eightfold path in particular. In other words, such monastic activities as studying or teaching the *dhamma* as well as chanting *suttas* or repetition of *gāthā* may equally be forms of *bhāvanā*. This is certainly the position of the *aṭṭhakathā* and was probably that of traditional Theravāda Buddhism. Many *samatha* meditators today would still have some such understanding. In this view of the matter, *bhāvanā* is very widely practised indeed, both by virtually all monks and by most of the more committed laity.

While such a view of 'meditation' is indeed still widely held, it is precisely not the position which is frequent in some schools of insight meditation. For them, such activities as chanting and repetition of traditional formulæ are either not meditation at all or only an inferior form of meditation and that only when they are in a very orthodox form. Note then that for such monks or lay followers there is relatively little meditation in present-day Buddhism—by definition.

Such a position can be a product of reformism, the frequently recurring tendency in the history of Theravāda Buddhism to seek to restore Buddhism in general and the *saṅgha* in particular to an idealized state conceived of as their original and proper condition. Reformist movements have in fact recurred fairly frequently throughout the last thousand years of Southern Buddhist history, if not longer. However, there is little evidence to suggest that in the past this was associated with insight meditation. In some cases at least, it was much more concerned with monastic practice and traditional scholarship. On the whole it seems that it is not possible, at present, to trace the lineage of the present-day insight meditation tradition beyond the nineteenth century (in Burma).

Ironically, the only form of meditation whose lineage appears to be provably older than this is the esoteric tradition. One branch of this tradition was certainly introduced into Ceylon by monks sent by the King of Siam in the eighteenth century. The practice of this method appears to have died out on the island in the course of the nineteenth century, but, as mentioned above, it is still extant in

Cambodia. It must in the past have been more widespread and is in any case clearly affiliated to some methods still surviving in Thailand. Indeed it is likely that there must have been an ongoing tradition of practice of a number of methods of *samatha* meditation.

In contrast the practice of insight meditation as a separate method is probably a revival based at least in part upon the texts. (Of course, it must always have existed as an adjunct to *samatha* meditation and as a practice for advanced *samatha* meditators.) We can in fact be more precise than that. Its primary source is the commentarial writings of Buddhaghosa, particularly the *Visuddhimagga*. Undoubtedly, some of the monks who have been influential teachers of *vipassanā* in Burma were very learned in *abhidhamma*, but, as we shall see, this is not the main basis for their presentation of insight meditation. (I do not mean to suggest that they did not draw on their knowledge of canonical Buddhism. Indeed, they certainly did. The point is that their presentation is structured on the *Visuddhimagga* model.)

Characteristic features of insight meditation

In order to delineate the main features of insight meditation today, I shall take as my paradigm the school of Mahāsi Sayadaw. This is perhaps the most influential single school at the present time and, more importantly, is probably one of the more extreme in its advocacy of insight and distrust of concentration.[16] (This is particularly the case in conversation with adherents of this approach; in some of his writings the Mahāsi himself seems to take a more moderate position.) The most distinctive element in the practice of this school is undoubtedly its technique of watching the rise and fall of the abdomen, but I shall pass over this as it seems to be an innovation of the Mahāsi himself.

The method of practice of this school is highly intensive, involving the maintenance of mindfulness and clear comprehension over long periods of time, ideally with very little sleep—eighteen to twenty hours of continuous meditation is normative. Usually sitting meditation and walking practice are alternated. The walking practice involves the systematic breaking down into named stages of the process of movement. Initially, each of these stages is noted mentally and at the same time all external distractions or internal wanderings of the mind are similarly noted. It is in fact recommended that the walking practice (and any other necessary activities) should be carried out as slowly as possible.[17] This slowing down is sometimes criticized by devotees of other schools of insight[18]

16. Outside Burma (but not within) the tradition of U Ba Khin is very nearly as influential, but this school is much more moderate in its approach.
17. Mahāsi, Sayadaw, *Satipaṭṭhāna Vipassanā*, Bangkok, 1975, 22: "It is therefore instructed that slow motion exercises be carried out at all times."
18. *e.g.* by the disciples of the well-known Thai female teacher, Acharn Naeb.

and does not in fact seem to be clearly authorized in the texts, although the differentiation of movement into stages is found.

As with most other schools of insight meditation the stages of the path are mapped out in accordance with the seven purifications and the various kinds of insight knowledge. On the whole the *Visuddhimagga* account is followed fairly closely with a few variations (usually justified by reference to other texts). I shall not give a detailed account of this, as I have outlined Buddhaghosa's description elsewhere.[19] The most important features for present purposes are set out in Table One. The third and fourth columns set out (in ascending order) the seven purifications (*visuddhi*) which form the structure of the *Visuddhimagga*. The first two columns give the corresponding insight knowledges which occur in each stage of purification.

The point at which controversy has sometimes arisen in relation to Mahāsi Sayadaw's approach lies in relation to the second purification: *cittavisuddhi*, always understood as equivalent to concentration (*samādhi*). For the Mahāsi, all that is required to practise insight meditation is the weakest of the three degrees of concentration, i.e. *khaṇikasamādhi* or momentary concentration. Of course, if this means that this degree of concentration is all that is required to *start* meditation, then it is not controversial and in fact applies to any kind of meditation. However, Mahāsi Sayadaw seems to mean more than this. Again, it is often stated that the various insight knowledges are experienced in momentary concentration. This seems to follow from the fact that they do not have a *paṭibhāganimitta* or non-sensory mental object, as the two higher kinds of concentration do. By elimination therefore they must be developed with momentary concentration.

There are two problems with this. The first is historical. Buddhaghosa uses the term *khaṇikasamādhi* only rather rarely. The list of the three kinds of concentration (momentary, access and absorption) occurs in a passage which explains how the five kinds of *pīti* (energization/joy), when they are conceived and mature, bring about the tranquillization of mind and body. When that matures, it brings about bodily and mental happiness. When that in turn matures,

19. L.S. Cousins, "The Stages of Christian Mysticism and Buddhist Purification: the Interior Castle of St. Teresa of Avila and the Path of Purification of Buddhaghosa," in *The Yogi and the Mystic—Studies in Indian and Comparative Mysticism*, ed., K.Werner, London, 1989, 103–120.

avasiṭṭhakilesa-paccavekkhaṇa	recollection of remaining defilements		
pahīnakilesa-paccavekkhaṇa	recollection of defilements abandoned		
sotāpatti, etc.	stream-entry, etc.	*ñāṇadassana-visuddhi*	purification by knowing and seeing
gotrabhu	lineage		
anuloma	inflow		
saṅkhārupekkhā	equipoise as to constructions		
paṭisaṅkhānupassanā	deep analysis	*paṭipadāñāṇa-dassanavisuddhi*	purification by knowing and seeing the path
muñcitukamyatā	desire to be free		
nibbidānupassanā	distaste	*(balavavipassanā)*	(strong insight)
ādīnavānupassanā	wretchedness		
bhayatupaṭṭhāna	establishing the sense of danger		
bhaṅgānupassanā	breaking up		
udayabbayadassana	seeing rise and dissolution	*maggāmaggañāṇa-dassanavisuddhi*	purification by knowing and seeing true and false ways
kalāpasammasana	laying hold in groups	*(taruṇa-vipassanā)*	(young insight)
paccayapariggaha =	comprehending conditions	*kaṅkhāvitaraṇa-visuddhi*	purification by crossing through doubt
(cullasotāpanna)	(lesser stream-enterer)		
nāmarūpavavatthāna	determining name and form	*diṭṭhivisuddhi*	purification of view
(saṅkhāraparicchedа)	(defining constructions)		
		cittavisuddhi	purification of mind
		sīlavisuddhi	purification of precept

Table One

it brings about the three kinds of concentration.[20] It is not entirely clear what Buddhaghosa (as opposed to later interpreters) means by that. The only other passage in which Buddhaghosa refers to momentary concentration is in the *Saṃyutta Commentary*.[21] Here *ekodibhūta* is explained as concentrated with momentary concentration, while *ekagga-citta* is understood to refer to access and absorption. The *ṭīkā* understands momentary concentration in this passage as referring to the concentration of the prior stage which brings access *jhāna*. In other words it would seem to be simply the momentary occurrence of access concentration, rather than a different level of concentration as such. Buddhaghosa also uses a somewhat similar term: *khaṇikacitt(ass') ekaggatā* — momentary one-pointedness of mind.[22] This is used to explain how someone practising breathing mindfulness emerges from *jhāna* and contemplates the mind associated with *jhāna* as subject to destruction and liable to disappear. As he is doing so, at a moment of insight momentary one-pointedness of mind arises as a result of penetrating the (three) characteristics (of impermanence, etc.). Subsequently he fixes the mind on the object by means of this momentary one-pointedness of mind. This seems to imply that the term momentary concentration would be applied by Buddhaghosa to the earlier stages of insight.

---

20. Vism, 144. Virtually the same passage is given in the *Abhidhamma Commentary* at Dhs-a, 117. This reference in Dhs-a is likely to be the source of the passage in the *Visuddhimagga* or else both are drawing from an earlier *Abhidhamma* commentary. The Dhs-a adds that only the kinds of *pīti* which produce the first two kinds of concentration apply i.e. in commenting on skilful, sense-sphere consciousness. Upasena and Mahānāma also give this passage (Nidd-a , I, 129; Paṭis-a, I, 183), but it is noteworthy that Dhammapāla does not. Indeed, Dhammapāla uses the term only once in his commentaries (at Th-a, III, 208) and Buddhadatta apparently never uses it. It is possible that there is a difference here between the Indian and the Sinhalese Pali commentators.
21. Spk, III, 200. Spk-pṭ, II (Be, 2521) 469: *Paṭipakkha-dhammehi anabhibhūtatāya eko udetī ti ekodī ti laddha-nāmo samādhi bhūto jāto etesan ti ekodibhūtā. Etttha ca ekodibhūtā ti etena upacāra-jjhānâvahā pubba-bhāgiko samādhi vutto; samāhitā ti etena upacār'-appanā-samādhi. Ekagga-cittā ti etena su-bhāvito vasi-ppatto appanā-samādhi vutto ti veditabbo.*
22. Vism, 289 = Sp, II, 433; cf. Paṭis-a, II, 503. The *Mahāṭīkā* comments: momentary one-pointedness of mind is concentration which lasts for just a moment (at a time); for that fixes the mind unshakably on the object as if in absorption, through occurring continuously in a single manner without being overcome by opposing qualities (*paṭipakkha*) (Vism-mhṭ, [1928] I, 278). Sometimes, Buddhaghosa does refer to: "factors of awakening in insight, which have various qualities and characteristics and last for one moment only"—Ps , IV, 143; Spk, III, 274 (v.l.). Note that in the same place there is mention of concentration which is "as if attained to absorption". There are also two passages referring to momentary attainment of fruition attainment (*khaṇikasamāpatti*): Sv, II, 547 (pṭ: II, 186); Spk, III, 292 f., but this expression is not used elsewhere or by other commentators.

This suggestion gains some support from the use of another term in the earlier commentators. Mahānāma (early sixth century A.D.) in fact distinguishes four kinds of concentration, of which the first two are: momentary concentration and insight concentration (*vipassanāsamādhi*).[23] This latter term is sometimes used by Buddhaghosa,[24] but more often, when referring to the higher stages of insight, he uses either a simple reference to insight or such expressions as signless liberation (*animitto vimokkho*) or signless attainment of mind (*animitta-cetosamāpatti*).[25] The higher knowledges are treated at a much later point in the *Visuddhimagga* and are perhaps considered by Buddhaghosa as something *sui generis*.

Let us note here that these rather few passages, in which momentary concentration is referred to, must stand against numerous references to concentration as having just the two kinds: access (*upacāra*) and absorption (*appanā*).[26] Access concentration is in fact fairly ancient as a concept, with roots in the canonical literature.[27] It is generally characterized in the commentaries in terms of the abandonment of the hindrances and the arising of the abstract or semblance sign (*paṭibhāga-nimitta*). It is possible that momentary concentration is intended to apply to the stage in meditation before this, when an acquired sign (*uggahanimitta*) or eidetic image is the object of the mind (as well as to the parallel stage in insight meditation). However, it is more likely that Buddhaghosa simply means by momentary concentration a stage in which moments of access concentration with a semblance *nimitta* as their object occur in between moments with other objects.

---

23. Paṭis-a, I, 125. Paṭis-gp, (c. 1962) 86: *Paramatthakkhaṇamattena yutto samādhi khaṇikasamādhi, Ekattavasena vā santānena vā abhāvita-samathass' ev' etaṃ nāmaṃ*; *cf.* also Paṭis-a, I, 130; 281.

24. Spk, II, 303; III, 90; Mp, II, 362; III, 402; IV, 40. Some of Buddhaghosa's references seem to be related to the defilements of insight (*vipassanūpakkilesa*) and others to strong insight. The expression *vipassanā-samādhi* is also used by Dhammapāla: Ud-a, 191; It-a, I, 175; Th-a, II, 270; III, 118; Thī-a to Thī, 144. It is used twice in Vism-mhṭ.

25. For textual references, see Peter Harvey, "'Signless' Meditations in Pāli Buddhism," *JIABS*, 9.1, 1986, 25–52.

26. *e.g.* Vism, 85 ff.; 11; 126; Sp, II, 427 ff.; VII, 1317; Sv, I, 217; Ps, I, 108; 113; II, 83; Spk, I, 27; III, 254; 277; Mp, II, 153; III, 345; V, 67; Vibh -a, 75; 261; 269; 284, etc. Other commentators: Abhidh-av, 93 f.; Nidd-a, I, 131; 133; III, 79; Cp-a, 49; 315; It-a, I, 139; 169; 173; II, 13; Ud-a, 32; 190; 268; 407, etc.

27. The concept, if not the term, is shared with the northern *abhidhamma* schools (and the Northern Buddhist traditions derived from them). In particular, note the ninth *samādhicariyā* of the *Paṭisambhidāmagga* (Paṭis, 99), which is rightly interpreted by Ud-a, 196 and Paṭis-a, 316 as referring to access *samādhi*.

This seems also to be the position of the author of the *Mahāṭīkā* to the *Visuddhimagga*.[28] Commenting on Buddhaghosa's use of the term 'preparatory concentration' in his description of the process of developing *deva* hearing (Vism, 408), he makes it clear that momentary concentration is for him a concentration that arises easily after emerging from the preceding (fourth) *jhāna*. He indicates that preparatory concentration has been referred to (by others) as the stage of access to the *deva* hearing element,[29] but suggests that this was said with regard to multiple advertings. Obviously he is correct in regard to the consciousness process, since in this case auditory consciousnesses must be interspersed. The implication for our purposes is that momentary concentration is simply access concentration occurring with sensory consciousnesses interspersed rather than, as normally, in a series of successive mind door processes with the semblance *nimitta* and *jhāna* factors as object.

The second problem is practical. In terms of meditation experience it is quite possible that a lower degree of concentration experienced after attaining a higher one is something quite different to the same degree of concentration when a higher level has not been achieved.

This brings us to the key area of debate. On the authority of the canonical *Rathavinītasutta* (M I 145–151), the seven *visuddhi* are held to be successive stages, referred to as like a relay of chariots. It follows therefore that it is not possible to achieve the insight knowledges of the sixth purification unless the earlier stages have been completed. The particular point of relevance here is the second *visuddhi* which is traditionally defined as either access concentration or full absorption (*appanā*). Indeed Mahāsi Sayadaw himself recognizes in his Pali work *Visuddhi-ñāṇa-kathā*[30] that this is the authoritative definition. However, he argues that here the term 'access concentration' is inclusive of momentary concentration, particularly that degree of momentary concentration which can still the five hindrances (*nīvaraṇa*). "For otherwise purification of mind would be very hard to arouse for someone whose vehicle is just insight (*suddhavipassanāyānika*) (and) who is experiencing insight without having aroused either access concentration or absorption concentration."[31]

In the Mahāsi's understanding then, momentary concentration is itself something which admits of various degrees. So he speaks of the stage of

---

28. *Khaṇikasamādhi* is mentioned six times in the *Mahāṭīkā* to the *Visuddhimagga* (Mahidol CDROM). Ñāṇamoli translates five of these (see Vism Trsl. Index s.v. momentary concentration), omitting only that to Vism, 144. See note 22 above.
29. *Parikamma-samādhi nāma dibba-sota-dhātuyā upacārâvatthā ti pi vadanti.*
30. Appended to: Mahāsi, Sayadaw, *The Progress of Insight*, Kandy, 1965. See p. 42: *Nanu aṭṭhakathāsu upacāra-appanā-samādhīnaṃ yeva citta-visuddhi-bhāvo vutto ti ? Saccaṃ ...*
31. *ibid.*, (my translation, correcting misprints).

purification of mind being accomplished by momentary concentration which is similar in strength to access. Likewise the highest stage of the sixth purification is explained as being accomplished by momentary concentration which has a strength equivalent to that of full absorption. Since it is difficult to imagine how someone could achieve such a degree of momentary concentration without having at some point experienced (at least briefly) access concentration, this is perhaps not really very different to saying that the higher stages require the prior development of access. What it apparently does differ from is the position of a number of Sinhalese scholar monks.[32] They, and others, argue that it is not possible to achieve the stage of the transcendent path (*lokuttaramagga*) without having previously achieved at least the first *jhāna*. Even here, however, if the momentary concentration in strong insight were taken as momentary experiencing of absorption interspersed with insight knowledge, the difference would be rather small in practice.

The canonical texts clearly give considerable importance to *jhāna*. So at first sight it is surprising that there should be a tradition which regards it as unnecessary for some. Even the canonical *abhidhamma* texts make it clear that the transcendent path must be of at least the degree of the first *jhāna*.[33] It is true, however, that they do not in fact specify that *jhāna* is attained beforehand; in principle it could be achieved at the path moment itself. (Equally, they could be assuming that higher *jhānas* have previously been achieved.[34]) The fact remains that this seems an unexpected development and not really what is envisaged in the *suttas*. How then did such a possibility arise ?

The literary sources of the vipassanā tradition

If we take the two main features of the insight tradition as, firstly, the acceptance of routes to enlightenment which bypass the development of *jhāna* and, secondly, the mapping of the sequence of insight knowledges, then the immediate source is no doubt the *Visuddhimagga*. In a former article[35] on the distinction between *samathayāna* and *vipassanāyāna*, I have surveyed the main

32. Soma Thera, "Contemplation in the Dhamma," in *The Path of Freedom by the Arahant Upatissa*, eds., N.R.M. Ehara *et al.*, Colombo, 1961, 353–362; Kheminda Thera, *Path, Fruit and Nibbāna*, Colombo, 1965. Note that these monks have connections with other Burmese insight schools.
33. *e.g.* Dhs, 60; 69 f.
34. From this interpretation, we should understand *e.g.* Dhs as describing the specific occasion on which the path is developed. This may be of the level of any one of the four *jhānas*, but previous experience of all four may be assumed, at least in the case of the *arahant* or never-returner.
35. L.S. Cousins, "*Samatha-yāna* and *Vipassanā-yāna*," in *Buddhist Studies in Honour of Hammalava Saddhātissa*, eds., G. Dhammapāla *et al.*, 55–68, Nugegoda, Sri Lanka, 1984.

THE ORIGINS OF INSIGHT MEDITATION

Eleven knowledges from the *Paṭisambhidāmagga*		The eighteen great insights (arranged after Mahānāma)		Way of the (seven) Purifications		Suttanta	
14. paccavekkhaṇa	reviewing (recollection)	*[tadā samudāgate dhamme vipassanā]*	[insight into the dhamma arisen then]	*avasiṭṭhakilesa-paccavekkhaṇa*	recollection of remaining defilements	*khayasmiṃ khaye ñāṇa*	knowledge of destruction of the destroyed
13. vimutti	freedom	*[chinnam-anupassanā]*	[contemplation of what has been cut]	*pahīnakilesa-paccavekkhaṇa*	recollection of defilements abandoned	*vimuttasmiṃ vimuttam iti ñāṇa*	knowledge that what is freed is freed
12. phala	fruit	*[payogapaṭipassaddhi]*	[the complete stilling of effort]				
11. magga	path	*[dubhatovuṭṭhāna-vivaṭṭana]*	[turning around that emerges in both ways]	*sotāpatti, etc.* *vuṭṭhāna*	stream-entry, etc. emergence	*dassana* or *virāga*	vision or greedless(ness)
10. gotrabhu	lineage	*vivaṭṭanānupassanā*	turning around	*gotrabhu*	lineage		
9. saṅkhārupekkhā	equipoises as to constructions	*paṭisaṅkhānupassanā*	deep analysis	*anuloma* *saṅkhārupekkhā* *paṭisaṅkhānupassanā* *muñcitukamyatā*	inflow equipoise as to constructions deep analysis desire to be free	*nibbidā*	distaste
8. ādīnava	wretchedness (disadvantage)	*[nibbidā]* *ādīnavānupassanā* *yathābhūtañāṇadassana*	[distaste] wretchedness knowing and seeing things as they are	*nibbidānupassanā* *ādīnavānupassanā* *bhayatupaṭṭhāna* *(balavavipassanā)*	distaste wretchedness establishing the sense of danger (strong insight)	*nibbidā*	distaste
7. vipassanā	insight	*adhipaññādhamma-vipassanā* *suññatānupassanā* *appaṇihitānupassanā* *animittānupassanā* *vipariṇāmānupassanā* *vayānupassanā* *khayānupassanā*	dhamma insight through higher wisdom emptiness without aim signless changing dissolving destruction	*bhaṅgānupassanā*	breaking up		
6. udayabbayānupassanā *5. sammasana*	contemplating rise and fall laying hold	*paṭinissaggānupassanā* *nirodhānupassanā* *virāgānupassanā* *nibbidānupassanā* *anattānupassanā* *dukkhānupassanā* *aniccānupassanā*	releasing ceasing greedless distaste no-self suffering impermanence	*udayabbayadassana* *(taruṇa-vipassanā)* *kalāpasammasana* = *maggāmaggañāṇa-dassanavisuddhi*	seeing rise and dissolution (young insight) laying hold in groups = purification by knowing and seeing true and false ways	*yathābhūtañāṇadassana*	knowing and seeing things as they are
4. dhammaṭṭhiti	dhamma abiding	*[yathābhūtañāṇa sammādassana kaṅkhāvitaraṇā]*	[knowing things as they are right seeing crossing through doubt]	*paccayapariggaha* = *kaṅkhāvitaraṇavisuddhi* *(cullasotāpanna)*	comprehending conditions = purification by crossing through doubt (lesser stream-enterer)	*yathābhūtañāṇadassana*	knowing and seeing things as they are
[phussana ekarasa pariccāga tīraṇa ñāta]	[touching single taste renouncing causing to enter into known]	*[sacchikiriyā bhāvanā pahāna pariññā abhiññā]*	[witnessing bringing into being abandoning thoroughly knowing deeply knowing]	*nāmarūpavavatthāna* *(saṅkhārapariccheda)* = *diṭṭhivisuddhi*	determining name and form (defining constructions) = purification of view	*yathābhūtañāṇadassana*	knowing and seeing things as they are

Table Two

The underlined terms are also found in the list of knowledges in the *Ñāṇakathā* of the *Paṭisambhidāmagga*.

to awakening. It suffices to say here that the possibility of omitting *jhāna* is reasonably well-established in the *aṭṭhakathā* literature. Its ultimate source appears to lie in a particular interpretation of a passage in the *Paṭisambhidā-magga* (II, 92–103).

It is with the second of these features that I am more concerned with here—the insight knowledges. Again, the *locus classicus* is no doubt the *Visuddhimagga*, which describes what later tradition takes to be the sixteen insight knowledges in considerable detail. In the earlier *Vimuttimagga*, which was probably Buddhaghosa's model, most of these (if not all) are present, but in a very abbreviated form.[36] The additional material, as so often in the *Visuddhimagga*, is derived from the *Paṭisambhidā-magga*. This is best set out in tabular form as shown in Table Two.The underlined terms are also found in the list of knowledges in the *Ñāṇakathā* of the *Paṭisambhidāmagga*.

The first two columns of the table list the fourth to the fourteenth kinds of knowledge given in the *mātikā* to the first (and longest) section of the *Paṭisambhidā-magga*, the *Ñāṇakathā*. Since the first three kinds of knowledge are concerned with learning, precepts and concentration, while the fifteenth and those following turn to the objects of insight knowledge, this can be treated as a distinct list of eleven knowledges. In fact, each knowledge is given a definition and it is sometimes this definition which is used in the later commentarial tradition. Where this is the case I have indicated it by underlining in the fifth column.

Perhaps even more important in the *Paṭisambhidā-magga* than the knowledges of the first section is a list of thirty seven (or forty one) experiences of the Buddhist path, a list which recurs on at least thirty different occasions. (There are some variations in application which make the exact count arbitrary.) Part of this list, following the eight '*jhānas*' and preceding the four paths is the sequence known to the commentaries as the eighteen *mahāvipassanā*. It is given in the third and fourth columns of the table. (The bracketed items also occur in the *Paṭisambhidā-magga*, but elsewhere.)

It is fairly obvious that the commentarial account of the stages of insight is largely built up from the materials provided by the *Paṭisambhidā-magga*.[37] This is not to say that the *Visuddhimagga* account would have been completely acceptable or even recognisable to the author of the *Paṭisambhidā-magga* (traditionally Sāriputta, the exemplar of wisdom). Looking at it the other way sophisticated account of the stages of insight—an account which does provide

36. *e.g.* N.R.M. Ehara *et al.*, *The Path of Freedom by the Arahant Upatissa*, Colombo, 1961, 298–302.

37. There, is of course, also material from the *suttas* and the term *anuloma* from the *Paṭṭhāna*.

the main features of the later model. This is clear enough if we note that it begins with detailed analysis of phenomena, moves on to contemplation of rise and fall, then to breaking up (*bhaṅga*), to the experiencing of some kind of sense of danger and subsequently to the establishment of a settled state of equipoise. After all this, there follows the transitional stage of gaining the lineage, prior to the path knowledge itself.

The historical context of the Paṭisambhidā-magga

A.K. Warder has discussed the date of the *Paṭisambhidā-magga* and concluded that, apart from a few later additions, the main parts of this text were composed in the late third century and the early second century B.C..[38] It would be possible to argue for a slightly earlier range of possibilities and in fact Warder's assumption that the work grew over a period of time could be questioned. The work is sufficiently well-integrated that a single authorship is not beyond the bounds of possibility. For present purposes, however, Warder's dating is close enough. It situates the composition of this text in a specific historical context.

That context is of some interest in itself. It is clearly subsequent to the division of the *mahāsaṅgha*, which took place at some point not too long after the Second Communal Recitation, probably as a result of a reformist move to tighten up the discipline of the community. Such movements are common in the history of religious groups which place a high value on spiritual development or moral purity. They were mentioned above in relation to the history of Southern Buddhism over the last thousand years or so. The evolution of mediæval Christian monastic orders also provides many parallel cases, to mention only one example from a wider context. It is probable that the first division of the order did not have doctrinal implications, but it is also likely that distinct schools of thought already began to emerge in this period or soon afterwards, centred around particular teaching lineages and/or specific monastic centres and regions.[39]

In terms of dating, we can suppose that three major trends had already emerged by the third century B.C.. One of these new schools of thought was the little known Pudgalavādin tradition, which seems to have been concerned, partly with a type of dialectical exploration of and/or meditation on the nature of self and partly with investigating the nature of the process of rebirth.[40] More relevant to the history of insight meditation are the two other schools of thought: the Sarvāstivādins and the Vibhajyavādins, the latter being the ancestors of the

38. Paṭis Trsl., xxix–xxxix.
39. L.S. Cousins, "The 'Five Points' and the Origins of the Buddhist Schools," in *The Buddhist Forum*, ed., T. Skorupski, Vol. II, 27–60, London, 1991.
40. See L.S. Cousins, "Person and Self," to appear in a volume to be produced following the 'Buddhism into the Year 2000' conference (Bangkok, 1990), 1995.

Ceylon tradition. When considering the Sarvāstivādins, it is customary to focus on their specific doctrine of *dharmas* as, in some sense, transcending time. Here, however, I am not so much concerned with that as with the reasons why they were interested in the subject at all.

After all, the subject of *dharmas* is precisely the subject of the fourth foundation/establishing of mindfulness: *dhamma* contemplation in regard to *dhammas* (*dhammesu dhammānupassanā*). In other words, the concerns of the early *abhidhamma* are closely related to insight meditation. In this sense one might expect these early schools of thought to share a common interest in insight meditation in so far as they are *abhidhamma*-based in their orientation.[41] Probably, in fact, that interest precedes the crystalization of distinct schools of thought. More specifically, one of the key areas of debate which eventually separated the two *abhidhamma* traditions of Sarvāstivāda and Vibhajyavāda is the exact nature of the process by which enlightenment is attained.

This debate focussed precisely upon the realization of the four noble truths at the time of achieving the 'stages of sanctity': stream-entry and so on. For the Sarvāstivādins this was a process of gradual realization (*anupūrvâbhisamaya*) in which the sixteen aspects of the four truths were separately known in successive moments. The Vibhajyavādins on the other hand taught that the truths were realized simultaneously in a single moment (*ekâbhisamaya*). Of course the contrast between 'sudden' and 'gradual' enlightenment is one with a long subsequent history,[42] but we should none the less be careful not to exaggerate the difference. Even sixteen moments is quite a brief period in terms of *abhidharma* and it is not clear whether the Sarvāstivādins supposed that the distinction could be observed in experience. Conversely, contemplation of different aspects of the four truths in the stages shortly before realization is quite acceptable to the tradition of the Pali commentaries. Again, it is not clear how far it was thought that this could be distinguished in practice.

The *Paṭisambhidā-magga* is in many ways a text of the *ekâbhisamaya* tradition.[43] The exact historical relationship between it and the developments in the canonical Sarvāstivādin *abhidharma* is not yet known, but it is certain that

41. One might also speculate that the Pudgalavādins might have been more orientated towards *samatha* meditation, as the early Sarvāstivādins certainly were towards insight meditation. In that case the Vibhajyavādins would be seeking a compromise (as in other areas). It is certainly noticeable that the *Paṭisambhidā-magga* contains important developments in the area of calm meditation as well as the insight-orientated materials with which I am concerned in this paper.

42. David Seyfort Ruegg, *Buddha-nature, Mind and the Problem of Gradualism in a Comparative Perspective, On the Transmission and Reception of Buddhism in India and Tibet*, London, 1989, 150–192, discusses the earlier sources.

43. A.K. Warder, "Introduction," in *The Path of Discrimination*, London, 1982, v–lxiv, espec. xxiii ff.

each cannot be fully understood without the other. One might compare the way in which the availability of previously inaccessible literature of the Buddhist logical tradition has made it possible to understand many aspects of the ancient Nyāya which were otherwise unclear. So it is not surprising that the articulation of the Vibhajyavādin insight tradition which we see already well under way in the *Paṭisambhidā-magga* is paralleled by similar developments in the Sarvāstivāda.

The formulation in that tradition which corresponds to the insight knowledges is the sequence of the set of the four skilful roots connected with penetration (*nirvedhabhāgiya*).[44] The term itself is not as frequently used in the Pali tradition, although *nibbedhabhāgiya* does occur.[45] The list of four is well-known:

1. The little flame (*ŭṣmăgata*) i.e. of understanding;
2. The culmination (*mūrdhan*) i.e. of understanding;

---

44. On the *nirvedhabhāgiya*, see: R.E. Buswell, Jr, "The Path to Perdition: The Wholesome Roots and Their Eradication," in *Paths to Liberation, The Mārga and Its Transformations in Buddhist Thought*, eds., R.E. Buswell, Jr & Robert M. Gimello, Honolulu, 1992, 107–34; C. Cox, "Attainment through Abandonment: The Sarvāstivādin Path of Removing Defilements," *ibid*., 63-106, 76 nn.; E. Frauwallner, "Abhidharma-Studien III," *WZKS*, 1971, 69–121, 83; 98–101; H.V. Guenther, *Philosophy and Psychology in the Abhidharma*, 2nd ed., Berkeley, 1974, 200; L. Hurvitz, "The Abhidharma on the 'Four Aids to Penetration'", in *Buddhist Thought and Asian Civilization.* (Guenther vol.), ed., L.S. Kawamura, Emeryville, Calif., 1977; E. Lamotte, *History of Indian Buddhism, From the Origins to the Śaka Era*, Louvain, 1988, 613 f.; Louis de La Vallée Poussin, "Pārāyaṇa cité dans Jñānaprasthāna," in *Études d'Orientalisme publiés par le Musée Guimet à la mémoire de Raymonde Linossier*, Paris, 1932, 323–327; Louis de La Vallée Poussin, *Abhidharmakośabhāṣyam*, tr. by L. Pruden, Berkeley, 1988–90, Vol. III, 930–43; D. Seyfort Ruegg, *op. cit.,* 176; Śānti Bhikṣu Śāstrī, *Jñānaprasthāna-śāstra of Kātyāyanīputra Retranslated into Sanskrit from the Chinese Version of Hiuan Tsang*, Śāntiniketan, 1955; José Van Den Broeck, *La Saveur de L'Immortel* (A-p'i-t'an Kan Lu Wei Lun). *La version chinoise de l'Amṛtarasa de Ghoṣaka* (T. 1553), Louvain-la-neuve, 1977, 15, 70–72, 156–160; C. Willemen, *The Essence of Metaphysics*, Brussels, 1975, 68–72, 86 f.

45. The canonical passages are: D, III, 277; S, V, 87; A, II, 167; III, 427; Paṭis, I, 27; 35ff.; 48; II, 201f.; Vibh, 330 f. (°*in*). Closely related terms occur at: D , III, 251; A, III, 410; 417; It, 35; 93, while the term *nibbedhika-* (usually applied to *paññā*) is quite frequent—PṬC lists more than forty occurrences in the Pali Canon. The source of the term *nibbedhabhāgiya* seems to be the *Nibbedha-sutta* where we find the idea of the factors of awakening, when well-developed, penetrating and breaking up the mass of greed which has never previously been penetrated and broken up (and similarly with the masses of hatred and delusion) (S, V, 87). Most commonly, however, especially later, it is found last in the sequence: connected with decline, connected with stability, connected with something special, applied to types of *samādhi*, wisdom, *saññā*, etc. The *Mahāṭīkā* to Vism, 696 explains *nibbedhabhāgiya- samādhi-* as *vipassanā-samādhi*.

3. Acceptance (*kṣānti*) i.e. when it seems good to one;
4. Highest *dharma*.

I have translated the first a little loosely to get the metaphor. The source is probably M, I, 132 where Ariṭṭha who thinks he has a highly developed understanding is told that he has 'not a glimmering' (*na … usmīkato*).[46] Skilful roots in *abhidharma* are the three of non-greed, non-hate and non-delusion i.e. the seeds in the mind of generosity, loving-kindness and understanding or wisdom respectively. Here the skilful root of non-delusion is intended.[47]

At first sight the set of four may not look very close to the *Paṭisambhidāmagga*'s sixteen great insights (*mahāvipassanā*) or the list of eleven knowledges which are abstracted in Table Two. In fact, however, the last four and probably the first two of the eleven knowledges need to be omitted for comparison purposes. This leaves just five (i.e. knowledges 5–10 of the *Ñāṇakathā*) to correspond with the set of four. A case could be made for matching more exactly, but that perhaps goes beyond the evidence. Turning to the great insights, obviously sixteen is a much larger number than four ! Yet, when the objects of consciousness are considered, and these are the principal concern of the eighteen *mahāvipassanā*, the similarity is striking. The eighteen are concerned with various degrees of the three universal characteristics of all *dhammas*, while the set of four have as their object the sixteen aspects of the four noble truths. Since one of the three characteristics is precisely suffering (*dukkha*) and the other two can be considered as ways of looking at suffering,[48] the eighteen are in effect concerned with the first noble truth.

The similarity is even closer, when it is noted that contemplation of the three (or rather four) characteristics is usually said to lead to the set of four.[49] Moreover, the highest *dharma* and the most advanced degree of acceptance are said to focus specifically on the first noble truth.[50] In fact some of the Pali

---

46. Note that in some forms of Middle Indic where -k- is voiced (and long vowels not written) *usmīkata* and the ancestral form(s) of *ūṣmăgata* would be very close, if not identical.
47. See Abhidh-k-bh, 19, which indicates that the *nirvedhabhāgiya* are *prajñā*, but can be considered as all five aggregates when their accompaniments are taken into account.
48. The first truth is often analysed in terms of the three levels of *dukkhadukkha*, *vipariṇāmadukkha* and *saṅkhāradukkha* i.e. literal suffering, suffering as change and suffering as constructed existence (the five aggregates produced by clinging). The second and third of these are clearly related to impermanence and no-self.
49. Abhidh-k, VI, 16—emptiness is added as the fourth. Note that this too is one of the sixteen great insights.
50. Abhidh-k, VI, 19. This is already implied in the *Jñānaprasthāna*: Louis de La Vallée Poussin, "Pārāyaṇa cité dans Jñānaprasthāna," in *Études d'Orientalisme publiés par le Musée Guimet à la mémoire de Raymonde Linossier*, Paris, 1932, 325. In fact, since the preceding *nirvedhabhāgiyas* have all four truths as their object and so do

sources do relate the insight knowledges to all four truths, or at least three of them.[51] An even more striking resemblance, at least in the later versions of the two descriptions of the process leading to enlightenment, is the way in which the culmination of that process is described. The first three *nirvedhabhāgiya* are now each divided into weak, middling and strong degrees. This gives a total of ten stages for the four sets as a whole. This enlargement parallels the enlargement in the later Pali sources quite closely—there are in fact ten knowledges from knowledge of rise and fall up to lineage knowledge. This of course could be quite coincidental. What is hardly likely to be an accident is that the last stage in each case lasts for a single moment only and the preceding stage is also very brief.[52] So in each system we have eight stages, followed by two stages that transit very rapidly to enlightenment (*bodhi*).

The third of the *nirvedhabhāgiya* is acceptance (*kṣānti*), a term which is also central to the Sarvāstivādin account of the realization of the truths at awakening. The same duality is also present in the *Paṭisambhidā-magga*. On the one hand, acceptance (*khanti*) occurs as one of the knowledges of the Knowledge Discourse. "Acceptance knowledge is understanding as a result of having known (the aggregates, etc. as impermanent, etc.)."[53] Later in the Insight Discourse (*Vipassanākathā*) (based on A, III, 437; 431–433) the term occurs as *anulomikā khanti* (suitable acceptance).[54] Here it is in close association with 'certainty of rightness' (*samattaniyāma*), a term which is linked with stream-entry.

Insight in the earlier period

If then the period of the development of the *abhidhamma* schools is the time when the elaborated versions of the path of insight begin to take form, the question arises as to the source material for these enlarged versions. In fact, the *Nikāyas* contain a large quantity of such material — too large to examine here.

---

the sixteen moments of *abhisamaya* (taken collectively), the difference is a product of the difference between *ekâbhisamaya* and *anupūrvâbhisamaya*. See Abhidh-k, VI, 17.

51. Vism, 638; the application of all four truths at the moment of Stream-entry (Vism, 689 ff.) is also relevant. Compare Paṭis-a, III, 542–543: "In the noble truths" was said with reference to the comprehension of the truths separately by means of ordinary (*lokiya*) knowledge of the truths in the prior stage.
52. For the Sanskrit system, the third degree of acceptance lasts for one moment only as does the highest (ordinary) *dharma*. This is perhaps already implied in the *Jñānaprasthāna* (cited above). For the Pali system, lineage is a single moment, but two or three *anuloma* moments immediately precede it. See Vism, 673–675; Dhs-a, 231 ff.; Abhidh-av, 125. The sequence from *anuloma* to lineage to path is given in the *Paṭṭhāna*, e.g. at Tikap, 159.
53. Paṭis, I, 106.
54. Paṭis-a, II, 236–242. The same expression is at I, 123; cp. also II, 171; 183. At, I, 176 it occurs as a synonym for *satthusāsana*.

In Table Two I gave as an illustration the sequence from *yathābhūta-ñāṇadassana* to *nibbidā* to *virāga* to *vimutti*.[55] Since the first of these may represent the beginnings of insight and the last its result, we can take the two central terms as representing the heart of the process of insight. Indeed they or their verbal forms occur quite frequently in the Canon. There are of course many parallel sequences, in some of which one or more of these terms are omitted.[56] Overall, however, *nibbidā* (distaste or disenchantment) can be seen as the parallel in insight meditation to *pīti* (joy or energization) in calm meditation. So, in the one case, joy if successfully tranquillized, leads to happiness and success in controlling one's emotional life. In the other, disenchantment with the things with which one identifies or to which one clings leads to a mental clarity and a deepening of knowledge.

The importance of what is later referred to as the insight knowledges is then already clear in the *Nikāyas*. What is less clear is the context in which we are to understand this. Where insight occurs in a sequence, it usually comes after concentration or after emerging from one of the *jhānas*. Often it occurs without such a context, but in dealing with some aspect of what may be called fundamental theory. I mean, such lists as the aggregates, bases, elements, truths, conditioned origination and the like. It is quite impossible to be sure whether in these passages it is intended to operate as an exercise for even a beginner or whether all these passages are addressed to someone who has already developed *jhāna*. I incline to suspect that in most of these cases it is the latter which is envisaged because they can all be viewed as elaborations of the teaching which is particular to the Buddhas (*sāmukkaṃsikā desanā*). That teaching is specifically stated to be given when the hearer's mind is in an appropriate state. The terms used to describe his mind recall the standard descriptions of the state which is appropriate to develop the *abhiññās* i.e. after the fourth *jhāna*.

In the Canon the development of insight after the *jhānas* is certainly the normative pattern, where a full process is described at all. I exclude from consideration those cases where the *dhamma* eye, etc. are said to arise at the end of a discourse, apparently spontaneously. There is no indication, or at least not much indication, of the prior background in most such cases and hence no way of telling if it is envisaged that *jhāna* had already been developed.

The kind of modern tradition of insight meditation with which we were concerned at the beginning of this paper often lays stress on insight as the

---

55. e.g. S, II, 30 ff.; III, 189; A, V, 311–317. Various other formulæ give parts of this process.

56. See, for example, the discussion of the *vivekanissita* formula in: R.M.L. Gethin, *The Buddhist Path to Awakening, A Study of the Bodhi-Pakkhiyā Dhammā*, Leiden, 1992, 162–168 or the last of the four tetrads of breathing mindfulness.

Buddha's particular achievement. In this view calm (*samatha*) meditation involving the development of the four *jhānas* is something pre-Buddhist, even perhaps Hindu—something which is not necessary for enlightenment. It is interesting to contrast this with the view of some modern scholars that the development of the *jhānas* is the typically Buddhist form of practice or at least that most likely to have been developed by the Buddha himself.

I will return to the views of scholarship shortly, but first it is useful to consider how far the view that only insight is the proper or specifically Buddhist practice is actually justified in the canonical works. It is certainly true that there is some stress in that literature on the fact that the stages of sanctity are not found outside the Buddhist tradition. There is also, as was mentioned above, some emphasis that the teaching of the four noble truths is particular to the Buddhas. Sometimes too we read that the four establishings of mindfulness are a path which is *ekâyana*. This is often explained as 'the only way', but Rupert Gethin's excellent discussion of this term states the situation quite clearly:

> "Given that nowhere is the sense 'one and one only' clearly and definitely the proper sense, and in most cases definitely not, it seems rather perverse to adopt this sense in the *satipaṭṭhāna* context."[57]

We should probably think rather of mindfulness as leading to only one destination, i.e. *nibbāna*.

To set against this are many passages where the relationship between *samādhi* and *paññā* or between calm and insight is stressed. The later tradition does accept that there were *arahats* 'liberated by wisdom' (*paññāvimutta*) who had not developed all or even any of the four *jhānas*.[58] However, the actual references to such *arahats* in the earlier texts seem mostly to say that they had not developed the formless attainments or the first five *abhiññā*. The first four *jhānas* are conspicuously not mentioned.[59]

---

57. R.M.L. Gethin, *op. cit.,* 1992, 63.
58. e.g. Sv, II, 512.
59. See for example M, I, 477; S, II, 121–123; 126–127. D, II, 70 is less clear. At AN, IV, 452f. one who has not attained all eight attainments can only be regarded as 'liberated by wisdom' by way of exposition (*pariyāyena*). It is very striking that in this passage the destruction of the *āsavas* is applied to the *nevasaññānâsañña* sphere, but not to the first *jhāna* (and according to C^e 1971 not to the following *jhānas*). C^e 1971 rightly corrects the absence of reference in E^e and N^e to destruction of the *āsavas* in regard to the *nevasaññānâsañña* sphere in the case of the individual who is 'both ways liberated'. However, in the *Mahāmāluṅkya-suttanta* (M, I, 435–36) it is explicitly stated that it is possible to reach arahatship or at any rate never-return after entering the first *jhāna*. Even here it would be possible to suppose that only the immediate process of attainment is referred to. In that case the possibility that prior development of the four *jhānas* is assumed could not be ruled out. It may also be a rather later discourse in view of the relatively developed subject matter and some possibly later terminology.

Already in 1927 E.J. Thomas wrote:

> "...the jhānas are only four stages in a much more extended scheme. It may of course be the case that they once formed the whole of the mystic process."[60]

Most recently, both Johannes Bronkhorst and Tilman Vetter have for different reasons taken up the view that the *jhānas* are likely to be the original core of Buddhist meditative practice.[61] It is interesting to note the contrast here with the view of many modern interpreters of Buddhism, for whom it is precisely the insight approach which is the innovative creation of Buddhism—the thing the Buddha added to what was known before. Of course, it does not necessarily follow that adding a rung or two to the top of the ladder means you can dispense with the ladder !

Given that we do not know precisely what developments had already occurred before the time of the Buddha and given that developments in teaching must have occurred during the long life-span of the Buddha himself as well as afterwards, it is difficult to say with any certainty what exactly was taught by the Buddha himself. No doubt, like any good teacher, he would have wished his followers to develop his teachings in a creative and fruitful manner. The subsequent history of Buddhism is clear enough proof that this was the case. What we can, however, say is that for most later forms of Buddhism, in India and elsewhere, the typical Buddhist approach is a synthetic one which seeks to combine differing approaches in a higher ideal.[62]

---

60. Edward J. Thomas, *The Life of Buddha*, London, 1975 [1927], 181 n.
61. J. Bronkhorst, *The Two Traditions of Meditation in Ancient India*, Stuttgart, 1986; T. Vetter, *The Ideas and Meditative Practices of Early Buddhism*, Leiden, 1988.
62. See: L.S. Cousins, "*Samatha-yāna* and *Vipassanā-yāna*," in *Buddhist Studies in Honour of Hammalava Saddhātissa*, eds., G. Dhammapāla *et al.*, Nugegoda, Sri Lanka, 1984, 55–68. For the integration of the ethical and the intellectual, see D. Keown, *The Nature of Buddhist Ethics*, London, 1992, and C. Cox, "Attainment through Abandonment: The Sarvāstivādin Path of Removing Defilements," in R. E. Buswell, Jr & R.M. Gimello, eds., *op. cit.*, for the view that "...the final goal ... subsumes knowledge and concentration as equally cooperative means rather than mutually exclusive ends." (page 66).

Buddhist Values of the Traditional Sinhalese Village

J.B. Disanayaka

1. Introduction

Values, in everyday life, cut across a wide range of interests: monetary values, functional values, utilitarian values and so on. In ethics, the science that deals with morals, the central concern is the concept of 'moral values' or 'ethical values'.

All religions, whether they believe in a God or not, whether they believe in one omnipotent God or many, whether they believe in a permanent soul or not, share in common one element: a code of moral values. There is, thus, an essential corelationship between religion and moral values.

Morality is, basically, a matter that relates to the concepts of 'right' and 'wrong'. What is morally right and what is morally wrong are not, however, absolutely objective. Although all religions share a code of moral values, these codes are not always identical. The differences stem from their histories and cultural conditioning.

The cultural milieu that gave birth to religions such as Judaism, Christianity, Islam, Hinduism and Buddhism vary and as such their codes of moral values also exhibit certain features that are distinctly of one religion or another.

The few moral values that religions share in common may be considered as those having universal validity. However, followers of a particular religion uphold such values not as part of a universal religious order but as part of their own religion. Hence, all moral values, whether of universal validity or not, carry the stamp of a particular religion.

For example: both Christianity and Buddhism share the moral value that it is not morally right to destroy the life of beings, human or animal. However, followers of each religion will consider this value either as a Christian value or as a Buddhist value. The Christians derive its moral validity from the first of the Ten Commandments: 'Thou shalt not kill', and the Buddhists derive its validity from the first of the Five-Precepts (*panca-sīla*)[1] that every Buddhist is expected to observe in daily life: 'I undertake to observe the precept to abstain from destroying the life of beings' (*pāṇātipātā veramaṇī sikkhāpadam samādiyāmi*). Buddhist values are, thus, those moral values that are upheld by Buddhists and derive their validity from some specific Buddhist source. It must be noted that these Buddhist sources have drawn their inspiration from several contemporary schools of Indian philosophical thought.

Values are, however, mere abstractions. They exist only at a conceptual level. They become externally manifested only in the form of habits and customs within a specific cultural framework. Hence, the same moral value may find expression in two different cultures in two different ways: by means of different habits and customs.

Cultures change in time and so do the habits and customs that manifest moral values. Values are also subject to change but their rate of change seems to be slower than that of other elements of culture. They are relatively more resistant to change because they provide the moral basis of a culture, and this moral basis is its most distinctive feature.

The aim of this paper is to present a few of the more important moral values of Buddhism and the way they are reflected in the habits and customs of the traditional Sinhalese village. As a preamble to this discussion, attention will be focussed on two preliminary themes: (a) the sources of Buddhist values and (b) the distinctive features that characterize the traditional Sinhalese village.

2. Sources of Buddhist Values

The Buddhist sources in which Buddhist values are embedded are basically of four kinds: (a) the discourses of the Buddha as recorded in the *Suttapiṭaka* of the Pali Canon; (b) the life of the Buddha as recorded in Buddhist literature and art; (c) the life of the Bodhisatta as recorded in the *Jātaka* tales and art, and (d) the codes of moral conduct (*sīla*) prescribed for the use of the Buddhist laity.

The most important discourse (*sutta*) of the Buddha in which his moral values are defined is his very first discourse, "The Discourse that sets in motion the Wheel of the Law" (*Dhammacakkapavattana-sutta*). In this discourse, the Buddha reveals that the path leading to the cessation of suffering (*dukkha*) is the Middle Path (*majjhimā paṭipadā*) and that it consists of eight stages of moral upliftment. This Eightfold Path (*aṭṭangika magga*) consists of the following: (1) right understanding (*sammā diṭṭhi*), (2) right thought (*sammā sankappa*), (3) right speech (*sammā vācā*), (4) right action (*sammā kammanta*), (5) right livelihood (*sammā ājīva*), (6) right effort (*sammā vāyāma*), (7) right mindfulness

1. Words within brackets are in Pāli unless otherwise stated. 'S.' indicates Sinhala, and 'Sk.' indicates Sanskrit.

(*sammā sati*) and (8) right concentration (*sammā samādhi*). In expounding each of these factors, the Buddha and later commentators have set out in detail the fundamental principles that govern the Buddhist way of moral conduct.

Among the other *suttas* that present Buddhist values are the *Sigālovāda-suttanta,*[2] which enumerates the duties and responsibilities of the householder, the *Mangala-sutta,*[3] which enumerates the ideal factors that are conducive to lead a Buddhist way of life, the *Parābhava-sutta,*[4] which enumerates the factors that cause the downfall of a householder, and the *Karanīyametta-sutta,*[5] which extols the value of universal love (*mettā*).

The life story of the Buddha, the historical figure who lived in India in the seventh century BC provides the second source that exemplifies the moral values of the Buddhists. The most important biography of the Buddha Gotama in Pali is the *Nidānakathā,* which forms a part of the *Jātakaṭṭhakathā.* The *Nidānakathā* is "the earliest attempt in Pali to give a connected life-story of the Buddha".[6]

In the life story of the Buddha Gotama, there are many episodes that exemplify the values of moral principles. For instance, the Buddha has shown, by example, that the ministering of the sick (*gilāna upaṭṭhāna*) is a moral value of the highest order. In the *Mahāvagga,* the Buddha has said: "Let him who would look after ıne look after the one who is sick."[7] He has also shown, by spending one whole week gazing unwinking at the *bodhi* tree, under which he attained enlightenment, that gratitude (*kataññutā*) is a value to be cultivated in one's heart.[8]

The third source is the collection of *Jātaka* tales, which narrate the life stories of the Buddha in his previous births as a Bodhisatta. The *Jātakaṭṭhakathā* contains two kinds of tales: first, the stories of the Bodhisatta performing the perfections (*pāramitā*), the conditions necessary for the attainment of Buddhahood, and second, the five hundred odd stories, each embodying a moral of practical significance.

The perfections, which are ten in number, are: (1) generosity (*dāna*), (2) morality (*sīla*), (3) renunciation (*nekkhamma*), (4) wisdom (*paññā*), (5) effort (*viriya*), (6) patience (*khanti*), (7) truth (*sacca*), (8) resolution (*adhiṭṭhāna*), (9) amity (*mettā*) and (10) equanimity (*upekkhā*).[9]

---

2. *Dīghanikāya*, PTS, vol. III, 180-93.
3. *Khuddakapāṭha*, PTS, pp. 2-3.
4. *Suttanipāta*, PTS, 18-20.
5. *Khuddakapāṭha*, PTS, 8-9.
6. *The Story of Gotama Buddha (Jātaka-Nidāna)*, tr. N.A. Jayawickrama, PTS, xii.
7. *Mahāvagga, Khandaka* 8.
8. Bhikku Ñāṇamoli, *The Life of the Buddha*, Kandy, Buddhist Publications Society, 1978, 30.
9. *The Story of Gotama Buddha,* 25-31.

The life of the Buddha as well as of the Bodhisatta has become the perennial source of inspiration for the Buddhist painter and sculptor. The last of the *Jātaka* stories, the *Vessantara Jātaka,* which extols the values of generosity and sacrifice, is one of the commonest themes of Buddhist art.

Finally, the codes of moral conduct provide the Buddhist with a practical guide to Buddhist values. For the Buddhist laity, the most important code is that known as the Five-Precepts (*panca-sīla*), which makes the Buddhists undertake to observe daily the precepts of abstaining from (1) destroying the life of beings (*pāṇātipātā*), (2) taking things not given (*adinnādānā*), (3) sexual misconduct (*kāmesu micchācārā*), (4) speaking falsehood (*musāvādā*) and (5) taking spirituous drinks, malt liquors and wines—foundations for heedlessness (*surā-meraya-majjapamādaṭṭhānā*).

On days of religious significance (*uposatha,* S. *pōya*), Buddhists observe the Eight-Precepts (*aṭṭanga sīla*). These include the Five-Precepts and three additional ones: to abstain from (6) taking food at an unseasonable time, (*vikāla bhojanā*), (7) dancing, singing, music and unseemly shows; the use of garlands, perfumes and unguents; things that tend to beautify and adorn the person (*nacca gīta vādita visūka dassana mālā gandha vilepana dhāraṇa maṇḍana vibhūsanaṭṭhānā*) and (8) using high and luxurious beds (*uccā sayana mahāsayana*). The Ten-Precepts (*dasa sīla*) are observed by those men and women who have committed themselves to lead a saintly life, outside the order of monks and nuns. The Ten-Precepts are made by dividing the seventh precept of the Eight-Precepts into two separate ones, and adding a new one: to abstain from accepting gold and silver (*jātarūpa rajata paṭiggahaṇā*). When the third of the Five-Precepts forms part of the other two sets, it is changed from 'sexual misconduct' to 'all unchastity' (*abrahmacariyā*).

The difference between the Five-Precepts, on the one hand, and the Eight-Precepts and the Ten-Precepts, on the other, is not merely a matter of number but a matter of scope. The former aims to promote harmony between oneself and others, and the latter aims to establish harmony with oneself, through self-discipline.

The Buddhist monks and laity who had access to these Buddhist sources transformed the moral values enshrined in them into action by evolving a repository of habits and customs peculiar to their own cultures. The present paper seeks to study the relationship between Buddhist values and the habits and customs of the traditional Sinhalese village in Sri Lanka.

3. The Traditional Sinhalese Village

The term Sinhalese denotes both an ethnic group as well as a language. There is today a tendency among some writers to make a stylistic distinction between Sinhalese and Sinhala, the former referring to the ethnic group and the latter, to the language they speak. Broadly, then, the Sinhalese are those who speak Sinhala as their first language.

The Sinhalese form one of the four ethnic groups that constitute Sri Lanka's population of sixteen million, the other three being Tamils, Muslims and Burghers, the descendants of the Portuguese and the Dutch. The Sinhalese are predominantly Buddhist, the Tamils are predominantly Hindu, all Muslims are followers of Islam, and the Burghers are Christian. The Sinhalese Buddhists and the Tamil Hindus share a cultural core, the source of which can be found in their Indian origins.

The origin of the Sinhalese Buddhist culture goes as far back as the third century B.C., when the Indian emperor Asoka sent his son Mahinda and daughter Sanghamittā to the island to establish Buddhism. The fact that Asoka sent his own children to Lanka shows the special regard he had for this island and its ruler, Tissa, who was given the title *Devānampiya,* Beloved of the Gods, a title which Emperor Asoka himself used in his famous edicts.[10]

In spite of the influence of three European colonial powers and their religions since the beginning of the sixteenth century, the Sinhalese culture has succeeded in retaining its essential Buddhist ethos.

Except for a few urban centres such as Colombo, the capital, Kandy, Galle and Jaffna, Sri Lanka is basically a land of villages (*gāma,* S. *gama,* Sk. *grāma*). The difficulty in defining the concept of the 'village' has been discussed in recent anthropological literature.[11] Although the precise boundaries of villages are not very sharp, every Sinhalese claims that he or she belongs to a specific village, the village that has his or her ancestral home (S. *mul gedara*). Even those who are born and bred in the cities will claim a particular village as his or her own, and it is a common social custom among the Sinhalese to begin a conversation with a stranger by inquiring "*gama koheda*?"—"Where is your village?" During the holidays for the national new year in April, Colombo becomes almost a ghost city because almost all its dwellers leave for their villages in order to pay respects to their parents and grandparents who live in their ancestral homes.

The traditional Sinhalese village, for the purpose of the present discussion, is a hypothetical construct. It does not refer to any particular village with a specific name or geographical location, such as Leach's Pul Eliya,[12] Yalman's

---

10. R. Mookerji, *Men and Thought in Ancient India*, London, Macmillan, 1924, 139.
11. R. Pieris, *Sinhalese Social Organization: The Kandyan Period*, Columbo, Ceylon University Press, 1956.
12. E.R. Leach, *Pul Eliya: A Village in Ceylon*, Cambridge, Cambridge University Press, 1971.

Terutenna,[13] Obeyesekere's Madagama[14] or Gombrich's Migala.[15] As a hypothetical construct, it represents an ideal, and in reconstructing such an ideal, I have been influenced by my training in comparative linguistics.

Comparative linguists reconstruct, on the basis of actually available data extracted from different languages of the same family, hypothetical forms of their parent language, which does not exist any longer. Although all these hypothetical forms do not actually occur in any single daughter language, they succeed in explaining the interrelationship among the daughter languages and their relationship with the parent language. On the basis of such hypothetical forms, linguists reconstruct what they have termed proto-languages, such as Proto-Indo European, Proto-Dravidian and so on. Proto-Indo-European is considered the parent language of Greek, Latin and Sanskrit, and Proto-Dravidian is considered the parent language of Tamil, Telugu, Malayalam and Kannada.

On the same methodological basis, one may be able to reconstruct a proto-village based on actual, extant data, collected from different villages of a given culture. No actual village has all the elements of the proto-village, but each element of the proto-village is found in some village or another. My traditional Sinhalese village is such a proto-village. In a Buddhistic sense, it is there and it is not there!

The traditional Sinhalese village is basically agrarian, with rice as its main sustenance crop. Yalman distinguishes four types of villages among Sinhalese agricultural settlements:

a. the tank-villages (S. *vaev gam*) of the Northern Dry Zone,

b. the tank-villages of the Central Highlands,

c. the rain-dependent villages of the Eastern Province, and

d. the *chena* villages—villages on highland with no irrigation facilities.[16]

The traditional Sinhalese village is essentially Buddhist. Most of the villages have temples (S. *pansal*) of their own, and smaller villages owe their allegiance to these temples. Temples that had the patronage of kings (S. *raja*) were named 'Great Royal Monasteries' (S. *raja maha vihāra*). Clusters of villages over which the temple has jurisdiction in religious matters are called 'subsistence-villages' (S *goduru gam*).

---

13. N. Yalman, *Under the Bo Tree*, Berkeley, University of California Press, 1967.
14. Obeyesekere, Gananath, *Land Tenure in Village Ceylon*, Cambridge, Cambridge University Press, 1967.
15. R.Gombrich, *Precept and Practice: Traditional Buddhism in the Rural Highlands of Ceylon*, Oxford, Clarendon Press, 1971.
16. N. Yalman, *op.cit.*, 21.

A typical Buddhist temple consists of three main objects of worship: (a) the hemispherical structure which enshrines some sacred relic of the Buddha or of some other sacred personage (S. *dāgaba, vehera, vehera vahanse*), (b) the tree which botanists have termed ficus religiosa (S. *bōdiya, bōdinnānse*) and (c) the shrine which houses the images of the Buddha and other religious personages, and contain mural paintings and sculptures depicting the life of the Buddha and Bodhisatta (S. *budu gē, vihāre*).

In addition, the temple has a sermon-hall (S. *bana gē, bana maḍuva*), a small library (S. *pot gula*), a bell-tower (S. *ganṭāre*) and the residential quarters of the monks (S. *āvāse, ārāme*). Large temples run an educational institution where both monks and laity study (*pariveṇa*, S. *pirivena*), and maintain a house where monks assemble to perform certain religious rites such as the recitation of *Pātimokkha* (*uposathāgāra,* S. *pōya gē*).

The monks follow the Theravāda tradition, and remain celibate. A temple has three kinds of monks: (a) novices (*sāmaṇera*), (b) monks who have attained higher ordination (*bhikkhu*), and (c) monks who have spent more than ten years after higher ordination (*thera*).

There is a special link between the village and the monk; for when a Sinhalese enters the order of monks (*saṅgha*), he gives up his personal name and takes a new name consisting of two parts: (a) a religious name such as Rahula or Saddhatissa and (b) the name of the village of his birth, such as Walpola or Hammalawa. The monks will bear names such as Walpola Rahula and Hammalawa Saddhātissa, which reveal their village links.

The temple which is located either in the centre of village or in the highest point overlooking the village served as the most important link in the communication network. The temple was the school 'without walls', where the laity received their education in living. It is at the temple that the monks and laity learned, both in precept and practice, the moral values of Buddhism.

4. Buddhist Values and Sinhalese Customs

The Buddhist values that underlie the customs of the traditional Sinhalese village may be classified, for the convenience of analysis, into two broad categories: (a) values that are related to others, and (b) values that are related to oneself.

Among values that relate to others are values such as (a) respect for the life of others, (b) respect for the property of others, (c) respect for the knowledge of others, (d) respect for the wisdom of others, and (e) respect for the well-being of others.

Among values that relate to oneself are values such as (a) humility, (b) contentment, (c) generosity, (d) self-discipline relating to one's body and (e) self-discipline relating to one's mind. Since it is not possible to deal with all these values in a single paper, I propose to select one from each category and discuss it in some detail, so that it gives a general picture of the impact of Buddhist values on the traditional Sinhalese village.

The two values selected for discussion are: (a) respect for the life of others, from the first category, and (b) humility, from the second category. Customs embrace both verbal and non-verbal modes of behaviour.

4.1 Respect for the Life of Others

Life (*pāṇa*), in a Buddhistic sense, encompasses not merely the life of human beings (*manussa*), but also that of animals (*tiracchāna*), gods and godlings (*deva*) and the departed (*peta*). The Buddhistic Pali terms *sabbe sattā, sabbe bhūtā* and *sabbapāṇi* denote life in all realms of existence in the cycle of rebirths (*samsāra*).

Since life is a continuum through *samsāra,* the boundaries between certain forms of life are not always sharp for the Buddhist. For instance, the Sinhalese Buddhist peasant does not kill or harm a snake (S. *nayā*) that visits his house frequently because he thinks that it is one of his dead relatives (S. *nāēyā*), that keeps on visiting its old family because it has been unable to give up its craving for the family and household even after being reborn as an animal in the next birth. The peasant thus speaks to the snake in Sinhala, politely and respectfully, as if it were a human being, addressing it as "*nay hāmi*" (Mr. Snake) and requesting it to carry itself away with respect, "*yahapat venḍa*".

Respect for the life of others means basically the recognition of the right of others to live. The Buddhist's recognition of this right finds expression in two complementary modes of action: negatively, by avoiding the wilful destruction of life (*pāṇa-atipāta, pāṇa-ghāta, pāṇa-vadha,* or *pāṇa-hara*), and positively, by cherishing the life of others.

The right of human beings to live, of course, has been recognized by all religions, at least in their original forms. Buddhism takes it further by recognizing the right of even non-human beings to live and to be protected. The Buddhist's wish is: "May all beings be happy" (*sabbe sattā bhavantu sukhitattā*).

The most common Buddhist formula that guarantees the life of all beings is the first of the Five-Precepts, which persuades the Buddhist, whether monk or peasant, to undertake to observe (*samādiyāmi*) the precept (*sikkhāpadam*) to abstain (*veramaṇī*) from the destruction (*atipāta*) of life (*pāṇa*).

According to Buddhism, life comes into being in four ways: (a) *anḍaja,* to be born from an egg, (b) *jalābuja,* to be born from a womb, (c) *sansedaja,* to be born from moisture and (d) *opapātika,* to be born spontaneously.[17] Any attempt to obstruct these ways of birth are avoided by the Sinhalese peasant.

17. Majjhima Nikāya, PTS, vol.1, 73.

The Sinhalese peasant avoids eating eggs because he is aware that they have life in the making. Even urbanites who eat eggs avoid eating eggs on *pōya* days. Others refuse to break an egg on a *pōya* day, even for the sake of someone else. Poultry was not practised in the traditional village because neither eggs nor fowl formed a part of the day's meal. Recently, when steps were taken by the government to introduce poultry farming into traditional villages as part of their development-programme they were met with resistance by the Buddhists.

Abortion was not tolerated in the traditional village. The dangers of abortion were described in vivid terms in a story named *Kāli Yakinnagē Katā Vastuva*—the tale of the female demon, Kāli—in one of the most popular works of Sinhala literature, the *Saddharma-ratnāvaliya.*[18] According to this tale, a woman aborts another woman in one life, and the latter aborts the former in the next life, and this goes on until one woman was born a female demon (S. *yakinna*) during the lifetime of the Buddha and the other a daughter of a noble family. When the demon was getting ready to avenge, the Buddha saw her with his divine-eye and advised both that "hatred never ceases through hatred" and that it can be overcome only through love. Buddhist women are very familiar with this tale and shun abortion as an evil means.

Killing harmless animals irritated the peasant the most. Among the animals that are considered harmless are the rat-snakes (S. *gaerandi*) and ants (S. *kurā kūmbi*). Hence, the proverbs: "Do not commit sin by killing rat-snakes" (S. *gaerandi marala pav ganda epā*) and "Do not kill even an ant" (S. *kurā kūmbiyek vat maranda epā*). An innocent man, according to the Sinhalese, is one who does not harm even an ant (S. *kurā kumbiyekuta vat hinsāvak naeti minihek*).

When little children play with ants, they are always reminded that it is a sin (*pav*) to do so because the ants might get killed in the process. On the other hand, if a child sees an ant or any other insect in water, struggling to survive, he will do everything possible to save it, because he has been told that saving the life of animals is a meritorious activity (S. *pinak*).

The animals that come closest to the peasant's life are cattle (S. *harak, gavayo*). The possession of cattle (S. *gava sampat*) is considered a blessing, like that of having children (S. *daru sampat*). The bull (S. *gonā*) and the cow (S. *eladena*) are given names such as Handaya—The Moon-faced One, Pohori—The Spotted One, or Ratti—The Red One, and they are addressed by a kinship term *duvē* (daughter) or *putē* (son), as the case may be. In folk songs sung during agricultural activities, cattle are addressed as *mage vahu daruvanē* (my cattle children), and their forgiveness is sought for making them work in the fields.

---

18. *Saddharmaratnāvaliya*, ed., D.B. Jayatilaka, Columbo, Svadesha Mitraya Press, 1930, 86-94.

When a bull becomes old and is unable to work, it is never taken to any slaughter-house. Instead it is allowed to roam freely in the village and is called *pin gonā* (merit-bull), meaning, the one who depends on the kindness of others. No peasant ate beef (*harak mas*) and when the Sinhalese spoke in derogatory terms of beef they called it *geri mas*. A Sinhala commentary of the thirteenth century says "*geri mas kat nam bera gasat nam ū beravāyō yi*"[19] meaning, if any one eats beef and beats the drum, he is a drummer, and a drummer is one who is considered as belonging to a low caste.

The Sinhalese peasant follows the custom of releasing a bull or a cow that is taken to a slaughter-house in order to acquire merit that can then be transferred to a person who is critically ill in his or her death-bed. It is believed that the life so saved will help the person in the death-bed to live for a longer period. This rite of releasing cattle is called in Sinhala *gō dāne* (cattle-offering).

Agriculture involves, invariably, the death of certain animals such as worms that subsist on soil. The peasant is aware of this and in order to clear his conscience of this guilt, as it were, he refuses to till his field on *pōya* days. Most interestingly, even those Buddhists who live in fishing villages by the sea, do not go fishing on *pōya* days to save, at least, a few fish from death.

The peasant handles the problem of pests that attack his crops in a Buddhist way, by resorting to certain magical practices known in Sinhala as *kem*. *Kem,* in general, refers to a form of magical practice performed by ordinary peasants to cure certain simple ailments, such as tooth-ache, stomach-ache or sprains.

When *kem* magic is used to control pests, it is believed that it prevents birds and insects from coming to the fields. In one form of *kem* magic, the peasant goes to the temple on a Sunday, makes some wicks from an old discarded robe (S. *sivura*), takes them to the paddy field and lights three oil lamps with the wicks, places them facing three directions on three spots at sunset, and hoots three times. The peasant strongly believes that this will keep the birds and other pests away from his field.

In another form of *kem,* the impact of Buddhism is strikingly conspicuous. The peasant takes a tender coconut leaf (S. *gokkolē*) and inscribes on it a Pali stanza, which has now assumed the status of a magical formula. The Pali stanza, which is used in many other instances of magic, is one that sums up the essence of the Buddha's teaching:

Sabba pāpassa akaraṇam
Kusalassa upasampadā
Sacitta pariyodapanam
Etam Buddhānasāsanam.

---

19. *Jātaka Aṭuvā Gaeṭapadaya*, Chapter 59, *Bherivāda Jātaka*.

"Not to do any evil,
To cultivate good,
To purify one's mind,
This is the teaching of the Buddha".[20]

The leaf is then placed at a central spot in the field.

Some of the pre-Buddhist rituals that were assimilated into the fold of the traditional Sinhalese village have also undergone certain changes as a result of the Buddhist value of protecting the life of animals. In some of the healing rituals (S. *tovil pavil*) performed in the South even today, the devils (S. *yakku*) have to be appeased by offering them the food that they relish. In pre-Buddhist folk religion, this was done by offering an animal as a sacrifice (S. *billa*). However, since Buddhists cannot sacrifice animals, this is replaced today by the offering of some blood taken from a fowl.[21]

Positively, the Sinhalese Buddhist follows many customs that tend to cherish animal life. Birds (S. *kurullo*) that are found in abundance in this tropical setting, are among the animals that are looked after well by the peasants. In the village, an entire tract of land, bordering the stretch of paddy fields, is set apart for the exclusive use of birds, and this land is called in Sinhala *kurulu pāluva*.

Individual varieties of birds, such as paddy-birds (*vī kurullo*) and sparrows (*gē kurullo*) are provided with dwellings inside houses, by placing on the wall, just below the roof, a clay pot with an opening. The birds build their nests inside these pots and tend their little ones without any fear from the human presence. The Sinhala word for sparrows, *gē kurullo,* means literally, house-birds.

Birds often get fed with human food because of a certain custom followed at the offering of alms (*dāne*) to monks either at the temple or at a household. Just before the monks begin to partake of the food, the chief householder goes from monk to monk with a small plantain-leaf (S. *pat kolē*) collecting into it the first handful of rice from each plate offered to the monks. This rice is then placed outside the house for the use of birds and other animals, like dogs.

The common crow (S. *kapuṭa*) is, in the belief of the Sinhalese, an animal that is eternally hungry. Thus, feeding such an animal is considered a highly meritorious act. To achieve this, the peasant performs a special offering of food to the crows and the dogs, and this is called *balu kapuṭu dāne*. This rite is done specially when someone is afflicted with certain diseases which the villagers think are caused by planetary-gods. Ghee (S. *gitel*), in particular, is mixed with rice on this day because it is believed that the crow relishes ghee.

---

20. *Dhammapada*, tr. Ven. Narada, verse 183.
21. E.R. Sarathchandra, *The Sinhalese Folk Play and the Modern Stage*, Columbo, The Ceylon University Press Board, 1983.

In certain jungle (S. *vanni*) villages of the Northern Central Province the peasant sets apart a small paddy field for the exlusive use of cattle, and this is also called in Sinhala *gō dāne* (cattle-offerings). When cattle are used at the threshing floor (S. *kamata*) to thresh paddy, they are never prevented from eating the corn even though this certainly leads to a slight reduction in the yield! In order to encourage the peasant to allow the cattle to be fed on the corn, it is said that if cattle ate corn on the threshing floor, it increases the yield!

Although the peasant finds his cattle very helpful in his activities, it is the custom to allow the cattle to rest at certain times of the day. For instance, the pair of buffaloes that are tied to the plough is let loose at midday when the peasant retires for his meal. This allows the animals to wander about grazing along the ridges (S. *niyara*) while the peasant himself enjoys his meal. Forcing cattle to work at midday, particularly under the tropical sun, is considered by the peasant as a grave offence that calls for severe punishment. There is, in the Southern Province, some interesting folklore relating to an incident when a peasant forced his buffaloes to plough his field even at midday. This folklore concerns the mountain known as Gon-gala-Kanda near Deniyaya in the South. Folklore has it that it was so named because its peak resembles a buffalo and a man, and that they were placed there by the Lord of the Gods, Sakra, in order to punish the farmer who was ploughing his field at midday. Sinhalese peasants say that the farmer and his bull were transformed into stone and were placed on this peak so that the whole world would not forget the message: that even animals need the love of human beings.

In the mountain villages of the Central Highlands, there is a custom known as *haetapum arinava,* whereby bulls are not made to work every day but only every other day, allowing them to rest (S. *haetapum*) in between. When cattle fall ill, they are looked after by a physician specially trained in the treatment of cattle diseases. He is called *harak-vedā* (cattle-physician). Even though Buddhists do not consider the cow a sacred animal, as do the Hindus, they care for it, as if it were a member of their family. Every year the mountain villages in the upper reaches of the Mahavaeli river also perform a ritual for the well-being of their cattle. It is called in Sinhala *mēsa maḍuva,* the word *mēsa* being perhaps a derivative from the Pali word *mahisa* denoting buffalo. This is a folk ritual performed all night invoking the blessings of gods, such as *Gopalu dēvatāvunnānse* (God of the Cow-herd) to protect cattle. The ritual comes to an end with the rite known as *kiri itiravīma,* the over-flowing of milk by boiling a pot of milk. Milk, taken from the cow, is a symbol of fertility and its over-flowing suggests abundance and well-being.

Among the non-human beings that arouse the concern of the Sinhalese peasant are the departed ones (*peta,* S. *malagiya aetto, malagiya prānakārayo*).

According to Buddhist belief, the departed ones may be born in certain realms of miserable existence, such as spirits and ghosts. These beings cannot perform meritorious acts and as such cannot improve their lot. They thus depend on the kindness of human beings to seek release from that realm of existence. In order to help such beings, the Buddhist follows the custom known as the transference of merit to the departed (S. *pin denavā*). The peasant who visits the temple engages himself in several meritorious acts and at the end says the following stanza in Pali to transfer some of his merits to the departed ones:

Idam vo ñātīnam hotu
Sukhitā hontu ñātayo.
"Let this merit accrue to our relatives
And may they be happy."

Merit is transferred to the departed on other occasions as well, particularly, at the end of an alms-giving held in remembrance of a dead relative. A pitcher of water and an empty bowl are kept beside the monks who are seated on the floor. The relatives of the dead come together and begin to pour water from the pitcher into the bowl slowly, as the monks chant the following stanzas in Pali:

Yathā vāri vahā pūrā
paripūrenti sāgaram
Evameva ito dinnam
Petānam upakappati.
"As the full water-bearing rivers fill the ocean
So indeed does what is given here benefit the dead".

Unname udakam vaṭṭam
Yathā ninnam pavattati
Evameva ito dinnam
Petānam upakappati.
"As water rained on a height reaches the low land
So indeed does what is given here benefit the dead."

The monks chant these verses until the water overflows the bowl.

In the view of the Buddhist, animals and the dead are not the only beings whose life has to be protected. The gods and godlings who live in the heavens are also dependent on human beings for their well-being. From a Buddhist point of view, the heavens are just another realm of existence, and their dwellers cannot acquire merit on their own, although they can enjoy pleasures. Thus, the Buddhist feels that it is his duty to transfer merit to these divine beings (*deva*, S. *deviyo*) too. This rite involves the recitation of the following Pali stanza:

Ākāsaṭṭhā ca bhummaṭṭhā
Devā nāgā mahiddhikā

Puññantam anumoditvā
Ciram rakkhantu sāsanam.
"May beings inhabiting space and earth
Devas and Nagas of mighty power share this merit.
May they long protect the Dispensation."[22]

Thus the Buddhist value that protects and cherishes the life of other beings at all levels of existence has given the traditional Sinhalese village one of its most pervasive features: its Buddhist ethos.

4.2 Humility

Humility (*nihatamānatā*) is one of the Buddhist values that relates to oneself. Even though the Sinhalese Buddhist uses Sinhala words such as *mama* (I), *mage* (my, mine) and *tamā* (oneself) in everyday communication, he is told that a belief in a permanent self (*atta,* S. *ātmaya*) is unrealistic. Hence any effort to exhibit one's attainments or possessions is, in the ultimate analysis, futile.

On the other hand, the Buddhist is taught to feel humble in spite of any such attainments or possessions, because beings are, after all, equal when it comes to the basic nature of life: its unsatisfactoriness (*dukkha*) and impermanence (*anicca*). Every human being, of whatever station in social life, is subject to decay (*jarā*), sickness (*vyādhi*), death (*maraṇa*) and so on.

The culture in which the individual grows up contributes many things to make him what he is: his family, house and property, dress and ornaments, social status, skills and so on. These things cannot be helped as long as the individual lives as a member of his social organization.

Society also uses these elements as symbols of social status to indicate that an individual is relatively higher or lower than another in a social scale that is purely subjective. The Buddhist is made to realize that such evaluations are futile because they have absolutely no bearing on human suffering in the world.

The traditional Sinhalese village maintains certain customs to show the importance of being humble. These apply both to monks and peasants, men and women.

In Sinhalese culture, the family name of an individual is an index of his or her social background, because the name betrays certain caste connotations. As such, the layman who enters the order of Buddhist monks is made to give up his family name in preference to a Buddhist name, which is not caste-bound.

The monk, of whatever social background, is trained to beg for his daily food once he enters the order. At the same time, the monk is made to visit all

22. Ven. Narada, *The Mirror of the Dhamma,* Singapore, Singapore Buddhist Meditation Centre, 1991, 29.

households of the village, irrespective of their caste and social rank, to collect his food and take part in other religious rites.

The life of the laity is also influenced by this value. Firstly, every devotee is made to part with all the symbols of social identification as he or she enters the sacred precincts of the temple, where secular symbols cease to function. In terms of dress, one is encouraged to wear something simple, preferably in white. On *pōya* days, when devotees observe the Eight-Precepts, they are made to wear a dress that is completely white, so that all devotees, of whatever social background, tend to look alike.

Laymen and lay women are made to remove, as they enter the temple, their head-gear and foot-wear, because they also serve to identify the social background of the user. Women do not wear jewellery to the temple. Stripped of all symbols of social identity, the laity who gather at the temple begin to look alike, which makes them feel that they are, after all, equal as human beings.

Secondly, the laymen are made to respect the monks at the temple by making them touch the feet of the monks. When monks enter a lay household for an alms-giving, or a *pirit* chanting ceremony, it is the custom to wash the feet of the monks by the chief householder, at the main doorstep. The main purpose of this custom is not so much to clean the feet of the monks in a physical sense as to make the chief householder humble enough to touch the feet of the monks, an act which only a person who has suppressed his pride and vanity can do; for, touching the feet of another in secular life implies that one is lower in status than the other. However, in the presence of the Buddhist monks, who are themselves humble, this secular rule ceases to operate, since no layman is higher than a monk, in terms of morality.

When Buddhist monks are offered alms at the temple or in a household, laymen are also made to carry and hold the spittoon (S. *paḍikkama*) for monks to pour water to wash their hands and mouths. The spittoon is a lowly thing, and no one who is proud would ever hold it for others in secular life. But the Buddhist monks make the laymen hold it for them, and the laymen hold it, suppressing their feelings of pride, if any.

Outside the temple, men and women sit on high chairs or low chairs, depending on their social status for it is the custom among the Sinhalese that only people of the same caste or social rank can sit together as equals, on high chairs. However, the temple provides no high chairs for anyone. All devotees, irrespective of social rank, sit on the floor, usually on mats, to listen to the sermons (S. *bana*) or the chanting of *pirit.*

The pilgrimage (S. *vandanāva*) is another Buddhist custom that is designed to teach the value of humility to the laity. In fact, the Buddhist pilgrimage is less of a tour to visit a place than a period of training to live an ascetic and humble life.

The food the pilgrims eat, the dress they wear, the words they speak, while on a pilgrimage, reflect that they are, in the last analysis, humble men and women who are on a common mission to visit a pilgrim-centre to pay homage to the Buddha.

To make the laity feel that they are equal at the temple, the monk also addresses them with special words in place of the usual secular words, such as ladies (S. *nōnāvaruni*) and gentlemen (S. *mahatvaruni*). The words the monk uses recognizes only one factor: that the laity is endowed with merit (S. *pin*). Thus, laymen are called *pinvatuni* and lay women *pinvatiyani* (those blessed with merit). Merit, not social rank, is all that matters to the monk.

What these customs aim to achieve is to make the laity less conscious of their differences of social standing, and to make them more conscious of their similarities as human beings who are, from a Buddhist point of view, caught up in the wheel of rebirths, characterized by impermanence (*anicca*), unsatisfactoriness (*dukkha*) and selflessness (*anattā*).

5. Conclusion

Some of the habits and customs discussed in this paper are gradually being replaced by others, making the Sinhalese village less traditional. This cannot be helped in the face of social forces such as westernization, modernization, technological advancement and so on. For the Buddhist, who understands that everything is in a state of flux, this causes no alarm.

From a Buddhist point of view, what is important is not to hold on to old customs uncritically but to hold on to the values they express. If, however, Buddhist values begin to change, modify or disappear completely, then, it will be a matter of grave concern since Buddhist values have a great relevance for mankind, and its survival on this planet in the future.

The Pāli *Nidānakathā* and its Tibetan Translation: Its Textual Precursors and Associated Literature

Sean Gaffney

The *Nidānakathā* as it is preserved in the Pāli Canon, and in the Tibetan *bKa' 'gyur,* has come to us via canonical traditions and an extensive network of commentarial traditions that began in India and were continued later in Ceylon. These commentarial traditions began at a very early period, possibly from the time of the death of the Buddha, and were inspired by the need to establish certain facts concerning the life of the Buddha. The commentarial traditions associated with the *Jātaka* were centred on the *Jātakatthavaṇṇanā*, consisting of prose elucidation on the *gāthās* of the *Jātaka* text. This work, or at least its core, was possibly in existence at the time of the first Council, and is known to have been a part of the Canon at the time of the Council of Vaiśālī. That there is evidence of a *Jātaka* and commentary from such an early stage is an indication of its antiquity, its contents being drawn from earlier Indian sources with some elements of it probably reaching back to the lifetime of the Buddha.

The Pāli text of the *Nidānakathā* forms an introduction to the *Jātaka* collection contained in the *Khuddaka-nikāya* (Minor collection). The precise number of texts collected in this *Nikāya* has varied widely according to the Pāli tradition at different times in Buddhist history, from as few as nine to as many as nineteen. The number of texts that have been accepted as constituting this *Nikāya* in Ceylon, from at least the fifth century A.D., are the fifteen now included within that collection in the Pāli *Tipiṭaka.*[1] That different traditions existed concerning the contents of one of the five *Nikāyas* of the *Suttapiṭaka*, which are all accepted as canonical by the Pāli tradition, in no way invalidates the *Khuddaka-nikāya's*

1. K.R. Norman, *Pāli Literature*,Wiesbaden, 1983, 9, gives the lists of twelve texts, excluding the *Buddhavaṃsa*, *Cariyāpiṭaka* and *Apadāna*, as recorded by the *Dīgha-bhāṇakas* and included by them in the *Abhidhammapiṭaka*, while page 31 gives the fifteen texts reckoned by Buddhaghosa to constitute the *Khuddaka-nikāya* and which he incorporates within the *Suttapiṭaka*. M. Winternitz, *History of Indian Literature,* vol. 2, 1933, 77 adds that the Burmese tradition includes four texts in their *Khuddaka-nikāya* that are not regarded as canonical in Ceylon, namely: *Milindapañha, Suttasaṃgaha, Petakopadesa* and the *Nettipakaraṇa.* See also W. Geiger, *Pāli Literature and Language*, New Delhi, 1978, 19.

claim to be considered as an extremely ancient collection of texts. This is not to maintain that all the texts collected within the *Khuddaka-nikāya* are of equal antiquity, for clearly many of its works date from a later period. In regard to its age, it may be noted that other works from within the first four *Nikāyas* quote from some of the texts that are contained in the *Khuddaka-nikāya.*[2] The position of the various texts of the Pāli *Khuddaka-nikāya* that are included or omitted by the different Pāli Buddhist traditions may at least be ascertained with some certainty, in that it is possible to see how these traditions classified the texts.

The *Khuddaka-nikāya* is comprised of a group of disparate texts that seem to have proved something of a problem to the compilers of the *Nikāyas*. The Pāli tradition has placed all these miscellaneous texts that did not fit into the scheme of the four *Nikāyas* into this *Khuddaka-nikāya* or fifth *Nikāya*. It is possible that not all the texts of the *Khuddaka-nikāya* were originally accepted as equally authoritative, in that they were not *Buddhavacana* in the strict sense of the term, and so they were classified as *Khuddaka* or Minor works.[3] Whatever the initial standing of this *Nikāya* may have been, it is apparent that the division into five *Nikāyas* is an old one, for according to Theravāda sources, the last work to be added to their Canon was the *Kathāvatthu*[4] at the time of the Third Council in the third century BC. If this is the case, it can be surmised that the *Khuddaka-nikāya,* in either its twelve or fifteen text format, or both, had been known in Ceylon from a very early time. Whatever the date of its introduction, it became a well established part of the *Suttapiṭaka* for the Theravādins. The importance of the Pāli *Khuddaka-nikāya* is that it represents the only complete and extant specimen of this fifth *Nikāya* from amongst all the Buddhist traditions.

Given that the *Khuddaka-nikāya* was known to Ceylon from a very early period, it is unusual that the term for the transmitters of this *Nikāya*, the *Khuddakanikāyabhāṇakas*, does not occur in the commentarial literature of that country. The first reference to this school of *Khuddakanikāyabhāṇakas* only occurs in the *Milindapañha,*[5] a work of a later date than the five *Nikāyas*, and which came to Ceylon from the Indian mainland.[6] Although there is no term used to describe the transmitters of the *Khuddaka-nikāya*, there is reference

---

2. E. Lamotte, *History of Indian Buddhism*, Louvain-Paris, 1988, 157. He gives two reasons for believing the antiquity of at least some of the texts of the *Khuddaka-nikāya;* firstly, they are used as sources by the first four *Nikāyas* and secondly, most of them have corresponding versions in Sanskrit or Prakrit.
3. Bh. Sangharakshita, *The Eternal Legacy*, London, 1985, 45.
4. K.R. Norman, *Pāli Literature*, 1983, 84.
5. V.Trenckner & P.S.Jaini, *Milindapañho with Milindaṭīkā*, PTS, London, 1986, 342, where, interestingly, a list of six groups of *bhāṇikas* is given: *Jātakabhāṇikā*, *Dīghabhāṇikā*, *Majjhimabhāṇikā*, *Saṁyuttabhāṇikā*, *Anguttarabhāṇikā* and *Khuddakabhāṇikā*.
6. E.W. Adikaram, *Early History of Buddhism in Ceylon*, Colombo, 1946, 25.

made to the transmitters of the *Jātaka* collection who were known as the *Jātakabhāṇakas*. These *Jātakabhāṇakas* were supposed to learn not only the *Jātaka* and its commentary but also the text of the *Dhammapada*. There is no record of how the other texts of the *Khuddaka-nikāya* were to be transmitted, but it is likely that there were *bhāṇakas* of the other *Khuddaka-nikāya* texts.[7] It may be that the other texts of the *Khuddaka-nikāya* were grouped in a different way for the purpose of transmission, perhaps being categorised in groups, as in the case of the *Jātaka* and *Dhammapada*.

The contents of the Sanskrit *Kṣudraka-nikāya* or *Kṣudrakāgama* and its full list of works is a much more problematic issue. This classification using a fifth *Āgama* appears to have been used, in the same way that it is used in the Pāli tradition, as a convenient place to locate miscellaneous texts that had not been included in the four *Āgamas*. Their position within the Sanskrit Canons is by no means fixed, with the different schools resorting to diverse methods of classifying them. Some sources, notably the Sarvāstivādins used the texts from within the *Kṣudrakāgama*[8] referring to them as *Kṣudraka* (Minor works) but only recognised four *Āgamas*. Others such as the Mahāsāṃghikas, Haimavatas, Mahīśāsakas and the Dharmaguptakas[9] did not have a *Kṣudrakāgama* but collected the texts that formed this *Āgama* in other schools into what they termed the *Kṣudrakpiṭaka,* the fifth collection of their *Sūtrapiṭaka*[10].

The exact number of texts comprising the Sanskrit *Kṣudrakāgama* is as yet an unresolved area of research that can only be satisfactorily resolved by the discovery of either the texts themselves or of references to them in the works of the other four *Āgamas*. This fifth *Āgama* seems to have been for the Sanskrit tradition, or at least for sections of that tradition, a notional or theoretical possibility rather than an actual collection of texts that was accepted as being canonical. As with the Pāli recension of this *Nikāya,* the Sanskrit is also a series of works in verse, with its contents varying greatly. However, the texts: *Udāna, Dharmapada, Sthaviragāthā, Vimānavastu, Pretavastu, Avadāna* and

7. K.R. Norman, "Pāli Language and Scriptures", in *The Buddhist Heritage*, ed., T. Skorupski, Tring, 1989, 33.
8. A.C. Banerjee, *Sarvāstvāda Literature*, Calcutta, 1979, 19, and E. Lammote, *History of Indian Buddhism*, 1988, 152. Although the Sarvāstivādins list only four *Āgamas* in their *Sūtrapiṭaka* they had and used texts that they refer to as coming from the *Kṣudrakāgama*.
9. A. Hirakawa, *A History of Indian Buddhism*, Hawaii, 1990, 128.
10. E. Lamotte, *History of Indian Buddhism*, 159. Sometimes they are assigned to the *Kṣudrakāgama* or *Kṣudrakapiṭaka*, and sometimes they are classified as a fourth *Piṭaka* distinct from the *Tripiṭaka*.

Buddhavaṁśa are known to have existed in the Sanskrit Canons.[11] It is noteworthy that the Chinese sources only know of four *Āgamas,*[12] but fourteen of the texts which constitute the *Kṣudrakāgama* of other schools appear as individual works in the Chinese canon, which includes a version of a work entitled the *Jātakanidāna*, though whether this corresponds to the Pāli text of the same name is another matter.

The Tibetan Buddhist tradition of cataloguing canonical works, as established by Bu-ston 1290-1364 A.D.,[13] sets out its literary works in quite a different manner to that of the Sanskrit canons of the early Indian schools. The primary distinction for the Tibetans is between *bKa' 'gyur* and *BsTan 'gyur*. For, while the Tibetans obtained scriptures, teachings and methods of classifying teachings from India, they have largely followed their own scheme when designating these scriptures into their respective places in the collections of *bKa' 'gyur* and *BsTan 'gyur.*

The Tibetans of course were following the *Mahāyāna* tradition, but even the *Mahāyāna* recognised the authority of the *Sūtrapiṭaka* with its four or five *Āgamas*. Moreover, they also admitted the existence of texts of the three turnings[14] of the wheel of the doctrine. That the Tibetans knew of the division of works into *Āgamas* can be seen by references to the four *Āgamas* in the *Mahāvyutpatti.*[15] The Tibetans, ignoring the four or fivefold classification into *Āgamas* or *Nikāyas*, instead set out the *Sūtra* material under four headings: *Śer-phyin* (*Prajñāpāramitā*), *dKon-brtsegs* (*Ratnakūṭa*), *Phal-chen(Avataṁsaka)* and *mDo-sna-tshogs* (Miscellaneous *Sūtra*). In the Peking edition of the *bKa' 'gyur,* the *mDo-sna-tshogs* section contains works that can be traced in Pāli to three *Nikāyas* including a work corresponding in part to the *Dhammapada* of the *Khuddaka-nikāya.*[16] With the addition of the texts in the *Śer-phyin* section, texts of all five Pāli *Nikāyas* can be located in the *bKa' 'gyur*. For the Tibetan canon, as with the Chinese, some of the texts of the *Kṣudrakāgama* are known but are

---

11. K.R. Norman, "The Value of the Pāli Tradition", in his *Collected Papers,* vol. 3, Oxford, PTS, 1992, 40-41. See also Winternitz, *History of Indian Literature*, vol. 2, 236.
12. A.C. Banerjee, *Sarvāstivāda Literature*, 20; also E.J. Thomas, *The Life of the Buddha as Legend and History*, 1933, 272.
13. D. Seyfort-Ruegg, *The Life of Bu-sTon Rin-po-che*, Rome, 1966, 20, says that the impetus for the compilation of a definitive collection of texts in Tibet was probably due to the sharp decrease of Indian texts coming into the country.
14. D.Snellgrove, *Indo-Tibetan Buddhism*, London, 1987, 79-109; F.D. Lessing & A.Wayman, *Introduction to the Buddhst Tantric Systems*, The Hague, 1968, Indian reprint 1983, 45-49.
15. R. Sasaki, *Mahāvyutpatti*, Tokyo, 1925, Nos: 1421–4.
16. The Tibetan *Tripiṭaka*, Peking Edition, *Catalogue and Index*, Kyoto, 1985, vol. 39, No. 992: *Ched-du brjod-paḥi tshoms (Udānavarga).*

not grouped together or classified as belonging to a *Ksudrakāgama*; instead they appear as individual texts.

The Tibetan translation of the *Nidānakathā* is found in the *bKa' 'gyur*[17] grouped together with twelve other texts also translated from Pāli.[18] These and ten other complete texts, also from Pāli sources, appear to be the only texts translated directly from Pāli into Tibetan. This is not to say that Pāli sources were not cited in other Tibetan works, but these references would have been to portions of text only.[19] The group of thirteen texts that includes the *Nidānakathā* is located, in the Peking *bKa' 'gyur*, at the end of the *Śer-phyin* section. There is no apparent reason for their inclusion at this particular location in the *bKa' 'gyur*, since they are not *Prajñāpāramitā sūtras*, and it does seem an incongruous point at which to insert this group into the collection. It has recently been suggested that the *paritta* (protective) status of these texts was perhaps recognised by the Tibetans and that they were used as *dhāraṇīs* (charms) to end a section of the *bKa' 'gyur,*[20] a practice that is not without precedent in the Tibetan canon.

The Tibetan *bKa' 'gyur* traditions do not appear to assign a definite location in the *bKa' 'gyur* for this group of texts, and at least one of these traditions omits many of the thirteen texts. The earliest systematic account in Tibetan of the Buddhist scriptures and their ordering comes from the thirteenth century AD with the writings of Bu-ston. In the final part of the third section of his *Chos-ḥbyuṅ* (History of Buddhism in Tibet), he mentions that his teacher, Ñi-ma-rgyal-mtshan-dpal-bzaṅ-po, had spent a fourteen year period in Nepal during which time he translated the group of thirteen texts[21] at the invitation of the monk Paṇḍita Ānandaśrī. At the end of the catalogue of the *Śer-phyin sūtras*, Bu-ston says that some teachers recognise there is also a group of recently translated sūtras which are to be added to this section, but he gives no elaboration on this matter[22] regarding the names of the texts. The detailed reference to the group of thirteen texts is found later on in section four of his work. There, he lists all the texts by name and comments that all these were recently translated by Paṇḍita Ānandaśrī and Lama Ñi-ma-rgyal-mtshan-dpal-

17. The Tibetan *Tripiṭaka*, Peking Edition, Catalogue and Index, Kyoto 1985, 94-5. Here the *Nidāna*kathā is found at the end of the *Śer*-phyin (*Prajñāpāramitā*) section, volume 21, no.748.
18. P. Skilling, "Theravādin Literature in Tibetan Translation", *JPTS*, 19, 1993, 69–183, provides the most up-to-date study of these Pāli texts that were translated into Tibetan. See also L. Renou and J. Filliozat, *L'Inde Classique* vol. 2, 1953, 393.
19. *ibid.*, 143, 182.
20. *ibid.*, 83.
21. Bu-ston, *Chos-ḥbyuṅ-gsuṅ-rab-rin-po-cheḥi-mdzod*, 1988, 206.
22. Bu ston, *Chos-ḥbyuṅ*, 1988, 217.

bzaṅ-po;[23] these are also the names that are given in the colophons of those texts as being the transmitters of the texts and their translators into Tibetan.

Within Bu-ston's descriptions, there are two possible locations for the group of thirteen texts. The first is at the end of the *Śer-phyin* section while the second, where Bu-ston himself places them, is at the end of the section of his catalogue entitled *Theg pa chen poḥi mdo sde sna tshogs* ("Miscellaneous Section of Mahāyāna *Sūtras*"). While all of the thirteen texts, apart from the *Nidānakathā*, are sūtras they are not Mahāyāna works, and it raises the question of whether Bu-ston was aware of their school affiliation, or if he was aware of it why he decided to add them to the *Mahāyāna Sūtra* section. That Bu-ston should mention them as recently translated texts may be significant, for if the texts were relative latecomers to the compilers of the various editions of the *bKa' 'gyur* and since they came as a distinct group, translated by the same two personages, it is not unreasonable to suppose that they would be kept together even if the *bKa' 'gyur* traditions placed them within different sections. The consensus of evidence within the different editions of the *bKa' 'gyur* regarding the location of these texts is divided between the two above mentioned sections of the *bKa' 'gyur*.

The seven editions of the *bKa' 'gyur* consulted here can be divided into two groups on the question as to where to record the thirteen texts within their respective *bKa' 'gyurs*. The first group has the texts at the end of the *Śer-phyin* section and within this group are the Peking, Urga and sDe-dge; the second group records the texts at the end of the *mDo-sde* section and is comprised of the sTog, sNar-thaṅ, Lha-sa and Śel-dkar. This difference between the two groups in locating the thirteen texts is hard to explain; it may be that they were following Bu-ston's suggestions. The problem is not solved by dividing the groups into Eastern and Western[24] traditions for there is no unanimous agreement between them as to whether the texts should be at the end of the *Śer-phyin* or *Mdo-sde* sections.

The Pāli text of the *Nidānakathā* as it now exists forms an integral part of the *Jātaka* collection. This, however, has not always been the case. The *Jātaka* collection together with its commentary, the *Jātakaṭṭhavaṇṇanā,* was probably known in Ceylon in some form or other from the introduction of Buddhism into that country. The tradition there considered that only the *gāthās* were to be taken as canonical[25] and not the commentary on them. This division into canonical and commentarial literature is extremely important for the history of Buddhist

23. *ibid.*, 225.
24. H. Eimer, "Some Results of Recent Kanjur Research", *Archiv für Zentralasiatische Geschichtsforschung, VGH Wissenschaftsverlag*, Sankt Augustin, 1983, 13.
25. See K.R. Norman. *Pāli Literature*, 1988, 77; W. Geiger, *Pāli Literature and Language,* 21.

literature in Ceylon, as it was only the commentarial material that was translated from Pāli, or whatever other Middle Indo Aryan dialect it may have been composed in, into the Sinhalese language.[26] This process of translation probably began at an early stage; it has even been suggested that the translation into Singhalese began during the time of Mahinda in the third century BC and was in fact instigated by him.[27]

This method of translating the Pāli commentarial material into Sinhalese became the normal way of recording the commentaries in Ceylon. By the time of Buddhaghosa in the fifth century AD, there was a vast amount of commentarial literature in Sinhalese; how much of this material was derived from Indian sources and how much from indigenous Sinhalese sources is difficult to determine.[28] What can be said, however, is that when Buddhaghosa arrived in Ceylon from India he was confronted with at least six[29] different commentarial traditions preserved in Sinhalese and Dravidian. So his work was not simply a matter of translation but of editing and evaluating the different commentarial traditions. Buddhaghosa is the pivotal figure in beginning the process of translating and editing the Sinhalese commentaries into Pāli, a process taken up by succeeding writers, and leading to the composition of works in Pāli by Sinhalese and Indian authors, some of them contemporaries of Buddhaghosa.

The text of the *Nidānakathā* belongs to that part of Buddhist commentarial tradition that is primarily concerned with the portrayal of the life of the Buddha. The *gāthās* of the *Jātaka* collection provided the basis around which there grew an elaborate system of commentary that dealt with the Buddha's relationship to these *gāthās*. The express purpose of the *Jātaka* commentary is to place the *gāthās* within an understandable and Buddhistically meaningful context. This was achieved by presenting the central character of each of the *Jātakas* as being the Buddha in one of his previous existences. That a commentarial tradition of some kind was linked to the *Jātaka gāthās* from the very earliest period is

---

26. E. Frauwallner, *The Earliest Vinaya and the Beginnings of Buddhist Literature*, Rome, 1956, 186, draws attention to another level of classification of the literature of Ceylon: "the essential distinction (regarding Ceylon) is not that between canonical and non-canonical scriptures, but between local (Sinhalese) literature and the literature of the home (India) country. "
27. G.P. Malalasekera, *Pāli Literature of Ceylon*, 73.
28. See G.P. Malalasekera, *op. cit.*, 81, where he quotes the *Sāsanavaṁsa* in order to show that even in Buddhaghosa's time, the *Aṭṭhakathas* were not extant in India.
29. *ibid.*, 91, Malalasekara gives a list of six commentarial traditions in Ceylon that would have been available to Buddhaghosa. E. W. Adikaram, *Early History of Buddhism in Ceylon*, 10, gives a list of twenty-eight commentaries, but says that only a few of these were distinct works while others were simply alternative names for some of the other works. See also T.W. Rhys Davids and J.E. Carpenter, *Sumaṅgala-Vilāsinī*, PTS London, 1968, ix-xi.

beyond dispute[30] and, given the terse and cryptic nature of those *gāthās*, understandable. The explanatory material provided by the commentary served a dual purpose; it allowed for an exposition of the doctrinal aspects of the *gāthās*, and also furnished concrete examples of how the Buddha had behaved in his previous lives.

The genre of texts dealing with the life of the Buddha and later with the Buddha legend, while represented in its fully developed form by the commentarial tradition, and especially for the Pāli tradition by the *Nidānakathā*, was not an independent section of Buddhist literature from the inception of that literary tradition. The rise of the genealogical class of works purporting to represent the Buddha's spiritual lineage and progress from one existence to another were not in themselves innovations within the existing Indian religious tradition. Texts dealing with spiritual or temporal genealogies, whether it be of kings or religious teachers, were a shared feature of Indian literary works. The intention of such texts was to establish that a particular person or tradition was important or in some way significant not only because of any individual or specific achievement, but primarily because of the weight of the tradition that preceded them. By setting out a detailed genealogy, the compilers provided evidence that enhanced the standing of that person or tradition, and by presenting them as belonging to an extremely well attested lineage showed that they were not fleeting phenomena but part of an authentic and ancient process.

The predilection in India for this form of literature that authenticated a person or tradition is present even from the Vedic period. In Vedic literature it is the *ṛṣis* who are depicted as having individual family lineages reaching back to the very origin of the *Vedas*. The rationale behind these genealogies is to demonstrate that the *ṛṣis* are the direct heirs to an unbroken line of human teachers and by implication bearers of an authentic religious and literary tradition. This form of literary record was continued and developed in later Indian history reaching its most complex form in the *Purāṇas*.

This biographical or genealogical genre of literature was already a recognised and developed form for representing persons or traditions prior to the advent of Buddhist works on the life of the Buddha. Perhaps the closest to the Buddhist tradition, and for comparative purposes the most interesting, is that of the Jainas with their genealogy of Mahāvīra. The case of the Jaina tradition that records the life of Mahāvīra yields numerous correspondences to that of the Buddhist compilations on the life of the Buddha. Jaina sources catalogue events connected with the conception, birth, early life, renunciation, enlightenment and nirvāṇa of Mahāvīra[31]. These events have obvious parallels to the Buddhist records on the

30. W. Geiger, *Pāli Literature and Language*, 21.
31. P.S. Jaini, *The Jaina Path of Purification*, 6–10.

life of the Buddha. The similarities are more striking when the Jaina tradition regarding the lineage of the twenty-four *Tīrthaṅkaras*[32] is taken into account. Whether the Jaina textual sources were influential in leading to the creation of the Buddhist tradition of the life of the Buddha and of the twenty-four previous Buddhas will not be investigated here; suffice it to say that the concept of a genealogical tradition that had as its purpose the establishment of an authentic and unbroken lineage was part of the general Indian cultural background, and certainly not a purely Buddhist innovation.

Given the prevalence of the literary tradition of recording genealogies in ancient India, it cannot be considered unusual that the Buddhists should have evolved their own textual traditions dealing with the life of the Buddha Gotama. The events that are presented as a continuous biography in the *Nidānakathā* have some precedents in the texts of the Pāli canon. Though the early Canonical works attempt no systematic or coherent life of the Buddha, references to the various important events in the Buddha's life are scattered throughout the texts of the *Suttapiṭaka* and *Vinayapiṭaka* as integral parts of individual texts.

Precisely when the attempt was made to begin the production of a connected life story of the Buddha is not known. Although from a very early period there had been isolated attempts to present a more or less connected series of episodes from certain parts of the Buddha's career, the text of the *Mahāparinibbāna-sutta* is an example of this stage of development. It has been suggested that the later works centring on the biography of the Buddha were in fact based in part on an old *Skandhaka,*[33] this being a proto-biography of the Buddha and a part of the *Vinaya*, which was compiled shortly before or after the Council of Vaiśālī. This text was a partial biography but it dealt with the parts of the Buddha's life that were most important for the establishment of a thoroughgoing Buddhist history. Here, the life of the Buddha is important in the sense that it allows for an elucidation of the history of the doctrine and how that doctrine was first introduced to the world.

The earliest occurrence in the Pāli Canon of the depiction of events in the life of the Buddha revolve around the personal recollections of Gotama Buddha about particular events in his life. These early records of the life of the Buddha appear to reflect the concern of the early compilers to establish a tradition that could be seen to derive directly from the founder's own experiences and which had been transmitted by him to his followers during his lifetime. These early fragmentary glimpses of the life of the Buddha are of a historical and utilitarian

---

32. P. Dundas, *The Jains*, 1992, 20–1, assigns the earliest Jaina biography of Mahāvīra to the second or first centuries B.C. In this work, the *Acaraṅga*, the Mahāvīra is first associated with the twenty-three preceding Tīrthaṅkaras. See also Jaini, *op. cit.*, 164–166.

33. E. Frauwallner, *op. cit.*, 163. See also E. Lamotte, *op. cit.*, 176.

nature. Although even here, in texts like *Acchariyabbhutadhamma-sutta* of the *Majjhima-nikāya*, the description of his birth is full of what might almost be called doecetic tendencies. The events are usually related to specific occasions in Gotama's life and are important in that they provide information on both the pre-enlightened and post-enlightened parts of Gotama's life.

The *Nidānakathā*, in contrast to other canonical sources, represents the biography of the Buddha not in the narrow or restrictive sense of only the life of Gotama but rather on the macrocosmic scale. The purpose of the text is to show the spiritual lineage of the Buddha Gotama through the presentation of the lives of the twenty-four Buddhas who preceded him. This scheme seeks to normalise the notion of Buddhahood by setting out an unbroken succession of Buddhas that reaches back in time for many aeons and culminates in a depiction of the life of the Buddha Gotama and his attainment of Buddhahood.

Though the *Nidānakathā* occurs at the head of the Pāli *Jātaka* collection belonging to the Theravāda school, it is still not fully understood from which school's sources it originally stems. From the internal evidence of the text, or at least from its introductory verses, it is apparent that the Theravādins themselves believed that the text represented their own doctrinal position. The evidence for this view is contained within the dedicatory verses that precede the text of the *Nidānakathā*.[34] The introductory verses begin with praises to the Buddha and his teachings and then proceed to state the reasons for the compilation of this introductory section to the *Jātakaṭṭhakathā*.

The authorship of these dedicatory verses and the *Nidānakathā* remains an undecided issue. It is assigned by the Pāli tradition to Buddhaghosa but this has been called into question by modern scholars and some think it more likely that it was Buddhadatta. The date of the work is thought to be fifth century AD[35] but certainly no earlier. The author makes it known that the impetus for the compilation of the *Nidānakathā* lies not with his own decision but is at the request of three *theras*, Atthadassi, Buddhamitta and Buddhadeva, of whom at least one belonged to the Mahiṁsāsaka school. There are differing views regarding just which one of these *theras* is referred to as being of the Mahīṁsāsaka[36] school.

The Tibetan text omits these introductory verses and so makes no reference to the Mahiṃsāsaka school. The existence of this school in Ceylon during the fourth and fifth centuries AD is attested to by Chinese sources; the accounts of Fa-Hien's travels in Ceylon show that he obtained copies in Sanskrit of a

34. V. Fausboll, *The Jātaka* vol. 1, 1.
35. E.J. Thomas, *History of Buddhist Thought*, London, 1933, 283.
36. K.R. Norman, *op. cit.*, 128, says it is Buddhadeva who is meant ; G. P Malalasekera, *op. cit.*, 117, says all three belonged to the same school.

Vinayapiṭaka of the Mahiṃśāsaka school as well as a number of other works also in Sanskrit.[37] What their precise connection with the Mahāvihāra was remains unclear and to what extent they exerted influence on the Mahāvihāra is even more difficult to determine although it seems likely that they had some texts in common with the Mahāvihāra, in particular the Mahiṃsāsaka *Vinayapiṭaka* that contained correspondences with both the *Dīgha-nikāya* and the *Khuddhaka-nikāya*[38] of the Pāli canon. Whatever the influence of the Mahiṃsāsaka may have been the author of the introductory verses concludes that he intends to present the commentary in accordance with the tradition of the Mahāvihāra.

The Tibetan text has its own short introduction, with no parallel in the Pāli. It is very like the introduction or *nidāna* found in *sūtras*. Here, the Buddha is approached by the gNas-brtan-chen-po Don-mthoṅ (Mahāsthavira Arthadarśana) and asked to teach about the lineage of the Buddhas. This coincides with the sense of the Pāli introductory verses in that it identifies the Mahāsthavira Arthadaśana as the person at whose request the *Nidānakathā* is related.

The main body of the first section of the text of the *Nidānakathā* is in prose and relates the life stories of the twenty-four Buddhas preceding the Buddha Gotama. The structure of the text shows it to be a composite work consisting of layers of Buddhist tradition, drawing on both canonical and non-canonical sources. That non-canonical or apocryphal materials are added to the existing stock of the traditional accounts of the Buddha's life is an innovative turn in Pāli Buddhist literature. It represents the evolution of the Buddha legend from an original core of canonical traditions concerning the life of the Buddha to a fully developed genealogical history of Buddhas in general. What sources the author of the *Nidānakathā* utilised for his work and what their age was cannot be accurately known. All that can be said is that the earlier commentaries that had been translated from Pāli into Sinhalese provided the basis for the *Nidānakathā* and that the growth of this Sinhalese commentarial tradition is thought to have come to an end during the first century AD.[39] It is possible that commentaries still came from India for some time, for Frauwallner maintains that the connection with India went on until the second century AD.[40]

The Pāli canonical sources in the *Nidānakathā* are represented not only by *gāthās* taken directly from canonical texts but also by themes that occur in canonical works. The principal canonical text that is commented upon in the

37. E. Frauwallner, *op. cit.*, 156; also J. Legge, *A Record of Buddhistic Kingdoms*, New York, Dover Publications, 1965, 111.
38. A. Hirakawa, *op. cit.*, 121.
39. E.W. Adikaram, *op. cit.*, 42.
40. E. Frauwallner, *op. cit.*, 186.

Nidānakathā is the *Buddhavaṃsa*; the second chapter, the *Dīpaṅkara-Buddhavaṃsa,* is found almost in its entirety and individual gāthās from the remaining chapters are cited. The other canonical works quoted in the *Nidānakathā* are also works of the *Khuddaka-nikāya, gāthās* from the *Jātaka, Dhammapada,Theragāthā* and *Cariyāpiṭaka*, and from the *Vinayapiṭaka* there are *gāthās* from the *Mahāvagga.* The themes that the *Nidānakathā* includes are a mixture of old and new. While taking the traditional themes about the Buddha's life, such as birth, renunciation, enlightenment and death, it details, however, these events in a way not seen in the *Nikāya* works. It also introduces themes that do not seem to have a counterpart in any other Pāli canonical works apart from the *Buddhavaṃsa* and the *Cariyapiṭaka.*[41] The sources that the *Nidānakathā* cites come from extremely early texts as well as later additions to the Pāli canon. In this respect the text represents a synthesis of the earlier and later traditions and their treatment of the life of the Buddha.

The first section of the *Nidānakathā,* the story of the remote past (*dūrenidāna*), contains large segments of *gāthās* from the text of the *Buddhavaṃsa*. These *gāthās* provide the canonical framework around which the commentary builds up a synchronic account of the path to Buddhahood of the Bodhisatta who was to become Gotama Buddha. The *dūrenidāna* deals with the period from his initial resolve to attain Buddhahood as the brahmin Sumedha to his rebirth in the Tusita heaven prior to his rebirth as Gotama. In this section the events that are claimed by the *Nidānakathā* to be common to all Buddhas are presented, such as the prediction to Buddhahood, by the Buddha of that age.

Both the *Buddhavaṃsa* and *Cariyāpiṭaka* are *gāthā* works that treat in detail topics that are not dealt with in such an ordered and systematic manner in any other work of the Pāli canon. The *Buddhavaṃsa* gives a full history of the lives of the twenty-four Buddhas, and in so doing shows the enormously long path to Buddhahood of the Buddha Gotama, who made his resolution to become a Buddha during the time of Dīpaṅkara, the first Buddha, and became a Buddha after Kassapa the twenty-forth Buddha. This scheme of twenty-four Buddhas found in the *Buddhavaṃsa* is an increase.on the six Buddhas that are referred to in other works of the Pāli canon. There is also a different ethos present that sets these two works apart from the other *Nikāya* texts.

Both the *Buddhavaṃsa* and its commentary record the incident where Sāriputta's request leads to the Buddha teaching the *Buddhavaṃsa.* The fact that the text is said to be the word of the Buddha should have been sufficient to ensure that it was accepted as canonical by all, although as is known, the *Dīghabhāṇakas* and *Majjhimabhāṇakas* disagreed over this. That these

41. These two texts have long been known to be later additions to the Pāli Canon; see E. J. Thomas, *op. cit.*, 171.

differences existed regarding the various ways of assigning the text to different *Nikāyas* can be taken as evidence in favour of the *Buddhavaṃsa* being a late work. Certainly the consensus among scholars is that it is a late text,[42] being placed by Warder as no earlier than the second century B.C,[43] while Gombrich thinks it is probably a work of the third century B.C.[44].

The dating of the *Buddhavaṃsa* owes much to the recognition that the ideas and content found in the text belong to a different phase in the development of Buddhist thought and doctrine. Some have argued that it belongs to a different school altogether. The variations found in the text when compared to other canonical works go beyond the simple differences over the number of Buddhas, for the *Buddhavaṃsa* contains doctrines that are not explicitly formulated in any other Pāli canonical works. These expound the doctrine of the Bodhisatta who strives for countless aeons to achieve Buddhahood and his practice of the ten *pāramī* (perfections) that must be perfected before Buddhahood can be achieved.

The term Bodhisatta is of course known to the other works of the Pāli canon but seems to be used there in a much more limited and restricted sense. In the many examples of the use of the term in Pāli canonical works, it is invariably used by the Buddha Gotama when referring to himself in his pre-enlightened state and is also usually confined to his existence as Gotama rather than to all his previous lives. In the *Nidānakathā,* the term and the number of individual lives it is connected with is extended to encompass all the previous lives of Gotama Buddha that occurred during the time of the twenty-four Buddhas that are mentioned in that text. This is an innovative development in the Buddhology and doctrine of the Pāli canon, for it does not possess anywhere else such elaborate and detailed schemes setting out the Bodhisatta's long and arduous career and his development over many lifetimes of the ten *pāramīs*.

The *pāramīs*, like the term Bodhisatta, are also known to the Pāli canon. The principal Pāli canonical sources dealing with the *pāramīs* are the *Jātaka* collection, thirty-two of the thirty-five *cariyās* in the *Cariyāpiṭaka* can be related to the *Jātaka* collection. There the *pāramīs* are treated as individual qualities that have been developed by the Buddha during various previous lives. There is no systematic presentation of the *pāramīs* in the *Jātaka* but only the bare mention of them as qualities that are developed by the Bodhisatta, much less is there anything approaching a doctrine of the *pāramīs*. The *Jātakas* certainly do not deal exclusively with the *pāramīs*, there being many *Jātakas* that have no

42. K.R Norman, *op. cit.*, 94. ; Thomas, *op. cit.*, 171; Winternitz, *op. cit.*, 162.
43. A. Warder, *op. cit.*, 298.
44. R. Gombrich, "The Significance of Former Buddhas in the Theravādin Tradition", in *Buddhist Studies in Honour of Walpola Rahula*, eds., S. Balasooriya *et als.*, London, 1980, 68.

reference to the *pāramīs* at all. They appear scattered throughout the *Jātakas* and some of the *pāramīs* have only one or two *Jātakas* representing them[45] from among the entire collection.

The *Buddhavaṃsa* and the *Cariyāpiṭaka* represent quite a sophisticated and evolved level of Buddhist doctrine. These doctrines, if we are to take the paucity of evidence for them in other works of the Pāli canon into account, seem to have appeared almost without canonical precedent. Both these works are the only two Pāli canonical sources that treat of the Bodhisatta and the *pāramīs* in anything like a coherent and systematised fashion. These two texts represent the epitome of Theravāda Buddhology for the doctrines found in them are not developed further in that tradition.

Because of the developments found in the *Buddhavaṃsa* and *Cariyāpiṭaka*, but absent in other works of the Pāli canon, the source of origin of these texts has been called into question. The doctrines that they contain, and they must be taken as doctrines for they are not merely random teachings as in the *Jātaka*, but fully set out and interconnected schemes of the path to Buddhahood, have led some to assume that the two texts were imported in their entirety from another school altogether.[46] It is known that a *Buddhavaṃsa* existed in the Sanskrit canon and reference is made in the *Tarkajvāla* to a text of that name belonging to the Abhayagiri school of Ceylon, who adopted the *Vaitulya-piṭaka* purportedly a Mahāyāna canon.[47] However, locating the sources for the *Buddhavaṃsa* and deciding whether it is a borrowing from another school or simply drawing on earlier material that had not previously found its way to Ceylon are in all likelihood impossible tasks given our incomplete knowledge of the canons of the mainland schools and of the *Vaitulyapiṭaka* that existed in Ceylon.

While the *Buddhavaṃsa* provides the biographies of the twenty-four previous Buddhas, the *Nidānakathā*, as a biography of Gotama Buddha, is concerned with the various accounts of the lives of the Bodhisatta but also pays particular attention to the life story of Gotama from birth to the donation of the Jetavana park. The second and third sections of the *Nidānakathā*, the *avidūrenidāna* (middle era) and *santikenidāna* (present era), deal solely with the life of Gotama before and after enlightenment. The accounts are found not only in the Pāli canon but also in the Vinaya texts of the Sanskrit canons, although they are only extant in Sanskrit in the Mūlsarvātivādin recension. The material in the Vinayas dealing with the life of the Buddha probably represents the oldest strata of this tradition that sought to flesh out the life story of the Buddha Gotama. For the

45. I.B. Horner, *Ten Jātaka Stories*, Bangkok, 1974, x.
46. E.J. Thomas, *op. cit.*, 172.
47. P. Skilling, *op. cit.*, 142–3.

Pāli canon, the principal source as a starting point for the life of Buddha was the *Mahāvagga* section of the *Vinaya-piṭaka*, though this was an extremely restricted account of a short period of the Buddha Gotama's life. The existing Sanskrit Vinaya sources for a biography of the Buddha are contained in the final two sections of the Mūlasarvāstivādin *Vinaya*, the *Saṃghabhedavastu* and the *Kṣudrakavastu*, which provide a fairly detailed account.

It has been shown by Frauwallner that the old *Skandhaka* text provided the basic materials for the stories about the life of the Buddha compiled by the different schools after the period of the schisms. From a very early time, each school equipped itself with a biography of the Buddha that can be seen to stem from this extremely ancient common source. The Chinese recension of a text questions what the text dealing with the life of the Buddha is called, and gives the answer that the Mahāsāṃghikas call it the *Mahāvastu*, the Sarvāstivādins call it the *Mahālalitavistara*, the Kāśyapīyas call it the *Buddhajātakanidāna*, the Dharmaguptakas call it the *ŚākyamuniBuddhacarita*, and the Mahīśāsakas call it the *Vinayapiṭakamūla*.[48] The common feature of all these biographies is that they depended on the old *Skandhaka* text, since it provided them with canonical authority and a precedent for their compilation.

The *Nidānakathā* is, like the early biographies of the Buddha that were based on the old *Skandhaka*, an incomplete biography in that it does not give any details about a large part of his life that culminates in his *parinibbāna*. The text only covers the period of the Buddha's life that ends with the donation of the Jetavana park by Anāthapiṇḍika. That the text ends here is significant, for it indicates that it shares with the *Mahāvastu* and the *Lalitavistara*, the feature of being a partial biography; on the basis of which Frauwallner and Lamotte have concluded that all these biographical texts derive from the same source. If the *Nidānakathā* is reliant on this source, it would explain why there are similarities between it and these other two biographies mentioned, and why its method of ordering events is not found elsewhere in the Pāli canon.

The *Nidānakathā,* incomplete as it is, still represents the fullest account of the life of the Buddha that is available to the Pāli tradition. Though it is primarily a commentarial work, it has come to provide for the Pāli tradition what is considered to be the most authoritative and extended account of the life of the Buddha. That it is set out in the form of an introduction to the *Jātaka* collection has perhaps aided its acceptance by the Pāli tradition as an ancient and reliable source of biographical material on the Buddha's life. Because, as an integral part of the *Jātaka* collection, it may have come to be regarded as being a valid part of the *Khuddaka-nikāya*, and therefore have acquired some sort of canonical or quasi-canonical status, Thomas has referred to what he terms the spurious

48. E. Frauwallner, *op. cit.*, 50; Lamotte, *op. cit.*, 177.

authority accorded to the *Nidānakathā*.[49] It should be remembered, however, that it was only the *Jātaka gāthās* that were technically recognised as canonical, but it is possible that the distinction between canonical and commentarial traditions became blurred. This process is all the more probable with the *Jātaka* collection where the commentary is so closely connected with the elucidation of the *gāthās* that form its canonical basis.

The treatment by the Tibetan tradition of the *Nidānakathā* has to be taken as an indication that they, for whatever reason, considered the text to be canonical. All the seven Tibetan *bKa' 'gyur* traditions used in this paper have included the text in the *bKa' 'gyur* section, even though they might not have agreed on its exact location in that collection of canonical works. There could be any one of several reasons for its inclusion in the canonical section. The fact that it came with the twelve *sutta* texts may have led to its being taken as a *sutta* of some kind, or at the very least a fully canonical work. The Tibetan translator Ñi-ma-rgyal-mtshan-dpal-bzaṅ-po may have been informed that all thirteen texts were canonical by the Sinhalese monk Ānandaśri who is named in the colophons as the person from whom the texts were obtained. If this is so, it could reveal the standing of the *Nidānakathā* in northern India, and possibly Ceylon, in the early part of the twelfth century AD. There is also the possibility that the Tibetans gave the text canonical status due to the introductory section, found in the Tibetan but not the Pāli, which states that it was the Buddha who initially taught the text. Alternatively, the inclusion of the *Nidānakathā* in the *bKa' 'gyur* may be a simple mistake or oversight, for Bu-ston is uncertain whether the thirteen texts were duplicates of earlier translations or even if they were *sūtras* of the Māhayāna or the Hīnayāna.[50]

The Tibetan *bKa' 'gyur* and *BsTan 'gyur* contains some other texts dealing with the life of the Buddha. There are four well known biographical works in these two collections. The *bKa' 'gyur* has in its *mDo-sde* ("*Sūtra Section*") the *Lalitavistara* and the *Abhiniṣkramaṇa-sūtra*. The *BsTan 'gyur* contains at least two texts dealing with the Buddha's life story, the *Jātakamāla* and the *Buddhacarita*. The *Nidānakathā*, as a commentarial text arranged into its present form in the fifth century AD, would seem to have more in common with these last two texts, since the *Jātakamāla* and the *Buddhacarita* are both earlier than the *Nidānakathā* in its present form, so that if the age of the text was any

49. E.J.Thomas, *op. cit.*, 283.
50. P. Skilling, *op. cit.*,78–9.

criterion for its acceptance as canonical, the *Nidānakathā* would be excluded, unless of course its date of retranslation and re-editing into Pāli was not known to the Tibetans. The problem is that it is not always possible to know exactly what criteria were used by the Tibetans, or what information was available to them when assigning these works to the *bKa' 'gyur*.

For the Pāli tradition, the *Nidānakathā* text is their record of the life of the Buddha, in the same way as the *Mahāvastu* and *Lalitavistara* represent the record of other schools. The text in its present form is a relative latecomer to the Pāli canon and represents a compilation of various traditional accounts of the life of the Buddha. It is an unusual work in that it spans both the canonical and commentarial traditions in the presentation of the Buddha's life. The canonical sources that it utilizes are equally diverse, both in their age and in their subject matter, covering the early period as represented in the *Vinaya* and a later period as shown in the *Buddhavaṃsa.* The principal doctrines that are dealt with are the Bodhisatta and the ten *pāramīs*, and the treatment of these two aspects of Buddhist doctrine is the most detailed in Pāli sources.

The study of the Tibetan translation of the *Nidānakathā* allows for a thorough comparison of the two versions to be made. It is admittedly unusual to find Pāli texts in the Tibetan *bKa' 'gyur*, but given the eclectic nature of the Tibetan translators it should not be thought that the texts represent translations from Sanskrit sources rather than Pāli. The Tibetan translation of the text provides a valuable witness to the version of the text preserved in Pāli, for it is a record of that Pāli text as known in north India in the thirteenth century AD. Any complete study of the *Nidānakathā*, however, cannot ignore the Sanskrit sources for the life of the Buddha, in particular the *Mahāvastu* and the *Lalitavistara* for these two texts contain certain parallels with the *Nidānakathā*.

General Munthe's Chinese Buddhist Sculpture: An Embarrassment of Riches?

Derek Gillman

Chinese Buddhist stone sculpture after the Tang dynasty

In 1942, Osvald Sirén reconsidered a number of Chinese Buddhist figures first published by him in 1925, in order to present a more coherent picture of the production of stone sculpture made in north China between the end of the Tang (618–906) and the beginning of the Yuan (1279–1368).[1]

An interesting aspect of his 1942 foray into what was then relatively uncharted territory was the identification of two 12th century tendencies, separate but related by some of the same features: a more naturalistic 'baroque' manner, ranging from the truly expressive to the merely decorative, and an archaistic one, referring directly back to 6th century modes of representation. Although he had previously thought that some dated to the latter part of the Tang, Sirén now reassigned almost all of the images, naturalistic and archaistic, to the Jin period, seeing them as an expression of the enthusiasm for Buddhism by a nomadic conquering power.

The artistic landscape mapped out in 'Chinese Sculptures of the Sung, Liao and Chin Dynasties' was revisited in 1984 in an article entitled "Buddhist Sculptures of the Liao Dynasty, A reassessment of Osvald Sirén's Study", by Angela Falco Howard.[2] Because Sirén's study made little difference between the Khitan Liao (907–1125) and the Jurchen Jin (1115–1234), Howard felt it necessary to distinguish more precisely the sculpture made under the two dynasties, and in particular to examine Liao production.[3] In an epilogue, she

1. O. Sirén, "Chinese Sculptures of the Sung, Liao and Chin Dynasties", *BMFEA*, 14, 1942, 45–64; Sirén, *Chinese Sculpture from the Fifth to the Fourteenth Century*, 4 vols, London, 1925, pls. 541–6 are attributed to the Tang, pls. 584–5 to the Liao and Jin.
2. A.F. Howard, "Buddhist Sculptures of the Liao Dynasty, A Reassessment of Osvald Sirén's Study", *BMFEA*, 56, 1984, 1–95.
3. The Liao co-existed with the Northern Song (906–1127); the greater part of their territory was north of the Great Wall. The Jin occupied the whole of north China down to the Huai River, the boundary with the Southern Song (1127–1279).

revised his Jin dating of at least some of the naturalistic images, placing them firmly into the 8th century by comparison with material excavated in 1950 from the ruins of a pagoda in Shanxi province.

The images that Howard thus dated were part of a rather homogenous body of work recorded by Sirén (in 1925) as having come from a pagoda in Dingzhou, west Hebei.[4] In 1942, Sirén reported that:

> "They were all said to have come from a place 'near Pao-ting or Ting-chou', an indication that is fully supported by the quality of the marble and the workmanship, and to judge from the fact that some of these figures are attached to slabs of varying size and form, they must have formed part of the decoration of an architectural monument, probably a pagoda. I have seen at least a dozen of them, all about one metre high, executed in the round, though in many cases attached to background slabs, partly cut off, and in addition to these there are some larger statues of Buddhas and Bodhisattvas belonging to the same group."[5]

He also remarked that a number of the images had passed through the hands of various dealers in Peking some twenty years previously. At least eighteen images from the 'architectural' group are known to exist, and thirteen of the larger 'free-standing' group (the tallest over two metres). Sirén was taken by the smaller figures, finding two images in particular remarkable for their emotional ennervation—a guardian warrior *(lishi)* and the *luohan* Kāśyapa; the Kāśyapa he described thus:

> "The monk, who stands absolutely motionless, steeped in fervent prayer, appears like a symbol of deep spiritual devotion. The figure, which is completely covered up by the thick mantle and placed almost in profile against the background slab, is quite simple, but so striking is the attitude that the monk may be considered one of the most expressive human representations in Chinese sculpture."[6]

He thought that the large Buddhas failed to reach the level of the metre-high images; they were carved for the pagoda's parent temple perhaps two or three decades later. The larger seated Bodhisattvas (Mañjuśrī and Samantabhadra) were somewhat effeminate. More satisfactory were the tall standing figures. They all represented "the most naturalistic phase of what we have called the dec-

---

4. O. Sirén, *Chinese Sculpture from the Fifth to the Fourteenth Century*, pls. 541–6. Zhou and Xian are Chinese administrative districts. Prior to the 20th century, the region was known as Dingzhou, as was the city; in the 20th century, Dingxian has also been used to describe the city and its surrounds (e. g. recent gazettes are the *Zhili Dingzhou zhi*, 1849, and the *Dingxian zhi*, 1934).
5. O. Sirén, "Chinese Sculptures of the Sung, Liao and Chin Dynasties", 55–6.
6. *ibid.*, 56.

orative style of this epoch" made "while the Chin dynasty was in its heyday".[7] The images were compared, on the one hand, with architectural decoration on datable pagodas and memorial pillars, and on the other with sculpture in the round.[8] Laurence Sickman commented on the material thus:

> "One of the most important centres for sculpture of this kind was the Hopei school centred around Pao-ting, Chü-yang, and Ting-chou, where so much excellent work in white marble had been produced from the latter part of the sixth century to the end of the T'ang Dynasty ... There is also a large group of sculpture that combines certain purely twelfth-century elements of naturalism, of pictorial composition and dramatic modelling, with archaic stiffness, grooved drapery, and flat folds of a much earlier time. These elements appear to be not so much conscious revivals of an archaic style as merely provincial relapses into relatively flat and linear manners of representation. They are for the most part heavy, ill-conditioned products of fairly skilled but uninspired stone-cutters ... The true spirit of the age found its happiest expression in sculpture done in the more pliable materials of clay and wood."[9]

The discussion of 12th century Hebei marble carving highlights the general decline of Buddhist stone sculpture from the later 9th century on. Chinese Buddhism recovered from the devastating suppression of 845, (although, as is often noted, the vigour of the Sino-Buddhist philosophical schools was now a thing of the past); yet apart from additions to the walls of existing cave temples, both in the north and south—most notably at Dazu in Sichuan during the Song, and Feilaifeng, near Hangzhou, in the Yuan—and bas-relief carving on Yuan and Ming Buddhist monuments in and around Peking, there seems to have been a general run down of free-standing Buddhist stone sculpture. By contrast, a

7. *ibid.*, 59. "The work of decorating the pagoda and the temple, for which all these sculptures were made, may have continued for some time, the architectural pieces being executed a little earlier than the free standing cult-figures, but they must all have been products of the same workshop and were probably made within two or three decades."
8. O. Sirén related the style firstly to decoration on the Southern Pagoda (Nan ta) and its associated octagonal pillars at the Yunju temple, Fangshan, near Peking (in the southern part of Liao territory)—the Nan ta is dated to 1117 and one of the pillars to 1118, the other is probably contemporary; secondly, to several free-standing figures, including two Jin dynasty *luohan (arhats)*, one found in the Bao'an temple, Baidu village, Tangxian, west Hebei, dated 1146, and the other dated to 1158 (inscribed with a village name, illegible in reproduction). It is not evident from the 1878 Tangxian gazette that there was a Baidu in the district; it is possible that Sirén has mis-transcribed the name of Baita cun ('white pagoda' village), which lies a short distance to the south-west of Tangxian city (see *Tangxian zhi*, preface 1878, Zhong'guo fangzhi congshu, 183, 1969, 154).
9. L. Sickman and A. Soper, *The Art and Architecture of China*, Harmondsworth, 1971, 189.

Confucian tradition continued strongly in the monumental spirit figures at the Song and Ming tombs. What emerges from Sirén's 12th century dating of the Hebei material is something of an oasis in the context of later Buddhist sculptural production. Although another significant body of stone sculpture, this time in sandstone (mostly) and limestone, was made around 1159 for the Chang'le temple, near Handan, south Hebei, in general little has been published to contradict the impression that energy was diverted after the Tang into other materials.[10]

By the 10th century, for large-scale images clay and wood were probably the most widely used materials in the metropolitan areas of China. Clay was surely always a cheaper alternative to stone. The evidence of temple decoration from the Song, Liao and Jin points not only to widespread use of such imagery, but also to an increase in the number of images. Very noticeable from the 10th century in both painting and sculpture, for example, is the development of the cult of the *luohan*, represented in groups of eight to five hundred.[11]

The more images commissioned for a temple, the more attractive the price of clay would have become to patrons (although economic considerations are always relative). It was also a natural medium to depict a wide range of facial expressions, and we certainly see Song, Liao and Jin sculptors exploring naturalism in different but no less interesting ways than that seen in the 7th and 8th centuries. In the longer term, we might say that clay lost out, the archaeological record constantly reminding us of the great stone monuments of the Six Dynasties and Tang Buddhism, and only infrequently of the more fragile and friable work.[12] On reflection then, the architectural images reported by Sirén as

---

10. The Chang'le si was reconstructed and re-equipped *ca.* 1159; a guardian king, *tianwang*, found there, resembles quite closely one of the free-standing figures under discussion, *cf.* figure 3 and *Wenwu*, 1982, 10, 41, pl. 53. Monika Thowsen, a student from Oslo with a special interest in the 'Dingzhou' pagoda/temple sculpture visited the site in 1991.
11. Until the end of the Tang, *luohan* were generally represented in sculpture by the disciples Ānanda and Kāśyapa, flanking the historical Buddha Śākyamuni along with the Bodhisattvas Avalokiteśvara and Mahāsthāmaprāpta, in hieratic representations of paradise. The pentad became widespread from the 6th century onwards, with the spread of the *Lotus Sutra*, encouraged by Tiantai Buddhism. Wen Fong has surveyed the textual authority for the grouping of sixteen, eighteen and five hundred *luohan*, the cult of which has been linked with Chan Buddhism (Wen Fong, *The Lohans and a Bridge to Heaven*, Freer Gallery of Art Occasional Papers, vol. 3, no. 1, Washington, 1958, 23–43). The addition of *luohan* halls to Chinese temple complexes was probably, at least in part, to stimulate pilgrim visits.
12. See D. Gillman, "Chinese Buddhist Art", *Apollo*, 122 (285), 1985, 328–331, for a discussion of the importance of clay sculpture in Chinese Buddhist art. It was common in the north, where the earth is naturally rich in alumina and very plastic; mixed with fibre to bond it, modelled over armatures, and dried in the air, the material is described in Western texts as stucco, although it obviously materially

having been removed from a Dingzhou pagoda together with a group of free-standing images (from the parent temple) should be understood not so much as representing the end of a long tradition, but as an intrusion into something else that had become well-established; hence Sickman's comment about 'provincial relapses'. Whether we regard individual pieces as amongst "the most expressive representations in Chinese culture" or the product of "fairly skilled but uninspired stone-cutters", the investment in this rather substantial body of work was considerable, both in time and money.

The purpose of this paper is firstly to look afresh at the 'naturalistic' figures, consider some very damaging comments made about them within the last few years, and look again at Angela Howard's dating; secondly, to investigate further the context for the production of Buddhist marble sculpture in west-central Hebei during the Jin.

The marble sculpture at Bergen

The Vestlandske Kunstindustrimuseum (West Norway Museum of Applied Art) at Bergen is not one of the places traditionally visited by specialists in Chinese art. Known for its collections of European art, particularly 20th century Norwegian art and crafts, it nevertheless holds a significant collection of Chinese art, including bronze vessels, paintings, sculpture and ceramics.[13] All of these were acquired for the city by Johan Munthe, a native of Bergen who lived in China from the closing years of the Qing Dynasty to the Japanese occupation of the thirties.

Born in 1864, Munthe grew up in Oslo, and trained as a young man with the Norwegian cavalry. In 1886 he left for China, where he was accepted into the Customs Service, then under British administration.[14] After China's defeat by

---

differs from western stucco. The earliest surviving examples are 5th century, in the dry desert oases of west China—images in cave 169 at Bingling si, Gansu province, can be dated to the 420s. Apart from tomb figurines, larger scale fired ceramic images are quite rare in the north until the Ming, when polychrome stoneware figures were produced in quantity at Yangcheng, Shanxi province, during the 16th and 17th centuries. The magnificent exception is the 11th century set of *luohan* from the Yizhou region, some 200 miles north of Dingzhou (see below, f.n. 60).

13. The Vestlandske Kunstindustrimuseum is one of three such museums of applied art in Norway; it was founded on the model of the Victoria and Albert to promote good design in industry. The Munthe Collection is about two thousand five hundred pieces strong.

14. P. Ankar and P. O. Leijon, *Chinese Sculpture and Painting in General J. W. N. Munthe's Collection in the West Norway Museum of Applied Art*, Bergen, 1980, 4. The Customs Service was a major point of contact between the foreign powers and the Chinese government. Munthe arrived during a period when Britain, Germany, France, the U. S., Russia and Japan were competing vigorously for territorial and economic advantages in China. The Chinese for their part were willing to exploit foreign skills where it was expedient, as with, for example, von Mollendorf,

Japan in 1895, when moves were being made to reorganize the Chinese military, Munthe asked for secondment from the Customs Service to assist with the cavalry. That December, he moved to the brigade base of the so-called Newly Created Army, under the command of Yuan Shikai, together with two German military instructors. As an aide to Yuan Shikai, his position was unusual insofar as it allowed him to move easily between one of the strongest Chinese military cliques of the time and the foreign powers.[15] At the time of Yuan's death in 1916, Munthe was responsible for the protection of the legation quarter at Peking.[16]

He began acquiring Chinese works of art before the turn of the century, perhaps as early as the late 1880s, and from 1907 was sending works back to the Bergen Museum on a periodic basis. Munthe started collecting sculpture in 1914, and in July 1915 we find him considering the logistics of shipping over to Norway a three-metre high Sui dynasty (581–618) marble Bodhisattva, which originally accompanied the great Amitābha Buddha now in the British Museum.[17] Probably between 1915 and 1917, Munthe acquired four of the architectural pieces and twelve of the free-standing figures discussed by Sirén.[18]

---

appointed customs commissioner and foreign affairs adviser in Korea in 1882; see I.C. Y. Hsu, "Late Ch'ing foreign relations 1866–1905", in J.K. Fairbank and Liu Kwang-Ching, eds., *Cambridge History of China*, vol. 11, *Late Ch'ing, 1800–1911*, part 2, Cambridge, 1980, 104.

15. He first joined a brigade under the command of Hu Yufen, together with a German instructor named Schaller. The brigade base of the Newly Created Army (Xinjian lujun) was Xiaochan, near Tianjin. The three foreign instructors were responsible for infantry, artillery and cavalry (R. L. Powell, *The Rise of Chinese Military Power 1895–1912*, Princeton, 1955, 77). When the Boxers laid seige to Peking in 1900, we hear from an English witness of Munthe's place in the thick of the action:

    "Captain Munthe, a Norwegian cavalry officer in the Chinese Customs, who had volunteered to go with the Russians as interpreter, greatly distinguished himself during this attack, General Vasilievski and he being the first to rush through the Tung-pien gate when it was blown in. He it is who has reconstructed Yuan-Shih-Kai's army and brought it to so remarkable a condition of efficiency. His services all through the campaign were, indeed, invaluable, no one having so intimate a knowledge of the organisation of the Chinese troops, and of what they were capable, as he had."

    (H. C. Thompson, *China and the Powers, A Narrative of the Outbreak of 1900*, London, 1902, 102).
16. P. Anker and P. O. Leijon, *op. cit.*, 4. He eventually reached the rank of general; Powell refers to him as colonel (R. L. Powell, *op. cit.*, 72-3).
17. Munthe favoured Bergen over the museum in Oslo, on account of his good relationship with the then Director, Johan Bogh (Anker and Leijon, *op. cit.*, 5). The shipment of the figure is mentioned in a letter to Bogh, dated 2 July 1915, (see also below, f.n.68).
18. Munthe acquired twelve free-standing figures—all but one are now at Bergen; a seated Maitreya has since been alienated from the collection.

The death of his wife in 1916 changed Munthe's attitude towards the objects he had accumulated, and by 1917 he was considering disposing of part of the collection in order to establish a charitable fund to help alleviate the poverty he saw about him; it is reasonable to suppose that he began winding down his collecting activities around this time.[19] Ten years later he sent a large part of the collection over to the United States for sale, initially to the Los Angeles County Museum. Negotiations were interrupted by the Depression, and when Munthe died in Peking in 1935, his collection was still largely intact. Much of it remained in the States until the beginning of the 'sixties, when the West Norway Museum began proceedings to recover what it could.[20]

At the time when restitution of the collection was very much an issue, John Ayers reviewed the marble sculpture at Scripps College, California, which then held the free-standing figures, as well as an associated group of small *luohan* images (not mentioned by Sirén), and some other pieces which Munthe had acquired.[21] Ayers referred to and agreed with Sirén's assessment, concluding that many of the sculptures, despite the damage, were of distinct artistic merit and of interest for the study of Chinese sculpture of the period, and there was much to be said for ensuring their preservation, in a museum or museums in Europe.[22]

Everything retrievable was back in Bergen by 1964. In 1978, the first western exhibition of Johan Munthe's collection was mounted at the National Gallery in Oslo, alongside the already widely-known Chinese works of art assembled by King Gustav VI Adolf of Sweden. In 1983, when the Museum received a visit

---

19. The extreme political and economic uncertainty at the beginning of the warlord era, and his prior conversation with Christian science, goes some way to explaining the change of direction. It is possible that some works may have been purchased as late as 1924.
20. The fund was to be administered by the Bergen Museum. In his last year, Munthe established a foundation to complete the sale of the collection; a 25–year limit set for the disbursement of monies in China ran out in the early sixties, and the free-standing marble sculptures were released from Scripps College, a Christian missionary school in Claremont. Anker and Leijon, *op. cit.*, 5.
21. Ayers, then Assistant Keeper in the Far Eastern Department at the V&A, reviewed the collection at the request of the Director of the West Norway Museum, Robert Kloster.
22. Preceded by the following comments:

    "In general the sculptures are of a somewhat homogenous character, both as regards style and material, suggesting common origin, and the majority are executed in a more or less white marble which is characteristic of the province of Chihli [Hebei]. Certain pieces, however, reveal a style which belongs properly to the period of the Six Dynasties, while others suggest that of the Tang; and others are frankly conceived in a manner corresponding to that of the known work of the Liao and Chin Dynasties (10th–13th centuries). It is my opinion that all are likely to have been produced at some time during this period … ." (Report for the West Norway Museum).

from Angela Falco Howard, then researching her article on Liao sculpture, the free-standing figures were still crated and she was able only to see the architectural pieces. Despite this, she was convinced that the architectural images dated to the mid-Tang, circa 750–800, and at least one of the free-standing images (photographed for the 1978 exhibition) to ca. 750. This was by virtue of their stylistic resemblance to two marble *luohan* and a Buddha image made for the Undefiled Pure Radiance pagoda at the Foguang si, (a well-known temple some 150 miles to the west of Dingzhou at Wutai shan, itself a major centre of Chinese Buddhism since the Tang).[23] Munthe himself believed much of the 'Dingzhou' pagoda/temple material to be Tang.[24]

Howard's assertion that the Munthe sculptures were radically different from those produced under the Liao was supported by Marylin Gridley. Gridley, however, strongly contested the mid-Tang argument, upholding instead the reliability of Sirén's Jin dating; she also observed that the association (by Sirén) of Liao art with "this mid-twelfth century style, a style which at times can be undeniably gross, has quite likely contributed to the neglect of Liao sculpture".[25]

In July 1990, the museum staff were greatly disturbed by an opinion given by Ma Shizhang, from the Department of Archaeology, Peking University. In the written report on a review of the Munthe collection by several outside scholars, in which Professor Ma participated, it is recorded that he took the view that not only was almost all the sculpture of low quality, but it was also made relatively recently—some time in the latter half of the Qing dynasty (1644–1911). He thought that the pieces seemingly of common origin (Sirén's pagoda/temple figures) might conceivably have been produced in an archaistic style for a Buddhist temple in the 19th century; others were straight fakes. His analysis was based on inconsistencies in motifs and styles in individual pieces. I accepted an invitation from the West Norway Museum to give a further opinion, and visited Bergen in November last year.[26] The task was to assess how much of General Munthe's riches were in fact an embarrassment.

23. A.F. Howard, "Buddhist Sculptures of the Liao Dynasty, A Reassessment of Osvald Sirén's Study", *BMFEA*, 56, 1984, 18–21. In the Oslo exhibition catalogue, the free-standing figure (the *luohan* Ānanda) was coincidentally dated to the Tang.

24. Attributed as such in Munthe's personal catalogue of the collection, compiled also in 1925 with the help of an American, Charles Arrott.

25. H. Gridley, *Chinese Buddhist Sculpture under the Liao, Free Standing Works in Situ and Selected Examples from Public Collections*, (doctoral dissertation, 1985, UMI), Ann Arbor, 1988, 9–10. Gridley's late medieval dating is supported by the opinion in 1989 of Professor Luo Zhao, a member of the Chinese Academy of Social Sciences, Peking, who did believe the material to be Liao.

26. Professor Ma was accompanied by Professor Lothar Ledderose from Heidelberg. My thanks are due to the Director, Professor Peter Anker, for his help in providing extracts from the Munthe archive and other information relating to the sculpture, and

Archaism, fakes and the market

One problem with Ma Shizhang's hypothesis, that the figures may have been carved in an archaistic style for a late Qing temple, is that even by the 12th century free-standing Buddhist stone sculpture in north China is notable for its relative scarcity in comparison with the production of gessoed wood and cheaper clay images—and that at a time when the *saṅgha* was still wealthy, and Buddhism a major force in Chinese religious life. Six hundred years later Chinese Buddhism was much changed. The Manchu rulers patronised Lamaism, together with the associated Sino-Tibetan style of representation. Beyond the court, the religion had absorbed elements of indigenous official and unofficial cults, and had, in turn, been partly assimilated by them. The idea that in the 19th century a non-Lamaistic temple in west Hebei had the patronage and resources to construct a suite of stone temple images on this scale is intriguing, but difficult to accept readily. The alternative 'late' hypothesis is that the material is simply fake, made in the early 20th century for sale to foreigners.

The archaistic argument would presumably run like this: a body of work in the manner of the past (reaching back before the influence of Tibetan Buddhism) was commissioned by wealthy patrons for a Buddhist temple in the Dingzhou region. The images were made locally, drawing on material to hand (Sirén's comparative sculpture and architectural decoration *in situ* in Hebei).[27]

I should make it clear that I agree with Ma Shizhang's comments on a considerable number of the stelae, smaller figures and individual heads presently in the storerooms of the West Norway Museum, which we can readily dismiss as clumsy attempts to deceive, made in a variety of styles during the early 20th century—a time when the Peking market for Chinese sculpture was mined with fakes—perhaps initially for the Japanese, but then for the French, Americans and other Westerners. Munthe's own collection has a variety of images weakly imitating Buddhist art of the 6th century, a period highly regarded by all the foreigners. Also, that some Peking dealers were capable of great resourcefulness in tricking their clients is indisputable—Grice tells about the entrapment of a party of overzealous and insufficiently sceptical European buyers.[28] But deviousness in selling requires different talents from production of the goods themselves. As

---

to Monika Thowsen, whose interest in, classification and study of the Munthe material contributed most usefully to the discussion on dating.

27. The quarries of west Hebei quite probably contributed much of the material for the marble terraces and facades of Ming and Qing buildings in Peking.
28. They were taken on a treasure hunt, using a map purportedly discovered in the Imperial Library. The trail ended at a large tree, amongst the roots of which was buried a rotting chest filled with jades and bronzes. It subsequently transpired that the tree had been planted over the chest six years earlier; the antiquities can hardly have been much older. J.W.H. Grice, "Faking and Selling Chinese Antiques", *Country Life*, July 29, 1954, 350–1.

fakes, the free-standing and architectural figures would be very superior examples.

In the West, the taste for early Chinese art was led from about 1900 by a select group of connoisseurs' who had already moved well beyond Whistler's appreciation of 17th and 18th century Chinese ceramics. Charles Freer and W.C. Alexander, two of Whistler's patrons were amongst them. Freer was perhaps the first major Western collector in modern terms, seeking out sculpture, archaic bronzes and paintings in north-central China, in 1909 and again in 1910.[29] Chinese dealers were there earlier; the Peking dealer Paul Houo-Ming-Tse, for example, was searching out antiquities in Shanxi around 1907/8.[30] It is worthy of note that when Johan Munthe became really interested in early Chinese sculpture, in 1914/15, it was still a relatively unknown area to Western collectors.

The early Republican period, following the Revolution of 1911, was characterised by weak central control—ever more so during the warlord era of 1916 to 1928. In a letter to Bergen, Munthe indicated that the market for Chinese sculpture had, as he saw it, taken off around 1911; certainly there was activity during the second and third decades of the century by the Japanese, Americans, French and British. The disorder of the time, and the greater access allowed to foreigners, created new conditions for the study, purchase and, sadly, vandalism of early Buddhist monuments.[31] In Japan, Buddhism was still very much a living religion, and China a major source of religious art. When Sirén first published the 'Dingzhou' material, at least four of the architectural figures were then divided between Yamanaka's galleries in Peking, Kyoto and New York.[32]

---

29. French sinologist, Eduard Chavannes, surveyed some of the earliest monumental sculpture in north China during the 1890's. The Parisian dealer, Charles Vignier, was also a key figure in introducing early Chinese art to the avant-garde. It was from Vignier that Roger Fry purchased in 1913 a 6th century Buddhist figure, subsequently exhibited at the Burlington Fine Arts Club exhibition of 1915. For a history of Western collecting, see Basil Gray, "The Development of Taste in Chinese Art in the West 1872 to 1972", *Transactions of the Oriental Ceramic Society*, 1971–1973, vol. 39, 19–41.
30. Houo-Ming-Tse (Huo Mingzhi), a missionary-educated Chinese dealer opened his gallery in Peking around 1906/1907; Houo-Ming-Tse, *Preuves des Antiquités de Chine*, Péking, 1930, introduction.
31. "Regrettably, the vandals (foreign) during the time of the revolution have succeeded in persuading the inhabitants to knock off the heads of those figures", letter to Johan Bogh, 8 June 1914. Yuan Shikai's revolutionary government held power only tenuously between 1911 and 1916.
32. Yamanaka and Co. were major players in the Peking art market in the first half of the 20th century. The company expanded from Japan to Peking, New York, Boston and London. C.T. Loo also had a gallery in Paris, where another of the architectural figures was held in stock. Two more figures were probably then with Houo-Ming-Tse in Peking (see appendix).

An embarrassment of riches?

Let us put aside the miscellaneous pieces and focus now on the three groups of pagoda/temple material (architectural, free-standing and *luohan*), which together form the principal holding of sculpture at Bergen. The free-standing group comprises eleven micaceous marble figures of roughly life size, nine carved from a fine-grained greyish-white stone, and two from the coarser, yellowish-white stone used also for the smaller architectural and *luohan* images.[33]

1–3. Three seated Buddhas.[34]

4. Standing Buddha: possibly Amitābha.[35]

5–6. Two *luohan*: the disciples Ānanda and Kāśyapa.[36]

7. Standing Bodhisattva.[37]

8–9. Two seated Bodhisattvas: Samantabhadra mounted on an elephant, and Mañjuśrī accompanied by, but detached from, his original lion mount.[38]

---

33. Howard notes that, mineralogically, the material is magnesian limestone, A.F. Howard, "Buddhist Sculptures of the Liao Dynasty, A reassessment of Osvald Sirén's study", 19.
34. The three Buddha images are similarly represented: each seated on a stepped Sumeru-type throne, the right arm raised, the left lowered to the lap, hand palm-up by the right foot. The larger figure measures 200 cm from head to base. One of the smaller Buddha images now has the head of a Bodhisattva, with the nose cut off; the original height of the smaller Buddhas was approximately 145 cm (the pedestals have been switched since the sculpture was displayed in Munthe's garden; see Sirén, "Chinese Sculptures of the Sung, Liao and Chin Dynasties", pl. 10:3; each pedestal has a pair of lions emerging from the front, and one also has a pair of Atlantean supporters also). Munthe originally owned four seated Buddha figures; the fourth represents Maitreya seated in the so-called 'western position' with the legs pendent (illustrated Sirén, *Chinese Sculpture from the Fifth to the Fourteenth Century*, pl. 542a, where the height is given as 6 ft; there are two small guardian kings at the rear of the throne).
35. The standing Buddha image at Bergen possibly represents Amitābha, Buddha of the Western Paradise. Like the other Munthe Buddhas, the figure is bulky, with a wide pear-shaped head, again badly disfigured, resting on a massive neck. The full height is 211 cm, including the dowel under the lotus base.
36. The overall height of the headless Ānanda is 163 cm, excluding the domed pedestal (probably Ming and unrelated to the figure it supports). The lotus pod base is incised with small circular seed pockets, as is the base of the standing Buddha. The Kāśyapa has a Buddha's head, too small for the body. The lobed base here belongs to the body, which stands at about 162 cm—the overall height (with head) is 186 cm.
37. The figure, which may represent Avalokiteśvara or Mahāsthāmaprāpta, wears looped and hanging sashes now partly broken away together with the arms; and a chamfered rectangular belt buckle of the type also worn by the two smaller Buddhas. The nose has a groove around it. Like the *luohan* Ānanda, the figure stands on a pedestal from a different scheme; disregarding that, the height is 168 cm.
38. The Mañjuśrī figure, separated from the companion lion (itself broken across all four legs), sits in *lalitāsāna* with the left leg pendent (height 107 cm). A section of the

10–11. Two guardians.[39]

Some of the figures, like the standing Bodhisattva and the two *luohan*, were intended, it seems, to be viewed principally from the front, others, like the seated Bodhisattvas, are conceived more fully in the round. There has been considerable 'mixing and matching' within the free-standing group: marriages with pedestals from other Buddhist or secular architectural schemes, bases switched, heads swapped. In addition, several of the images have neatly cut-out noses, a point noted by Sirén in 1942; we know from photographs that this was done no later than 1925.[40] If the figures are fake, then they were probably manufactured shortly before Munthe bought them, and the rather considerable damage to most, and at least some of the mismatching of heads and bodies, was designed in from the outset.

All these figures seem to have been severely cleaned, so much so that there are only traces of pigment on the flat surfaces, although the crevices reveal more extensive evidence of a pinkish-buff and maroon colour scheme (the elephant was also once painted lurid pink). One explanation for this is that Munthe or his servants, or dealers, exhaustively scrubbed the marble.[41] The statuary must also have been weathered during the period (perhaps twelve years) that it stood in Munthe's Peking garden.[42]

---

lotus throne beneath the right knee has been replaced—the figure is presently cemented to yet another unrelated base—at Scripps College both Bodhisattvas were placed on such square plinths. The Ṣamantabhadra figure, which has lost all of the left legs, was remounted at Bergen using a new lotus element to fit it sideways onto the circular sockle. Taking into account the Norwegian fixings, the full height is about 220 cm. Sirén's photographs show both Mañjuśrī and Samantabhadra seated facing forwards on their mounts (Sirén, *Chinese Sculpture from the Fifth to the Fourteenth Century*, pls. 585 a & b). The carving of the elephant and lion seems to me to be consistent with that of their riders, notwithstanding Sirén's comment that they are "out of proportion" and "can only be explained as later substitutes". The harness on the elephant has a toggle under the left ear for attaching a rein; the lion was led from the right side, the rein stopping above a collar studded with the already familiar chamfered buckles or studs, here used to suspend a series of tassles.

39. The two guardians may either be *tianwang*, heavenly kings, or attendants to Mañjuśrī and Samantabhadra. Both wear armour: the more complete figure has horned animal-masks emblazoned at the belt and epaulettes (height 159 cm), the other, lozenges and rosettes at the belt. Compare the groups of Mañjuśrī and Samantabhadra and their two attendants at Dazu Beishan, cave 136 (*Dazu Shike*, Sichuan meishu xueyuan diaosu xi, Beijing, 1962, pls. 40, 43).
40. Munthe's original photographs, taken under the supervision of Charles Arrott in 1925, show noses on heads where there are presently none (on the standing Buddha for example), but only incision marks. This indicates that the restoration had taken place before Munthe acquired them.
41. Munthe writes that he had cleaned a Wei head, hoping thereby to ascertain the period from the composition and state of the marble; letter to Bogh, 12 January, 1915.
42. Sirén, "Chinese Sculptures of the Sung, Liao and Chin Dynasties", 58.

The four architectural pieces at Bergen are cut, like the free-standing guardians, from the coarser marble.[43]

1. A Buddha carrying a staff: probably Śākyamuni.[44]
2. A *luohan*: Kāśyapa.
3. An eleven-headed Avalokiteśvara.
4. A guardian warrior, *lishi*.

The description by an American visitor to Munthe's house in 1925 gives the barest glimpse of how the sculpture was shown:

> "On our knocking we were admitted by a servant into a quiet and sombre garden of breath-taking beauty, the chief feature of which was an avenue of tall trees leading toward the house with large stelae and sculptured figures of stone placed between the trees on either side of the path—stelae and figures which, I was to learn later, dated back two, three and even four thousand years."[45]

Among these sculptures must have been placed the five *luohan* figures that make up the third distinctive group at Bergen, in size and material similar to the architectural figures. Four are seated (three of them headless), and one is standing. From the carving, it is evident that they form a further part of the 'Dingzhou' material: the rounded sleeve bunches of the complete seated *luohan* echo those of the free-standing *luohan* Kāśyapa (figure 4).[46]

Two of the *luohan* sit on tall plinths, a combination both unfamiliar and unsettling, since the fancy flower vase and scrollwork decoration is reminiscent of Qing dynasty art made under European influence. Intriguing though the plinths are, they have nothing to do with the *luohan* they bear. The Munthe Collection is rich in such prints, and I suspect that all were made for the Old Summer Palace in north-west Peking, obliterated during the Second Opium War.[47]

---

43. See appendix for the full list. There is a fragment of a fifth figure at Bergen—the head and shoulders of a guardian—which probably also relates to the architectural group.
44. Compare the staff-carrying Buddha to a Kamakura painting of Śākyamuni in the Kozan-ji Temple, Kyoto (*Special Exhibition: Arts of Buddha Śākyamuni*, Nara National Museum, 1984, 214, pl. 42); Howard describes the figure as Kṣitigarbha.
45. Charles Arrott, then travelling the world, paused for longer than anticipated in Peking, persuaded by Munthe to assist in photographing and recording the entire collection (*ms.* with the Vestlandske Kunstindustrimuseum).
46. Catalogued by Munthe as Song.
47. The Yuan Ming Yuan was an expansive exercise in 'sino-Versailles', designed in the mid-18th century under the supervision of the Jesuit, Guiseppe Castiglione. The palace was destroyed by Lord Elgin as personal reprisal against the emperor for the death of twenty British troops seized while under a flag of truce; its ruins have lain scattered for over a century. Sales of the more salvagable architectural fragments are easily imagined, particularly in the years immediately following the dissolution of

The free-standing figures in particular reveal, when we examine them, Tang, Northern Song and Jin features, the compound of which explains why stylistically they might appear 'inconsistent'. To understand further the disposition of these elements, let us look at five specific aspects.

1. The Bodhisattvas Mañjuśrī and Samantabhadra

In medieval Chinese painting and sculpture, when Mañjuśrī and Samantabhadra are shown with pendent legs, the two are often mirror-images. The Munthe figures part from that convention (figure 1). Mañjuśrī sits in *lalitāsana* with the left leg pendent; the carving around the missing left leg of the Samantabhadra suggests that the Bodhisattva was seated in *dhyānāsana*, with both legs folded on the lotus; (if the image was fake, there would have likely never been a leg).[48] In a painting executed by Zhang Shengwen during the 1170's for the Da Li court in present day Yunnan province, south-west China, we see the two Bodhisattvas represented so: Mañjuśrī with both legs on the lotus; Samantabhadra with the right leg pendent.[49] More significantly, the painted figure of Mañjuśrī resembles in general appearance the Munthe Mañjuśrī, and we should note in each case the frontal scarf snaking down over the lap, tied with a broad decorative ring (figure 2). When Helen Chapin first saw the painting in Peking during the winter of 1931-32, it was relatively unknown.[50] The Munthe Mañjuśrī and Samantabhadra seem, therfore, to be representing a mode of depicting Bodhisattvas current in the 12th century.

2. The rectangular buckles

Although rectangular buckles are worn by Bodhisattvas and guardians from the Tang onwards, the chamfered studs or clasps on the Mañjuśrī figure, and several of the architectural images, are very distinctive.[51] Identical to these is the belt

---

the dynasty. The flower vases mostly follow an ancient bronze shape, *fang'gu;* as much as we can tell from surviving engravings, the Yuan Ming Yuan 'belvedere' (Fangwai Guan) seems to have had balustrades of just this type; C.M. Beurdeley, *Guiseppe Castiglione, A Jesuit Painter at the Court of the Chinese Emperors*, London, 1972, 71.

48. Sirén's 1925 photograph shows the figure damaged as it is now.
49. H. Chapin, *A Long Roll of Buddhist Images,* revised by Alexander C. Soper, Ascona, 1972, pls. 26, 27.
50. At a meeting of the Committee on Paintings of the Palace Museum:
"At the time I first saw the long roll, only about three tenths of the paintings in the museum had been examined by the committee. This one among others was brought out on that memorable day from the hidden closets of the Palace, probably for the first time since the fall of the empire." (*ibid.*, 7).
51. Bodhisattvas of the architectural group now in the University Museum, Philadelphia, and Asian Art Museum, San Francisco, wear these buckles. Rectangular buckles can be seen in 9th and 10th century banners from Dunhuang (see Whitfield and Farrer, *Caves of the Thousand Buddhas, Chinese art from the Silk Route*, London, 1990, pls.

stud worn by a small gilt bronze guardian, excavated in 1969 at the Jingzhi temple, in the north-east sector of Dingzhou (Dingxian) city.[52] Dated to the early Northern Song, ca. 977, this image not only has the same belt decoration, but the pleating on the underskirt is of a type that appears frequently on the Munthe images.

3. Relationship with the images found at the Undefiled Pure Radiance pagoda, Foguang temple, Wutai shan, Shanxi province

In 1950, five white marble figures were unearthed from the site of the Undefiled Pure Radiance pagoda (Wugou jing'guang ta), attached to the Foguang si at Wutai shan, east Shanxi, the neighbouring province to Hebei. The images were two *luohan* (Ānanda and Kāśyapa), each just under a meter high, a guardian king *(tianwang)*, a guardian warrior *(lishi)*, and a small Bodhisattva. The *luohan* are dated to *ca.* 752 by comparison with the base of a marble Buddha also made for the pagoda.[53]

Within the framework of known examples of Chinese Buddhist sculpture it is hard to deny a direct stylistic link between the two free-standing Munthe *luohan* and those found at the Foguang si (figures 3-5). The relationship between the pairs of images is close indeed, and although the hands of the Ānandas are

---

9, 10). Something close to the pierced buckles on the smaller seated Buddhas and standing Bodhisattva of the free-standing group is worn by a small clay figure excavated from the White Elephant pagoda at Wenzhou, south-east China, dating from the 990's, *Wenwu*, 1987, 5, 23, pl. 11. Although Chinese Buddha images rarely wear buckles, an 11th century Liao example is illustrated by Howard; A.F. Howard "Buddhist Sculptures of the Liao Dynasty, A Reassessment of Osvald Siren's study", pl. 22.

52. Shi Yan, *Zhong'guo Meishu Quanji, Wudai Song diaosu, diaosu bian 5* (sculpture, vol. 5, Five Dynasties and Song), Beijing, 1988, pl. 78; for the archaeological report on the foundations of the Zhenshen sheli pagoda, Jingzhi si, Dingzhou, see *Wenwu*, 1972, 8, 39–47. Two similarly made gilt bronzes were excavated, the *tianwang* (15. 4 cm), and a *lishi* (15. 2 cm). The *lishi* is illustrated in Shi, *Zhong'guo Meishu Quanji, Sui Tang diaosu, diaosu bian 4*, (sculpture, vol. 4, Sui and Tang), Beijing, 1988, pl. 58, where it is dated to 713–765; a strong case can be made, however, for giving it the same date as the *tianwang.*

53. The base of the Foguang si Ānanda is inscribed, but not dated; the calligraphy is believed to be identical in style to that on the dated base of the Buddha figure. The latter was removed by 1924 to the Mañjuśrī Hall of the main temple, and is now located with the two *luohan* in the main (eastern) shrine hall. Also discovered was the head of another Bodhisattva, resembling in its pear-shaped outline the head wrongly fitted onto one of the two smaller Buddhas at Bergen. The Ānanda is 88 cm high, the Kāśyapa 83 cm, and the Buddha 112 cm. See *Shanxi wenwu jieshao*, Beijing, 1953 (section on the Foguang si); Shi, *Zhong'guo Meishu Quanji, Sui Tang diaosu, diaosu bian 4* , pls. 47, 48; also A.F. Howard, "Buddhist Sculptures of the Liao Dynasty, A Reassessment of Osvald Siren's study", 19–20. The Wugou jing'guang ta was formerly raised up on the hill behind the Foguang si.

crossed differently, the disposition of the robe folds is almost parallel.[54] The two Munthe figures were either made contemporaneously with the Foguang si *luohan* as Howard thought, or were copied later from them, or from very similar Tang images that are no longer known.[55]

There is also a strong resemblance between the three Munthe seated Buddhas, and the metre-high Foguang si Buddha (figures 6,7). Gridley believed that the Foguang si Buddha was itself a 12th century replacement, fixed to a mid-Tang base, but the better photograph recently available makes the 8th century date reasonably convincing.[56] The two Munthe *luohan* point quite precisely in style towards the mid-8th century, as Howard observed. The seated Buddhas do so in a more general manner; a Buddha image from the Xiude hoard, dated to 746, where the baldachin is carved with rounded-over folds as we see on the throne-drapes of the Munthe Buddhas, lends further weight to this conclusion (figure 8).[57] However, that the Bergen figures were actually made in the Tang is not proven.

4. Relationship to clay images

Sirén noted that on some of the free-standing figures, the Ānanda and the standing Buddha in particular, the robes were represented with unusually smooth and rounded folds and pleats; he accommodated this as a development of style.[58]

---

54. The shoes on the two Ānanda figures are identical: the Munthe Kāśyapa has lobed shoes whereas the Foguang si Kāśyapa is barefoot. Another point of note is that a similar arrangement of lotus petals decorated with rosettes enclosing a ring of stamens features on the bases both of the Foguang si Ānanda and the Munthe large standing Buddha (the Ānanda has one tier, the Buddha two).
55. A.F. Howard dated the free-standing Ānanda (from its photograph) to *ca.* 750 by comparison with the Foguang si Ānanda; A.F. Howard, "Buddhist Sculptures of the Liao Dynasty, A Reassessment of Osvald Siren's study", pl. 56. We should remember that when she visited Bergen, the free-standing figures were still crated.
56. M. Gridley, *Chinese Buddhist Sculpture under the Liao* 9. Howard thought the Buddha contemporary with the mid-8th century base; *op. cit.*, 20. The device of alternate lozenges and rosettes on the Sumeru throne of the Buddha also appears on the belt of the headless free-standing guardian.
57. 29 cm high. A hoard of over two thousand white marble figures was excavated in 1954 from the site of the Xiude temple, Quyang district (adjacent to Dingzhou); they are now held in the Palace Museum, Peking. See Yang Boda, "Quyang Xiude si chutu jinian zaoxiang de yishu fengge yu tezheng", Weng and Yang, *The Palace Museum Peking, Treasures of the Forbidden City*, 237, pl. 134.
58. Sirén, "Chinese Sculptures of the Sung, Liao and Chin Dynasties", 59:
"The tall standing figures are perhaps more satisfactory from a sculptural point of view [than the other free-standing figures] particularly the Buddha and the monk, both of whom are draped in mantles of soft and heavy material, which fall from the shoulders over the elbows and lifted arms in broad folds without any sharp edges. The linear stylisation of the folds which seemed so prominent in some of the preceding statues [e. g. the architectural group and large seated Buddhas] is here

We can find a little of this both on the architectural Kāśyapa, and also on the Foguang si *luohan*, but the fluency of the drapery treatment compares particularly well with clay modelling of the 11th and 12th centuries, notably with the figures surviving in temples in Shanxi and Shandong. Although not a new feature in Chinese sculpture (*cf.* also the Xiude Buddha, above, and footnote 57), the rounding off of edges is especially developed in clay imagery.

For example, there is similarity between the handling of the upper edge of the outer robe of a *luohan* (datable to 1079) in the Chongqing temple, Shanxi, province, and that of the Munthe large standing Buddha. Whilst the Buddha also resembles generally the architectural Śākyamuni, the former's robes are closer in manner to the clay *luohan* (figures 11, 12, 9). Further, the bunching of the robe in the lap of the Chongqing figure can be usefully compared with the lobes of material at the right sleeve of the free-standing Kāśyapa (the genesis of which was a Tang image).

The gentle smoothing-out of the robe that we see on the left side of the free-standing Ānanda, reminiscent of waves on a pond, is likewise seen on a number of the forty *luohan* images at the Lingyan si, Shandong province, which probably date from 1124 (figure 10).[59]

At once marvellous and domestic, Song, Liao and Jin images of *luohan* captured the appearance of the real monastic community in China; the Munthe free-standing Ānanda, Kāśyapa and Buddha robes seem to reflect something of this late medieval naturalism.[60] In general, the carving of detail is rather fine, for example on the braids holding up the outer robes of the standing Buddha and Ānanda, and the knuckles and fingernails of Ānanda's hands.[61] What comes through from this exercise is the sense that although there was a Tang precedent for some of the free-standing images, the treatment has been modified by the in-

---

substituted by a more naturalistic treatment, which may be a sign of a somewhat more advanced stage in the evolution of style … ."

59. Gridley argued that the date previously given for this set (1056–63) is too early for their appearance, and that if the bodies are mid 11th century, the faces must have been remodelled; the present author considers that scenario unlikely, and prefers to follow the later of two dating traditions connected with the Lingyan si images (1124), which would meet Gridley's reservation (Shi, *Zhong'guo Meishu Quanji, Wudai Song diaosu, diaosu bian 5*, 18).
60. Compare also the celebrated 11th century set of eight *luohan* from Yizhou, on the southernmost part of Liao territory from the 10th to the early 12th century. Gridley devotes a chapter of her dissertation to the set, challenging the traditional view that there were sixteen or eighteen figures. She relates them, as does Gillman, to the clay *luohan* at the Lower Huayan si, Datong, dating to 1038: M. Gridley, *Chinese Buddhist Sculpture Under the Liao,* 205–7; W. Zwalf, ed., *Buddhism: Art and Faith*, London, 1985, pl. 295.
61. The fashion in which the robes of the standing Buddha and Ānanda are fastened and drape at the left shoulder is consistent with Song and Jin practice.

fluence of the increasingly developed clay modelling tradition in the post-Tang era.

5. The elephant's saddle cloth

Let us move back to the Bodhisattva images, this time to Samantabhadra's elephant. Below the band of egg-and-dart lotus petals are lobed panels at either side of the saddlecloth.[62] These are unusual insofar as the shape is rather different from the common decorative lappet used from the Tang period onwards (the so-called cloud collar, or *ruyi* head, with pointed apex and upturned side lobes).[63] It seems to represent the profile of a lotus leaf, in a specific form widely used on northern stonewares between the later 11th and early 13th centuries (Dingyao, Cizhou and Yaozhou celadon), on metalwork, and possibly on textiles also. This is an appropriate saddle decoration, below the tiers of lotus petals.[64]

When we put together the points discussed above, the overall picture is of a group of images made sometime between the late 10th and early 13th centuries, and more probably between the late 11th and early 13th. Some of the figures are directly modelled on Tang prototypes, others are drawn straight from contemporary figuration—but even those which imitate 8th century sculpture are affected by the conventions of the time.

For the images to be archaistic or fake, the makers would have needed access to the Foguang si *luohan* (excavated in 1950), or very similar images which are presently unknown. Also, access to something like the Dingzhou guardian (excavated in 1969) for the belt clasps would have been needed, as would a familiarity with currents in Song/Jin Buddhist representation (as seen in the Zhang Shengwen painting). It is difficult to conceive how a Qing exercise in archaism could so reproduce the conditions of a late Northern Song/Jin attempt to make a suite of sculptures, where possible, in Tang style.

For the large Munthe *luohan* to be modern imitations of the Foguang si images, we would be left with a conspiracy of the sort revealed by Grice (above footnote 28). These Tang *luohan* were unearthed at the Undefiled Pure Radiance

---

62. Each lotus petal terminates in a neatly made curlicue. Sirén's 1925 photograph shows that the Bodhisattva was linked to the elephant in the "twenties by another lotus support."

63. For a discussion of the development of lobed panels in China, see J. Rawson, *Chinese Ornament the Lotus and the Dragon*, London, 1984, 125–138. If we flatten out the panels, we can see three lobes to the left and right.

64. By the late 11th and 12th centuries, the side lobes have developed a distinct inward-curving profile. This type of leaf appears in scenes of lotus flowers rising from a pond, sometimes accompanied by a pair of swimming ducks; such scenes also decorated Jingdezhen blue and white procelain in the Yuan and early Ming. Lotus foliage is seen on the saddlecloths of Samantabhadra groups in Song/Jin and Kamakura painting. Something of this leaf profile carried on into the Qing.

pagoda at least 25, if not 35 years after the Bergen figures were acquired by Munthe. The Foguang si figures would have to have been known in the late Qing or early years of the Republic, replicated and then buried. That would be an exceptional thing: dealers do not generally conspire to bury genuine antiquities.

If we reintroduce the comparative material put forward by Sirén in 1942, we are back in the 12th century, most probably in the Jin, rather than Northern Song. Of the four scenarios on offer (8th century, 12th century, 19th century and early 20th century), the evidence is firmly on Sirén's side.

Why did Ma Shizhang dismiss the pagoda/temple imagery so readily? I suspect that a contributory factor was seeing them amongst the fake stelae, figures and heads which created a distorting frame around the Jin images and skewed the whole picture. A second factor was probably the cleanness of the free-standing group; cleanness and newness tend to be associated psychologically. The process of attribution and accreditation, in which museums play a major role, can be a nervous one where doubt and conviction displace each other, and the ease with which one can move between them is at times disturbing, but the anxiety is perhaps a healthy one, reminding us of the limits of certainty. The original disposition of the architectural pieces is probably best understood by reference to mid-12th century wall images within the Duobao (Prabhūtaratna) pagoda at Dazu Sichuan, where high-relief carvings with back slabs are set into brick niches. The question of the cut noses remains. It was done precisely, and suggests restoration rather than vandalism, but by whom and when?

Buddhist stone sculpture in 12th-century west-central Hebei

One of the seated figures from the *luohan* group bears an inscription at the front of the base recording the name of the village that donated it: Da Liu cun ('great wave' village). With the proviso that we are dealing with the 12th century, when villages appear and disappear, we do nevertheless find in the 1849 Dingzhou and 1934 Dingxian gazettes just such a place.[65] It lies in the north-west of the Dingzhou (Dingxian) region, on the south bank of the Tang river, close to the border (at Xi Pan) with Quyang to the west, and Tangxian to the north.

The nearest surviving temple to Da Liu village in 1849 was the Tiantai si, sited on the other side of the river, in the vicinity of Xi Ban village, but we have no further information about it. We may however surmise that the pagoda/temple was somewhere to the north-west of Dingzhou city, near the boundaries with Quyang and Tangxian. In itself, this clarifies the dynastic placement of the imagery, as this area was only briefly controlled by the Liao (in the 10th century), otherwise it was under the jurisdiction first of the Northern Song, then of the Jin.

65. *Zhili Dingzhou zhi*, 1849, Zhong'guo fangzhi congshu, 204, 1969, ps. 490, 790. This is the earliest gazette for the region available in the UK.

For convenience, rather than absolute precision, I shall henceforth refer to the pagoda/temple material as the Da Liu sculpture.

Sirén also found several sizable Jin period Buddha images in the manner of the 6th century at places around Quyang and Dingzhou; the most impressive he thought was at Zhu He village, about six miles east of Quyang.[66] That area generally was a major centre for the production of Buddhist marble sculpture between the 6th and 8th centuries, responsible for the variety of images excavated from the site of the Xiude temple. It is not clear when the Xiude images were buried, it may have been in 845 (but stone figures were excluded from the edict ordering the destruction of Buddhist imagery), or alternatively at the coming of the Mongols in the early 13th century. Certainly we know that at least some larger scale 6th century sculpture survived *in situ* into the present century.

One of the greatest examples of this tradition, an almost six-metre high Amitābha Buddha dated to 585, now in the British Museum, stood most probably some six miles to the north-east of Wanxian, at the Chong'guang temple, Pushang village.[67] In 1915 Munthe purchased a three-metre high

---

66. Chu-ho (Sirén's transcription). Also at Xi Gu, near Quyang, and in the Dingzhou museum, Sirén, "Chinese Sculptures of the Sung, Liao and Chin Dynasties", 60–1.
67. Given to the B. M. by the Chinese Government and C. T. Loo in 1936, following the Burlington House exhibition of 1935–1936. The full height is 578 cm. The figure was known by its inscription to have come from the Chong'guang si (temple of Lofty Radiance) in a village called Han Cui that no longer exists. Sirén wrote that its 20th century location was Hsiang-pei (Xiangbei) near Wanxian, south-west of Peking (Sirén, "Chinese Marble Sculptures of the Transition Period", *BMFEA,* 12, 1940, 494). The Amitābha was taken from Xiangbei to Fangshun qiao railway station, and from there to Peking. The Xiangbei provenance was accepted by Gray and Watson in their article on the figure for the British Museum (*BMQ*, 16, 1951–52, ps. 81, 84), where it was noted that no record of a Chong'guang si had yet been found.

    Although no Xiangbei is shown on the 1934 Wanxian district map, the gazette texts record that a Chong'guang si once stood at Pushang, 'village above the reeds'. The village is shown in the 1732 Wanxian gazette, and also in the late Ming edition of the Baoding gazette. As this Chong'guang si is the only temple bearing the name in the Baoding/Dingzhou area, it seems likely to be the one in question; according to the gazettes, the hall was founded in the early Tang, between 627 and 649—the authors having 'lost' the first half century of its existence (the sculpture is 585). Sirén's Xiangbei, which he never visited, may have been a misunderstanding of local information—possibly that the figure came from "Wanxian xiang bei"—the northern part of the countryside around Wanxian. The place where Pushang village was located is marked on the 1934 map by a swastika (cartographic symbol for a Buddhist monument). See *Wanxian xinzhi*, 1934, Zhong'guo fangzhi congshu, series 4, 164, vol. 1, 1968, 149; *Zhili Wanxian zhi*, 1732, Zhong'guo fangzhi congshu, series 4, 523, 1976, 167, *Wanli Baoding fuzhi*, preface 1607, Rare Books of the National Library, Beijing, 604, j. 2, 42–3.

attendant Bodhisattva to this Buddha, which subsequently passed via Baron Kawasaki to the Tokyo National Museum.[68]

Another example is the beautiful three-metre high late Northern Qi Buddha (*ca.* 570s) in the Nezu Art Museum, Tokyo, which stood in Yamanaka's courtyard in Peking from 1921–36, reportedly having come from "a ruined temple in Dingzhou".[69]

A third example is a late 6th century headless Buddha figure, formerly in the Dingzhou Museum (on a sculptured base which Sirén believed was 12th century, and may once have formed part of a *sūtra* pillar).[70] If west-central Hebei has yielded these marble sculptures in the 20th century, it is clear that in the 12th century local sculptors had source material in depth, which explains a convention common to both the 'archaistic' and 'naturalistic' figures, derived from the 6th century: the use of doubly deep grooves to represent drapery folds.[71]

The more general question that arises is: why does the material appear at this time? Sirén put it down to the patronage of foreigners keen to participate in China's mainstream culture. Of Liao and Jin endeavour in this direction, he wrote:

> "Their system of government was organized according to indigenous traditions, carried out by Chinese officials, and they made the best to

---

68. Munthe wrote to Bogh of his recent purchase:
"It is from the last years of the Sui dynasty—the inscription is on the base—as far as I remember 385 AD [actually 585], it is a Kuan Yin and very beautiful, worth at least some 20,000 dollars … . The figure itself is 8.1/2—9 ft high. How to get it home, I do not know yet."
The figure is 256 cm; 305 cm with the base. At some point after 1918, the Bodhisattva passed to Baron Kawasaki in Kobe, and thence to the Tokyo National Museum. In discussing the figure in his 1940 article, Sirén was unaware of its relationship to the 'parent' Buddha, exhibited only 4 years earlier at Burlington House. A vague tradition had it that the figure came from a place in west Hebei (Sirén, "Chinese Marble Sculptures of the Transition Period", 482). There is also an interesting Buddha torso at Bergen which is stylistically close to the British Museum Amitābha, particularly in the detailing of the sash and hem, and the carving of the sleeves. When the smaller figure was published (*ibid.*, pl. VII:d), it then had a head with a restored nose (in the manner of some of the free-standing figures). Sirén dated it to the early Sui dynasty, commenting on the technical skill of the sculptor, revealed both in the carving of the sash and the surface treatment of the chest. Ayers thought that, in common with the free-standing and architectural pieces, it dated to somewhere between the 10th and 13th century, and was executed in an archaistic manner.
69. *ibid.*, 482, pl. IV:a; Mizuno, *Bronze and Stone Sculpture of China, from the Yin to the T'ang Dynasty*, Tokyo, 1960, pl. 61.
70. *ibid.*, 485, pl. V:d.
71. The double fold is quite common on 6th century images from the region; see for example the 541 dated Maitreya from the Xiude hoard, Weng and Yang, *The Palace Museum Peking, Treasures of the Forbidden City*, pl. 132.

support the old cultural institutions of the country. Most remarkable in this respect were their efforts to protect and enliven the Buddhist religion, which at the end of the T'ang dynasty had suffered greatly through official persecution and consequent indifference on the part of the people."[72]

We know that in the late 1130's and 1140's a second wave of sinicisation was felt at the Jin court, supported by the emperor Wanyan Tan (r. 1123–49), who instigated reforms to emulate Chinese bureaucratic and court practice—to the extent of offering sacrifices in person at the Temple of Confucius in 1141.[73] To suggest however that the Jin were behind all developments in religion during the period of their rule in north China would be somewhat like suggesting that the British are behind all cultural events in Hong Kong. Admittedly, Quyang/Dingzhou was in the north of China proper, where Jin influence was strongest, but again, the Jurchen practice was to rule China where possible through Chinese civil servants. The Jin exerted their sovereignty over a vast area of China by means of an effective but numerically modest army. To put this in perspective, in the late 12th century the Chinese outnumbered them in north China by about 15:1.[74]

When the Jurchen invaded, north-east Quyang was already enjoying prosperity. In the Northern Song, the ivory-glazed stonewares produced about 18 miles north of Quyang city (around Longquan) were highly regarded across China.[75] Dingware was accepted at court, and generally treasured; the pagoda at the Jingzhi si (from which the gilt bronze *tiangwang* was excavated) contained dozens of Ding pieces, including Buddhist vessels.[76] Production continued on into the Jin and ceased probably in the 13th century.

It is possible that the Jin did exercise some control over these kilns, but rather more likely that they were clients. The kilns were probably owned by Chinese landlords, who as Tregear argues, would have amassed considerable wealth from their operation.[77] If we link together the profitability for the regional gentry of the Ding kilns (and their market in Buddhist wares) with the earlier Quyang/Dingzhou tradition of Buddhist marble sculpture, we can perhaps make more sense of the later stone production. Expressions of piety and prosperity

---

72. O. Sirén, "Chinese Sculptures of the Sung, Liao and Chin Dynasties", 50.
73. J-S. Tao, *The Jurchen in Twelfth-Century China, a Study of Sinicisation*, Seattle & London, 1976, 41–2.
74. *ibid.*, 51.
75. The principal kilns were sited at present-day Jianci village.
76. Such as water-sprinklers. Rawson has pointed to the Buddhist market for Ding ware, and the dependency of some of its ceramic shapes on Buddhist metal prototypes; J. Rawson, *Chinese Ornament the Lotus and the Dragon*, 81–3.
77. M. Tregear, *Song Ceramics*, London, 1982, 16.

often unite in religious patronage. The Hebei material, archaistic and naturalistic, quite conspicuously signifies wealth within the context of its time, when clay and wood imagery were predominant. The Da Liu material is yet more interesting because it demonstrates a particular focus: on the Foguang si, one of the better known temples in north China, sited at Wutai shan.

Wutai shan was one of the major Buddhist centres in China from the Tang onwards, associated particularly with Mañjuśrī, its presiding deity. A brick pagoda in the vicinity of the Foguang si houses the remains of the priest Jietuo, a famous resident of the 7th century, later widely believed to have been an incarnation of the Bodhisattva.

Following the destruction of the Foguang si in Wuzong's 845 purge, the eastern (main) shrine hall was rebuilt in its present grand form. As Wutai shan became increasingly popular in the 10th century—as a destination for pilgrims, and an icon of worship itself—so the temple continued to be important. Amongst the evidence for this is a late 10th century map of the mountain painted at Dunhuang, which includes the Foguang si and the Jietuo pagoda.[78] In 1137 a Mañjuśrī hall was added at the north side, (opposite was a Samantabhadra hall, no longer standing, and for which presently there is no date).

Conclusion

Let us conclude with a hypothesis. The Da Liu material represents the pious sponsorship of a temple and pagoda (or pagoda alone if it was very large) by the families of a wealthy region; a region moreover with its own long-standing tradition of marble sculpture. Possibly inspired by new building at the Foguang si, a celebrated temple 150 miles to the west, the patrons—including the inhabitants of villages like Da Liu—commissioned a sculpture which resembled, where possible, the existing marble statuary of the Undefiled Pure Radiance pagoda. This accounts for the creation of the free-standing *luohan* and seated Buddhas. The Foguang si could not provide marble prototypes for all the images required, and further figures, including Mañjuśrī and Samantabhadra, were made in a more contemporary manner, by clay-modelling, and perhaps also by painting and wood carving. Most of the images shared some stylistic features with other current stonework in the area. As far as the archaistic Buddhas are concerned, Sickman's 'provincial relapses' may hold some truth, but as a description of the overall Jin production in marble, it does little justice to attempt, in west-central Hebei, to build on a distinguished history of Buddhist statuary.

Appendix: Architectural Group

78. M.M. Rhie, *The Fo-kuang ssu, Literary Evidences and Buddhist Images*, New York and London, 1977, chs. 1–4, *passim*.

1. Standing Bodhisattva, 3'2"[79]	(l.)[80] University Museum, Philadelphia; (ill.)[81] Sirén, 1925, pl. 543a; Howard, 1984, pl. 51.
2. Standing Bodhisattva, 3'2"	(l.) University Museum, Philadelphia; (ill.) Sirén, 1925, pl. 543b (ex. C.T. Loo, Paris); Sirén, 1942, pl. 9:2.
3. Standing Bodhisattva, 3'2"	(ill.) Sirén, 1925, pl. 544a (ex.Yamanaka, Kyoto); Sirén, 1942, pl. 8:2.
4. Standing Bodhisattva, ? 3'2" (Avalokiteśvara)	(ill.) Sirén, 1925, pl. 544b (ex. Yamanaka, New York).
5. Standing Bodhisattva, 3'10" (Mahāsthāmaprāpta)	(l.) Asian Art Museum, San Francisco; (ill.) Lefebvre d'Argencé, 1974, pl. 132.
6. Standing Bodhisattva, 2'7" (11-headed Avalokiteśvara)	(l.) West Norway Museum; (ill.) Howard, 1984, pl. 49.
7. Seated Bodhisattva, 3'6"	(ill.) Sirén, 1925, pl. 542b (ex. Yamanaka, Peking).
8. Seated Bodhisattva, 2'11"	(l.) British Museum (ex. Houo-Ming-Tse, Peking).
9. Seated Bodhisattva (?)	(ill.) Houo-Ming-Tse, 1930, 30.
10. Standing Buddha, 3' (Śākyamuni)	(l.) West Norway Museum; (ill.) Sirén, 1925, pl. 546a; Howard, 1984, pl. 50.
11. Standing Buddha, approx. 3' (Śākyamuni)	(1.) Spink & Son, 1992.
12. Standing Buddha, 3'3"	(l.) Asian Art Museum, San Francisco; (ill.) Sirén, 1925, pl. 546b (ex. Yamanaka, Kyoto); Lefebvre d'Argencé, 1974, pl. 131.
13. Seated Buddha, 3'5" (Cosmic Vairocana)	(l.) Asian Art Museum, San Francisco; (ill.) Lefebvre d'Argencé, 1974, pl. 134.
14. Seated Buddha, 2'7"	(ill.) Eskenazi, *Ancient Chinese Sculpture,*, 1978, no. 27.
15. Seated Buddha Trinity, 2'	(ill.) Sotheby's New York, 9.12.87,

79. Dimensions are given in feet, following Sirén, 1925.
80. (l.): Located
81. (ill.): Illustrated

'ig. 3

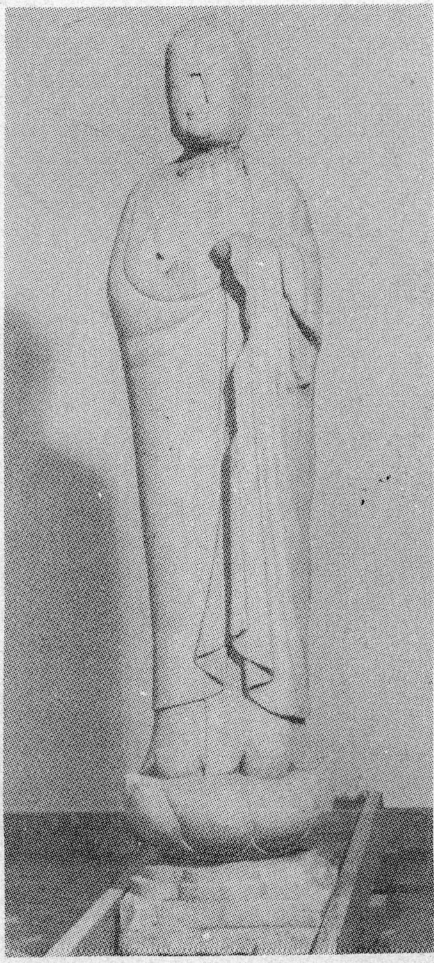

Fig. 4

Fig. 5

Fig. 6

Fig. 7

Fig. 8

Fig. 9

Fig. 10

Fig. 11

Fig. 12

An American Appropriation of Buddhism

Ian Charles Harris

A. Setting the Scene

It is rather difficult to get an accurate picture of the number of practising Buddhists in the United States. In 1975, Barrett[1] estimated 190,000 persons, or approximately 0.1% of the population and one would expect this figure to be mainly composed of descendants of Chinese and Japanese immigrants affiliated to the Jodo shinshu inspired Buddhist Churches of America with some Nichiren shoshu of America thrown in for good measure. Barrett goes on to predict an approximate 30% decrease within American Buddhism by 2000 presumably on the basis of assimilation to the dominant Christian atmosphere of the host culture.

Now, it is likely that these statistics significantly underestimate the true extent of Buddhist influence in the country today. Of course, Buddhist affiliation is notoriously difficult to determine for there is no easy answer to the question, "Who is a Buddhist ?" Again, with the exception of death, life-cycle rites are studiously avoided by most traditional forms of Buddhism so that documentary information on adherents is necessarily sketchy and this situation is likely to be further complicated by the relative youth of recently engaged Buddhists, and their fellow-travellers in contemporary America. Anecdotal evidence does, however, suggest a fairly major explosion of interest within the last 25 years with successive waves of mainly Japanese and Tibetan teachers attracting and sustaining large, though fluctuating, numbers of followers.[2] It is no exaggeration to say that virtually all extant forms of Buddhism are now established and prospering in the United States, often in conditions far more

1. D.B. Barratt, ed., *World Christian Encyclopedia: A Comparative Survey of Churches and Religions in the Modern world AD 1900-2000*, Nairobi, OUP, 1982, 711.
2. The triennial, New York based, magazine *Tricycle*: The Buddhist Review is a reasonable barometer of the present scene. With its high production values and sponsors, including Leonard Cohen, Richard Gere, Philip Glass and several Rockefellers, *Tricycle* represents a quantum leap away from the more sedate and academic popular Buddhist journals of Europe and Asia.

satisfactory than are possible within the old Asian homelands. A variety of reasons are given in the literature to account for this state of affairs ranging from a general decline in traditional religious beliefs to the apparent harmony that Buddhism shares with the antinomianism of the beat, hippie and new-age variants of the counter-culture. On a more specifically regional level, W.I.Thompson argues that the steady movement of European people's on their westward journey to America should not be seen simply in geographical terms, it is also a movement of the mind from the old certainties of occidental civilisation towards a fruitful encounter with the East. As such contemporary Californian society, the spatial and logical terminus of this movement, is experiencing the birthpangs of a new planetary culture which will be most appropriately supported by the purified world philosophy (Heidegger's *planetarische denken*) that Thompson terms "reformation Buddhism."[3] Thompson's millenialism, with California (the so-called 'edge of history') as the promised land, is shared by many within the new-age sub-culture, though this need not incline us to regard the growth of Buddhism as a purely West Coast phenomenon. The fact is that, alongside the traditional 'school-based' meditation and retreat houses, single issue Buddhist activist groups, gay and lesbian *sanghas*, Buddhist healing and therapy centres and the like are springing up throughout the length and breadth of the land.[4]

Superficially much here seems novel, but on closer examination the American transformation of Buddhism, which in some respects runs parallel to the Chinese reception of that religion at the beginning of the present epoch, has roots which extend well back into the nineteenth century. Thomas Tweed,[5] in a recent study of this formative period in American Buddhism, offers a useful three-fold typology of the forms into which Buddhism had crystallised by the end of the last century. His scheme encompasses firstly an occult or esoteric type strongly influenced by popular Neoplatonism, Swedenborgian ideas, Mesmerism, Spiritualism and Theosophy; secondly, a Rationalist or Scientific type arising from a Unitarian, free-thinking background, in which the influence of New England Transcendentalism can be clearly discerned, and finally a Romantic or Exotic type primarily associated with a small, though influential group of wealthy East Coast aesthetes and intellectuals, many of whom had first-hand

---

3. W.I. Thompson "Pacific Shift", in J.B. Callicott & R.T. Ames, eds., *Nature in AsianTraditions of Thought: Essays in Environmental Philosophy,* Albany, SUNY Press, 1989, 25. *Cf.* also W.I. Thompson, *At The Edge of History*, New York, Harper Colophon, 1971.
4. Listings located at the back of Tricycle are particularly enlightening in this respect.
5. T.A. Tweed, *The American Encounter with Buddhism 1844-1912: The Victorian Culture and the Limits of Dissent,* Bloomington, Indiana University Press, 1992.

acquaintance with East Asian culture, mainly through their interests in fine art, ritual, drama, customs and the like.

However, if we look back half a century, to a time before the crystallisation of Tweed's three types, it would be unwise to underestimate the considerable influence of Henry David Thoreau of Walden Pond fame, who brought Buddhism to a popular audience by preparing and publishing the first American translation of a Buddhist text, a fragment of Burnouf's edition of the Lotus Sutra.[6] Thoreau clearly represents an important link in the chain that leads from the wilderness ideal of the early settlers, so well documented in Nash's classic study *Wilderness and the American Mind*,[7] to contemporary Eco-Buddhism, a movement to which this article is primarily intended to give prominence. That Thoreau was considered a guru-like figure in his lifetime, there can be little doubt. Here is his friend Moncure Conway eulogising his sojourn at Walden:

> "Like the Yogi so long motionless whilst gazing on the sun that knotty plants encircled his neck ... and the birds built nests on his shoulders, this poet and naturalist, by equal consecration, became part of field and forest."[8]

Thoreau represents a figure, then, who popularly symbolises the initial encounter with Buddhism, still at this period insufficiently differentiated from its Hindu background side by side, or, more accurately in harmony with, the various benign powers of nature; a highly potent image and one that has continued to flourish up to the present day!

A preliminary survey of the forms of contemporary Buddhism in America suggests that Tweed's threefold typology will remain a useful explanatory tool, though more work clearly needs to be undertaken here with regard to movements of Buddhist fusion with New-Age thinking. Nevertheless, I hope that the following discussion will convincingly demonstrate that Eco-Buddhism, with its eclectic intellectual tastes and strong sense of identification with the natural world, may usefully be seen as a close amalgam of the rationalist and romantic encounter types. The writings surveyed in the body of the article certainly show a minimal inclination towards the esotericism characteristic of Tweed's first grouping.

---

6. Henry David Thoreau, "The Preaching of the Buddha", *The Dial 4*, Jan.1844, 391-401.
7. R. Nash, *Wilderness and the American Mind*, 3rd edition, New Haven, Yale University Press, 1982.
8. Quoted in R. Fields, *How the Swans Came to the Lake: A Narrative History of Buddhism in America*, 3rd edition, revised and updated. Boston & London, Shambala, 1992, 64.

B. General Features of Eco-Buddhism

A recurring theme in writings concerning the Buddhist engagement with the natural world is the obstructive and destructive character of the dominant Western model of the self. Some authors attribute responsibility for this state of affairs to the general Judaeo-Christian character of our culture, others mention the Greeks, while others pointing an accusing finger at Descartes. However, a detailed critique of the self and its place in Western thought is not a major concern for Eco-Buddhism - it is bad and there is an end to the matter! The present condition of extreme individualism, conceived of as the final stage in the disease of the Western self, is a major occasioning factor behind the present eco-crisis. As such, this post-modern apocalypse can only be arrested by a kind of radical restructuring of the self to which Buddhism alone holds the key. Nolan P. Jacobson, for instance, holds that, only by relinquishing our barbaric and illusory sense of the self can we hope to establish a "future planetary civilisation"[9] of the sort prophesied by W.I.Thompson. Elsewhere, Joanna Macy, one of the more prolific of Eco-Buddhists, argues that below the level of our dysfunctional and pathologic empirical self, which she regards as the great "epistemological error of Occidental civilisation",[10] lies a true or ecological self just waiting to germinate. The greening of this eco-self need not be sought through any specific process of mental and ethical cultivation. On the contrary it rather curiously manifests itself through something "very close to the religious concept of grace."[11] We shall return to Macy in more detail later but two points immediately spring to mind at this stage. In the first place, the views expressed above, with their dependence on a hierarchical stratification of the self, are at least superficially closer to *vedantic* notions, particularly those advanced in the *Visistadvaita* of Ramanuja, than to any known variety of Buddhism. Secondly it is clear that the outlook owes as much to a longstanding American engagement with nature as it does to any Indian-based tradition of thought, be it orthodox or heterodox. As the philosopher George Santayana noted during an address to the University of California:

> "things would have been different if [Western] philosphers had lived among your mountains ... [which] suspend your forced sense of your own importance not merely as individuals, but even as men."[12]

---

9. N.P. Jacobson, "A Buddhist-Christian Probe of the Endangered Future", *EB*, 1[illegible] 1982, 38-55. In particular *cf.* 41-3.
10. J. Macy, "The Greening of the Self", in A. Hunt-Badiner, ed., *Dharma Gaia: Harvest of Essays in Buddhism and Ecology*, Berkeley, Parallax, 1990, 53-63; 53-7.
11. *ibid.* 63.
12. Quoted in W. Fox, *Toward a Transpersonal Ecology: Developing New Foundations for Environmentalism*, Boston, Shambala, 1990, 18.

In a similar vein, Allan Hunt-Badiner, the editor of a recent collection of essays on Buddhist environmentalism,[13] stresses the essential harmony between autochthonous Native American traditions of respect for nature and those found in Buddhism, though he does little for his case by listing additional parallels with the Gaia hypothesis of scientist James Lovelock, Central Asian Shamanism, the economics of E.F. Schumacher, the Orphic and Dionysian mysteries, modern physics, eco-feminism, cybernetics, general systems theory and the Christian creation-centred spirituality of the renegade Dominican monk, Matthew Fox. This embarrasment of riches calls to mind Stcherbatsky's rather ambitious attempt in *Buddhist Logic* to show that every conceivable Western thinker from Parmenides to Hegel is either pre- or post-figured in the writings of Dignaga and Dharmakirti. The problem with this kind of approach is that it tends to deprive the subject under examination of any fundamental core. In our case, it deprives Buddhism of the freedom to exist 'in itself' and, as such, is reminiscent of the nineteenth century liberal protestant reduction of Biblical tradition by the method of documentary source criticism, an activity which the celebrated rabbinic scholar, Solomon Schechter, regarded as the higher anti-semitism".

In a parallel, which again is reminiscent of the much earlier Chinese transformation of Buddhism, many Eco-Buddhists have attempted a reformulation of basic terms and concepts. The nature of the *sangha* is a particularly good case in point. Thus, in a rather obscure passage, Macy talks of the ancient "sacramental life"[14] of *bhikkhus* and *bhikkhunis*, perhaps referring to their role as a conduit through which the benign powers of nature can flow to their lay supporters who by force of circumstance are necessarily alienated from, and fearful of, the natural world. This restructuring of terminology is made more explicit elsewhere. Hunt-Badiner, for example, takes the term *sangha* to apply, not to the traditional "community of monks and nuns ... [but] more informally ... to mean all practitioners [of Dharma-Gaia] and kindred spirits."[15] The most obvious source for this innovation within contemporary American Buddhism is Gary Snyder, in many respects the modern day incarnation of Thoreau. Perhaps best known as Japhy Ryder, the 'factional' hero of Kerouac's beatnik mountain-dwelling novel *The Dharma Bums*, Snyder is also a prolific poet and pamphleteer. In a short essay, first published in 1969, he maintains that the term *sangha* is, in fact, the proper designation for the totality of all beings.[16] In a romantic development of this idea, he goes on to argue that traditional

---

13. A. Hunt-Badiner, ed., *op. cit.*
14. J. Macy, *Mutual Causality in Buddhism and General Systems Theory: The Dharma of Natural Systems*, Albany, SUNY Press, 1991, 204.
15. *op.cit.*, xviii.
16. G. Snyder, "Buddhism and the Possibilities of a Planetary Culture", reprinted in B. Devall and G. Sessions, *Deep Ecology*, Layton, Utah, Gibbs M. Smith, 1985, 251-3.

societies of the past, specifically those that dwelt harmoniously as part of this totality of beings, such as Native Americans and Australian Aborigines, may be said to have "accomplished a condition of *Sangha*."[17] Being *sangha*, then, does not entail particular assent to the doctrine and practice of the Buddha as embodied in the Pali Canon, the Mahāyāna sutras or to any of the schools of northern and eastern Buddhism. On the contrary, what we have here is essentially an ethical orientation towards the natural world. One could easily dismiss this point of view as part and parcel of the paraphernalia of Beat Zen, an immature transitional movement, now moribund, on the way to a more informed instantiation of Buddhism in America, yet this does not seem to be supported by the evidence. The anti-traditional view is quite widespread and is perhaps given greater weight by figures like Thich Nhat Hanh, a reasonably traditional Vietnamese representative of the Lin-chi school of Ch'an, now active in America. The first precept of the Order of Interbeing, a movement based on Thich Nhat Hanh's reformulation of Buddhism states that no-one is to be "bound to any doctrine, theory or ideology, even Buddhist ones."[18]

In line with this reworking of Buddhist concepts it is perhaps unsurprising to discover that Eco-Buddhist literature has further redefined the nature of the Mahāyānist practitioner par excellence, the Bodhisattva. The Bodhisattva is now quite simply an ecologically active member of the great community of biospiritualists and other assorted eco-activists busy hugging trees[19] and practicing insight meditation ouside nuclear power stations and waste dumps for the benefit of all sentient beings. Social activism is the order of the day, as it is throughout much of the traditional Asian heartlands with engaged environmentalism now very much part of the modern agenda of Protestant Buddhism, be it amongst Tibetan refugees in India, in rural Thailand or in northern California. Gary Snyder believes that this change in emphasis is a natural reaction to the reality of traditional Buddhism, bogged down as it has been in scholastic examination of recondite epistemological and psychological problems. Even in its Mahāyānist forms, and despite the altruistic rhetoric, meditational procedures have been employed "toward the end of liberating a few dedicated individuals."[20] In short, institutionalised Buddhism has become dead to "any meaningful function of compassion."[21]

---

17. *ibid.*, 252.
18. Quoted by Sulak Sivaraksa, "True Development", page 177 in A. Hunt-Badiner, ed., *op. cit.*, 169-177.
19. *cf.* J. Macy, "The Greening of the Self", in A. Hunt-Badiner, ed., *Dharma Gaia: A Harvest of Eddays in Buddhism and Ecology,* 54ff.
20. Snyder, *op. cit.*, 251.
21. *ibid.*

Beyond his emblematic presence within the counter-culture as guru and eco-activist, Gary Snyder is the one of the more significant post-modern poets of nature in America today. The growing number of doctoral theses on his work eloquently attest to this fact. I do not possess the critical apparatus to assess the quality of his work myself but two contrasting examples of informed criticism will give a flavour. For Charles Altieri, Snyder's rejection of the tragic/heroic convention of earlier American poetics, such as that found in Pound, successfully enables him to "put mind more directly into the impersonal processes of the world."[22] By evoking "a metaphysical state [earlier] described by Fenellosa (incidentally, Tweed's prime example of the nineteenth century Romantic/Exotic type of Buddhist) and Whitehead",[23] Snyder is able to articulate the "radiant nodes of the process"[24] that constitutes the world. In a less flattering light, the critic, Robert Boyers, regards Snyder simply as "the poetic Marlboro man."[25]

Snyder's short work, *Smokey the Bear Sutra* (1969), brings together the Buddhist and environmental concerns of the author quite neatly. As the poem unfolds, the Buddha predicts a future rebirth in the land of Walden Pond, the Grand Canyon and Big Sur. He will take the wrathful form of Smokey the Bear, clad in blue work overalls and a stetson hat. With a halo of smoke and fire produced by the man-made forest fires of *kali yuga* he will trample "underfoot wasteful freeways and needless suburbs; smashing the worms of capitalism and totalitarianism."[26] He will teach the great *mantra* : "Drown their butts, crush their butts. Drown their butts, crush their butts."[27] And with his *vajra*-shovel he will dig out and dump the enemies of nature. A millenial era of peace, free from the dangers of oil slicks, will ensue and all will win the highest perfect enlightenment.

Joanna Macy approaches the environmental question in a quite different way. She is convinced that the "political values ... implicit ... in early Buddhist teachings"[28] require an active engagement with the State understood in socio-political terms. Not only that, but at present this kind of engagement is of the utmost urgency. "The very viability of our societies and ecosystems necessitates

22. C. Altieri, *Enlarging the Temple: New Directions in American Poetry during the 1960s*, Lewisburg, Bucknell University Press, 1979, 144.
23. *ibid.*, 136.
24. *ibid.*, 147.
25. R. Boyers, "A Mixed Bag", *Partisan Review*, 36, 1969, 313.
26. G. Snyder, "Smokey the Bear Sutra", (1969), reprinted in Devall and Sessions, *op. cit.*, 25-7.
27. *ibid.*, 26.
28. *Mutual Causality in Buddhism and General Systems Theory: The Dharma of Natural Systems*, Albany, SUNY Press, 1991, 198.

it."[29] It is encumbent on responsibly committed Buddhist activists to be guided by the ideal of "reverence for natural systems", an ideal she derives from both early Buddhism and from the work of the general systems theorist Ervin Laszlo. However, further investigation reveals another source for Macy's message of redemptive work. At an earler stage in her career, as a Peace Corps volunteer, she came in contact with the Sri Lankan, Buddhist-inspired Sarvodaya movement of A.T. Ariyaratna. This led to the publication of a book *Dharma and Development* [30] in 1981. Now Gombrich and Obeyesekere identify Sarvodaya as a prime example of a Protestant Buddhist movement. Its rise to prominence is closely associated with the injection of large sums of rural development money from foreign donor countries and though an example of "practical this-worldly asceticism of an altruistic"[31] kind, it is not at all clear that its basic orientation is uniquely Buddhist. In fact, there is reasonable evidence to suggest a strong Gandhian source for much of Ariyaratna's thought. In a rather fulsome attack on the Buddhist authenticity of Sarvodaya, Gombrich and Obeyesekere claim that:

> "Much of what has been written on Sarvodaya is by good-hearted but naive Western intellectuals who see the movement in terms of their own utopian fantasies of a benevolent social order."[32]

Not that Ariyaratna is free from utopian and romantic fantasy himself. Critics have regarded the goals of the movement as both simplistic and unattainable, based as they are on a sentimental, bourgeoise projection back into Sri Lanka's Buddhist-inspired village past.

> "Ariyaratna's disembodied village has little recognition of social conflict, of the vice and folly that constitute part of our humanity and were clearly recognised by the great religious teachers of history, including the Buddha."[33]

Further scrutiny reveals a number of parallels between the Sarvodaya movement and Eco-Buddhism. In the first place, the need for "a clear beautiful environment",[34] the first of ten basic village needs according to the teachings of Ariyaratna, meshes nicely with the environmental concerns of contemporary American Buddhist activists. From another perspective, both Ariyaratna and Macy make determined efforts to establish the validity of their positions, by a romantic appeal to antiquity. In Airyaratna's case, this relates to the concept

29. *ibid.*, 195.
30. J. Macy, *Dharma and Development: Religion as a Resource in the Sarvodaya Self-Help Movement*, West Hartford, Conn., Kumarian Press, 1983.
31. R. Gombrich & G. Obeyesekere, *Buddhism Transformed: Religious Change in Sri Lanka*, Dehli, Motilal Banarsidass, 1990, 245.
32. *ibid.*, 243.
33. *ibid.*, 251.
34. *ibid.*, 248.

(borrowed from Gandhi) of selfless labour (*sramadana*). This may be all very well in the Sri Lankan context where Singer's "symbolic traditionalization"[35] appears necessary for new ideas and practices to become established, but why Macy feels the need for this procedure remains a bit of a mystery, especially when set against the wider background of innovative activism of the Snyder variety. Nevertheless, Macy and Snyder are often of one mind. The former writer regards Sarvodaya and Eco-Buddhism as both providing contexts for the positive evolution of the role of the traditional monk, who by leaving his solitude and becoming part of the wider community of eco-activists, is transformed into the altruistic Bodhisattva of the Mahāyāna. This is the sort of confusion of traditions relished by both authors. Snyder on his side derives a similar conclusion from his contact with Chinese and Japanese sources. Quoting the Ch'an maxim, "a day without work, a day without food",[36] he concludes that Buddhism in the present epoch implies "real work", i.e. meaningful, environmentally positive work, not the foppish or artificial work predicated by a decadent, late capitalist economy. The message of redemptive work is never far from the surface here.

A final factor, though rarely made explicit, in the composition of Eco-Buddhism is Spinozism, or more specifically a variant on Spinoza's philosophy developed in recent decades by Arne Naess and presented under the title 'Deep Ecology' Naess, Norway's first academic professor of philosophy, and a noted mountaineer, having conquered peaks in the Hindu Kush and the Himalayas, has a massive bibliography under his belt, concentrating since the 50's on the application of Spinoza to environmental problematics. While recognising that an ecological interpretation of Spinoza's logical monism cannot, of itself, be fully justified, Naess has worked hard to tease out potentially useful elements in Spinoza so that they may be blended with other thought patterns, the most notable being Buddhism and the teachings of Gandhi, though in practice, Naess sees little difference between the two holding, as did Gandhi, that Buddhism is a reformed version of Hinduism.[37] Rather surprisingly, a number of other important, mainly Scandinavian, Spinoza scholars also see substantial parallels between Spinoza and Buddhism. Jon Wetlesen, for instance, in a highly detailed treatment of the ethics of freedom, notes significant points of contact between

---

35. discussed at *ibid.*, 251.
36. G. Snyder, *The Real Work: Interviews and Talks 1964-1979*, New York, New Directions, 1980, 104.
37. A. Naess, "Through Spinoza to Mahayana Buddhism or Through Mahayana Buddhism to Spinoza?", in J. Wetlesen, ed., *Spinoza's Philosophy of Man: Proceedings of the Scandinavian Spinoza Symposium 1977*, Oslo, University of Oslo Press, 1978, 136-158. In particular pages 138 & 141.

the Four Noble Truths and Spinoza's treatment of liberation and bondage.[38] Again, Paul Wienpahl, author of *The Radical Spinoza*[39] and advocate of an egoless, mystic intuition as the highest level of knowledge for Spinoza, a kind of "seeing things as they are",[40] came to his studies after a clearly influential spell in a Japanese Zen monastery in the late 1950's.

Wetlesen, though a self-proclaimed eco-catastrophist and admirer of Schumacher's 'Buddhist economics',[41] holds that the teachings of the Buddha and Spinoza share a certain otherworldliness. This makes it difficult for either system of thought to provide a satisfactory foundation for any meaningful environmental activity. However, Naess disagrees with this, preferring instead to align himself with the fashionable trend, recently identified by Lambert Schmithausen,[42] which aims to reject the traditional view of Buddhism as escapist. This makes it a rather more straightforward matter for Naess to erect an ecological ethic upon quasi-Buddhist foundations than it would be for Wetlesen. In its developed form, Naess's deep ecology maintains that God or Nature (Spinoza's *Deus sive Natura*) is perfect in itself.[43] All things are said to be possessed of intrinsic value and the "richness and diversity of life forms contribute to the realization of these values."[44] Similarly, all things are interconnected. "There is a network of cause-effect relations connecting everything with everything"[45] yet all things strive towards higher and higher levels of self-realisation, not in a narrow, atomic manner but in the sense that one comes to see that which is real as that which binds us to the whole. This is Spinoza's *conatus*, a drawing near to the "realisation of union with the whole of nature",[46] an understanding love of nature which aims at the most extensive vision of things possible. In a sense then, the goal of deep ecology is a this-

38. J. Wetlesen, *The Stage and the Way: Spinoza's Ethics of Freedom*, Assen, van Gorcum, 1973,13f. See also J. Wetlesen, "Body Awareness as a Gateway to Eternity: a Note on the Mysticism of Spinoza and its Affinity to Buddhist Meditation", in S. Hessig, ed., *Speculum Spinozanum 1677-1977*, London, RKP, 1977, 479-494 on the relations between Spinoza and Buddhist insight meditation (*vipassanā*).
39. P. Wienpahl, *The Radical Spinoza*, New York, 1979.
40. cf. P. Wienpahl, "Spinoza and Mysticism", in J. Wetlesen ed., *op. cit.* 211-224.
41. Wetlesen, *op. cit.*, 405-6.
42. Noted by L. Schmithausen, *Buddhism and Nature: The Lecture Delivered on the Occasion of the EXPO 1990*, An Enlarged Version with Notes, Studia Philologica Buddhica, Occasional Paper Series VII, Tokyo, The International Institute for Buddhist Studies, 1991, 12, paragraph 18.1.
43. A. Naess, "Spinoza and Ecology", in S. Hessig, ed., *op cit.*, 418-425. In particular 419ff.
44. Fox, *op. cit.*, 115ff.
45. Naess, *op. cit.*, 420.
46. *ibid.*, 421.

worldly inflation of the self such that it may eventually become co-terminate with the boundary of the known. The process shows a marked similarity to Macy's greening of the eco-self. Now this looks all very well from a Gandhian perspective, in fact Naess admits to such an influence,[47] but it seems a little curious from the Buddhist point of view. In other words, what is specifically Buddhist about deep ecology ?

Although I have seen no specific reference to Far Eastern forms of Buddhism in any of the writings I have consulted by Naess, Hua-Yen teachings appear to be the nearest equivalent to the position outlined above, particularly if we disregard the apparent theism of Spinozism. This connection is explicitly, though more regularly implicitly, endorsed by Eco-Buddhists. Snyder, for instance, mentions the Hua-Yen vision of "the world as a vast interrelated network in which all objects and creatures are necessary and illuminated"[48] in the context of a powerful antidote to the scholasticism of the early schools. In other words, its doctrine of interdependence acts as a welcomed balance to the infuriatingly intellectual felicities of mainstream Buddhist debate. Similarly, by rejecting the Abhidharmic linear understanding of the causal process (*pratītyasamutpāda*) and insisting that the position of archaic Buddhism is one of mutual interdependence or reciprocal causality,[49] Macy moves rather close to a position that unites Hua-Yen teachings on identity and total intercausality with the original teachings of the Buddha.

Superficially, then, Hua-Yen appears to be the ideal Buddhist support for an ecological ethic maintaining, as it does, the interpenetration of all things. However, there is a problem, for in the *dharmadhātu*, the non-obstructed '*dharma*-field' of suchness (*tathatā*), past, present and future are said to be harmonised within a single moment. Quoting from the Ocean Seal of Uisang (625-702):

> "One is identical to all and all is identical with one.... The incalculably long aeons we identified to a single thought-instant.... All epochs are mutually identical.... *Samsara* and *Nirvana* are always harmonized together. Particular and Universal are completely merged together without distinction."[50]

47. A. Naess, *Freedom, Emotion and Self-Subsistence: The Structure of a Central Part of Spinoza's Ethics*, Oslo, University of Oslo Press, 1975, 98. The ramifications of this are also discussed in Fox, *op. cit.*, 107ff.
48. G. Snyder, in Devall and Sessions, *op. cit.*, 252.
49. Macy, *Mutual Causality in Buddhism and General Systems Theory: The Dharma of Natural Systems*, 59-62.
50. Quoted in S. Odin, "A Metaphysics of Cumulative Penetration: Process Theory and Hua Yen Buddhism", *Process Studies*, 11.2, 1981, 65-82: 66.

If this is so, if the future inheres in the past and vice versa, then the Hua-Yen position on causality is one of rigid determination, for if:

> "...each *dharma* is simply an 'effect' reducable to its manifold of 'causes': there is no creativity, novelty, or freedom of decision.... There is complete mutual penetration and mutual identification between all *dharmas* of the universe."[51]

The Hua-Yen realm of total togetherness then is completely devoid of a *telos*. It is going nowhere! Now, I would argue that this is probably the position of early Buddhism, but we must remember that this way of presenting Buddhist thought has been chosen by proponents of Eco-Buddhism specifically because it avoids the constraints of other options, ie. the strict determinism and non-teleological flavour of Spinoza for Naess, the simplistic linearity of the Abhidharma for Macy and the arid scholasticism of early Buddhism for Snyder. Such a formulation is supposed to open up the possibility of a better ordering of man's relations with the natural world in its infinite diversity and complexity, yet as Odin rightly notes:

> "Hua-yen Buddhism is deficient in categoreal equipment or adequate conceptual apparatus to argue both for the retention of a single determinate form by each *dharma*, as well as the 'total fusion of all that is.' For if any actuality is to possess definiteness of structural pattern or uniqueness and singularity of form, there must be some theoretical mechanism in the Hua-Yen system for the 'gradation, selection and elimination' of alternative patterns; but then one cannot argue for the 'total fusion of all that is'."[52]

In a highly stimulating article, Robert C. Neville shows that a two level[53] interpretation of Hua-Yen causality, such that total mutual penetration is only understood to be true from the ultimate perspective, is in harmony with the tradition itself. On the conventional level, indeterminacy with regard to the causal realm of process may continue to be retained. But as Schmithausen has so clearly pointed out,[54] this solution, one which is also maintained within the Japanese Tendai school, fails to address the problems of the environment. If we accept indeterminacy within the mundane realm, we must, willy nilly, also accept that ordinary unenlightened beings are unlikely to be aware of the true nature of things. This will inevitably incline them to be out of harmony with the total togetherness of nature. If, on the other hand, one sees things from the

---

51. *ibid.*, 71.
52. *ibid.*, 76.
53. R. C. Neville, "Buddhism and Process Philosophy", in K. K. Inada & N. P. Jacobson, eds., *Buddhism and American Thinkers*, Albany, SUNY Press, 1984, 121-142; 137.
54. *op. cit.*, 24-5, paragraph 31.

ultimate perspective, with the fully deterministic consequences that this implies, one must accept the full perfection of nature. This is clearly a recipe for inaction and equanimity, for:

> "If Buddha-Nature, being identical with the true essence of all entities, pervades everything, it follows that not only natural beings but also products of civilisation possess Buddha-Nature, and not only walls and tiles, as some texts actually state, but even cars, highways, dumping places, toxic waste, nuclear bombs, etc."[55]

The Eco-Buddhist is in a bit of a double bind here and I have the strong feeling that this is realised by some authors, though never explicitly stated. Now, American Buddhist studies are littered with scholars who at some stage in their career have been strongly influenced by Christian process theology of the Harshornian kind. It is also fairly well known that process theologians like John B. Cobb[56] and David Griffin[57] have led the way in developing a coherent Christian response to the present environmental crisis. A number of authors under discussion in this paper actually owe more than a passing alliegance to process thought; Nolan P. Jacobson[58] even going to the extent of dedicating his book on contemporary Buddhism to Charles Hartshorne himself. In an earlier article, the same author, paraphrasing Hartshorne, reports that:

> "In both Christian and Buddhist thought, the art of loving involves the penetration of all ego-centred compulsive drives and delusions that prevent men and women from participating in the fullness of experience and *taking responsibility for preserving the endangered future* (my italics)."[59]

This certainly harmonises with the evolutionary cosmic purpose ethics of a Christian like John Cobb who holds to the Whiteheadian doctrine that "God's persuasive power lures all aspects of the universe toward the realisation of instances of ever greater richness of experience or intensity of feeling",[60] but how close is it to the traditional Buddhist position? To my mind, it is not very close, but this turns out to be a positive advantage to the Eco-Buddhist, for the idea of creative novelty, of a *telos*, really needs to be injected into traditional

---

55. *ibid.*
56. *cf.* C. Birch & J. B. Cobb Jr., *The Liberation of Life: From the Cell to the Community*, Cambridge, CUP, 1981.
57. *cf.* D. Griffin, "Contributions to a Theology of Nature", Buckwell Review, 20, 1972, 3-24.
58. N. P. Jackson, *Buddhism and the Contemporary World: Change and Self-Correction*, Carbondale, S. Illinois University Press, 1983.
59. N. P. Jacobson, "A Buddhist-Christian Probe of the Endangered Future", *EB,* 15, 1982, 54-5.
60. *cf.* Fox, *op. cit.*, 181.

Buddhism so that it may fully open itself to ecological concerns. Process thought can do this job admirably, for it shows a marked congruence with Hua-Yen yet lacks the negative consequences described above. Not only that, process thinkers and Buddhist academics have been in dialogue for a considerable time making borrowings on both sides commonplace. Whitehead is often said to have had a view of things: "... uniquely available and publicly penetrable through the language and imagery of Buddhism."[61]

Nevertheless, and despite obvious similarities, recent work in dialogue between the two camps has identified a significant difference between Buddhism and Whitehead over the nature of causation. As we have already seen, Buddhism, in its Hua-Yen form, cannot account for change. Hartshorne [62] tries to show, though I do not entirely follow the argument, that a similar charge may be laid against the door of Nagarjuna, but even if we accept that Nagarjuna is an authentic representative of mainstream Buddhism, hardly a controversial suggestion, we are, it seems to me, led to accept that the realm of causal relations works in a non-teleogic or, in process jargon, in a symmetric manner. There can be no emergent novelty, no creative freedom and "no cumulative or incremental change in the structure of reality."[63] Whitehead and his followers, on the other hand hold to an asymmetric causal process in which past events are creatively synthesised at each node of the process such that the many become one and are increased by one.[64] This emergent togetherness, a creative advance into novelty, is at odds with the cosmic togetherness of Buddhist symmetrical arrangements. Cobb's Christian enviromental ethic is clearly built on this principle.

Neville[65] has argued that Buddhists would do well to take the principle of asymmetry on board. Of course, this would supply a much needed teleological element, not the straightforward pre-existing or supratemporal *telos* of traditional Christianity but, nevertheless, an idea of emergent purpose. Not unsurprisingly, in that it solves a substantial dilemma, Macy argues that this is the position of archaic Buddhism, though in the discussion leading up to this point she admits her debt to both process thought [66] and to general systems theory.[67] Perhaps,

61. Neville, *op. cit.*, 133, quoting from T.J.J. Altizer, "The Buddhist Ground of the Whiteheadian God", *Process Studies*, 5.4, 1975, 227-236.
62. C. Hartshorne, "Whitehead's Differences from Buddhism", in *PEW,* 25.4, 1975, 407-413. Also *cf.* C. Hartshorne "Toward a Buddhistico-Christian Religion", in K. K. Inada & N. P. Jacobson, eds., *Buddhism and American Thinkers*, Albany, 1984, p. 2-13.
63. Odin, *op. cit.*, 70-1.
64. *ibid.*
65. *op cit.*, 123.
66. Macy, *Mutual Causality in Buddhism and General Systems Theory: The Dharma of Natural Systems*, 177.
67. *ibid.*, 208-9.

knowing full well the difficulties of imposing a full teleology on Buddhism, she uses the term "telenomic or telic"[68] to define the principle.

In conclusion then, Eco-Buddhism, in its most developed form to date (i.e. in the work of Macy *et als*) is informed by a variety of extraneous factors. On the Buddhist side, it accepts *pratītyasamutpāda* as the central element of the Buddha's teaching though in a symmetric i.e. non-linear form not characteristic of the ancient sources. Then, in order to protect the activist message of engaged Buddhism, a telenomic principle of emergent purpose is introduced, probably from the direction of process theology. This is quite an intriguing procedure, and represents an attempt, though not a fully successful attempt, to steer a middle path between the two extremes of monism and complete pluralism, which is after all the Pali canonical position on causality.[69] Ecologic activity is seen as a function of 'seeing things as they are', i.e. as interdependent, yet Macy and her co-workers fail to offer, and in fact seem often to reject, any special soteriological method that might be used to achieve this vision despite the fact that this was, for the Buddha himself, an arduous and lengthy process.[70] The only necessary requirement in order to receive a vision of the world *sub specie aeternitatis* is something "very close to the religious concept of grace."[71] The parallels with Spinoza are very clear here. The final debt of Eco-Buddhism is to deep ecology, particularly to its reformulation of the Spinozan *conatas*, yet Arne Naess' concept of self-realisation as expansion to the furthest limits of the cosmos certainly appears rather too *vedantic* to fit our Buddhist context.

Despite the problems, which I hope that I have successfully indicated, the generality of Eco-Buddhist views have received significant endorsement from a variety of influential directions, not least from H. H. The Dalai Lama[72] himself. As such they represent an important and perhaps seminal American appropriation of Buddhism and clearly require further examination.

---

68. *ibid.*
69. S, II, 77; *cf.* also Y. Karunadasa, *Buddhist Analysis of Matter*, Columbo, Department of Cultural Affairs, 1967, 175-6.
70. On the necessity for training to 'see' *pratītyasamtpāda cf.* S, II, 131-2.
71. Macy, in A. Hunt-Badiner, ed., *Dharma Gaia: A Harvest of Eddays in Buddhism and Ecology,* Berkeley, 1990, 63.
72. H.H. Dalai Lama "Forward", dated 9 February 1990, to A. Hunt-Badiner, *op. cit.*.

The *Vinaya*
Legal System or Performance-Enhancing Drug?

Andrew Huxley

What can a lawyer say about the Pāli canon? If the lawyer happens to be T.W. Rhys David, the answer is "a lot". Although a lawyer by profession, he preferred to expound doctrinal and historical matters. Buddhism for him was an escape from the nit-picking legalisms of the colonial bureaucracy. Perhaps this point may be generalised: most westerners who are drawn to Buddhism are in search of the exotic as well as the true. They tend to dislike the "legalistic" *Vinaya* and the "scholastic" *Abidhamma* because, though true, these most nearly approach European forms of intellectual discourse. It is not surprising, then, that *Vinaya* studies are a comparatively neglected corner of Buddhology. What is surprising, in a world which still thinks of law as a masculine profession, is that women have written the leading works in this field[1]. So what can we lawyers say about the *Vinaya*? We have tended to concentrate on the *Suttavibhanga* rather than on the *Khandaka*: we have been more interested in the *Vinaya* as a duty-imposing criminal law than as an institution-creating constitutional law. We have analysed the saṅgha's legal procedures and punishments to the near exclusion of its claims about power and authority. In this paper, I take the less trodden path. By doing so I hope, to suggest explanations for the success of the *Vinaya*. Hammurabi's legislation may be older, Justinian's *Digest* more informative about its sources, but the *Vinaya*, unlike them, is still in force. It continues to govern the daily behaviour of thousands of people and continues to produce its own specialists and literature. Which of its qualities have contributed to its survival? The apparent answer is: precisely those qualities which are the least legal. Law operates by way of sticks—"Do this, or you'll go to prison"—while the *Vinaya* operates by way of carrots—"Do this, and you're one step nearer to enlightenment". Law, with its heirarchy of courts, can dispose

---

1. I.B. Horner, *The Book of Discipline*, London, PTS, 1938-52; D. Bhagvat, *Early Buddhist Jurisprudence,* Poona, Oriental Book Agency, 1939. Male contributions include: J. Holt, *Discipline: The Canonical Buddhism of the Vinayapiṭaka,* Delhi, Motilal Banarsidass, 1981; M. Voyce, "The Legal Aspects of Early Buddhist *Vinaya*", PhD thesis, Law Department SOAS, held by the Senate House Library, London, 1982.

of questions finally while *Vinaya* disputes can rumble on undecided for millenia. The *Vinaya*, I am tempted to say, has outlasted Hammurabi and Justinian because it is a set of spiritual exercises rather than a legal system. But what would Loyola or à Kempis think of a set of spiritual exercises offering an analysis of 25 kinds of theft? Or an analysis of *mens rea* into motive and intention which matches many contemporary codes in sophistication? My problem with the *Vinaya* is that it will not fit comfortably into either of these categories. It is neither fish nor fowl.

The Pāli *Vinaya* (to which this paper is restricted) expresses the contrast between law and spiritual exercise by using two stock metaphors. *Vinaya* processes are compared either to a king giving judgement or to a doctor prescribing medicine. The medical trope sees the *Vinaya* as the super-drug, the anabolic steroid, which the trainer urges on his athletes to help them run that extra mile to *nibbāna* [M, I, 446]. This was probably not original to the Buddha (it is also found in the Jain monastic code[2]), but it conveniently encapsulates a message that the Buddha repeats endlessly in the *Suttapiṭaka*: "The training may be hard, it may be unpleasant, but it is good for you!" When the Buddha speaks in this way, he sounds like a parent urging a child to drink up the whole spoonful of medicine. But in other contexts he can sound the authentic legal note of e *cathedra* promulgation:

> "Then the lord gave Dhaniya, the potter's son, a lengthy telling-off for his misdeeds. 'Monks', he said, 'I set forth the following rule of training: If a monk should take what does not belong to him, then he suffers the penalty of defeat, provided that on similar facts he would be liable for flogging, prison or exile in the kings' courts.'" [Vin, III, 44][3].

This suggests one simple rule: we find the medical metaphor in the *Suttapiṭaka* and the legal metaphor in the *Vinayapiṭaka*. This is a useful starting point, but, given the haphazard way in which text has been assigned to each *Piṭaka*, and given the amount of material which is common to both, it is unlikely to be the whole truth. Another simple rule would focus on the Buddha's death: while the Buddha was alive he talked of the *Vinaya* as a drug, but after his death he was credited with speeches treating the *Vinaya* as law. I shall examine both these possibilities, but reject them. Pāli literature uses both metaphors to describe the

2. C. Caillat, *Atonements in the Ancient Rituals of the Jaina Monks*, Ahmedabad, LD Institute of Indology, 1975, 130.
3. All quotations from the Pāli are my paraphrase of the standard English translations found in the Pali Text Society and the Sacred Books of the Buddhists series. This unscholarly procedure is bound to introduce some inaccuracies (as I don't read Pāli), but it has one advantage. Since I indicate what I want the texts to say in my own words, it will be easier for the reader to judge whether I have mistaken the meaning of the English translation or drawn wrong conclusions from it.

Vinaya because the nature of the *Vinaya* is poised halfway between the medical and the legal model. In the first half of this paper I shall examine this proposition in four of its aspects. In the second half, I shall offer an account of the institutional rivalry in which the Pāli approach to the *Vinaya* was honed. I derive my account from an analysis of three familiar texts which discuss the implications of the Buddha's death.

1.a. Obedience

One implication of the contrast between law and medicine relates to obedience. There is a difference between taking the doctor's advice and obeying the jurist's rule. I take the medicine which the doctor has prescribed for teleological reasons: the doctor and I share the aim of improving my health and I understand him to be the better informed partner in our joint enterprise. But I obey a rule of law for reasons of legitimacy or authority. In Weber's celebrated analysis, we classify these reasons as either traditional ("because we've always done it this way"), rational ("because it makes sense to do it this way") or charismatic ("because my hero has told me to start doing it this way"). The *Vinayapiṭaka* appeals to all three of these arguments. Each rule has been kitted out with an account of the occasion on which the Buddha promulgated it (its own charismatic legitimation) and the circumstances (its own rational legitimation in terms of policy). Some of the rules are also justified in traditional terms: "this is what hermits in general do" or "this is what past Buddhas have ordained as correct behaviour". It shows us a codifying Buddha who is not quite a god-like king like Hammurabi, nor an appointed sage like Solon, but who recognisably belongs to the same club of charismatic legal innovators. The *Suttapiṭaka*, however, portrays him as a salesman, a purveyor of snake-oil, who must persuade volunteers—against their natural inclinations—to submit to a rigorous discipline. In short, he is a doctor who must first persuade his patients that they are ill, and then persuade them that he knows the cure. He must use rhetoric and public relations ploys to achieve this end. Notice the way in which he creates a climate of opinion:

> "Kassapa, I speak in praise of the monk who ... himself speaks in praise of the training. I praise the monk who persuades others to commit themselves to the training, who expounds its true virtues to the right people at the right time. I do this so that my praise will persuade other monks to spend time with him and adopt his ideas. This will be for their long-term benefit." [A, I, 238].

And notice how testimonials from satisfied customers appear at regular intervals:

> "Lord, when you told us to give up eating after midday, I was distressed. But when I recalled the unpleasant scrapes I used to get into when begging for alms after dark, I realised that you had made us happier and

> wiser." "And yet, Udayin, some silly people accuse me of overdoing the austerities!" [M, I, 448].

Such testimonials come from monks who have had glimpses of what it might be like to validate the Buddha's new causal theories through visionary experience. The Buddha himself can prescribe with confidence because he can see the connections between our morality, our psychology and our future.

From this angle, the Buddha seems more like a scientist than a legislator. His conclusion that five grievous sins lead straight to hell in this lifetime is based on his own observations [Vin, II, 201; A, I, 402]. Experimental data also led him to state that the four *pārājika* offences render a monk immediately unfit for meditation and the monastic life. The relationship between law and natural science raises tricky legal theoretical problems which I would prefer to sidestep. For our present purposes, let us think of the Buddha as the inventor of a game. We must accept his rules if we want to play his game: *nibbāna* means winning, and *pārājika* means losing. Only if we share the Buddha's aim should we follow his prescriptions:

> "If, monks, you observe the training in full, you will attain your object in full. If you observe partially, you will attain your object partially. I must emphasise that these rules of training do not fail to work." [A, I, 234].

We must obey the *Vinaya* rules in blind faith so that they will lead us to a state of mind which allows us to see why we were obeying them. To encourage us to make this leap of faith we are told of others who successfully followed the Buddha's training. Sona, having just experienced enlightenment, describes his experience to the Buddha, rather like a post-graduate student giving an oral defence of his thesis [Vin, I, 183]. He has learnt to concentrate on six things, one of which is the contrast between non-violence based on the essence and non-violence "due to the contagion of habit and custom" [*sīlabbataparāmāsa*]. Buddhaghosa glosses this fascinating expression as "the mere holding on to what is held onto, having rubbed up against moral habit and custom (as though this was enough)". I take this to mean that you know the medicine has finally worked when you cease thinking of it as law: when you do the right thing because you want to do it ["based on the essence"] rather than through mere obedience. This is the strongest statement I have found of the proposition that the *Vinaya* should be viewed as medicine rather than law: thinking of it as law is part of the very mindset which the medicine is designed to cure! That this occurs in the "legalistic" *Vinaya* rather than the "medical" *Suttapiṭaka* indicates the inadequacy of my first rule of thumb.

1.b. Two or three party procedures

Legal dispute-settlement characteristically involves three parties (two quarrelers and a judge) while medical problem-solving characteristically takes place between two (the doctor and the patient). Typical of the way the *Vinaya* straddles the division between law and medicine is that it envisages both models. *Vinaya* procedure is two-party for the good monk, but three party for the bad monk. By "good monk", I mean one who is both self-referring (he approaches his *Vinaya* teacher when worried that he might have committed an offence) and self-sanctioning (he will take whatever medicine he is prescribed). Buddhaghosa describes the procedure in relation to masturbation:

> "If a *bhikkhu* becomes guilty he must go to the *Vinaya* teacher who ... admonishes him: "I am like a physician, you are like a patient ... you must tell me each and everything ... There are eleven kinds of masturbation."[4]

In the least important breaches of discipline such self-referring, or confession, becomes its own sanction: it is good for the monk's mental development [M, I, 440]. In more serious cases, a public act of confession may be necessary, or a loss of seniority or a week's banishment from the monastery. Such sanctions have to be voluntarily undertaken, whereas the four most serious cases lead automatically to defeat. Their *kammic* effects are such that, though you may continue dressing like a monk and living like a monk, you can no longer meditate like a monk. Having lost your *raison d'être*, you should slink quietly back into lay life. If, nonetheless, you try to stay on, then the *saṅgha* can perform an act of formal expulsion, publicising the defeat that has already taken place, or, with less formality, it can simply refuse to acknowledge you[5]. Any monk good enough to be self-referring will be good enough to admit defeat, even when the bad news is broken as gently as this:

> "If [the senior *Vinaya* master] finds that there has been an offence of defeat ... he should give the *bhikkhu* thirty objects of meditation. If his conduct is unblemished ... he can enter *samādhi*. When it becomes dark the *Vinaya* master visits him ... 'Good friend, how is the state of your mind?' The *bhikkhu* replies 'No *samādhi*'. The *Vinaya* master says 'Good friend, you have to seek for yourself, as is befitting for you, some place where you can rest in peace.'"[6]

---

4. Smp, 359-362 = XII, 67-76. Since I am using P. Bapat & A. Hirakawa's translation of the Chinese version [*Shan-Chien-P'i-P'o-Sha, A Chinese Version by Saṅghabhadra of Samantapāsādikā*, Poona, Bhandarkar Oriental Research Institute, 1970.] all references to *Samantapāsādikā* are in this form: the page number of their translation is followed by the equivalent chapter and paragraph number of the Pāli original.
5. Buddhaghosa lists these three possibilities as "personal ruin by one's own actions, ruin by disassociation and ruin by punishment"; Smp, 386-7 = XIII.44.
6. Smp, 177 = VI.61.

In brief, the good monk submits to the will of the *saṅgha*, meaning his disciplinary community, the body of monks with whom he shares a *sīma*. His catchphrase should be, "What may I do to please the *saṅgha*?" [M, I, 443].

The bad monk is not self-referring: he tries to conceal his offences. If one of his colleagues accuses him, and if he then denies the charge, the *saṅgha* must step in as a third party judge to settle what, structurally speaking, has become a typically legal dispute. But "settle" is an inappropriate word when there is no Supreme Court of Buddhism to give a final judgement. The *Vinaya* is well aware that unsettled disputes can fester and lead to polarisation. It analyses the problem in its chapter "On the monks of Kosambī" but does not suggest a solution, unless we are to take the faithful laity as the Supreme Court of Buddhism:

> "Then the lay-followers of Kosambī neither greeted the monks, nor stood up before them, nor saluted them with joined palms ... they did not revere, respect, esteem or honour them and they did not give them almsfood ..." [Vin, I, 352].

But to recognise bluntly that the *saṅgha*, like Napoleon's army, marches on its stomach would be too great a loss of dignity. The *Vinaya* must protect its own autonomy by finding a solution that leaves monks in charge. Its attempts to do so are described in *Cullavagga IV*. The disputants must agree to be bound by arbitration. Contractual principles must make up for the absence of jurisdictional finality:

> "When monks go to another monastery for a ruling, they must agree to be bound by the decision, or the monks won't hear their case. If the disputants will still not agree, then a verdict by referendum can be given. Two *Vinaya* experts are appointed by order to conduct the referendum. If they cannot settle it by committee, they can use a majority vote. If the disputants go from monastery to monastery forum-shopping in search of a favourable verdict, then they must be convinced that the legal issue is settled for good by the three methods of taking the vote: the secret, the whispering in the ear, the open." [Vin, II, 92-8].

Buddhaghosa demonstrates how to wage psychological warfare against the bad monk until he agrees to be bound:

> "If the accuser and the accused approach the *saṅgha* asking for a decision, and they agree to follow its decision, the *saṅgha* can proceed. But otherwise they must be delayed three times[7] until the accuser's mind is pliable and properly subdued. If they still refuse to be bound by the decision, the *saṅgha* must say: 'This place is too small, no *Vinaya* teacher

7. Could this possibly mean "three days"?

> is available here: go to another monastery.' At the other monastery they will, after questioning, send the disputants on to a third, and so on, until they say: 'We shall gladly abide by your decision.'"[8]

Notice here that his accuser is considered equally reprehensible. To insist on the guilt of others is nearly as bad as to break a *Vinaya* rule. Anyone with an inquisitorial approach to his fellows is more than half way to acquiring a reputation for shamelessness.

A monk who does not refer himself for judgement is unlikely to punish himself after judgement:

> "Even at the third time of asking, the monk stayed silent and would not budge from the assembly. Then, Moggallāna seized him by the arm, thrust him outside the porch and bolted the door ... The Exalted One said 'It is very strange, Moggallāna, that that foolish person should have waited till he was seized by the arm.'" [Vin, II, 236].

This occurs at a significant moment: the Buddha is preparing his disciples to carry on after his death by instructing them in the fortnightly ritual of *Pāṭimokkha* recitation. On this occasion, he was certainly thinking of the *Vinaya* as law rather than medicine - the rules have been organised into the Pāṭimokkha code and Moggallāna, the role model for Buddhist bouncers, is there to enforce them. But it is by no means the only occasion on which the *saṅgha* applies violent sanctions:

> "'Off you go, Sāriputta and Moggallāna. Carry out a formal act of banishment from Kitagiri against those monks who follow Assaji and Punabbasu.' 'But, Lord, these monks are fierce and rough'. 'Then take a crowd of monks with you.'" [Vin, II, 11].

Muscular Buddhism (meaning the Shaolin temple traditions in China and the *pwe* monasteries of Burma which taught wrestling and sword-fighting) can find canonical justification in this passage. The legitimacy of violent *Vinaya* sanctions can also be supported by a simile which Ghokale describes as "almost a cliché within the canon":

> "Good to bad monks are like rulers and robbers—when one is strong, the other is weak." [A, I. 69; D, I, 115].

This must imply that good monks, like kings, have to wield the big stick of punishment. They must form a posse or inquisition:

> "There are monks who make their living in one of the twenty one acquisitive ways, such as practising medicine, acting as messengers, or usury ... They hear that monks who know the Three *Piṭakas* have set out on a mission to purify the *Sāsana* and will arrive today or tomorrow;

---

8. Smp, 390 = XIII.50-51.

> they go into the forest and sit behind a bush, and at the slightest sound of grass or leaf they are terrified, thinking 'Now we are lost', for they imagine those monks coming and catching them and making them put on white clothes."[9]

How effective is such an expulsion from the order? How long will the bad monk, X, stay in his white clothes? Both the local monasteries and the laity in the local villages will know that X has suffered defeat and been disrobed. But, if X is prepared to travel to a new region, there is no institution that can stop him getting hold of new saffron robes and presenting himself once more as a monk. Lay criminals can escape their reputation in much the same way, save that the judicial institutions of branding and amputation perform an advisory function. The defeated monk is branded in his mind, and only arahants have the necessary mental insight to recognise this. This begets a deep uncertainty within the *saṅgha*: a fellow monk may, as the Buddha warned, in fact be a layman:

> "As an ass can follow the herd of cows pretending to be one, so a 'monk' can pretend to be a monk." [A, I, 229]. "Though he sits in the middle of the assembled *saṅgha*, he is far away from it and it is far away from him." [A, IV, 201].

And any formal act of the *saṅgha* at which X was present must be regarded as void, having been carried out in the presence of a layman. If the formal act of the *saṅgha* happened to be a punishment directed against Y, Y has a perfect reason for ignoring it. In such circumstances, Kassapagotta had to ask the Buddha:

> "Is the punishment enacted against me *dhammika* [legitimate], *kuppa* [void] or *ṭhānāraha* [voidable]?" [Vin, I, 312].

But once the Buddha had passed into final *nibbāna*, no-one could definitively answer such questions. If Kassapagotta had lived a century later, he would have been left in doubt forever as to whether he was an ass or a cow. The pupils whom he had ordained and subsequent generations of his lineage would have had to memorise the details of the dispute and argue it afresh whenever their status was put in question. It is not surprising that contemporary Theravāda Buddhism sets so much store by ordination lineages which include reports of bygone *Vinaya* disputes: they are what you must have if you do not have a "Supreme Court of Buddhism". This lack of finality is one of the most important ways in which the *Vinaya* is not a legal system and one of the senses in which records of *Vinaya* disputes are not "case law" or "precedent". To state the difference formally: legal precedents accumulate arguments that will be

---

9. R. Gombrich, *Theravāda Buddhism: A Social History from Ancient Benares to Modern Colombo*, London, Routledge & Kegan Paul, 1988, 110, quoting Buddhaghosa's *Papañcasūdanī*.

useful in future similar cases. The position of the judge in the state heirarchy of courts is more important than his individual reputation for wisdom. The authority of legal precedent is based on the degree of similarity to the instant case. *Vinaya* precedents tell of decisions which are generally useless for the decision of future cases. Because there is no heirarchy (state or other), the purpose of the stories is to enhance an individual scholar's reputation for wisdom or to discredit his rival's reputation. They identify those trustworthy scholars of the past whose interpretations of the canon deserve the utmost consideration today.

1.c. General application

Characteristic of the legal model is that rules should apply to all citizens. "No-one should park here" is regarded as a better law than "No-one except Volvo drivers should park here". But medicine dare not deal in rules of general application: though penicillin is usually a useful drug, some people are allergic to it. "Most patients will find this treatment beneficial" is about as near as you can get to a rule in medical circles. That monks should be "trained in the training", that they should obey more of the *Vinaya* rules as they gain strength for further austerities, is a common theme in the canon. The dialogue between Bhaddāli and the Buddha [M, I, 437-47] discusses the jurisprudential implications of this. When the Buddha announces a new regime of one meal a day maximum, Bhaddāli does not think that he can manage it. The Buddha suggests that he wrap up a sandwich which he can eat in private later, but Bhaddāli now evinces the pride of the victimised—eating dinner is not enough: he must be seen in public to be eating dinner. For the whole three months of the rainy season, he lives apart from the community in disgrace. He apologises and gains re-admission just before the Buddha moves off on his annual travels. Bhaddāli submits to the Buddha's law-making, and is consoled by a conversation in which the Buddha agrees with his denigration of law-making. So far so good. The Buddha was willing to bend the rules a little for Bhaddāli, but not to grant him a public exemption. However, we must not expect consistency from an Omniscient Being. The next time a monk challenges the *Vinaya,* the Buddha gives in completely. When an anonymous Vajjian monk complains about having to recite more than 150 rules each fortnight:

> "Lord, I cannot stand such a training!" [A, I, 230].

The Buddha allows him to pursue the threefold training in higher morality, higher thought and higher insight, unmediated by the rules of the *Vinaya*. The Vajjian monk, having abandoned lust, malice and delusion for good, reaches the same point that others reach by diligently following the *Vinaya.* An alternative route to the legalisms of the *Vinaya* exists, but the Buddha only allows it to some. What has happened to such legal qualities as the universal applicability of rules, due process and fairness in application? As Bhaddāli puts it:

> "Your Reverence, why are some monks round here subject to constant legal harassment while others get off with an easy ride?" [M, I, 442].

The Buddha replies that it is those who cooperate with their accusers who get an easy ride. The ones who complain of legal harassment are the ones who will not say "What may I do to please the *saṅgha*?" To lawyers, this is ominously reminiscent of the commonest justification for torture, brutality and human rights abuse. But doctors might judge it more positively: those who refuse to take their medicine do not get better so quickly. The Buddha, in his omniscience, is the perfect prescriber of medicine. He knows that that which will speed recovery for the Vajjian monk might be poison to Bhaddāli. The *Vinaya* itself is too strong a medicine for certain monks with borderline faith and will-power. They need special treatment just as in lay life the disabled need special treatment [M, I, 444].

If the *Vinaya's* function is to help monks reach *nibbāna*, Bhaddāli's next question cuts at the roots of the whole enterprise:

> "What is the reason, your Reverence, why there were formerly fewer *Vinaya* rules and more monks who were established in profound knowledge? And why is the opposite now the case?" [M, I, 444-5].

Astonishingly, the Buddha accepts the factual basis of Bhaddāli's question and attempts to explain it:

> "The answer, Bhaddāli, is that the preponderance of rules and the scarcity of enlightened monks are both symptoms of the general deterioration in true *dhamma* and in life itself."

Small is beautiful. Though the *saṅgha* has no governmental heirarchy, once it reaches a certain size, it will develop a heirarchy of esteem. Once the well-endowed monk, the famous monk, the intellectually self-confident monk and the monk proud of his seniority appear on the scene, so do the blotches (*āsavas*) which prevent enlightenment. The *Vinaya* is designed precisely to remove these blotches, and is, therefore, an epiphenomenon of our troubled times. But so, we are told in the *Aggañña-sutta*, is the emergence of kingship, taxation and state-law. At this point in the cycle of world ages, we must all — monks and laity alike — put up with law. We have fallen from the Golden Age, the pre-juristic Eden. In Buddhism as in Marxism, law is specific to a certain stage in the development of human society. This historicist perspective means that neither the Buddha nor Marx need take law as seriously as liberal theorists do. People have got on without law in the past and will get on without law in the future. Law is not a deep part of being human and thus requires only superficial explanation.

1.d. Anarchy, ahiṃsā and autonomy

So far I have been conducting an exercise in literary appreciation: what is signified by the tropes of the *Vinaya* as law, the *Vinaya* as a drug? Let us shift the enquiry into the realm of theory by asking how the *Vinaya* relates to the three abstract nouns which head this section. Is the *saṅgha* anarchic? Is it non-violent? Is it autonomous? The answer to the first question, at anything above the micro-level, is a clear "yes". Beyond what takes place within the *sīma*, the *saṅgha* has no bureaucratic structure whatsoever. "The *Saṅgha* of the Four Quarters" is a pious fantasy. After the Buddha's death there was no person, no committee, no triennial conference which could speak for the *saṅgha* as a whole. The second question is almost as easy to answer. When dealing with "good monks" who impose sanctions on themselves, the *saṅgha* can afford to be non-violent. But when purging the order of "bad monks" the Buddha approved of whatever violence was necessary. Can such violence properly be called a sanction? Organised government, sensing a threat to its monopoly on punitive violence, tends to decry these acts as "lynch law" or "mob justice". This is mere propaganda. An anarchist community cannot have executions (which need an executioner who must be appointed by a government) or imprisonment (since prisons must be built and staffed by a government), but it does have access to a limited range of sanctions which depend on the mobilisation of popular anger and disapproval. Public shaming rituals (*charivari* or "rough music") is one such, and the forced social isolation of an offender (*brahmadaṇḍa* or "sending to Coventry") is another. The most important is ad hoc crowd violence, as in: "But Lord, these monks are fierce and rough!" "Then take a crowd of monks with you." In Burma, in the 1690s and again in the 1870s, monks from rival lineages fought in the streets. From their point of view, they were not infringing the virtue of *ahiṃsā*: they were engaged in a vigorous enforcement of the *Vinaya* by forcibly defrocking shameless monks. The third question—whether the *saṅgha* is autonomous—needs further explanation, since "autonomy" has become a legal buzz-word. To lawyers, an autonomous institution means firstly a self-regulating institution, secondly an institution which has carved out its own methodology and epistemology and thirdly an institution which has become a self-referential closed circuit or, as the latest wave of German social theorists puts it, an "auto-poietic" system[10]. The *saṅgha* at the local level is self-regulating: it can generally take care of itself. King Pasenadi was describing the *saṅgha* during the Buddha's lifetime, but his comments aptly describe most *saṅghas* most of the time:

---

10. For an introduction to Luhmann and Teubner's thought, see M.King, "The Truth about Autopoiesis", *JLS*, 20, 1993, 218-236.

> "When I am hearing a case, people interrupt me ... they spit and they cough. But when the Lord teaches *dhamma* to his disciples, they keep themselves in order. Indeed, it is striking how well-behaved the *saṅgha* is without *daṇḍa*, without the threat of the sword." [D, II, 122].

As for the second sense, I have no problem regarding the 2500 year succession of *Vinaya* experts and authors as an autonomous intellectual community. Indeed a major thrust of my South East Asian research is to describe how "*Vinaya*-thinking" influenced and inspired the state-law of Theravāda Buddhist kings: it is in this sense that we can talk about Pāli Buddhism as having a strong and influential legal tradition. As to "auto-poiesis", perhaps I can rephrase the issue thus: is the *Vinaya* in fact as self-sufficient as it claims? Or does it rely on unacknowledged help from outside its own closed system? Selvanayagam suggests that something is missing:

> "Further, as we learn from life in Buddhist *saṅghas* and from the rule of Asoka, punishment and some form of violence were unavoidable. But there seems to be no discussion about their degree and procedures."[11]

What is missing, he explains, is state enforcement and, he implies, it is therefore perfectly proper that in Sri Lanka, Burma and Thailand the state purports to exercise control over the local *saṅgha*. I am not convinced. At the local level Buddhism's approach to legitimate force may not be neat and tidy but, on the whole, it has worked. State control of the *saṅgha*, whether by Asoka in Mauryan India or by SLORC in contemporary Burma, seems to me an unwarranted intrusion on the order's autonomy rather than a necessary intervention to prop up the *saṅgha's* inherent weakness. To echo Rousseau—the *saṅgha* was born free but everywhere it is in chains. If the *saṅgha* does rely on unacknowledged help from outside its ranks, it is the faithful laity who supply it. Much more important than the very occasional royal purifications of the *saṅgha* were the quotidian acts of purification which the laity carried out. I have already cited the laity of Kosambī starving out the quarrelsome monks. This is not the optimum behaviour of a lay supporter, who should feed good and bad monks indiscriminately [A. IV. 212] but it is a predictable and effective way of pressurising defeated monks. We could think of it as "bottom-up purification" as opposed to the "top-down purifications" of Asoka and Parākramabāhu. Such acts are not going to be recorded in rock-edicts or chronicles. That they occurred throughout Buddhist history has to be inferred from a few scattered references, as for instance from this comment on 19th century Burma:

> "A monk is one who acts as a monk. Directly he breaks his laws, his holiness is gone. The villagers will have none such as he. They will hunt

11. I. Selvanayagam, "Asoka and Arjuna as Counterfigures on the Field of Dharma", *HR*, 32, 1992, 59-75, 74.

> him out of the village, they will refuse him food, they will make him a byword, a scorn. I have known this to happen."[12]

A recently published survey reaches the same conclusion:

> "It is important to note that just as the laity play an important role within *Suttavibhaṅga* literature by reporting infractions of discipline to the Buddha, so has the laity in modern times continued to display great interest in insuring that the *saṅgha* adheres to the *Vinaya*."[13]

2. The Pāli constitutional literature

The constitutional literature of Pāli Buddhism reveals a consistent set of preoccupations and beliefs. Just as we can attempt to reconstruct the doctrinal and philosophical positions of the 18 schools from the *Katthāvatthu's* denunciation of them, so we can infer a rival tradition against which the constitutional texts were composed. The claims about power and authority could not have become as precise as they are now unless they had been honed by honest argument with another *saṅgha*. I shall attempt to reconstruct the nature of that challenge by taking backbearings from the positions which the Pāli canon adopts. I hope my list of constitutional documents will not strike the reader as too eccentric: it consists of *Cullavagga VII* on schism, *Cullavagga XI* on the First Council and the *Mahāparinibbāna-sutta.*

Cullavagga VII is an action-packed popular drama, an epic in three acts designed to burn its way into the popular memory when recited or performed—Homer would have called it "The Upāliad" or "The Wrath of Devadatta". It is not just a highly structured work of art: it playfully flaunts its structural armature at the beginning and end of its text. These bookends which support the main narrative both feature Upāli, who is otherwise absent from events. At the start Mahānāma persuades his brother that they should leave home to follow the Buddha, and his brother then has to persuade Bhaddiya, their boss, to do the same. Bhaddiya offers to come in 7 years' time, alright, make it 6, what would you say to 5? perhaps we could agree on 4? This countdown runs all the way from 7 years to 1 year, 7 months to 1 month, half a month, then half a fortnight which is, of course, 7 days. It gives us notice that numbers are important to the work, and that the descending sequence from 7 to 1 governs the shape of the text. The countdown also builds up tension for the arrival of Upāli, who is suddenly transformed from personal servant to the 6 Sakyan nobles to seniormost of the newly ordained 7 monks. Twenty pages later, Upāli reappears for the climax where he joins the Buddha in a count up from 3+1 to 8+1 which defines the precise distinction between dissension and schism in the *saṅgha*.

---

12. H. Fielding, *The Soul of a People*, London, MacMillan, 1898, 147.
13. K.L. Hazra, *Pāli Language and Literature*, Emerging Perceptions in Buddhist Studies, no. 5, New Delhi, D.K. Printworld, 1994, vol.1, 135.

From a *Vinaya* point of view, this final conversation between the Buddha and Upāli is the point of the whole epic. The rise and fall of Devadatta has merely been an extra-long framing story, the moral of which is to lay down the point at which dissent becomes schism. Bearing in mind that Devadatta's schism has earned him an aeon in hell, the final words of the sutta are remarkably upbeat: "good schismatics" who do not misrepresent their opponents or manipulate public opinion will avoid Devadatta's fate.

The main narrative hangs on descending numerical pegs. In the first act we start with 6 + 1 (6 Sakyan Don Qixotes + Upāli, their Sancho Panza), and proceed via a 5 + 1 analogy (5 Television Evangelists + the Buddha) to 4 + 1 similes (4 similes for the causal link between Devadatta's ambitions and his imminent destruction). The second act with its three attempted Buddhicides culminates in a 3 + 1 plot (Kokālika, Kaṭamorakatissaka and Samuddadatta agree to join Devadatta in his plan to split the *saṅgha*). And the climax of act three, to which Devadatta's consignment to hell is a mere postscript, is the 2 + 1 chase and gunfight (Devadatta has rustled 500 head of cattle and is heading for the border. Sāriputta and Moggallāna ride out of town to head him off.) Within this structure there is scope for improvisation. The author of *Cullavagga VII* has added plenty of inessential but entertaining business—the ghost spy in Act 1, the clashing rocks and the limping hero in Act 2, the town drunk who comically misinterprets Sāriputta's motives in Act 3. However it is staged, this script makes good popular entertainment: in 4th century India it would be performed by live actors at pagoda festivals, 18th century Burma would have staged it using puppets and these days Bertolucci could shoot it as a cowboy movie. It is great popular art, but are we also to treat it as history? Dramatic logic demands that every hero needs a villain to thwart. In the higher worlds Māra plays this role, and it is tempting to consider Devadatta as a human *avatār* of Māra conjured up by literary necessity. He is Moriarty to the Buddha's Holmes, Lex Luthor to the Buddha's Superman—a plot device rather than a historical figure. My reading of the constitutional texts has led me to resist this temptation. The texts argue against a rival organisation, and Devadatta is the most promising candidate for leader of that organisation. My premise is that Devadatta was a historical figure, a younger contemporary of the Buddha who was treated by a large part of the original *saṅgha* as Gautama's legitimate successor. I believe that the *saṅgha* did vote on the question of the five austerities, and that the majority voted on Devadatta's side. The defeated minority, the Elders, then withdrew to form their own *saṅgha* from whom all present-day Buddhists descend. Whether this split took place before or after the *parinibbāna,* I could not say. Whether Devadatta was really a cousin of the Buddha or even a fellow Sakyan, I do not know. I am fairly sure, however, that Devadatta continues to suffer the fires of hell until this aeon comes to an end: dramatic conventions demand it.

To change the subject completely, a newspaper article carried the news that the chairman of the Rugby Union and the chief executive of the Rugby League will undertake joint discussions later in the month:

> "It is the first time that senior representatives of the two codes have met on an official basis since the great schism of 1895 when rugby league was founded."[14]

Here is a voluntary organisation which split a century ago in such acrimony that until recently the two halves did not explicitly recognise each other's existence. But implicitly they had to do so, since they had to develop "conflict of law" rules. Players sometimes switch from one code to the other, so each side must have rules governing the conversion process. These need not be the same: the League might let Union players straight in, while the Union might refuse to admit League players or makes them wait in limbo for a specified time. The development of such rules represents an implicit dialogue between the codes: a jockeying for prestige whereby the code with the stricter conversion rules could claim to be "the senior code". The battle for prestige is also pursued by representing your weak points as virtues: if the Union denounces the League for having broken the precept against taking gold and silver, the League can reply that the Union members are effete southern scum who do not have to work for a living. Another important factor is the precise history of the schism in 1895. Which of the rivals can claim institutional continuity with the united organisation of 1894? Who has physical possession of the minute books, the memorabilia, the relics of William Webb Ellis?

These issues—the rules for conversion, the jockeying for prestige, the claim to institutional continuity—are the main themes of the Pāli constitutional literature. Both sides claim institutional continuity with the pre-split *saṅgha* in which the Buddha was *primus inter pares* and Devadatta was recognised as "of great psychic power, of great majesty" [Vin, II, 188]. The Elders portray Devadatta as Jung to the Buddha's Freud: he was a brilliant pupil who went off the rails, resigned and founded a new organisation. The Devadattans must have painted the Elders as the new organisation—as Franco to the Spanish Republicans in 1937 or as the Provisional IRA to the Official IRA in 1973. I infer that the Devadattan claim rested on viewing the *saṅgha* as an elective democracy. If the majority so voted, new precepts could be added to the *Pāṭimokkha*. And if the majority voted for Devadatta as the new *saṅgharājā*, then *vive le roi*! There does not appear to be anything anachronistic or non-Indian about such an

---

14. O. Slot, "End in Sight to Rugby's 100-year War", *Independent On Sunday*, 8/01/1995, Sports Section, page 1.

election: the prime minister of Magadha naturally assumes that if the Buddha did not nominate his successor, the *saṅgha* would elect one themselves. He has great difficulty understanding Ānanda's concept of a *saṅgha* ruled by *dhamma* [M, III, 7]. Ānanda has to justify it by emphasising the very special qualities of the Buddha:

> "The Buddha blazed a new trail, he was the progenitor of a new spiritual lineage, he was author of a wholly new book - none of us can match that achievement." [M, III, 15].

But emphasising the Buddha's uniqueness is the first step towards deifying him. When the Elders credit the Buddha with the power to prolong his life almost indefinitely [D, II, 104], they are treading dangerous ground: virtual immortality is not normally a human characteristic. And when the Buddha's skin shines forth brighter than gold [D. II. 133], this recalls the iconography of Indian gods rather than human heroes. One of the few things we know about Devadattan doctrine is that they made "offerings to the three past Buddhas but not to Sākyamuni"[15]. For them, Gautama may not even have been the founder of the *saṅgha*, but merely one of a succession of the *saṅgha's* human leaders. The Devadattan loyalty was to the *saṅgha* which the Buddha once headed. Their claim to institutional continuity depended on the assertion: "we are what the original *saṅgha* has decided to become". The Elders' claim to institutional continuity had to be based on fidelity to the Buddha's intentions: "we are what the Buddha intended the original *saṅgha* to be". Hence, the leitmotif of their constitutional literature is "we have added nothing, we have taken nothing away."

Imagine a debate between these two positions. If I were briefed to argue the Devadattan case, I would put it thus:

> "The Enlightened One said that he did not aspire to lead the *saṅgha*. Yet you Elders behave as if his views on right training were an unalterable code of the *Vinaya*. You are treating him as a posthumous codifier. You regard him *ex post facto* as the *saṅgharājā*. But if he was the *saṅgharājā*, why does he have no successor?"

To which the Elders must reply:

> "We do not slavishly follow the Sakyamuni as the chariot follows the horse: we are in charge of our own destiny. It is by our own joint decision that we Elders have chosen to follow the Buddha's rules without addition or subtraction."

This would explain the otherwise baffling tradition that the Buddha signified his willingness for the lesser and minor rules to be rescinded [Vin, II, 286; D, II, 154; Mil, 143]. The Elders have had to invent this tradition, and the subsequent

15. H. Giles, *The Travels of Fa-hsien*, Cambridge, Cambridge University Press, 1923, 36.

discussion of it at the First Council, in order to meet the Devadattan argument. Their response utilises a technique known to contemporary lawyers as "autocthonisation of the grundnorm". By the grundnorm, alias the ultimate rule of recognition, we mean the source of validity beyond which we cannot go. The Pāli canon locates it in Mahākāssapa and his 500 arahants:

> "I put the motion three times—that the *saṅgha* should neither promulgate new rules nor abolish old ones ... I interpret the *saṅgha's* silence to mean that it approves the motion." [Vin, II, 287].

Superficially this motion changes nothing, but it implies that the *saṅgha* has the power to change the rules, though they are not in fact exercising it. Thus it shifts the grundnorm from the Buddha to the First Council. In the last 15 years the governments of Australia and Canada have gone through exactly the same exercise: by passing new constitutions which were identical with the old constitutions, they have autocthonised their grundnorm from London to Canberra and Ottawa. Such was the Elders' reverence for the precepts of the Buddha that they had to arm themselves with the Buddha's express permission before daring to take this step.

We know that the Devadattans were prepared to add new rules to those laid down by the Buddha, but there is no evidence that they abrogated existing rules. If the Elders wish to place themselves on the moral high ground—if they want the rhetorical advantage of taking the middle path between two extremes—then they need another bogeyman to advocate the jettisoning of rules of training. It is this dialectic which brings Subhadda into existence:

> "Subhadda, who had become a monk in old age, said 'Enough tears, Gentlemen! Dry your eyes! We are well rid of the great master. He used to annoy us by saying: 'You should do this, you mustn't do that'. But henceforth we can please ourselves!'"[Vin, II, 283; D, II, 162].

If we treat Subhadda as historical, then we can identify him as the ideologue of anarcho-Buddhism (with the Chabbaggiyas as the direct action wing of the movement)[16]. But he strikes me as a stock fictional character. He is there as a contrast to Subhadda the Brahmin, the last of the Buddha's converts and the audience for the Buddha's last definition of orthodoxy ["Wherever the noble eightfold path is practised"]. The Pāli commentaries labour to add detail and depth to the portrait (his profession was barber, his former home was the town of Atuma, his animus against the *Vinaya* rules can be explained by identifying him

---

16. In some of the non-Pāli *Vinayas* the Chabbaggiya monks play a prominent part in the First Council. A very useful comparison of *Vinaya* traditions on this point is J. Dhirasekera, "The Rebels against the Codified Law in Buddhist Monastic Discipline", *Buddhist Studies* (*Bukkyō Kenkyū*), 1, 1970, 90-77.

with the anonymous monk at Vin, I, 248) but I am unconvinced[17]. "Good" Subhadda was ordained when the Buddha was old. The Buddha ordained "bad" Subhadda when Subhadda was old. "Good" Subhadda was the last to be preached to by the Buddha. "Bad" Subhadda was the first to renege on what the Buddha preached. He is a creation of the Elders' story-tellers, a convenient fiction who enables them to boast: "The Devadattans would add new rules, Subhadda would abrogate old rules but we take the middle track of nothing added, nothing taken away."

I now turn to consider the *Mahāparinibbāna-sutta* as a constitutional document. It is, admittedly, a great deal more than that. It has been described as "the Buddhist Gospel", as a "final recapitulation of familiar themes" and as "Scenes from the Life of a Travelling Preacher"[18]. Its tempo is a stately *Marche Funebre* as the Buddha falls ill in chapter 2, rejects the rest of his life in chapter 3, reaches the spot where he will die in chapter 4, arranges his funeral in chapter 5 and dies in chapter 6. Other elegiac themes are sounded: preparations for the forthcoming war between Magadha and the Vajjians dominate chapter 1. We hear of Pāṭaliputta, a great city to come, and Kusinārā, a great city long in the past. The *sutta* ends with several parties competing for control of the Buddha's remains, all of whom have to put up with an unsatisfactory compromise. I think of the *sutta* as "The Buddha Makes his Final Dispositions". He makes his last visit to familiar spots, sums up his message to the laity in the discourse at Pāṭaligāma and declares his last will and testament, his "instructions as touching the *saṅgha*", at D, II, 154, (in words clearly taken from *Cullavagga XI*) and at D, II, 100-1 in the familiar but still moving speech starting "Be ye lamps unto yourselves". If we think of the *sutta* as composed by the Elders to justify their position vis-à-vis the Devadattans, the message becomes: "Let *dhammavinaya* [rather than Devadatta] be your teacher". "Be ye lamps unto yourselves [rather than basking in Devadatta's artificial illumination]". For the Elders there will be no Pope of Buddhism, no Rightly-Guided-Imam of Buddhism, because Buddhism will be ruled by a text instead of a human. Tradition has made Devadatta into the Buddha's cousin to emphasise this point: even the Gautamids, the Buddha's relatives, have no special claim over the faithful.

Slipping back into my role as Devadatta's advocate, I would reply:

---

17. The process of embellishing this story continued into the 18th century. Badon's *rajathat* of 28/01/1795 (which I think was drafted by the 1st Maungdaung sayadaw) adds a detail that I have not found in earlier accounts: "Mahākāssapa on hearing Subhadda's words said that the old man should be disrobed, sprinkled with ash and exiled." Than Tun, "The Royal Order (Wednesday 28 January 1795) of King Badon", *JAAS*, 26, 1983, 153-201, 189.
18. S. Collins, *The Perfect Moral Commonwealth* (forthcoming), n.d.

"Fine. Ok. You have enthroned a text rather than a human being. But what happens when there is a dispute as to the interpretation of the text? Whose reading will prevail then?"

Rule by a constitutional document will necessarily degenerate into rule by the Supreme Court empowered to interpret it. It is to answer this point that the Buddha preached the four Great Authorities [D, II, 124]. His argument is, we would now say, Dworkinian[19]: he asserts that there is enough overall consistency in the *dhammavinaya* that different interpreters must agree on the answer to controversial questions. There is "One Right Answer" both to questions of interpretation and to questions of canonicity: a pseudo-*sutta* can be spotted by its inconsistency with the rest of the material. Not only is the canon internally consistent: it has been well-published. The episode in which Māra tells the Buddha to drop dead (and the Buddha agrees to do so!) has been included so that the Buddha can express his confidence that his followers are now "well trained, carrying the doctrinal books in their memory, masters of the lesser corollaries that follow from the larger doctrine, ... able to preach it to others, establish it, minutely explain it and make it clear." [D, II, 104]. Likewise the episode of Subhadda the 'good's' conversion, prominently placed at the end of the penultimate chapter, allows the Buddha to define the true doctrine—"Void are the systems of other teachers" [D, II, 151], to extol Sāriputta's guardianship of the lineage of the faith [D, II, 83] and to lay down four months' probation for anyone converting to Buddhism "from another doctrine". Woe betide the Rugby League player who asks to play Rugby Union!

The last of my trio of constitutional documents is *Cullavagga XI*, the account of the First Council. Once more the tone is different: the author strives for an affectless, bureaucratic prose style as if he were writing "the Minutes of the *Saṅgha's* First Committee Meeting". But, as the overlapping material makes clear, the account is designed to complement the *Mahāparinibbāna-sutta.* The activities of the First Council can be minuted under six paragraphs: [1] The canon is defined and (theoretically) closed by Upāli and Ānanda's recitations. [2] The grundnorm underlying the *Vinaya* is shifted from the Buddha to the 500 arahants. [3] The policy underlying strict *Vinaya* observance is acknowledged. Lay opinion is a decisive factor in choosing not to change the precepts because prudence dictates that the laity must be given no opportunity to criticise the *saṅgha*[20]. [4] Ānanda demonstrates how the good monk responds to a judgement against him:

---

19. R. Dworkin, *Law's Empire*, Oxford, OUP, 1988.
20. This is not quite the same as saying that the laity are given the job of enforcing *Vinaya* rules: I argued above that this was true in practice, but the minutes of the First Council are not evidence for my case. The *Vinaya's* ideology is that the *saṅgha* is wholly autonomous.

"I do not myself see anything wrong in what I did, yet I trust my colleagues enough to confess it as an offence." [Vin, II, 288].

[5] Purāṇa demonstrates the polite way to differ from the Elders:

"Well chanted by the Elders are *dhammavinaya*, but I prefer to be guided by what I myself heard the Lord preach." [Vin, II, 289].

Purāṇa must presumably exemplify the "good schismatic"[21] mentioned at the end of *Cullavagga VII.* Compare and contrast with Devadatta. [6] Finally Channa provides an object lesson in how judgement should be enforced against the bad monk:

"How can I enforce the *brahmadaṇḍa* against Channa who is fierce and rough?" "Take as many monks as you need, Ānanda."

And the minutes end with a couple of items of good news: Ananda collects the largest yet lay gift of robes, Channa achieves enlightenment and the Elders live happily ever after. Date and place of the next meeting: at Vesālī in 110 years time.

These three constitutional documents rehearse the same themes for different audiences. "The Wrath of Devadatta" is addressed to the laity, whether Buddhist or non-Buddhist. It tells them that the Elders are the real thing and the Devadattans an inferior and evil-minded substitute. "The Buddha Makes his Final Dispositions" presents the same themes (along with much else besides) to the average monk, while "The Minutes of the First Council" summarise the nature of the *Vinaya* and the nature of authority within the *saṅgha* for a specialist audience of *Vinaya-dharas* and controversialists. It is *Cullavagga XI,* the most technically legal of the three, which provides the most obvious bridge between the constitutional literature and the issues I raised in the first half of this paper. I hope to have shown that the peculiar nature of the *Vinaya*—half drug, half legal system—can be largely explained by the Elders' quarrel with the Devadattans. The Elders must have been aware from early on that their policy of "no addition or subtraction from the *Pātimokkha*" could only work at a local level. Ānanda admits as much to Gopaka-Moggallāna:

"The truly enlightened Lord laid down *Dhamma* and *Vinaya.* We meet once a fortnight in groups which cluster round a single village neighbourhood to check what has happened to each other. If a monk has committed an offence, we deal with it according to the instructions of *Dhamma*. Consequently it is *Dhamma,* not our fellow monks, which rules us." [M, III, 10]

---

21. If Purāṇa is intended to exemplify the 'good dissentient' mentioned at V, II, 202, then someone has miscounted the number of his followers.

Above the local level, the *saṅgha* is merely an abstract notion. There is no Rome or Canterbury where bureaucrat monks administer the *Saṅgha* of the Four Quarters. And therefore there have been no inquisitions or heresy trials, and the *saṅgha* has split more often than interfering busybodies like Asoka have been able to clamp it back together. Herein lies its strength and longevity. Mendelson, in his discussion of the Burmese *saṅgha*, expresses a universal truth:

> "Its strength lies in adherence to *Vinaya*, relations with lay donors and ability to discipline itself by forming small governable monastic groups such as taiks or sects, which are the *saṅgha's* best defence against those who would use it for secular ends."[22]

That the longest lasting law code in human history operates on anarchist principles is a pleasing paradox. In South and South East Asia today, the best hope for the *saṅgha* is that contemporary governments have assimilated so many European dogmas about the state as to have forgotten what anarchy really means. The modern state creates a Devadattan "National *Saṅgha* Organisation" which it then manipulates and controls. But the real *saṅgha* of the Elders will continue to slip between its fingers and escape its grasp.

****

Postcript on dates, non-Pāli and extra-canonical Pāli sources

The relative dating of documents within the Pāli canon depends on linguistic considerations which are far beyond my competence. Insofar as I can judge from the translations I have read, I would put the composition of the "constitutional literature" in the second or third century after the Buddha's death. If that means they were written during Asoka's reign, so much the better. Whatever one thinks of the Third Council, the Theravādins clearly felt gratitude to Asoka for something. I have a pet theory—a flight of fancy—to explain what might have happened. What if the Devadattans had gained control of the Buddha's body (hence the Elder's hostility to Kusinārā as a "wattle and daub town") and were in control of some or all of the *stūpa* containing his relics? And what if Asoka's collection of all the relics and redistribution of them into 84,000 *stūpas* was a ploy to put them under the control of the Elders? Since control of the relics meant control of the *stūpa* festival and its revenues,[23] Asoka's "purification of Buddhism" meant prosperity for the Elders. But, as Devadatta himself could have told them, pride comes before a fall. If Asoka helped the

22. E. Mendelson, *Sangha and State in Burma*, ed. J. Ferguson, Ithaca, Cornell University Press, 1975, 172.
23. G. Schopen, "Death, Funerals and the Division of Property in the *Mūlasarvāstivāda Vinaya*", in D. Lopez, ed., *Buddhism in Practice*, Princeton, Princeton University Press, 1995.

Elders to supremacy over the Devadattans, he also presided over the disintegration of the *saṅgha* of the Elders.

Later Buddhist literature adds snatches of information to the Devadatta story. The *Dhammapada* commentary mentions a great popular festival "to celebrate Devadatta's death" [DhA, I, 126]. I presume this was the Elders' rationalisation of the fact that the Devadattans had their own equally popular *stūpa*, festival and market complexes. Buddhaghosa describes the Vajjiputtaka monks at the Second Council as Devadatta's party. He glosses the phrase "they came to grief at the hands of the laity" [Vin, III, 23] as "Some were expelled, some were punished by the king, some were separated by death"[24]. Another late Pāli source deplores the fact that Devadatta "passed separate ordinances and pro-claimed a separate *Pāṭimokkha*" [Ud, 60]. The Sanskrit *Mahāvastu* developed stories about the rivalry between the Buddha and Devadatta when they were young cousins and the *Vinaya* of the Mūlasarvāstivādins "conspicuously expands the history of the schismatic"[25] with new episodes such as a deathbed attempt to scratch the Buddha with poison-coated fingernails. Can we use this continuing demonisation of Devadatta as evidence that his cult continued to prosper? A recent book describes a similar dynamic against those whom early Roman Christianity regarded as heterodox[26]. Fa-hsien tells us of a Devadattan *saṅgha* in the early 5th century CE; Hsüan-tsang mentions three monasteries in eastern Bengal which followed Devadatta's restrictions on milk-products. But this does not conclusively prove the continuity of the Devadattan *saṅgha* over 1,000 years: they may have been "neo-Devadattans" inspired by literature. The *Jātaka* collected stories of the rivalry between Gautama and Devadatta in previous lifetimes. As *Milindapañha* notes, there are 16 *jātakas* in which the Buddha was born inferior to Devadatta (showing that at that point his kammic balance was inferior) and 6 more where they are born as equals. Nāgasena gives a fairly plausible explanation, but is it possible that these stories have infiltrated the Pāli from a Devadattan corpus? A feature of the later literature was to play Devadatta [the antinomian] against Upāli [the spirit of the *Vinaya*]. Devadatta wanted to lead the *saṅgha*: Upāli wanted to be a forest recluse. Devadatta was a nobleman: Upāli was his barber[27]. In the case of Kumāra-Kassapa's pregnancy,

24. Smp, 170 = VI.51.
25. E. Lamotte, *History of Indian Buddhism*, trans. by S. Webb-Boin, Louvain-la-Neuve, Publications de l'Institute Orientaliste de Louvain, 1988, 658.
26. E. Pagels, *The Origin of Satan*, New York, Random House, 1995. Reviewed by N. Cohn in *New York Review of Books*, 42.14, 21 Sept. 1995, 18-21.
27. For the *Apadana* Upāli's lowly status requires explanation. *Vinaya* connotes law and law connotes kings. Therefore, Upāli must have been a *cakkavatti* in 1000 previous lives and a king of the *devas* in 1000 other lives [Ap, I, 37].

Devadatta and Upāli give conflicting verdicts, and the Buddha (of course) supports Upāli [Th, 200].

The Evolution of the Buddhist Yama

Bulcsu Siklós

Preface

Selected evidence is presented here in the form of an 'evolutionary history' of the deity Yama. The intention is to provide a coherent picture of the development of Yama into an object of devotion for Buddhists. The stages identified here are perhaps not the only ones that could be used, and much depends on how widely the researcher is prepared to cast his net for evidence from Indo-European (IE) groups other than the Aryans and their Iranian relatives. Further comparisons of the IE Yama figure to similar Mesopotamian, Egyptian and Greek gods or heroes might be possible, but even without such expansion, the amount of Indo-Iranian and Buddhist material ensures that only a proportion of the references to Yama can be treated here.

1. The Early Yama

a. Yama as Puruṣa and Yama as Bull

The *Ṛg-veda* (X.90.1-16) contains a creation myth in which a primordial being known as the Puruṣa ('Man') is sacrificed by the gods to produce a new world. The Puruṣa is described there in these terms:

> "The Puruṣa has a thousand heads, a thousand eyes, a thousand feet. He pervades the earth everywhere and extends beyond for ten fingers' breadth. The Puruṣa himself is all this, whatever has been and whatever is to be... Al. him; three quarters are the immortal in heaven."

The sacrifice of the Puruṣa is then performed by the gods, *sādhyas*[1] and sages, and the creative result is described thus:

> "From that sacrifice in which everything was offered, the ghee was obtained, and they [= the gods *etc.*] made it into those beasts who dwell in the air, in the forest and in the villages. From that sacrifice in which everything was offered, the sacred verses (*rg*) and the chants (*saman*)

1. The *sādhya* are a group of 12 celestial beings inhabiting the region between the sun and the earth. Dowson describes them as the personified rites and prayers of the *Vedas*. J. Dowson, *A Classical Dictionary of Hindu Mythology*. London. 1957, 271

were born, the metres were born and the formulas (*yajur*) were born...When they divided the Puruṣa, into how many parts did they disperse him? What became of his mouth, what of his arms, what were his two thighs and his two feet called? His mouth was the priest (*brāhmin*), his arms were made into the warriors (*kṣatriya*), his two thighs were commoners (*viṣ*) and from his feet the servants (*śūdra*) were born. The moon was born from his mind; the sun was born from his eye. From his mouth came Indra and Agni, from his vital breath the wind was born; and from his head the heaven appeared. From his two feet came the earth and the regions of the sky from his ear. Thus they fashioned the worlds".[2]

The equivalent Iranian myth splits the creative act into two:

"It is said in the religion [=Avesta] ; when the sole-created [=created apart from other creatures] ox passed away, there where it sent forth its marrow, the fifty-five species of grain grew up, and the twelve types of healing plants...the semen of the ox was borne up to the moon. There they purified it and he [Ohrmazd] created animals from it".[3]

Then:

"I created men in ten species. The first was that which was radiant and white of eye, namely, Gayōmart, and the ninth from Gayōmart was Gayōmart again. The tenth was the monkey, said to be the least of mankind. When illness came over Gayōmart he fell on his left side. From his head, lead became manifest; from his blood, tin; from his marrow, silver; from his legs, iron; from his bones, copper; from his fat, crystal; from his arms, iron; and from his soul's departure, gold...From the left death entered the body of Gayōmart. [Therefore] death comes over all creatures until the Renovation".[4]

The text goes on to describe the creation of the ten types of mankind from Gayōmart's semen.

The Norse version of this IE myth[5] tells of the dual being Ymir (the word is cognate to Skt. Yama) who was produced from the meeting of heat and cold

---

2. W.D. O'Flaherty, *Hindu Myths, A Sourcebook Translated from the Sanskrit*, Harmondsworth, 1975, 28.
3. B. Lincoln, *Priests, Warriors and Cattle: A Study in the Ecology of Religions*, Berkeley, Los Angeles & London, 1981, 72.
4. *ibid.*
5. There are still more versions of this myth in the IE world, but perhaps only the heavily modified Old Irish and Roman versions of the tale can be considered primary. The first of these is preserved as a short section at the end of the epic poem the Cattle Raid of Cooley (the *Táin Bó Cuailnge*; trs. by C. O'Rahilly, *Táin Bó Cúalnge from the Book of Leinster*, Dublin, 1967, 270-2) and tells of a conflict

(originating from lands to the north and south) in the void between known as Ginnungagap. Ymir is the ancestor of both humans and giants, who first emerged from his left armpit and feet respectively. But Ymir is also the world itself, since he was slain by the gods Odin, Vili and Ve, taken to Ginnungagap, dismembered and used to make the world. The vault of the sky is his skull, the sea his blood, the earth his flesh, the clouds his hair - and as in the case of Yama it seems his death was the first in this creation. Ymir's primary slayer Odin was a result of the union between a giantess and a man licked into existence from the salted ice by the cow Auðumbla on whose milk Ymir had been fed.[6]

The equivalences are so clear that there can be little doubt concerning the identity of the Vedic Puruṣa, the Iranian Gayōmart/Bull combination and the Norse Ymir. While the Puruṣa alone is sacrificed in the Vedic version, the Iranian account describes a dual dismemberment of the primordial man and a bovine. Perhaps it is only to be expected that a scholarly solution incorporating a bovine element into the Vedic story should have been proposed. J. Otrebski argued that *puruṣa* be understood as a compound *pu-* 'man' (as in *pu-mān* 'human', *pu-tra* 'son') + *vṛṣa* 'bull' (>*ruṣa* by metathesis);[7] this interpretation brings the Aryan myth into line with the Iranian and Norse versions. The bovine association is to stay with Yama in some form or another[8] for the rest of his history.

---

between two bulls, one of which kills the other and tosses the remains to the four quarters creating the landscape of Ireland. Echoes of the Puruṣa myth are equally faint in Livy's account (I.6.3-7.3) of the founder twins of Rome, Romulus and Remus (*geminus* is again a cognate word to *yama*). Romulus kills Remus and on this possibly sacrificial basis Rome can be founded. The Greek and Russian versions seem to be secondary (see the discussions in A. Olerud, *L'idée de macrocosmos et de microcosmos dans le Timée de Platon*, Uppsala, 1951, and S. Schayer, "A Note on the Old Russian Variant of the Purushasukta.", *AO,* 7, 1935, 319-23.).

6. The primary source is Snorri's Gylfaginning 4-9 (relying on the Voluspá, 3 ff.); Ellis Davidson Ellis Davidson, *Gods and Myths of Northern Europe*, Harmondswort,1964, 27-8.
7. J. Otrebski, "Aind, Puruṣaḥ, Pumān und Verwandtes", *ZVS,* 82, 1968, 252-3.
8. Yama is associated with bovines of several different types in the course of his history. The Puruṣa Man/Bull is one, the *mahiṣa* associated with Yama, originally the Aurochs but later the Water Buffalo, is another. The Water Buffalo identification for the *mahiṣa* provides a clear link with the Dravidian myths surrounding the slaying of the monstrous Mahiṣa by Durgā (a comprehensive bibliography and summary of the South Indian buffalo sacrifice is given by Hiltebeitel ("Rāma and Gilgamesh: the Sacrifices of the Water Buffalo and the Bull of Heaven", *HR,* 1980, 188ff). The *mahiṣa* has also been associated with the horse (A. Wayman, "Studies in Yama and Māra." *IIJ,* 3, 1959, 49) though I am not convinced by the argument. In addition to the *mahiṣa,* Yama is also associated with a black decrepit barren cow (equated with the *anustaraṇī* cow slaughtered at funeral ceremonies) which in turn has a counterpart in the barren cow offered to Varuṇa at the conclusion of the *soma* sacrifice. The *anustaraṇī* cow, the pieces of which are burnt along with the corpse, is

b. Yama as Twins

While the Vedic Puruṣa is equated with Yama on the basis of internal evidence and of the related Norse myths where the name Ymir (=Yama) is preserved, in the *Ṛg-veda* the deity named Yama appears as one of a pair of twins born to Vivasvat the Sun and Saraṇyū the daughter of Tvaṣṭṛ the divine artisan. His younger twin sister is given the name Yamī. His twin nature is his defining characteristic—the Sanskrit word *yama* means 'twin'. And again the twin characteristic has a specific creative meaning, one that is different to the creative dismemberment of the Puruṣa/ Bull version of Yama[9]. An interesting passage in the *Ṛg-veda* (X.10.1-14)[10] tells of Yamī's attempted seduction of her twin Yama. She speaks thus in one verse:

> "the desire for Yama has come upon me, Yamī, the desire to lie with him upon the same bed. Let me open my body to him as a wife to her husband. Let us whirl about together like the wheels of a chariot".

Yama resists successfully:

> "Never will I agree to unite my body with your body. They call a man who unites with his sister an evil man. Seek your pleasures with some other man than me".[11]

This 'anticlimactic' tale is apparently not discussed further in Hindu mythology. It seems that the extant version is a prudish alteration of an earlier, more complex tale in which the incest does occur.[12] The Iranian Yasna suggests that Yamī's powers of seduction were originally greater—she and Yama had after all had intercourse before while in the womb, she persuasively argues. Yama does in fact succumb, creating mortality by the sexual act:

---

intended as an offering for Yama's dogs, Śyama and Śabala (equivalent to the Graeco-Latin Cerberus), enabling the deceased to pass them by safely en route to the Underworld.

9. In his discussion of Vedic sacrifice Aguilar concludes that Yama "no more than repeats at another level the creative immolation of the Puruṣa" (*The Sacrifice in the Ṛgveda (Doctrinal Aspects),* Delhi, 1976, 144); he is however probably wrong to claim that it is on account of Yama's self-sacrifice—that is to say the abandonment of his immortality as described in *Ṛgveda* X.13.4—that he is called 'Twin' since he is the twin of god, the perfect image of Prajāpati, the Lord of Creatures. The Iranian, Vedic and Scandinavian evidence has been presented and discussed in detail by Lincoln (*Priests, Warriors and Cattle: A Study in the Ecology of Religions*, Berkeley, Los Angeles & London, 1981, 69ff).

10. *Ṛgveda*, X.10, is analyzed in detail, both philologically and mythologically, by Schneider ("Yama und Yamī (RV, X, 10)", *IIJ*, 10, 1967, 1-32.) who also discusses the comparable Egyptian myths involving the twin Osiris (*ibid*., p19-22).

11. W.D. O'Flaherty, *Hindu Myths, A sourcebook Translated from the Sanskrit.*, Harmondsworth, 1975, 64.

12. S. Bhattacharji, *The Indian Theogony, A Comparative Study of Indian Mythology from the Vedas to the Purāṇas,* Cambridge, 1970, 94; also U. Schneider, *op. cit.*, 19.

"And when these two spirits [good and bad; called *yīma* 'twins' in the previous verse] first met, they instituted life (*gaya-*) and death, and how life should be in the end".[13]

Yama consequently becomes the first mortal and, as the first being to experience death, also becomes the first being in the Underworld.[14] His position as ruler of this realm, a role which gradually comes to supersede his other roles, is thus based on his twin aspect (the creation of mankind and of death) rather than on his Puruṣa/Bull aspect (the creation of the universe).

The two identifications of Bull and Twins for the same deity may seem contradictory. However there is one other location where this pairing occurs: the zodiacal constellations.

The earliest indisputable Mesopotamian evidence for astrological thinking dates from c. 4400 years ago, though doubtless much had been worked out earlier.[15] Evidence for the full celestial zodiac, the twelve zones into which the ecliptic is divided, appears somewhat later (indisputably from c. 700 BC). The zodiac is not merely applied on the annual scale (the year divided into 12 zodiacal months) but is also used to mark out periods of about 2160 years (cosmic months), this being the time it takes for the spring point of the sun to

---

13. B. Lincoln, *Priests, Warriors and Cattle: A Study in the Ecology of Religions*, Berkeley, Los Angeles & London, 1981, 76. Consideration of theories of genetics might lead to conclusions reminiscent of the twin myth of Yama and Yamī. In organisms which reproduce asexually, there occurs a simple duplicating process (cloning) whereby the organism genetically manufactures identical copies of itself. A colony of such organisms, bacteria for example, is made up not of many individuals but of many copies of the same 'individual'. In organisms which reproduce sexually, the procedure involves the alternation of haploid phases (where the nucleus contains a single set of chromosomes) and diploid phases (where the nucleus contains a double set). Sexual reproduction thus involves the union of two haploid cells from two different individuals of two different mating types (called male and female) to produce a single unique organism, composed of diploid cells, which produces, in turn, haploid gametes (sex cells). In the case of simple organisms, which reproduce asexually by repeated fission, it makes little sense to speak of the 'death' of individuals since these are all identical copies of the (hypothetical) source organism and can, in a sense, be traced back to it. In the case of sexually reproducing organisms, the mixing of chromosomes from two parent individuals ensures the uniqueness (and hence individuality) of the offspring—but at the cost of the eventual dissolution of that particular individual organism. As Lyall Watson puts it, "the price we have had to pay for sex is death" (*The Romeo Error: A Matter of Life and Death*, Falmouth, 1974, 30). But looked at from this point of view, Yama's creation of death must be concurrent with the creation of a new and complex type of life—life as lived by individuals.
14. *Atharvaveda-saṃhita*, 18,3,13; A. Parpola, "The Sky-Garment, A Study of the Harappan Religion and its Relation to the Mesopotamian and Later Indian Religions", *SO*, 57, Helsinki, 1985, 65.
15. L. Kákosy, *Egyiptomi és antik csillaghit*, Budapest, 1978, 111.

transit one zodiacal sign (these following each other in the reverse order to what we find in the 'normal' yearly cycle). Twelve of these 2160 year periods make up a cosmic year of 25,920 years, this being the time it takes for the precession of the spring point to complete a full round of the zodiac. The history of the universe is made up of a sequence of these cyclical cosmic years. The precession of the spring point in more recent human history has marked out, in sequence, the following periods: Gemini (c. 6700-4500BC), Taurus (c. 4500-2350BC), Aries (c. 2350-200BC), Pisces (c. 200 BC-1960AD) and Aquarius (c. 1960-). At around 4500 BC according to this scheme a cosmic transition from the Twins to the Bull took place, and this is reflected in a similar ritual and religious transition in some ancient civilisations in this period, as in the later transitional periods (2350 BC for Taurus-Aries and so on)[16]. Whether or not these transitions did actually take place in the religious life of a particular prehistoric group—such as the Aryans prior to their entry into India—at the astrologically predetermined time would be hard or impossible to ascertain. Nonetheless, the existence of Yama as Bull and Yama as Twins—consecutive signs in the zodiac—within Indo-Iranian mythology may suggest that knowledge of astrology had been acquired either directly or indirectly from a civilised source (Mesopotamia, Egypt or the Indus Valley)[17]. This astrological aspect of Yama is not necessarily in conflict with his death and knowledge-of-death associations discussed below (these being the philosophical-religious reflexes of the scheme). The fact that both the Twins and the Bull are bound up in the figure of Yama (and not some other figure) suggests the prominence of the deity amongst the early Aryans and

16. Such transitions can be detected at least in the Egyptian case. Egyptian civilization (the First Dynasty) begins, along with a new calendrical system, at c. 4000 BC with a fully fledged Bull cult, that of the bull Hapi, better known as Apis. This follows a Twins period apparently characterized by human sacrifice. Apis is associated with Osiris, who like Yama is a twin of solar origin (*cf.* note 4). The Amun ram cult officially replaces that of Apis after two thousand years or so at the time of the accession of the XIIth Dynasty and just after the era of the pyramids comes to an end; this cult in turn comes to an official end with the start of the Ptolemaic era (c. 300 BC) and the gradual rise to power of monotheism in the Near and Middle East (and it is no accident that the early Christians chose the Greek word ιχφυ′σ 'fish/Pisces' to summarize their doctrine). This discussion relies primarily on Várkonyi (*Sziriat oszlopai,* Budapest, 1972, 176ff). It is not necessary to involve the Zodiak to explain the Buull-Twins link since the original non-zodiacal Twins constellation is Orion (also next to Taurus in the sky). This association is millenia older than the early evidence for the Zodiak.

17. Mesopotamian and Egyptian astrology are certainly linked; the direct evidence for astrology (as for most else) in the Indus Valley may be slight but as Mesopotamian influence on the Indus Civilizations can clearly be detected in other areas, knowledge of astrology as a fundamental component of civilization is only to be expected. Fairservis (*The Roots of Ancient India*, London, 1971, 296-98) has a summary of the evidence for Mesopotamian influence on the Indus Civilizations.

points to a gradual 'demotion' in rank as the later Hindu pantheon coalesced from Aryan and Dravidian elements.

2. The Iranian and Kafir Yamas

a. The Iranian Yima

Since the rest of this essay will be taken up with the discussion of Yama in Hindu and Buddhist contexts, a brief account of the Iranian Yima and the Kafir Imra would help complete the Indo-Iranian picture, especially as the Kafir information has a bearing upon the evolution of the Buddhist tantric deity Yamāntaka as discussed in the closing section. Both the Gayōmart and the twin legends of Yama have been preserved in Iran. Yima as a creator-figure (initially bound up with Gayōmart) and as the first mortal has been present from earliest times providing opportunities for reinterpretation as religious conceptions changed. Yima may have lost his creative role but he did—and still does—survive in a heroic role. Earlier texts such as the Avesta (Yasna 9.3-5) describe Yama as the first king ruling over our world which was a deathless paradisaical place at that time.[18] In subsequent literature he drops to third in the list of early kings. His thousand-year reign ends with the loss of his immortality which, though seen as sacrificial in India, was interpreted as punishment for sin by Zoroastrianism. Zoroaster hints darkly at some deception perpetrated by Yima concerning the bull sacrifice as the sin in question (Yasna 32.8). Later sources (Pahlavi texts and Persian epic) say that Yima's claim to be creator was the lie that led to his fall.[19] Yama as first worldly king is conspicuously absent from the Indian myths though the progenitor of the human race Manu, a half-brother of Yama in Indian tradition, shows certain similarities.[20]

Yima's kingly role ending in death is altered in a curious legend preserved in the second chapter of the Vendidād. Yima is instructed by the gods to build an underground *var* (fortification) as a refuge from an ice age which will destroy the world above ground. Like the ark, the *var* is inhabited by pairs of the best men, women and animals and seeds of the most fragrant and delicious plants. This underground world has its own sun, moon and stars to provide light and the people live long, happy and secure lives. Yima still exists in his secret abode biding his time through our age waiting for the opportunity to re-emerge (this

---

18. A. Christensen, *Les types du premier homme et du premier roi dans l'histoire legendaire des Iraniens*, I-II, Stockholm, 1917, II, 3.
19. *cf.*, M. Boyce, *A History of Zoroastrianism,* Leiden & Koln, 1975, 93, and note 56.
20. *Markandeya-purāṇa*, 103, I; trs., W.D. O'Flaherty, *op. cit.,* 66. Perhaps as Dumézil suggests (*The Destiny of a King,* Chicago & London, 1973, 7), the less rigorous Iranian opposition to incest enabled Yama to make the twins—earthly king transition without the loss of status that characterises Yama's Vedic role.

being one of the events of the Zoroastrian apocalyptic in later descriptions.[21] It is this Arthurian role which enables Yima—now known as Jamšed—to become a standard hero of Iranian storytelling and thereby to survive the Islamicisation of Iranian religion.[22]

b. The Kafir Imra

Additional evidence for Yama's prominence in earlier (pre-Vedic) times can be adduced from his central role in the religions of the Kafirs of the Hindu Kush of Afghanistan and Pakistan. These groups are linguistically intermediate between their Iranian and Aryan neighbours forming a distinct third language family and possessing a 'third tradition' of Indo-Iranian myth existing only in orally-transmitted form. This tradition seems to retain Yama, known in Kafir as Imra, in a supreme role, while both Indian (whether Hindu or Buddhist) and Iranian traditions required Yama's demotion and altered his status. Robertson describes a tripartite cosmology ruled over by Imra for the Afghan Kafirs:

> "In the Kafir theology there appears to be both a heaven and a hell. It divides the universe into Urdesh, the world above, the world of the gods; Michdesh, the earth; and Yurdesh, the nether world. Both the heaven and the hell for mortals is in Yurdesh, which is reached through a great pit at the mouth of which a custodian named Maramalik [=Māra], specially created by Imra for the purpose, is always seated. He permits no one in Yurdesh to return to the upper world".[23]

As creator of Maramalik, Imra is master of death. He rules by proxy in Yurdesh and in person in Urdesh since all the other gods were brought to life by his breath. He is also creator of humanity whom he churned into existence inside a golden goat skin. Robertson gives the following description of the eight imposing wooden images of Imra which once stood in the main temple at Kushteki:

> "The figures are probably seven feet high and represent Imra seated and working a goat-skin butter churn. The face of each is prodigious. The square-cut chin reaches within a hair's-breadth of the goat-skin on the god's knees. The brows and nose are, in the majority of the figures, scored with lines, while those on the two practicable doors [of the temple] have rough iron bells suspended between the eyes...above the faces of the images a large circular head-dress appears with a horizontal

21. *cf.*, M. Boyce, *op. cit.*, 95-6.
22. A. Christensen, *op. cit.*, II, 81ff, provides a full listing and summary of the Islamic works featuring Yima/Jamšed.
23. G.S. Robertson, *The Kafirs of the Hindu-Kush,* London, 1896, 380.

line of carving across the middle and vertical cuttings running upwards and downwards from it."[24]

The most interesting question concerning the Kafir Imra is whether his identity as supreme creator god is a relic of some earlier pre-Vedic period when the Indo-Iranians worshipped Yama as supreme, or whether Imra's rise in rank has been of more recent origin. Karl Jettmar has proposed opposition to Buddhism as the goad for Imra's rise:

> "The Kafirs perhaps knew of a deity with the name and the attributes of Yama; but then they learnt that by the Buddhists this god was regarded as supreme ruler of all worldly affairs, full of temptation and splendour and therefore detested by the followers of the Saviour [=Buddha]. If they were already Kafir-minded in those days, i.e. reluctant to accept foreign values involving renunciation of their traditions, we may infer that they saw Yama as their 'chosen god', expressing their distinct group personality".[25]

It will be noticed that the Buddhist evidence discussed later does not support this view in the form stated since the Buddhist view of Yama (as opposed to that of Māra) was not a particularly hostile one. The closing paragraphs of this essay propose a different and distinct type of Buddhist influence on the Kafirs and Imra—but any such influence, whether Iranian, Hindu or Buddhist, does not rule out the possibility of the Kafir Imra being a direct continuation of the creator Yama, whether Puruṣa or Twin—of pre-Vedic times.

3. *The Hindu Yama*

We have seen how the Yama/Yamī legend has been sanitised in the *Ṛg-veda* in response to the rise of the incest taboo; Yama's role in the *Vedas* is consequently relatively minor. To find an effective way back into the Indian pantheon Yama has to abandon his Twin identity and adopt a new persona[26]. In the *Brāhmaṇas* he is no longer *yama*—'twin' but instead grows in stature and dread with the adoption of the etymology *yam,* 'restrain, curb, subdue'. This new Yama is

---

24. *ibid.*, 1896, 389-90.
25. K. Jettmar, *The Religions of the Hindukush,* Vol. I: *The Religion of the Kafirs*, New Delhi, Bombay & Calcutta, 1986, 133.
26. It was also impossible for Yamī to maintain any kind of effective religious role in post-Vedic India without transformation. She comes to be identified with the destructive earth goddess, Nirṛti, prior to the Epic-*Purāṇic* age; afterwards, Nirṛti's functions are distributed amongst various dread goddesses, both Aryan and Dravidian - Kālī (*cf.* Yama's *persona* as Kāla), Camuṇḍa (Yama's *tantric* consort in some later manifestations), Cinnamastā and Mānasa. In the *Purāṇas,* Yamī is identified with the river Yamunā bathing in which is said to prevent rebirth in Yama's realm. Full details are given in the fourth chapter of Bhattacharji's monograph (see note 12).

called Death (Mṛtyu) and Ender (Antaka); he is now the god of Death itself, not merely god of the dead. He grows in significance and menace along with the doctrine of transmigration which, in the *Brāhmaṇas,* is invariably seen as an unpleasant succession of deaths:

> "Verily there are deaths connected with all the worlds and were he not to offer oblations to them, Death would get hold of him in every world; when he offers oblations to the Deaths he wards off death in every world."[27]

As Death Yama has knowledge of death and knowledge of the means of escaping its clutches. Occasionally, he can be made to reveal aspects of this knowledge, which he does in ways which belie his dread nature. The most significant Hindu source revealing Yama in this role of guru is the *Katha-upaniṣad* in a tale based on an episode of the *Ṛg-veda* (X.135). The young brahmin Naciketas sent by his father finds his way to Yama who after much persuasion reveals certain secrets:

> "I know, Naciketas, that sacred fire which leads to heaven. Listen. That fire which is the means of attaining the infinite worlds, and is also their foundation, is hidden in the sacred place of the heart...and Death [=Yama] told him of the fire of creation, the beginning of the worlds, and of the altar of the fire-sacrifice, of how many bricks it should be built and how they should be placed."[28]

Performing the fire-sacrifice or burnt offering (*homa*) three times leads the officiant to the heavens where immortality can be enjoyed and death—Yama—can be avoided. Yama then discusses death. His attitude to reincarnation seems favourable (in contrast to the *Brāhmaṇa* attitude):

> "The soul may go to the womb of a mother and thus obtain a new body. It even may go into trees or plants, according to its previous wisdom and work. There is a spirit who is awake in our sleep and creates the wonder of dreams. He is Brahman, spirit of light, who in truth is called the Immortal. All the worlds rest on that spirit and beyond him no one can go."[29]

These dialogues take place in the after-death state and Yama's frank revelations to the self-sacrificing seeker after the truth are connected with the same righteousness that had made him fit to judge the deceased who follow him into death, the state which he pioneered:

27. *Śatapatha-brāhmaṇa* XIII, 5, 1, 2.
28. *Katha-upaniṣad*, I, 14ff; trs., Mascaró, *The Upanishads*, Harmondsworth, 1965, 56.
29. *Katha-upaniṣad,* V, 7-8. *ibid.*

> "Because he has the eye of dharma he is impartial to both the kindly and the harmful. Therefore the dispeller of darkness, his father, the lord, appointed him lord of the south[30] and made him a world protector, the overlord of the ancestors."[31]

Yama is further elaborated in the epic literature in which he appears with the additional persona of Time (Kāla) alongside Mṛtyu and Antaka, his *Brāhmaṇa* personalities. Bhattacharji describes the relationship between these various forms thus:

> "When a man's action nears final fruition, his span of life is measured accordingly—if his actions demand that his opportunities of life-on-earth are over, then Kāla, Time, comes in. Death as the Ender (Antaka) announces the end and Death as Mṛtyu carries him off to the other world. But who is to guarantee fair play in all this? This is the special province of Yama as Dharmarāja whose code of justice is immutable and infallible."[32]

In the *Mahābhārata* (XII.92: 38), Yama is subordinate to Śiva by whose appointment he becomes Lord of the Ancestors (Pitṛpati)—in other words Yama loses his automatic right to this position which he had initially earned through blazing a trail to the underworld as the first mortal. He does however gain compensation in other areas. As Bhattacharji observes:

> "Yama on his own is a minor god with limited jurisdiction confined to the after-life and consequently he cannot directly control the land of the living. Whereas by being associated with the Śiva-complex[33] he becomes an organic part of a much bigger whole, for, although Yama is frequently called Kāla, it is only as he imbibes the attributes of the Śiva-complex more and more that he becomes the true representative of Time, for Śiva is Mahākāla. And behind this we have the tremendously power-ful philosophical concepts of Karman, rebirth and metempsychosis."[34]

The path to the underworld of the ancestors through the gateway of death is called the Pitṛyāna; from the epic period onwards this is increasingly seen as contrasting with the Devayāna which involves liberation from existence through

---

30. Along with Indra (E), Kubera (N) and Varuṇa (W).
31. *Markandeya-purāṇa*, 105, 18-19; trs., W.D. O'Flaherty, *op. cit.*, 70.
32. S. Bhattacharji, *op. cit.*, 61.
33. This relationship to Śiva seems to supersede one with Varuṇa, the god of the waters. Both Yama and Varuṇa are recorded as appearing together before the deceased (*Ṛgveda,* X.14.7). The sacrificial animal associated with Varuṇa is the black ram—perhaps there is an astrological aspect to be clarified here. For further details on the Yama-Varuṇa link see A. Parpola, *op. cit.*, 64ff.
34. S. Bhattacharji, *op. cit.*, 53.

wisdom (*jñāna*). This division into ancestral (lunar) and divine (solar) 'vehicles' corresponds to the two sects Śaiva and Vaiṣṇava:

> "Devayāna is Viṣṇu's path, the path of the Pitṛyāna is dark; these are the two paths after death - the one leading upwards, the other below."[35]

The issue at this stage is whether or not Yama's new multiple persona can harmonise with the workings of *karma*. The ancestral Yama of the Underworld remains secure but one could argue that Yama as Time, as Ender, as Judge—Yama as karma itself—is in fact an emasculated Yama with no function apart from this vague identification with *karmic* processes. But this identification also results in a deification of *karma*—and with the rise of both Vedantic and Buddhist movements, both dominated by *karma* theories, Yama has to remain in place.

4. The Buddhist Yama

a. Yama in early Buddhism

While Yama as judge (Dharmarāja) of the intermediate state plays a not insignificant role in early Buddhism as a component of a common Indian cosmology, it would seem that the workings of *karma* according to any Buddhist interpretation might be in conflict with any judgement given by an external being. Marasinghe summarises the Devaduta-sutta in which the deceased is brought before Yama who questions him as to whether he has seen the appearance of the three messengers of old age, disease and death.[36] A negative answer implies that grave sins have been committed since these are avoided by taking heed of the messengers. Yama then cautions the sinner that only he is responsible for the consequences of his actions since these were committed by himself. Infernal beings then drag the sinner off to various tortures. Marasinghe comments:

> "that Yama neither does 'preside over judgement and punishment', nor is in charge of the tortures inflicted in the Niraya is quite clear from the above sutta...Yama appears as a sympathetic onlooker who does not interfere in any serious way with the operation of the karmic law. The commentary goes even further in saying that Yama's questions are intended to explore any possible chance of averting the suffering in Niraya [= the hells]...the vagueness in [Yama's] position also goes to show the subtlety of his adaptation by Buddhism: he appears to be almost the same, but yet [is] quite different."[37]

---

35. *ibid.*, 74, 76. *Mahābhārata*, XII, 315, 30.
36. G. Marasinghe, *Gods in Early Buddhism*, Kelaniya, 1974, 268; *Aṅguttara-nikāya*, I, 138.
37. *ibid.*, 269.

Buddhism seems to have avoided expelling Yama from the after-death state despite having an apparent excuse—the theory of karma—to do this. This may in part have been connected with a desire to give Yama his due as Lord of the Ancestors and—in so far as early Buddhism concerned itself with the laity—to provide the bereaved with intercessionary opportunities not available in the case of pure *karma* propelling the deceased towards a possibly unfavourable existence (a factor which came to dominate the human relationship to Yama in China). Cults of spirits or gods were in any case confirmed as suitable for humans by Śākyamuni Buddha himself in the *Suttanipāta*:

> "Whatever beings have come together, whether earthly or those of the intermediate space, let them be glad. Therefore, all spirits, all of you, take care of mankind and be friendly [to them] who bring you offerings day and night; therefore do protect them assiduously" (222-223).

There could be no reason therefore for the removal of Yama from the Buddhist intermediate state. Piatigorsky comments on the *Suttanipāta* passage thus:

> "the worship of spirits is not denied or rejected by Buddha here, but rather neutralised, ousted into the sphere of cult, of natural religion. And by this, the worship of spirits finds its place as a thing naturally appropriate to all sentient beings who have not yet realised the calm state."[38]

This would be particularly true of a being such as Yama who functions as Lord of the Ancestors since it is ancestral spirits just as much as local spirits or higher gods who were, and still are, chief objects of devotion for most Indians whether Hindu or Buddhist[39]. In this regard the *Vimalaprabha's* use of the word *preta* 'ghost, spirit' (Tib. *yi dwags*) to describe Yama is noteworthy.[40] Yama's position is therefore secure in the earliest stages of Indian Hīnayāna and thereafter in a way in which no other Indian deity's position can be.

While many canonical Buddhist texts, both Theravāda and Mahāyāna, refer to the hells either extensively or in passing, the number of direct references to Yama is fewer. In the Pali Tipiṭaka, apart from the *Devadūta-sutta* of the *Aṅguttara-nikāya* quoted above, there are references in the *Kathāvatthu* (a rare datable text contemporary with the so called Council of Patna of 246BC) where

38. A. Piatigorsky, *The Buddhist Philosophy of Thought: Essays in Interpretation*, London & Dublin, 1984, 25.
39. Reference may be made to the study by D. Shastri, *Origin and Development of the Rituals of Ancestor Worship in India*, Calcutta, 1963, who provides details of all the traditional rites of ancestor worship in India.
40. *cf.* note 69.

the question of the reality of Yama and the guardians of the hells is raised.[41] There are also references in the late text, the *Petavatthu* of the *Khuddaka-nikāya,*[42] and in the *Mahāsamaya-sutta* of the *Dīgha-nikāya* (II, 259). The third book of the Sanskrit Abidharmakośa of Vasubandhu (c. 316-396) contains several references to Yama,[43] as does the Mahāsāṅghika text, the *Mahāvastu* (properly part of the *Jātaka* literature) in which Yama is also invoked by the Buddha for the protection of some travelling merchants.[44] References are similarly scant in the non-tantric Mahāyāna literature. The *Saddharmapuṇḍarīka* mentions Yama in passing as ruler of the hells;[45] similarly the large *Prajñāpāramitā-sūtra*[46] and book VII of the *Śūraṅgama-samādhi-sūtra.*[47]

By the time of the formation of the Tibetan *Bar do* (intermediate state) literature (7-8th c.) tantric influence is evident, though a judgement involving Yama is still present. In the Rnying ma (Old School) versions of the *Bar do thos grol* (Liberation through hearing in the intermediate state) Yama appears to the deceased after the appearance of the directional colours (those of the five Tathāgatas (*pañcatathāgata*) to supervise the (*karmic*) judgement. The judgement itself does not fundamentally differ from the earlier Hinayāna accounts, though the appearances of the directional colours of the five Tathāgatas are a tantric addition. After the black and white pebbles representing the bad and good actions of the deceased have been counted out, the deceased may prevaricate or attempt to lie:

> "'I have not committed any evil deed'. Then the Lord of Death will say, 'I will consult the mirror of Karma'. So saying he will look into the mirror wherein every good and evil act is vividly reflected. Lying will be of no avail. Then the Lord of Death will place round thy neck a rope and drag thee along; he will cut off thy head, extract thy heart, pull out thy intestines, lick up thy brain, drink thy blood, eat thy flesh and gnaw thy

---

41. XX, 3; Aung and Rhys Davids, trs., *Points of Controversy or Subjects of Discourse, Being a Translation of the Kathāvatthu from the Abhidhamma-Piṭaka*, London, 1915, 345-6.
42. 11,9; Gehman, tr., *The Minor Anthologies of the Pali Canon, Pt.IV: Vimana-vatthu: Stories of the Mansions; Peta-vatthu: Stories of the Departed.* London, 1942, 163.
43. L. de La Vailée Poussin, *Abhidharmakośabhāṣyam,* II, (Eng. tr.), Berkeley, 1988, 458, 460.
44. J.J. Jones, *The Mahāvastu*, Vol. 3, London, 1956, 81.
45. H. Kern, *The Saddharma-puṇḍarika, or the Lotus of the True Law*, SBE, XXI, Oxford, 1884, 233, 248, 402, 415.
46. II, 11, 2; E. Conze, tr., *The Large Sutra on Perfect Wisdom,* Berkeley, 1975, 289.
47. C. Luk, tr., *The Śūraṅgama Sūtra*, London, 1964, 184.

> bones; but thou will be incapable of dying. Although thy body be hacked to pieces, it will revive again."[48]

This text does not hesitate to make a Buddhist addition, following the lead of the *Kathāvatthu*:

> "In reality thy body is of the nature of voidness...the Lords of Death are thy own hallucinations."[49]

But with this new role as *karmic* supervisor—hallucination or otherwise—in the intermediate state Yama has doubled his functions. He still remains ruler of the hells (*niraya*), one of the six major divisions of the Wheel of Transmigration; but he also appears whenever any being transmigrates from one life to the next regardless of which of the six divisions is the source or destination for that being. These two roles are occasionally merged.

Yama does have another, exclusively Buddhist, manifestation: Māra, the enemy of Buddha[50]. Buddhism in its earlier forms as a means for preventing rebirth through wisdom is a type of *devayāna* (divine vehicle) opposed to that which encourages continued transmigration. Encouragement for continued existence is provided by practices of the *pitṛyāna* (ancestral vehicle) type—practices which are sacrificial, which express gratitude for life, which generate more *karma* and rebirth, and which fuel *saṃsāra.* The personification of all such *saṃsāric*, or more emphatically, anti-*nirvāṇic* temptations is Māra (= Mṛtyu = Death = Yama). In the *Saṃyutta-nikāya,* Māra in the guise of a deity comes to the Buddha and says:

> "He who hates austerity and does not like to stay alone, who is addicted to beautiful forms and wishes to go to the heavenly realms, is competent to give advice regarding the attainment of the next world."[51]

Māra is shown repeatedly to have confidence in his own position as a promoter of the *pitṛyāna* (to use the Hindu terminology for a moment). The Buddha's primary adversary is thus not Ignorance nor Desire nor Aversion as

---

48. *Zab chos zhi khro dgongs pa rang grol las bar do'i thos grol chen mo chos nyid bar do'i ngo sprod*, II; trs., W.Y. Evans-Wentz, *The Tibetan Book of the Dead,* Oxford, 1927, 166.
49. *ibid.*, 166-7.
50. This extensive and complex topic can only be touched on here. For further information and references, the standard account of Windisch (*Māra und Buddha*, Leipzig, 1895) and Law's essay ("The Buddhist Conception of Māra", *Buddhistic Studies,* Calcutta & Simla, 1931, 257-283.) may be referred to. Though it is true that the Māra-Yama association is purely Buddhist, Hindu sources suggest Yama's association with Kāma ('Love'), who is identified with Māra (S. Bhattacharji, *op. cit.,* 107). Aśvaghoṣa calls Māra Kāmadeva 'God of Love' in the *Buddhacarita* (XIII, 2); trs.& ed. by E.B. Cowell, *Buddhist Mahāyāna Texts*, SBE, XLIX, Oxford, 1894.
51. Rhys Davids, tr., *The Book of the Kindred Sayings*, PTS, 1917, I, 67.

one might expect. Death fulfils this role—but Life, as the other side of the coin, would be just as good a name for a being encouraging transmigration and discouraging *nirvāṇa*. Life would be a much harder name to demonise, however. So it would seem that Buddhism possesses two Yamas with the first in two sub-forms: 1a. The *karmic* judge Dharmarāja (from a Buddhist point of view a 'neutral' being since there is just *karma*); 1b. Yama, the Ruler of the Hells; and 2. the pro-*saṃsāra* Māra (considered negative and anti-*dharma*).

b. Yen-lo

From the beginning, Buddhism took for granted many aspects of a common Indian heritage. A basically tripartite Indian cosmology was one of the most significant of these features. Buddhism without lower realms or hell realms is simply inconceivable since much of its moral teaching—not to mention its central *karmic* philosophy—would collapse without the provision of the 'natural justice' of *karmically* dispensed punishment. Such conceptions were however alien to peoples such as the Chinese who possessed cosmologies which excluded hell-type realms and to whom the concept of transmigration was unknown. In Chinese thought, the two components which remained after death started independent existences in differing realms. The 'heavy' part of the 'soul' (*p'o*) which initially stayed close to the corpse, eventually sank down to the underworld while the 'light' component (*hun*) could be induced to stay by a wooden tablet inscribed with the name of the deceased to partake of offerings left by descendants. The *hun* of a person of exceptional virtue would ascend to Heaven from where it would periodically visit the tablet.[52] All ancestors were able to help the living if properly tended; if ignored, they became pitiable and possibly vengeful ghosts. Descriptions of the various levels of the Buddhist cosmos including the hells were of particular interest to those concerned with the implications for their ancestors. The possibility that they might suffer terribly in a hell realm or in the realm of the *pretas* on account of their own misdeeds rather than merely being guaranteed well-being through filial offerings was disturbing enough to ensure that the possibility of Buddhism being right also had to be covered.

The Chinese texts that directed early conceptions of this novel Indian cosmology are in the main apocryphal (at least in the sense that their Sanskrit originals are not known). Significant material on Yama can be found in book VIII of the *Sutra of the Past Vows of Kṣitigarbha* (apparently not preserved in Sanskrit) where Yama appears before the Buddha with many other powerful hell-beings and spirits. Yama asks the Buddha why, given the power of

52. H. Welch, *The Practice of Chinese Buddhism 1900-1950*, Cambridge, Mss., 1967, 182.

Kṣitigarbha to save the damned, so few worshipped the Bodhisattva.[53] The Buddha gives human stubbornness as the reason. Yama and the assembled hosts of hell then pledge to protect all Buddhist worshippers from misfortune in this life and bad rebirths in the next. Pleased, the Buddha replies by placing Yama under the protection of Hindu gods:

> "It is excellent, excellent, that all you ghost kings and Yama are able to protect good men and women in this way. I shall tell Brāhma and Sakra to cause you to be protected as well."[54]

Also amongst these apocrypha is the 5th century *Consecration Sutra* which contains, amongst other material, an early version of the Mu-lien (Sk. Maudgalyāyana) legend.[55] Maudgalyāyana, one of Śākyamuni's disciples, is given permission by the Buddha to visit his deceased mother in the next world. He visits each realm in turn, first meeting Yama who is regretfully unable to release his mother from the hells due to the large number of sins she had committed. Eventually, Maudgalyāyana, with Avalokiteśvara's help, manages to liberate his mother from the hells and she is reborn in the ghost (*preta*) realm. A sequence of such visits takes place until the mother is born as the daughter of a wealthy man whom the Buddha himself instructs in the Dharma. The Buddha concludes by predicting the daughter's ultimate enlightenment and thereby her liberation from cyclic existence.[56]

The Maudgalyāyana legend and related descriptions of the transmigratory cycle introduced Yama to a Chinese audience in the early Buddhist *karmic* judge/ruler of the hells form.[57] A further development was the subdivision of the single judgement into a sequence of ten judgements taking place in ten different

53. H. Ching, *Sutra of the Past Vows of the Earth Store Bodhisattva*, New York, 1974, 180.
54. *ibid.*, 183.
55. The *Consecration Sutra* is evaluated by Strickmann ("*The Consecration Sutra*: A Buddhist Book of Spells", in R.E. Buswell, ed., *Chinese Buddhist Apocrypha*, Honolulu, 1990, 75-118.) in the context of a set of studies by different authors on the Chinese apocryphal tradition. One can assume that other Chinese material touching upon Buddhist cosmology and Yama's place in the process of reincarnation will be uncovered as these apocrypha become better known to the Western academic world.
56. Summarized on the basis of the Mongolian translation edited by L. Lörincz, *Molon Toyin's Journey into the* [sic] *Hell,* Altan Gerel's Translation, Budapest, 1982.
57. There is some confusion between these two separate functions of Yama. The description of Chinese folk cults given by C.B. Day, *Chinese Peasant Cults, Being a Study of Chinese Paper Gods,* Taipei, 1974, 117ff. suggests that the deceased initially travels to Yama's realm and thence passes through the various cosmological levels above this before incarnation in Heaven.

courts of the world of the dead.[58] Each such court has its own king[59] and each king judges the deceased in turn with the judgements of the first seven kings occurring at seven-day intervals (= the standard 49 days of the intermediate state). The eighth king judges on the hundredth day, the ninth after one year, and the tenth three years after death (corresponding to the standard memorial days for the deceased). Of these ten kings Yen-lo (Yama; Jap. Enma), though of primary importance, is only the fifth. It is said that he used to be king of the first court but was demoted (by the Taoist Supreme Ruler of Heaven, Yu huang shang ti) on account of his lenience.[60] Yen lo is also dominated by the Bodhisattva Ti tsang (Kṣitigarbha; Jap. Jizō) who descends to hell to rescue the damned:

> "With his magic wand he opens the portals of this dismal land and rescues tortured souls from the grasp of Yama (Yen-lo wang)...on [Ti tsang's] birthday which falls on the 30th of the seventh month, all the judges of the Ten Courts of Hades come and offer him their congratulations. On this occasion, he grants special favours to the damned."[61]

In the later Japanese assimilative *honji suijaku* (true nature-trace manifestation) theorizing each of the Ten Kings is associated with a Buddha or Bodhisattva whose manifestation each one is. According to this scheme Yama is a manifestation of Kṣitigarbha[62]. In Japan the Ten Kings were further discussed and promoted by popularizing teachers such as Nichiren (1222-1282), founder of the eponymous *Lotus Sutra* based sect which became numerically the most significant Japanese Buddhist school. A later Muromachi-period (15th-16thc) development saw the number of Kings increase to thirteen, possibly in response to the thirteen sections of the tantric Taizōkai (Sk. Garbhadhātu) *maṇḍala*.[63]

c. Yama in Indo-Tibetan Vajrayāna

A brief text from the Tibetan Kanjur with the appended Tibetan title *Gtam rgyud*[64] provides a description of Yama's entry into the Buddhist fold. According to this text, Vajrabhairava (a variant of the deity Yamāntaka, 'Ender of

---

58. A. Matsunaga, *The Buddhist Philosophy of Assimilation*, Tokyo, 1969, 37-38.
59. The full list is given in Matsunaga (*ibid.*, 37-8). Taiser has contributed an as yet unpublished study and translation of a primary Japanese apocryphal source for the Ten Kings.
60. C.B. Day, *op. cit.*, 121.
61. Fr. H. Doré, *Researches into Chinese Superstitions*, Vol. VII, Shanghai, 1911-34, VII, 252.
62. Matsunaga (*op. cit.*, 1969, 234) gives the full list of Kings with their corresponding Buddhas or Bodhisattvas.
63. S.F. Taiser, *The Scripture on the Ten Kings and the Making of Purgatory in Medieval Chinese Buddhism*, Honolulu, forthcoming, 75.
64. The Myth, Peking edition, no. 108.

Yama') went to the city of Yama across the Southern Ocean and subdued the deities there:

> "With his unendurable sixteen feet he trod on the sixteen gateless iron dwellings. With his single-pointed organ of wisdom he crushed the central great iron dwelling...the eight classes of gods offered their life-essences to him—Yama offered YA, the divine mothers MA, the ghouls offered RA, the spirits KṢE, the humans offered NṚ, the lords of the earth SA, the demons offered CCHA and the Maras offered DA."[65]

It is only from this moment onwards that Yama becomes a suitable object for Buddhist tantric worship[66]. His conversion enables him to take his place amongst the great protective divinities of Tantric Buddhism. He is found as one of the eight wrathful protectors of religion (Tib. *drag gshed brgyad*) along with (amongst others) Yamāntaka, the generalized title of the Mañjuśrī emanation which converted him. In the Gsar ma (New) tradition of Lamaism, the three forms of the converted Yama called Dharmarāja (Tib. Chos rje) are known as the Outer, Inner and Secret Forms.[67]

The Outer Form (Tib. *phyi sgrub*) is blue, naked, ithyphallic and buffalo-headed. He stands on a buffalo which is crushing—or, in certain representations, copulating with—a corpse. His right hand wields a club topped with a skull (Tib. *thod dbyug*) and his left, a noose. To his left, his twin sister Yamī offers him a blood-filled skull-cup with her left hand while holding a trident in her right.

The Inner Form (Tib. *nang sgrub*) is blue, *rākṣasa* (ghoul)—headed and wears a tiger skin. He holds a chopper and a skull- cup and tramples on a corpse.

The Secret Form (Tib. *gsang sgrub*) is red, buffalo-headed, naked, ithyphallic and tramples on a buffalo. He holds a jewel (a chopper, Sk. *kartari,* Tib. *gri gug*), in some illustrations), in his right hand and a skull-cup in his left.

---

65. *Gtam rgyud,* 158v of the Peking version.
66. This converted Yama is called Dharmarāja (with Dharma interpreted as the Buddhist doctrine rather than as 'righteousness'). Such acceptance of subordination by Yama is mentioned in several other *tantras*, eg. the *Sarvadurgatīpariśodhana,* (ed. & tr., T. Skorupski, Delhi, 1983, 52) where Yama bestows longevity on and obstructs untimely death for the initiate. It would seem that when the name Yama (Tib. Gshin rje) appears in Buddhist texts, it indicates that the deity is playing an earlier pre-Buddhist role. This is borne out by Yama's appearance in a list of divine mounts in the *Hevajra-tantra* (II, v) alongside Brahmā, Indra, Viṣṇu, Śiva, Kubera, Nairṛti and Vemacitrin (D.L. Snellgrove, *The Hevajra Tantra: A Critical Study,* I-II, London, 1959, 112).
67. See the detailed descriptions in R. Nebesky-Wojkowitz, *Oracles and Demons of Tibet*, Graz, 1975, 82ff.

These three forms[68] may seem to be the elaborations of later Tantric exegesis, but they are intended to be understood in terms of various aspects and consequences of death itself. Jaya Paṇḍita quotes the *Vimalaprabha* as saying that the three Yamas are:

> "the *preta* dwelling in the place, the lord of death which is in the body, the defilements (*kleṣa*) which are in the mind."[69]

Thus the Outer Form is the Dharmarāja who resides across the Southern Ocean. The Inner Form is personal mortality, the path which Yama was the first to follow. The Secret Form is mental defilement, those obscurations (desire, aversion and ignorance) which produce the sufferings of birth, old age, sickness and death (as opposed to the Inner Form, which is itself death and consequent birth, sickness and old age).

As protective deities of Lamaism, the three Dharmarājas are ritually invoked and worshipped mostly without a yogic union taking place between the practitioner and the deity. The offerings made to Yama are similar to those made to other protectors,[70] though with some small differences. These offerings are sometimes illustrated separately in Lamaist paintings of the type known as 'collection of ornaments' (Tib. *rgyan tshogs*) or 'materials for the banquet' (Tib. *bskang rdzas*). One such example from the Yung-ho-kung is described by Lessing as showing these offerings for Yama:

1. Offerings (Tib. *mchod rdzas*). These are the usual 'eight offerings' (minus one) in their tantric form offered in skull-cups: i. blood (= water for the face); ii. human organs, eyes *etc.* planted in a brain (= flowers); iii. smoke of burnt flesh (= incense); iv. lamp fed by human fat (= lamp); v. clotted blood and bile (= perfumed water) vi. human flesh (= food); and vii. the music of trumpets and drums made from human bone and skin. The missing item is urine (= water for the feet).[71]

---

68. According to Klong rdol bla ma, the Outer and Inner forms have retinues composed of yet more forms. The Outer form has a retinue of eight Yamas and eight Yamis (Tib. *gshin rje pho brgyad mo brgyad*) or alternatively a retinue of twelve *ma mo* (this alternative is given by Tucci, *Tibetan Painted Scrolls,* I-III. Rome, 1949, II, 582). The Inner form has a retinue of four Yamas, one each for the activities of calming, increasing, controlling and for fierce activities (R. Nebesky-Wojkowitz, *op. cit.*, 1975, 82-3). In addition, there are other forms of Yama found in the Rnying ma literature, for which see Nebesky-Wojkowitz, *op. cit.*, 83ff.
69. *Thob yig*, I, 272a ff. The relevant material from Jaya Paṇḍita's *Thob yig* has been presented and translated by A. Wayman in his extensive article on "Yama and Māra; Studies in Yama and Māra", 44-73, 112-31.
70. R. Nebesky-Wojkowitz, *op. cit.*, 398-408.
71. Lessing relates a popular tale according to which the 'water for the feet' was withdrawn from Yama by the founder of the Dge lugs pa school Tsong kha pa (1357-1419) as a punishment for the deity's lateness in completing an errand (F.D. Lessing, *Yung-ho-kung: An Iconography of the Lamaist Cathedral in Peking,*

2. Special dough offerings (*bali;* Tib. *gtor ma*) in a human skull surmounted by an arrow with a black veil with various ornaments.
3. The Inner offering. This is a boiling skull-cup containing the five types of flesh (those of the five domestic animals: cow, dog, horse, elephant and human) and the five nectars (blood, urine, excrement, marrow and semen).
4. Various animals as offerings to gratify the sight of a god.
5. Various goddesses making oblations.
6. The symbolic cosmos.[72]

d. Yamāntaka

The presentation of offerings befitting a great protective divinity does not in itself 'activate' Yama to perform any specific tasks assigned by a devotee. Yama can be generally propitiated by these offerings—but he may be commanded to perform desired tasks by the superior deity, Yamāntaka ('Ender of Yama'),[73] in one of his several forms (in a Gsar ma context, Kṛṣṇayamāri, Raktayamāri and Vajrabhairava) since it is Yamāntaka who binds Yama by oath to protect Buddhism. Since Yamāntaka/Vajrabhairava is a *yoga-tantra* deity (belonging to the Gsar ma category of the *anuttara-yoga-tantra*), the devotee is able to command Yama when correctly united with Yamāntaka. This adds an immediate active aspect to Yama which cannot be seen outside Tantrism:

> "If the devotee wants to drive someone away he should make a camel out of earth from the seven places and should then imagine on its back a wind-mandala in the shape of a half-moon transformed from the syllable YAṂ. Above this he imagines the victim and on [the victim's] back he imagines the form of Yama holding a staff in his hand. [The devotee] thinks that the victim is beaten with that staff and is led off towards the south."[74]

Stockholm, 1942, 105). The reason for the omission is probably far earlier—Yama, according to the *Mārkandeya-purāṇa* (103, 1, 3-40), was cursed by the shadow of his mother for raising his foot against the shadow. The sun Vivasvat, Yama's father, was unable to undo the curse ("there is nothing anywhere that can dispel the curse on those who have been cursed by a mother") and Yama's foot was devoured by worms (W.D. O'Flaherty, *op. cit.*, 65-7); consequently, no offering of water for the feet (= urine) is made.

72. F.D. Lessing, *op. cit.*, 100-1.
73. The name Yamāntaka is perhaps better translated as 'Ender of Yama' rather than 'Slayer of Yama' since, as the *Gtam rgyud* tells us, Yama merely becomes a protector of Buddhism (Dharmarāja) through Vajrabhairava's appearance and is not killed in the process. In Tibetan we find both Gshin rje gshed (Slayer of Yama) and Gshin rje mthar byed (Ender of Yama). The two Yamāri forms (Red and Black) are both 'Enemies of Yama'.
74. *Vajramahābhairava-tantra*; Peking edition,137r.

The cycle of Vajrabhairava, clearly a tantric Buddhist equivalent of Śiva-as-Bhairava, has always played a major part in the religious life of the various Gsar ma ('New') schools of Tibetan Buddhism though other schools prefer to evoke Yamāntaka in different forms. Amongst the Dragon Bka' brgyud and the Rnying ma pas, Yamāntaka appears as the Black Poison-faced One (Dug gdong nag po), also called Quicksilver (Khro chu), while the Kar ma bka' brgyud cultivate Yamāntaka in a form known as the Black Master of Life, Tshe bdag nag po.[75] Amongst those schools which relied on canonical works sanctioned by the primary compiler of the Kanjur Bu ston (1290-1364) and who therefore cultivated the *tantras* of Vajrabhairava, the two Yamāris and the Yamāntakas of the *Khrodavijāyakalpaguhya-tantra*, the Sa skya school was particularly noted for its mastery of Vajrabhairava's cycle (with notable works by 'Phags pa, Ngor chen kun dga' bzang po, Go ram bsod nams seng ge and others).

It is, however, amongst the Dge lugs pa that the cycle was most prominent. Vajrabhairava counts as one of the three central Highest Yoga Tantra cycles preferentially cultivated by Dge lugs pa yogins; the Tibetan phrase *gsang bde 'jigs gsum* is used to refer collectively to the three deities in question, *ie*. *Guhyasamāja* (*Gsang bsdus*), *Saṁvara* (*Bde mchog*) and of course *Vajrabhairava* (*Rdo rje 'jigs byed*). It is said that the cultivation of these three tantric cycles amongst the Dge lugs pa derives from the originator of the school Tsong kha pa (1357-1419) who performed the full evocations (Sk. *sādhana*; Tib. *sgrub thabs*) of these three deities as part of his daily practice, and who also performed an extensive retreat on the Vajrabhairava practice in his 55th year.[76] The Dge lugs pa also considered Vajrabhairava to be the special protector of the *anuttara-yoga-tantra* while Yama as Dharmarāja was pressed into service as the special (Tib. *thun mong ma yin pa*) protector of the Dge lugs pa themselves.[77] Numerous lamas and yogins of this school, including several of the Dalai Lamas, wrote commentarial and ritual works on Vajrabhairava and the related forms of Yamāntaka. The Yamāntaka cycle was equally important to the monks and yogins of Mongolia. It seems that the few members of the Dge lugs pa pantheons with animal connections were particularly popular in Mongolia, with only the deity Hayagrīva (Tib. Rta mgrin; 'Horse-necked') approaching the buffalo-headed Vajrabhairava in popularity. Perhaps more so than in Tibet, we find the practices of Yamāntaka widespread amongst the wider populace to whom these were dispensed by proselytizing monks or local princes without the full set of initiations required, much to the dismay of the Dge lugs pa establishment:

---

75. S. Beyer, *The Cult of Tārā, Magic and Ritual in Tibet,* Berkeley & London, 1978, 42-4.
76. R.F. Thurman, *The Life and Teachings of Tsongkhapa*, Dharmsala, 1982, 28.
77. F.D. Lessing, *op. cit.*, 76.

> "In order to begin the spread of the Buddha's doctrine with benevolent intention, the Tüsiyetü Khan of the Khorcin [Mongols] let it be publicly known: 'I will give a horse to whoever learns by heart the summary of the Doctrine, and a cow to whoever can recite the Yamāntaka dhāraṇī by heart!' Thereupon from the moment that they heard this announcement, all the poor and have-nots learnt the prayers according to their intellectual capacity. And since the Khan, as he had announced, gave horses and cows to those who had already learnt the prayers from other people, there were many believers..."[78]

Amongst the Mongols one therefore finds Yamāntaka invoked in spells for various worldly purposes—for example for adjusting one's gun and making it shoot straight (*qv*. the Mongolian texts entitled *buu-yin tarni* (gun-*dhāraṇī*) and *buu-yin sang* (gun incense offering).[79]

Yama's first appearance in Mongolia predates that of Yamāntaka since Yama's Mongolian name Erlik seems to be an early loan from Uighur. *The Ten Kings Sūtra* exists in early Uighur versions translated from Chinese, (in the 11-13th century) according to von Gabain,[80] but though the borrowing may have taken place in a Buddhist context, the time separating pre 13th c. Mongolia from the heavily Buddhicized 17th c. Dge lugs pa environment enabled Yama as Erlik to find his way into the shamanic pantheon as well[81] thereby adding meaning to the Yamāntaka cycle in Mongolia.

Yamāntaka/Vajrabhairava was also one of the most prominent deities evoked by the Manchu-supported Dge lugs pa community in Peking and associated Lamaist centres in China and Manchuria. The deity had a close relationship with the Manchu imperial family on the basis that the phonetic similarity between the words Mañjuśrī (the Bodhisattva of wisdom whose manifestation Yamāntaka/Vajrabhairava is considered to be) and Manchu (the wisest nation in the Empire) was no accident. Mañjuśrī came to be considered the special patron of the Manchus (just as Vajrapāṇi and Avalokiteśvara protected Mongols and Tibetans respectively, power and compassion being the characteristics which these nations saw in themselves). It is immediately understandable why Vajrabhairava as the wrathful form of Mañjuśrī should have been pressed into Imperial service. The sixth hall of the great Yung-ho-kung (Palace of Harmony) in Peking was devoted entirely to the evocation of Vajrabhairava and the other

---

78. W. Heissig, *The Religions of Mongolia*, London & Henley, 1980, 36-7; from a biography of the Mongol monk, Neici Toin, 1557-1653.
79. Rinchen, *Les matériaux pour l'étude du chamanisme mongol I. Sources littéraires*, Wiesbaden, 1959, 38-40.
80. A. von Gabain, "The Purgatory of the Buddhist Uighurs", *Colloquies on Art and Archaeology in Asia,* 2, ed., W. Watson, London, 1972, 25.
81. W. Heissig, *op. cit.*, 54; Rinchen, *op. cit.*, 26.

forms of Yamāntaka as was an entire temple in Peking (Yamāntaka-yin süme). During Manchu times, the city of Peking itself was topographically identified with Vajrabhairava and his *maṇḍala* as a means of protection (with a famous statue in Pei-hai representing the deity himself), and the Forbidden City, the Imperial City and the Outer City three concentric *maṇḍalas*.[82]

It remains to be explained why this particular relationship between Yama and Yamāntaka should have achieved such prominence in Tantric Buddhism. Other Indian deities, Brahmā for example, also have a place within Tantrism as protectors, but the status of their converters (if any) was never equal to that of Yamāntaka who remains one of the three primary *anuttara-yoga* deities cultivated by the Dge lugs pa. Yet Yamāntaka cannot be independent of Yama—the name and iconographic similarity are enough to prove this—and it is interesting in the light of Yama's long history to find the largest school of Tibeto-Mongolian Buddhism preferentially evoking a deity whose defining function is dominance over Yama—and thereby dominance over transmigration, over *karma* and indeed over Māra.

A clue to understanding the conditions in which the Yamāntaka cycle rose to prominence is provided by observing that the place of origin of the Yamāntaka *tantras* is given as U rgyan in the colophon of the *Vajramahābhairava-tantra* (147v of the version in the Peking Kanjur) and in the history of Jo-nang Tāranātha (b.1575).[83] U rgyan is the Tibetan equivalent of the Sanskrit toponym Oḍḍiyāna which is usually identified with the Swat region of northern Pakistan.[84] This area is precisely that inhabited to this day by the Kafirs who stubbornly maintain the worship of Yama as supreme deity. K. Jettmar made a case for the opposition between Buddhists in the larger valleys and the Kafirs in the mountains encouraging the promotion of the Kafir Imra to supreme status.[85] Consideration of the Yamāntaka *tantras* might suggest that the Kafir Imra represents the earlier Indo-European 'primary deity/creator' phase rather than a later demoted phase since the Tantric Buddhists of 8th c. Swat would hardly

82. F.D. Lessing, "The Topographical Identification of Peking with Yamāntaka", *CAJ*, 2, 140; also in his *Ritual and Symbol: Collected Essays on Lamaism and Chinese Symbolism*, Taipei, 1976.

83. D. Chattopadhyaya, ed. & tr., *Tāranātha's History of Buddhism in India*, Calcutta, 1980, 243.

84. Lokesh Chandra has argued for a South Indian location for Oḍḍiyāna ("Oḍḍiyāna: A New Interpretation", in M. Aris & A.S. Suu Kyi, eds., *Tibetan Studies in Honour of Hugh Richardson*, Warminster, 1980, 73-8) but the Swat interpretation is more likely. The faunal references (to camels and wild asses, for example) in the *Vajramahābhairava-tantra* certainly suggest Swat rather than South India as the point of origin.

85. K. Jettmar, *The Religions of the Hindukush*, Vol.I, *the Religion of the Kafirs*, New Delhi, Bombay & Calcutta, 1986, 52-3.

have bothered to promote a Slayer of Yama unless that Yama had been supreme amongst their opponents. They were engaged in the promotion of the same type of Śaivaite domination over Yama that had taken place in Hindu contexts. And since the devotees of the Slayer of Yama were engaged in yogic practice, they ended up being individually dominant over Yama (and all his manifestations—Death, Karma, Māra and so on) who could be made to perform desired tasks on account of his subjection to Yamāntaka. One can hardly imagine a stronger inducement to Yamāntaka practice than this.

The *Saṃpuṭa-tantra*
Sanskrit and Tibetan Versions of Chapter One

Tadeusz Skorupski

1. An Overview of the Saṃpuṭa-tantra

The *Saṃpuṭa-tantra* occupies an interesting and indeed important position among the Buddhist *tantra*s as a whole. As such it is classed by the commentators as a *yoginī tantra*, but when we examine its title, content, and the interpretation of the commentaries, we learn that its real position is not to be understood as being solely an independent *tantra* belonging to one particular class of *tantric* texts, but also as an epitome or recapitulation (*nidāna*) of all the *tantras*. Like many other *tantras*, the *Saṃpuṭa-tantra* has a short and a long or full title. The short title of this *tantra* has several variants: *Saṃputa* (sTog edition, Abhayākaragupta, Vīryavajra), *Saṃpuṭi* (Peking edition), *Saṃpuṭodbhava* (Sanskrit manuscripts), *Saṃpuṭitilaka* (Indrabodhi). The term *saṃpuṭa* or *saṃpuṭi*, which is included in all the titles, constitutes the principal name by which this *tantra* is normally known. When we examine its full titles as given in the Sanskrit and Tibetan versions, and the commentaries,[1] we realise that its name, apart from containing the key term

1. For the purpose of my introductory study of this *tantra* and the edition of the Sanskrit and Tibetan versions of Chapter One, I have employed three Sanskrit manuscripts, two Tibetan versions and three commentaries. The three Sanskrit manuscripts employed here are designated as A, B, and C. Manuscript A is kept in the Bibliothèque Nationale in Paris. Its identification number is give as Sansrit 148 and its microfilm number as R.19830. It is written in *devanāgarī* script and numbers 135 folios. Manuscript B is also kept in Paris and is numbered Sanscrit 144 and again R.19829. It is also in *devanāgarī* and it numbers 211 folios. Manuscript C is kept in Kyōtō and its identification number is given as 2739287. It is in Newari script and numbers 241 folios.
The two Tibetan versions employed here are the Peking and sTog Palace editions of the Kanjur (bKa' 'gyur); abbreviated to TTP (Tibetan *Tripiṭaka*, Peking Edition, Tokyo & Kyoto, 1957) and sTog:
rgya gar skad du Sampuṭi-nāma-mahātantra / bod skad du Yang dag par sbyor ba zhes bya ba rgyud chen po (TTP, vol. 2, 245-5-2 to 291-1-3).
rgya gar skad du Sampuṭa-nāma-mahātantra / bod skad du Yang dag par sbyor ba zhes bya ba'i rgyud chen po (sTog, vol. 93, *kha*, 301b6-450a4).
The Tibetan Tanjur (bsTan 'gyur) contains translations of three Indian commentaries written by Indrabodhi, Abhayākaragupta, and Vīryavajra.
Śrī-Saṃpuṭitilakā-nāma-yoginītantrarājasya-ṭīkā Smṛtisaṃdarśanāloka-nāma / dPal Kha sbyor thig le shes bya ba rnal 'byor ma'i rgyud kyi rgyal po'i rgya cher 'grel pa

saṃpuṭa, is not entirely uniform. The title folios in all three Sanskrit manuscripts are missing, but either its full or short titles are given at the end of individual chapters or sections and in the final colophons. In all three Sanskrit manuscripts the full title is given as *Sarvatantranidānarahasyāt Śrīsaṃpuṭodbhava*. On the initial folios of the two Tibetan versions we find short titles of this *tantra,* and a full title coinciding with the one given in the Sanskrit manuscripts is given at the end of individual chapters. The commentaries written by Abhyākaragupta and Indrabodhi provide only short titles, but in Vīryavajra's commentary we find a variant long title, namely *Sarvatantrasya-nidāna-mahāguhya-Śrīsaṃpuṭa.* Although this title is similar to the long title given in Sanskrit manuscripts, it is obviously different in wording and grammatical structure.

The term *saṃpuṭa,* in its general sense, means a hemispherically shaped dish or a hollow space between two dishes placed together. In the Tibetan versions of this *tantra* and in the commentaries, the term *saṃpuṭa* is translated either as *yang dag par sbyor ba* or as *kha sbyor.* Tentatively, these two Tibetan translations could be respectively rendered as "perfect union" and "mystic embrace". Fundamentally, there is a limited meaning that one can deduce from the Sanskrit term *saṃpuṭa* or from its Tibetan translations. However, the initial section of the *tantra* and the commentaries provide a whole range of complex interpretations all of which basically assert that it symbolises the non-dual union of wisdom (*prajñā*) and means (*upāya*), and other similar *tantric* pairs. Perhaps it should be mentioned that in Tibetan sources this *tantra* is known by its transcribed Sanskrit term or as either *Yang dad par sbyor ba* or *Kha sbyor*.

The structure of the Sampuṭa-tantra

Out of the three Sanskrit manuscripts of the *Sampuṭa-tantra*, manuscript A has ten chapters (*kalpa*) and manuscripts B and C have eleven chapters each. The Tibetan versions also have eleven chapters like manuscripts B and C, but in the Peking edition there is a colophon at the end of Chapter Ten.[2] We learn from it that the translation of this *tantra* into Tibetan was executed by the Indian master Gayādhara and 'Brog mi Śākya ye shes (992-1072), and that it was later revised and edited by Bu ston (1290-1364). The mere presence of this colophon at the end of Chapter Ten clearly suggests that during Bu ston's time there must have been

---

Yang dag par lta ba'i snang ba zhes bya ba, written by Indrabodhi; TTP, vol. 55, 1.1.4 to 104.1.2.

Śrī-Saṃpuṭatantrarājaṭīkā Āmnāyamañjarī-nāma / dPal yang dag par sbyor ba'i rgyud kyi rgyal po'i rgya cher 'grel pa Man ngag gi snye ma zhes bya ba, written by Abhayākaragupta; TTP, vol. 55, 105.1.1 to 249.1.5.

Sarvatantrasyanidānamahāguhya-Śrīsampuṭa-nāma-tantrarājaṭīkā Ratnamālā-nāma / rGyud thams cad kyi gleng gzhi dang gsang chen dpal kun tu Kha sbyor zhes bya ba'i rgyud kyi rgyal po'i rgya cher bshad pa Rin chen phreng ba zhes bya ba, written by Vīryavajra (dPa' bo rdo rje); TTP, vol. 55, 251.1.1 to 300.4.8.

2. See note 42.

some controversy about the nature and canonicity of Chapter Eleven as part of this *tantra*. In the sTog Palace edition, this colophon has been removed, which again would suggest that the editor of this Kanjur accepted Chapter Eleven as part of this *tantra*. The colophon at the end of Chapter Eleven is basically the same in both the Peking and sTog editions.[3] It is clear from it that after this *tantra* was translated by 'Brog mi, some Tibetan masters tried to impose their own translations, and that strange as it appears in the context of the previous colophon, Brog mi edited it once more. According to Abhayākaragupta's commentary, the *Sampuṭa-tantra* is in ten chapters (*kalpa*) and he comments on ten chapters only as does Vīryavajra. Indrabodhi states at the beginning of his commentary that this *tantra* is in eleven chapters[4] but again, like Abhayākaragupta and Vīryavajra, he provides an impressive and extensive interpretation of ten chapters only.

The origin and history of Chapter Eleven is not known but it seems apparent that its canonical position as part of this *tantra* was disputed by some *tantric* masters. The colophons at the end of Chapter Eleven in Sanskrit manuscripts B and C name this chapter as a *nidāna* of all the chapters. In addition to this, manuscript C also adds that it is a commentary (*ṭikā*) on the *Saṃpuṭa*.[5] An analysis of the actual text of Chapter Eleven clearly suggests that originally it must have been an independent work written as a commentary on the various passages of the *Saṃpuṭa-tantra*. It is not a particularly original piece of work as it merely provides further elaborations and comments on specific passages or topics already covered in the body of the first ten chapters. However, although this chapter is basically a commentary, in its present format it is written in the form of conversations between the Lord and his entourage just as it is done in other chapters. Since Abhayākaragupta and Vīryavajra do not mention this chapter, it would seem that they did not treat it as canonical. Indrabodhi, however, seems to have accepted it as belonging to this *tantra* but at the same time since he does not comment on it, he must have viewed it as being at least self-explanatory and not as a text that needed to be explained.

In addition to being divided into ten or eleven chapters, the first ten chapters of the *Sampuṭa-tantra* are further subdivided into sections (*prakaraṇa*). In all ten chapters, one finds short colophons marking three sections numbered one to three, and in most cases also providing their names. However, the end of the third section in each chapter does not coincide with the end of the chapter itself. In all instances, the text runs on and concludes with a colophon marking the end of the chapter. If we count the marked sections and ignore the fourth and final portion of the text which coincides with the end of the chapters, each chapter has three

3 See note 46.
4. Indrabodhi, TTP, vol. 55, 1.3.4.
5. See note 46. In the catalogues to the Peking and sDe dge editions, this chapter is listed as a separate work.

sections plus a portion of text. Thus, if we count the marked sections only, the *Sampuṭa-tantra* has thirty sections, and if we count the unmarked portions as well, it has forty sections.

According to Abhayākaragupta and Vīryavajra, the *Sampuṭa-tantra* is divided into forty sections. Abhayākaragupta divides his commentary into forty sections, called clusters (*mañjarī*), in which he explains the forty consecutively counted sections of the *tantra*. Both Abhayākaragupta and Vīryavajra count the marked sections and the final portion of each chapter as independent sections. According to Indrabodhi, this *tantra* is divided into thirty sections. He counts only the named sections as independent sections, and treats the unnamed portions at the end of chapters as further clarifications or elaborations on all or any of the three sections within the same chapters. Although he makes a distinction between as it were 'proper' sections and 'additional sections', it is evident from the structure of his commentary that he also comments on forty sections. In addition to counting the sections in a consecutive way throughout the whole *tantra*, Indrabodhi and Vīryavajra also make use of numbering them consecutively within individual chapters. In fact, the chapter and section divisions of their commentaries correspond to the structure of the *tantra*. However, whichever way we count the sections, for all practical purposes we can say that all three commentators are fundamentally in agreement on the number of sections as forty.

Abhayākaragupta explains in his commentary that divisions into chapters and sections constitute two different although related ways of dividing this *tantra*, and that the sections do not merely form internal subdivisions within individual chapters but also stand on their own and relate to each other throughout the whole text. He further explains that while individual chapters demarcate larger topical portions, the individual sections deal with specific topics which are arranged according to a certain logical sequence. Indrabodhi and Vīryavajra do not explicitly affirm Abhayākatagupta's observation but since they also count the sections in a consecutive way, they would seem to confirm his interpretation of the relationship between chapter and section divisions.

Now, we shall proceed to sketch the structure of the *Sampuṭa-tantra*. The chapter and section headings are culled from the *tantra* itself and from the commentaries. Not all the chapter and section headings are given in the Sanskrit and Tibetan versions. Abhayākaragupta and Vīryavajra speak of ten chapters and forty sections but do not provide their titles. Indrabodhi is the only one who provides the titles of all the chapters and thirty sections. As is well known, the chapter and section titles in Sanskrit and Tibetan texts are normally given at the end and not at the beginning unlike standard practice in western scholarship. Thus, the references to chapters and sections given here are to the places where they are actually located. In the left column are given the sections as marked in the Sanskrit and Tibetan versions. In the central column are given the sections as counted by

Abhayākaragupta and Vīryavajra, and in the right column as counted by Indrabodhi.

Skt/Tib Versions	Abhayākaragupta	Indrabodhi
Chapter I: The secret nature of all the *tantras*[6]		
Section 1	Section 1	Section 1
	Raising the *bodhicitta* and other matters[7]	
Section 2	Section 2	Section 2
	Unveiling the thought of enlightenment[8]	
Section 3	Section 3	Section 3
	Exposition of the essential nature[9]	
	Section 4	
Chapter II:[10]		
Section 1	Section 5	Section 4
	Consecration of the thought of enlightenment[11]	
Section 2	Section 6	Section 5
	Meditation on the meaning of wisdom and means[12]	

6. Sanskrit Version, A15b, B17b & C21: no title.
Tib Version, TTP, vol. 2, 249.5.7: no title.
Indrabodhi, TTP, vol. 55, 1.3.5: *rgyud thams cad gsang ba'i rang bzhin.*

7. Sanskrit Version, A5a & C7a: *abhidhānābhidheyabodhicittotpādādibhāvanātatva*; B5b: *abhidhānābhideyabodhicittotpāḍa*.
Tib Version, TTP, vol. 2, 246.5.7: *brjod par bya ba dang rjod par byed pa'i byang chub kyi sems bskyed pa la sogs pa'i bsgom pa*; sTog, 305a5: *sgom pa'i de kho na nyid.*
Indrabodhi, TTP, vol. 55, 1.4.3: *rjod par byed pa byang chub tu sems bskyed pa la sogs.*

8. Sanskrit Version, B11a: *bodhicittāvatāro*; A9b & C12b *pañcendriyapañcabalasapta-bodhyaṅgāryāṣṭāṅgamārgaparyantādivivaraṇaṃ bodhicittāvatāro.*
Tib Version, TTP, vol. 2, 248.2.5 (& sTog 309a3): *byang chub kyi sems la 'jug pa*.
Indrabodhi, TTP, vol. 55, 1.4.3: *byang chub kyi sems la 'jug pa.*

9. Sanskrit Version, A11a, B13a & C15a: *tatvoddeśa.*
Tib Version, TTP, vol. 2, 248.4.7: *de kho na nyid mdor bstan pa.*
Indrabodhi, TTP, vol. 55, 1.4.3: *de kho na nyid kyi man ngag.*

10. Sanskrit Version, A30b, B36a & C41a: no title.
Tib Version, TTP, vol. 2, 253.3.5 no title.
Indrabodhi, TTP, vol. 55, 1.3.5: *rjod par byed pa, brjod par bya ba, byang chub tu sems bskyed pa rnam par bsgom pa*. The title given to this chapter by Indrabodhi broadly corresponds to the title of section one in Chapter one. It remains unclear why he gives the same titles to the second chapter and section one in Chapter One.

11. Sanskrit Version, A20a, 24b & C27a: *bodhicittābhiṣeka.*
Tib Version, TTP, vol. 2, 251.1.4 (& sTog 317b4): *byang chub sems kyi dbang.*
Indrabodhi, TTP, vol. 55, 1.4.3: *byang chub sems kyi dbang.*

12. Sanskrit Version, A23b, B28b & C32a: *prajñopāyārthabhāvanā.*
Tib Version, TTP, vol. 2, 251.5.7 (& sTog 320b1): *thabs dang shes rab kyi don bsgom pa.*
Indrabodhi, TTP, vol. 55, 1.4.3: *shes rab dang thabs kyi don bsgom pa.*

Section 3	Section 7	Section 6
	Manifestation of all the retinues [13]	
	Section 8	

Chapter III: Drawing the great *Vajradhātu-maṇḍala* [14]

Section 1	Section 9	Section 7
	Generating the Herukas[15]	
Section 2	Section 10	Section 8
	Sādhana of the knowledge *ḍākiṇīs*[16]	
Section 3	Section 11	Section 9
	Section 12	

Chapter IV: The signs of the *vajraḍākiṇīs*[17]

Section 1	Section 13	Section 10
	Characteristics of speech symbols[18]	
Section 2	Section 14	Section 11
	Signs and *mudrās* of *kaṭapūtanīs* [19]	
Section 3	Section 15	Section 12
	Gestures of Lāmā [20]	

---

13. Sanskrit Version, A27b; B31a; C37a: no title.
Tib Version, TTP, vol. 2, 252.4.7: no title at the end of the section but at its beginning (251.5.7) it reads: *'khor lo thams cad kyis rnam par 'phrul pa*; sTog, 323a4: *de bzhin brgyad pa rdo rje sa.*
Indrabodhi, TTP, vol. 55, 1.4.4: *'khor lo thams cad kyi rnam 'phrul*.
14. Sanskri Version, A42a; B51a & C58b: no title.
Tib Version, TTP, vol. 2, 256.4.2: no title.
Indrabodhi, TTP, vol. 55, 1.3.6: *rdo rje dbyings kyi dkyil 'khor chen po bri ba.*
15. Sanskrit Version, A32b, B39a & C44b: *herukotpatti*.
TibVersion, TTP, vol. 2, 254.1.4 (& sTog 327b1): *he ru ka bskyed pa.*
Indrabodhi, TTP, vol. 55, 1.4.4: *heruka bskyed pa.*
16. Sanskrit Version, A35a, B42b & C48b: no title.
Tib Version, TTP, vol. 2, 254.4.6: no title.
Indrabodhi, TTP, vol. 55, 1.4.4: *ye shes mkha' 'gro ma'i sgrub thabs.*
17. Sanskrit Version, A47a, B57a & C65a: *vajraḍākinīsaṃketa.*
Tib Version, TTP, vol. 2, 257.4.8 (& sTog 339b1): *rdo rje mkha' 'gro ma'i brda.*
Indrabodhi, TTP, vol. 55, 1.3.6: *rdo rje mkha' 'gro ma'i brda.*
18. Sanskrit Version, A36b, B44a & C50b: no title.
Tib Version, TTP, vol. 2, 255.1.6: no title.
Indrabodhi, TTP, vol. 55, 1.4.5: *ngag gi brda'i yi ge'i mtshan nyid.*
19. Sanskrit Version, A44a, B53b & C61a: *kaṭapūtanīcihnamudrā.*
Tib Version, TTP, vol. 2, 257.1.3 (& sTog 337a2): *lus srul mo'i mtshan ma dang phyag rgya*.
Indrabodhi, TTP, vol. 55, 1.4.5: *lus srul po'i mtshan ma dang phyag rgya.*
20. Sanskrit Version, A46b has no title, B56a & C64a read *cihnamudrā.*
Tib Version, TTP, vol. 2, 257.4.2 (& sTog 339a1): *mtshan ma'i phyag rgya,* and at the beginning of this section *de nas lā mā'i mtshan nyid ni yang dag rab tu bshad par bya*.
Indrabodhi, TTP, vol. 55, 1.4.5: *lāma'i mtshan nyid kyi mtshan ma.*

Section 16
The character of *mudrās*[21]

Chapter V: The practice (*caryā*)[22]

Section 1 Section 17 Section 13
The nature of gathering places[23]

Section 2 Section 18 Section 14
The purity of the *skandhas* and *āyatanas*[24]

Section 3 Section 19 Section 15
Consolidating the practice[25]

Section 20

Chapter VI: The spring ornament[26]

Section 1 Section 21 Section 16
The character of the sixteen syllables[27]

Section 2 Section 22 Section 17
The arrangement of the *nāḍīs*[28]

Section 3 Section 23 Section 18
The body *maṇḍala* and the *homa*[29]

---

21. Tib Version at TTP, vol. 2, 257.4.2 (at the beginning of Section 4) reads *phyag rgya yi mtshan nyid yang dag rab bshad bya*.
Indrabodhi, TTP, vol. 55, 1.3.5: *phyag rgya'i rang bzhin.*
22. Sanskrit Version, A57b, B70a & C79b: *caryākalpa*.
Tib Version, TTP, vol. 2, 260.4.2: *spyod pa.*
Indrabodhi, TTP, vol. 55, 1.3.7: *spyod pa.*
23. Sanskrit Version, A48b, B58b & C67b: *melāpakasthāna.*
Tib Version, TTP, vol. 2, 258.1.6 (& sTog, 340b3): *'du ba'i gnas*.
Indrabodhi, TTP, vol. 55, 1.4.6: *'dus pa'i gnas kyi rang bzhin.*
24. Sanskrit Version, A52a, B63a, C71a: *skandhāyatanaviśuddhi.*
Tib Version, TTP, vol. 2, 259.1.5: *phung po dang skye mched rnam par dag pa*; sTog, 343b3. *gsang ba padma'i mtshan nyid.*
Indrabodhi, TTP, vol. 55, 1.4.6: *phung po dang khams dang skye mched kyi rnam par dag pa*.
25. Sanskrit Version, A55a, B66b, C75b: *caryāliṅgana.*
Tib Version, TTP, vol. 2, 259.5.5: *'khyud pa'i spyod pa*; sTog, 346a7: *spyod pas rtog pa rnams 'jig par byed pa.*
Indrabodhi: TTP, vol. 55, 1.4.6: *spyod pa dang ldan pa'i rang bzhin.*
26. Sanskrit Version, A70b, B85a & C98b: *vasantatilakā.*
Tib Version, TTP, vol. 2, 263.5.7 (& sTog 359a4): *dpyid kyi thig le*.
Indrabodhi, TTP, vol. 55, 1.3.7: *dpyid kyi thig le.*
27. Sanskrit Version, A61b; B74a; C84b: no title.
Tib version, TTP, vol. 2, 261.3.6: no title.
Indrabodhi, TTP, vol. 55, 1.4.6: *yi ge bcu drug mtshan bya dang mtshon byed.*
28. Tib Version, TTP, vol. 2, 261.3.6: *rtsa yi gzugs kyis yang dag gnas.*
Indrabodhi, TTP. vol. 55, 1.4.7: *rtsa'i gnas dgod pa.*
29. Sanskrit Version, Chap VI/Sec 2: A63b & C87b, B76b: *deśanyāsa.*
Tib Version, TTP, vol. 2, 262.1.2: *yul gyi dgod pa*.

Section 24

Chapter VII. The emergence of meditation on all rites[30]

Section 1	Section 25	Section 19
	The emergence of perfect knowledge[31]	
Section 2	Section 26	Section 20
	The *homa* rites[32]	
Section 3	Section 27	Section 21
	The emergence of all rites and *maṇḍalas*[33]	
	Section 28	

Chapter VIII. The emergence of all activities[34]

Section 1	Section 29	Section 22
	The nature of the bell[35]	
Section 2	Section 30	Section 23
	Recitation and meditation on *mantras*[36]	
Section 3	Section 31	Section 24
	Rejection of heretical knowledge[37]	

Indrabodhi, TTP, vol. 55, 1.4.7: *lus kyi dkyil 'khor dang sbyin sreg.*

30. Sanskrit Version, A111a & C159a: *sarvadhyānodaya*; B135b: *sarvakarma-dhyānodaya*.
Tib Version, TTP, vol. 2, 274.4.2 (& sTog 393b3): *las thams cad kyi bsam gtan 'byung ba.*
Indrabodhi, TTP, vol. 55, 1.3.7.: *las thams cad dang bsam gtan 'byung ba.*

31. Sanskrit Version, A83a, B100a & C117a: *sarvajñānodaya-nāma-āyur-vadaḥ/āyurvedaḥ*.
Tib Version, TTP, vol. 2, 267.2.4: *ye shes thams cad 'byung ba zhes bya ba tshe ring ba'i tshe'i rig pa*.
Indrabodhi, TTP, vol. 55, 1.4.7: *thams cad mkhyen pa'i ye shes 'byung ba.*

32. Sanskrit Version, A87a, B104b & C122a: *homavidhi*.
Tib Version, TTP, vol. 2, 268.2.2 (& sTog 372b4): *sbyin bsreg gi cho ga.*
Indrabodhi, TTP, vol. 55, 1.4.8: *sbyin sreg gi cho ga'i rang bzhin.*

33. Sanskrit Version, A98a, B118b & C138b: *sarvakarmaprasaracakrodcya.*
Tib Version, TTP, vol. 2, 270.5.8 (& sTog 381b3): *rgyas pa'i 'khor lo 'byung ba*.
Indrabodhi, TTP, vol. 55, 1.4.8: *las tshogs thams cad dang 'khor lo 'byung ba.*

34. Sanskrit Version, A122a, B147b & C174b: *sarvakriyāsamudaya.*
Tib Version, TTP, vol. 2, 276.5.8(& sTog 401b1): *bya ba thams cad yang dag par 'byung ba.*
Indrabodhi, TTP, vol. 55, 1.3.8: *bya ba thams cad yang dag par 'byung ba.*

35. Sanskrit Version, A113a, B137b & C161b: *ghaṇṭhatatva*.
Tib Version, TTP, vol. 2, 275.1.3 (& sTog 394b6): *dril bu'i de kho na.*
Indrabodhi, TTP, vol. 55, 11.4.8: *dril bu'i de kho na nyid*.

36. SanskritVersion, A115a, B139b & C164a: *mantrajāpabhāvanā*.
Tib Version, TTP, vol. 2, 275.3.1 (& sTog 396a5): *sngags kyi bzlas pa dang bsgom pa.*
Indrabodhi, TTP, vol. 55, 1.5.1: *sngags kyi bzlas pa dang bsgom pa.*

37. Sanskrit Version, A118a, B143b & C168b: *tīrthikajñānāparayaṇa*.

Section 32

Chapter IX. The nature of ritual activities[38]

Section 1	Section 33	Section 25
	Generating all the Tathāgatas[39]	
Section 2	Section 34	Section 26
	Offering *bali*[40]	
Section 3	Section 35	Section 27
	The execution of painted scrolls and books[41]	
	Section 36	

Chapter X. The *nidāna* of all the *tantras*[42]

Section 1	Section 37	Section 28
	The great *sādhana* of the master[43]	
Section 2	Section 38	Section 29
	Worship and veneration of the perfected great bliss[44]	

Tib Version, TTP, vol. 2, 276.2.1(& sTog 399a1): *mu stegs kyi ye shes 'jig pa.*
Indrabodhi, TTP, vol. 55, 1.5.1: *mu stegs pa'i rnam par shes pa bsal ba.*

38. Sanskrit Version, A129b: *catuḥkriyātatvarāja*; B157b & C187a: *catuḥkriyātatva.*
Tib Version, TTP, vol. 2, 279.1.4 (& sTog 408a6): *bya ba bzhi'i de kho na'i rgyal po.*
Indrabodhi, TTP, vol. 55, 13.9: *bya ba'i de kho na nyid kyi rgyal po*.

39. Sanskrit Version, A123b, B150a & C177b: *sarvatathāgatotpatti.*
Tib Version, TTP, vol. 2, 277.3.3 (& sTog 403a3): *de bzhin gshegs pa thams cad kyi bskyed pa.*
Indrabodhi, TTP, vol. 55, 1.5.1: *de bzhin gshegs pa thams cad bskyed pa.*

40. Sanskrit Version, A126a, B153a & C181b: *balyupahāra.*
Tib Version, TTP, vol. 2, 278.1.6 (& sTog 405a6): *gtor ba'i mchod pa.*
Indrabodhi, TTP, vol. 55, 1.5.2: *gtor ma dbul ba'i rang bzhin.*

41. Sanskrit Version, A127b, B155a & C184a: *paṭapustakanirṇaya.*
Tib Version, TTP, vol. 2, 278.3.8 (& sTog 406b5): *bris sku dang glegs bam gtan la dbab pa.*
Indrabodhi, TTP, vol. 55., 1.5.2: *bris skud dang glegs bam gtan la dbab pa*.

42. Sanskrit Version, A134b: *śrīsampuṭodbhavasarvatantranidāna-mahākalparāja-daśamaḥ samāptaḥ* (the end of text); B163a & C194a: *śrīsampuṭodbhava-sarvatantranidāna-mahākalparājadaśamaḥ samāptaḥ.*
Tib Version, TTP, vol. 2, 280.2.4 (& sTog 412b1): *de kho na nyid thams cad kyi gleng gzhi brtag pa'i rgyal po chen po*.
Colophon in Peking edition, 280.2.4: *rgyud kyi rgyal po 'di ni paṇḍita gāyadharma dang bdag nyid chen po 'brog mi śākya ye shes kyi bsgyur* (for *bskyur*) *ba las slad kyi thams cad mkhyen pa bu ston zhabs kyis rgya dpe rtsa 'gril dang bstun nas hor kong bas bas shing 'gyur bcos legs par mdzad las bris ba'o //.*
Indrabodhi, TTP, vol. 55., 1.3.8: *rgyud thams cad kyi gleng gzhi.*

43. Sanskrit Version, A131a & C189a: *ācāryamudrādhiṣṭhāna*; B159a: *ācārya-mahāsādhana.*
Tib Version, TTP, vol. 2, 279.3.1(& sTog 409b2): *slob dpon dang phyag rgya byin gyis brlab pa.*
Indrabodhi, TTP, vol. 55, 1.5.2: *slob dpon gyi sgrub thabs chen po.*

44. Sanskrit Version, A132a, B160a & C190a: *mahāsukhasiddhipūjāsatkāra*.

Section 3 Section 39 Section 30

The manifestation of the Buddha illusion[45]

Section 40

Chapter XI. The *nidāna* ornament of all the chapters[46]

Out of the various headings provided by our sources, I have given paraphrased translations of those which closely reflect the actual content of individual chapters or sections. As it can be seen in the above sketch, not all chapter and section headings are provided in all our sources, and when they are given, they are not always exactly the same. Some of the headings are somewhat mysterious and difficult to justify when one tries to understand the overall structure of the *tantra's* text, but hopefully their meaning will become clearer below when we analyse the content of the *tantra*.

Stages of Tantric Theory and Practice According to the Sampuṭa-tantra and its Commentaries

It is well known among Buddhist scholars that the Buddhist *tantras* as literary texts do not readily present themselves as logically structured expositions of *tantric* theory and practice. Although their compilers must have followed some kind of compositional plan, the *tantras* give an impression of containing haphazardly arranged materials which deal with a variety of theoretical and practical matters. The same or similar topics are often found scattered in different sections of *tantric* texts, and the logical structure of such topics within chapters or

---

Tib Version, TTP, vol. 2, 279.4.2 (& sTog 410a6) *bde ba chen po'i dngos grub kyi mchod pa dang rim gro.*
Indrabodhi, TTP, vol. 55, 1.5.2: *bde ba chen po'i dngos grub dang mchod pa dang bkur sti.*

45. Sanskrit Version, A132b, B161a & C191b: *buddhamāyāvikurvita*.
Tib Version, TTP, vol. 2, 279.5.4 (& sTog 411a3): *sangs rgyas kyi sgyu tshe (sTog: ma) rnam par mdzad pa*.
Indrabodhi, TTP, vol. 55, 1.5.3: *sangs rgyas kyi sgyu ma'i rnam 'phrul.*

46. Sanskrit Version, B211a: *śrīsampuṭodbhave tantrarāje sarvakalpanidānatilaka ekādaśaḥ samāptaḥ*; C240b: *śrīsampuṭodbhavasarvatantrarāje sarvakalpanidānatilaka ekādaśamaḥ iti sampuṭaṭikā-nāma-mahātantrarājasamāpta*.
Tib Version, TTP, vol. 2, 291.1.3: *rgyud kyi rgyal po chen po dpal yang dag par sbyor* ba'i (for *spyod pa'i*) *thig le zhes bya ba rdzogs te*.
Colophon: *rgya gar gyi mkhan po kāyasthāpa* (Pek. ed. *kayastapa*) *gayadhara'i* (sTog *gayadhāra'i*) *zhal snga nas dang / bod kyi lo tstsha ba dge slong śākya ye shes kyis bsgyur cing zhus te gtan la phab pa'o / slad nas yang bod kyi lo tstsha ba gzhan rnams* (Pek. ed. *gzhan*) *gyis bsgyur ba* (Pek. ed. *kha*) *la zur mi 'dra bar bcos nas / rang gi ming bcug cing gzhan gyi ming 'phye ba de dag dang / mi shes pa de dag sun dbyung ba'i phyir slad nas yang rgya gar gyi rgyud bzhi dang / dge slong śākya ye shes de nyid kyis gtugs nas bcos te gtan la phab pa'o //.*
sTog 446b4: *rgyud kyi rgyal po chen po dpal yang dag par sbyor ba'i thig le*.
Indrabodhi, TTP, vol. 55, 1.4.1: *rtog pa thams cad kyi gleng gzhi thig le thabs sna tshogs.*

entire texts is not easily recognisable. The commentaries generally provide meaningful interpretations but even with their help it is not always easy to unravel and establish the precise order and infrastructure of the various parts of *tantric* texts. This seemingly apparent lack of clarity and logic in the structure of many *tantric* texts must have been perceived at least by some Indian masters as the body of *tantric* texts continued to grow over centuries. The *Saṃpuṭa-tantra* and its commentaries appear to have been deliberately composed to address this problem. The *tantra* itself explicitly claims to offer a systematic exposition of *tantric* theory and practice as advocated in all the *yoga* and *yoginī tantras* and the three Indian commentators duly interpret it in that way.[47]

At first glance, the *Saṃpuṭa-tantra* does not appear to be especially different from many other *tantras*. It is a highly eclectic text which clusters together relevant materials derived from a number of *yoga* and *yoginī tantras*. As in other *tantric* texts the same topics are also found scattered in different sections of the *tantra*. There are places throughout the whole text which show that this *tantra* is very much a product of cut and pace procedure. Thus, in terms of originality, only some portions seems to be new and creative compositions. Otherwise, practically the whole *tantra* is composed on the basis of materials already found in other *tantras* such as the *Guhyasamāja*, the *Hevajra*, and other important *tantric* texts, which were already in existence before the composition of the *Saṃpuṭa-tantra*. However, the eclectic nature of this *tantra* is quite understandable and justifiable when one considers its purpose, namely, an exposition of *tantric* theories and practices taught in the *yoga* and *yoginī tantras*. It is precisely this effort to provide a coherent and systematic exposition of theoretical and practical assumptions of the Buddhist *tantras* that constitutes the originality and indeed contribution of the *Saṃpuṭa-tantra* and its commentaries to our understanding of the Buddhist *tantras*.

The whole structure of the *tantra's* text and its exposition of *tantric* theory and practice are hinged on several well-known *tantric* principles or categorisations. The Two basic approaches to the *tantric* theory and practice are the process of generation (*utpattikrama*) and the process of realisation (*saṃpannakrama*). Other categories frequently employed explicitly or implicitly by the *tantra* and its commentaries include the differentiation into outer, inner, and secret levels of the practice; the two levels of truth: conventional (*saṃvṛti*) and transcendent or absolute (*paramārtha*); mundane (*loka*) and transcendent (*lokottara*) attainments (*siddhi*), and the activities performed either for one's own or other people's benefit.

---

47. Indrabodhi commenting on the phrase "all the *yoga* and *yoginī tantras*", states that it implies thirty six *tantras* but he does not name them. Indrabodhi, TTP, vol. 55, 4.5.7. At the end of his commentary, However, Vīryavajra says that the ten chapters and forty sections of the *Saṃpuṭa* explain the meaning of five *upāya tantras* and four *prajñā tantras*. Vīryavajra, TTP, vol. 55, 300.3.5.

When we look at the *tantra's* text bearing in mind the above mentioned categorisations, it becomes possible to offer a general explanation as to why one finds the same topics scattered in different parts of the *tantra*. Depending on the context, some sections treat the same subject from a theoretical position while other sections set out its practical framework. Some sections explain the same doctrine or practice in relationship to three different levels of practice or from the perspective of the two truths, or again from the perspective of the two orders of spiritual progress, namely, the process of generation and the process of realization. For instance, the *homa* is treated in several places in our *tantra*. The explicit or intended presence and significance of these passages does not become readily apparent when one reads the *tantra's* text. However, the commentaries justify such repetitions by explaining that the *homa* is mentioned or treated in different sections because, depending on the context, it should be performed for some particular purpose, be it either as a meditational exercise or as an external ritual, or again in order to gain either mundane or supramundane attainments. More examples could be offered but instead we shall now proceed to sketch a broad outline of *tantric* theory and practice as presented in the *Saṃpuṭa-tantra* and its commentaries.

The first six chapters of the *Saṃpuṭa-tantra* explain the progressive stages leading to the attainment of the highest *siddhis* (*mchog gi dngos grub*). Or to put it differently, they provide the theoretical and practical framework of becoming an accomplished and indeed enlightened *vajra*-master. The *tantra* defines the nature and location of the *bodhicitta*, and then teaches in various ways how it should be consecrated and cultivated until it becomes entirely liberated from the bonds of *saṃsāra*. Chapter Seven teaches a variety of ritual performances through which one gains the worldly *siddhis* (*'jig rten pa' dngos grub*).[48] Within the context of the *tantric* practice, the primary dimensions of both the highest and worldly *siddhis* are constituted by the *yogin's* inner dispositions. The attainment of such *siddhis* means that the *yogin* has purified the *bodhicitta*, acquired the true and liberating knowledge, and gained control over phenomena and other people. Chapter Eight and Nine explain a number of important branches[49] of the practice, which involve certain specific activities which further perfect the *vajra*-master and enable him, as it were, to induce and to sustain a perfect and happy state within himself and the surrounding world. Chapter Ten outlines the *sādhanas* relating to a fully perfected *vajra*-master.[50] It basically shows how an accomplished and fully perfected *vajra*-master acts and behaves, and how he interacts with and is respected by gods and men.

48. Vīryavajra, TTP, vol. 55, 273.3.7.
49. Vīryavajra, TTP, vol. 55, 253.4.1.
50. Chapter Eleven is not included in our analysis. As already stated above it is fundamentally a commentary on certain passages in other chapters.

Chapter One, which is considered by the commentators as the most important, outlines the overall framework of *tantric* theory and practice. Section One, drawing on various *tantric* sources, unveils the nature of the thought of enlightenment (*bodhicitta*) according to the process of generation and the process of realization.[51] The *tantra* makes a fundamental assumption that the impurities of the embodied beings (*dehin*) become cleansed in emptiness (*śūnyatā*). This basic assumption is then expanded by asserting that the objects of cognition (*viṣaya*), form (*rūpa*) and the rest are empty. Since the objects of the sense-faculties (*indriya*) are empty and non-existent, there can be no consciousness (*vijñāna*) that arises in the empty sense faculties. Consequently, all the elements (*dhātu*). including the mind (*citta*) and mental states (*caitasika*), must be perceived as non-existent. However, the *tantra* promptly recognises the limitations of differentiation into subject and object, and at once proceeds to set out the essential (*tattva*) and non-dual (*advaya*) path (*mārga*) which is free of duality (*dvaya*), reasoning (*apratarkya*), and apprehension (*avijñeya*). In contrast to ordinary knowledge, the secret of all the Buddhas, which is like space (*ākāśa*), constitutes the sameness (*samatā*) of all *dharmas*.[52] It remains unknown to the *śrāvakas* and Pratyeka Buddhas but the Bodhisattvas submerged in *saṃsāra* lead towards liberation by means of appropriate meditational dispositions (*bsgom pa'i bsam*) and the very character of the four *abhiṣekas*.[53] Hence, the *tantra* states that the mind (*cetas*) freed from *saṃsāra* constitutes the liberating factor (*lakṣa*) that vibrates within the body. The knowledge-mind (*jñānacetas*) ascertains consciousness (*vijñāna*) in its various aspects, and once it perceives through knowledge the knowable world (*jñeya*), it understands its different pathways; it knows its nature and how it operates but does not become entangled in it. On the other hand, the mind drawn towards different paths of rebirth (*gati*) continues to be involved in the path of *karmic* retribution. Having made a basic distinction between two different ways of viewing the world, the *tantra* proceeds to explain matters concerning the path of liberation.[54] The *yogin* who perceives the empty character of all characteristics deposits a seed (*bīja*) into the empty field of the body. Following upon an understanding of the empty characteristics of things, one recollects with wisdom the emptiness of all *dharmas*, and casts the seed of bliss as the seminal consciousness of knowledge[55] into the field of the bodily *maṇḍala* inside three *maṇḍalas*, namely, the bodily *maṇḍala*, the *bhaga's maṇḍala*, and the *dharma-dhātu maṇḍala*. Such is the succinct presentation of the path of liberation.[56]

---

51. Abhayākaragupta, TTP, vol. 55, 107.2.8.
52. Vīryavajra, TTP, vol. 55, 254.5.8.
53. Vīryavajra, TTP, vol. 55, 255.1.3.
54. *grol lam pa'i shes bya.*
55. *ye shes kyi rgyu rnam shes.*
56. Vīryavajra, TTP, vol. 55, 255.1.7-8.

Next, the *tantra* sketches the various transfigurations and locations of the *bodhicitta*. The subtle mind (*sems*), emerges from the *avadhūtī* and has the nature of psychic channels (*nāḍī*).[57] The very thing that emerges from the hollow psychic channels constitutes the stainless *bodhicitta* which is luminous (*prabhāsvara*) and similar to the brightness of a pure crystal. It has the nature of the five Buddha *jñānas* and it is the size of a mustard seed. The deity (*deva*) abiding inside it has manifested (*vyakta*) and unmanifested (*avyakta*) forms. One half is subtle. It has the nature of the mind (*manas*) and the form of the primordial drop or essence (*bindu; thig le*). It always abides in the heart and shines with brightness. The mind (*sems*) manifested in the form of clear light (*prabhāsvara*; *'od gsal ba*) is taught to be the *bindu* of the *bodhicitta* that abides in the heart. The so called deity inside it denotes the central psychic channel (*avadhūtī*), and again the deity resting inside it represents the space wind (*nam mkha'i rlung*). Due to its unmanifested aspect, it is constant, and its manifested aspect is experienced by the wise. One half represents the steady wind[58] and the second half has the form of the abiding *bindu*, and it is experienced through the non-reasoning mind.[59] Next the *bodhicitta* is ascertained as the location of bliss(*sukha*).[60] It is located within the confines of the six faculties (*indriya*) and inside the heart permeated with the light of great brightness. It is free from reasoning.[61] Depending on the *yogic* method, it reaches from the feet to the top of the head or, as the *avadhūtī* thread, it is located inside the space of twelve fingers from the feet and nine fingers from the spot between the eyebrows. Or once again it abides at the top of the *avadhūtī,* nine fingers below the navel or again it is also said to rest at the extremity of the *brahma*-aperture.[62] The treatment of the *bodhicitta* in terms of psychic channels and winds is followed by explaining it in terms of the *mantra* procedure, which involves the wind endowed with heat.[63] This practice adheres to the so called one thread (*tantu*) located inside the navel. Although there is heat inside the navel, the bliss does not arise. A proportionate part of it is endowed with the properties of the five elements. It has the shape of a thumb or a coiled snake (*nāgendra*). When it becomes augmented and open, the region of the *bodhicitta* becomes activated inside the *vajra* at the navel. The place of the emerged *bodhicitta* constitutes the fire *maṇḍala*. And again when the *bindu* of the *bodhicitta* resting inside the triangular letter E is discharged, it constitutes the essence of the semen (*khu ba*). When it is duly augmented, it expands towards the extremities of the nine apertures, but it is retained within by means of the magic group (*'khrul 'khor*) of the eight seed

57. Vīryavajra, TTP, vol. 55, 255.1.8.
58. *mi shigs pa'i rlung*.
59. *avitarka / rtog pa med pa.*
60. Vīryavajra, TTP, vol. 55, 255.2.2.
61. *avitarka / rtog pa med pa.*
62. *brahmarandhra / tshangs pa'i bug.*
63. Vīryavajra, TTP, vol. 55, 255.2.7.

syllables (*bīja*) and ritualised procedures (*vidhi*). This means that following upon the meditation on emptiness, one meditates on the *jñāna-ḍākiṇīs,* and one becomes perfected by means of the *bījas* or their fully perfected deities.[64] This eventually leads to penetrating the entire sphere of the world, and further exercises in a particular *samādhi*[65] induce the emergence of the bliss.[66]

Next the *tantra* recounts the path of deliverance and its fruit in relationship to phenomenal existence and within the context of its understanding of the Four Noble Truths. With one foot, as it were, one stands in *nirvāṇa* and with the other in *saṃsāra.* It is due to this very fact that the mind is tied up, and so long as one abides in a body, it is governed by *karma* and non-*karmic* factors. While the mind's self-awareness (*sems rang rig*) is covered by the adventitious impurities,[67] it has no understanding of the bliss. At the time of rebirth, one acts by means of *karmic* and non-*karmic kleśas*, and through the power of *kuśala* and *akuśala* actions are produced the various heavenly (*svarga*; *mtho ris*) and evil (*durgati*; *ngan song*) rebirths. Thus, the *tantra* here affirms the truth of suffering (*duḥkha-satya*) and the truth of its arisal (*samudaya-satya*).[68] Next, it states the truth of the path (*mārga-satya*) and the truth of suppression (*nirodha-satya*) by declaring the practice of the *yoga* of sameness (*samatā*), and the practice of *pūjana* and *bhāvanā*. Once the *karmic* body becomes destroyed, one becomes like a deity (*devatā*). The yoga of sameness implies the four *mudrās*. When one meditates on the nature of the mind free from thoughts, one destroys the body of discursive thinking, and one acquires a form (*gzugs*) resembling the nature of bliss and emptiness. Then upon gaining the first *bhūmi* all the firm and moving phenomena become known as emptiness.[69]Then the *tantra* briefly unfolds the progress towards the fruit (*phala*; *'bras bu*), which is spoken of as the sameness resembling space that is gained through knowing the appearance of the manifested things. Once the *mudrā* of Vairocana is applied with regard to the elements (*bhūta*; *'byung ba*), the emptiness of the objects (*viṣaya*) becomes known, and when the mind is sealed by Akṣobhya, emptiness is perceived as being similar to space. One thus abides in *nirvāṇa* being "naked and stainless". This means that after contemplating the inconceivable clear light, and after executing the *mudrā* of Vajrasattva, the mystic fusion of the opposites (*yuganaddha*; *zung du 'jug pa*) becomes known. Thus, the truly knowing mind (*ngo shes pa'i sems*) is no longer clad with the obstructions of the *kleśas*, and the *jñeyāvaraṇas* also become abandoned. This also implies that upon going beyond the gross forms, one

64. Abhayākaragupta, TTP, vol. 55, 114.1.2.
65. *zhi gnas kyi bde ba'i ting nge 'dzin.*
66. Vīryavajra, TTP, vol. 55, 255.3.6.
67. *āgantuka / blo bur gyi dri ma*.
68. Vīryavajra, TTP, vol. 55, 255.3.1.
69. Vīryavajra, TTP, vol. 55, 255.3.3.

contemplates the mind's nature free from entities [70] but one does not examines the mind's nature since it is inconceivable. But the *yogin* abiding in the mind is not to be considered as having passed into *nirvāṇa*.[71]

The basic outline of the path of liberation is now followed by an exposition of the path of desire (*chags pa'i lam*). This path incorporates the consecrations and the various activities involving different categories of appropriate female partners categorised as mother, sister and so forth. [72] This is then followed by elucidating the *upāya* approach. The adept who is fond of the essence, should perform the acts of worship by means of the *prajñā* and *upāya* method (*vidhāna*). This procedure has the nature of joy free of discursive thinking. One gains the secret and becomes endowed with the pledge (*samaya*). One performs activities by means of veneration (*sevā*). Next, the text provides the categorisation of the four *mudrās*. Here, the exposition concerns the various Buddha Families. [73] The five families are the family of Mahāvairocana and the other four Buddhas. In this connection are also stated the various categories of female partners as *mudrās* of the different Buddha families. [74] The *tantra's* assertion that "the glorious one submerged and re-emerged from suchness (*tathatā*) should be considered as a Tathāgata attended by a *prajñā*" lays down a foundation for understanding the specific character of the Buddhas attended by goddesses. The Tathāgatas abide in the different families perceived as wisdom and emptiness. This concludes the sketch of the path of desire (*chags pa'i lam*). [75]

Finally the *tantra* sets forth the self-abiding path. [76] When there is no discursive development (*niṣprapañca; spros pa med pa*), there is no differentiation into subject and object, no adherence to the notion of the one who meditates and the meditated objects, no *mantra* recitation, and no deities, but only a meditation on the nature of the clear light. The very freedom from discursive development (*prapañca*) constitutes the nature of the five Buddhas abiding in the five wisdoms.

After defining the nature and configurations of the *bodhicitta*, and outlining the pathways of deliverance, Section Two of the *tantra* teaches how to induce the manifestation of the *bodhicitta*. In addition to describing the thirty-seven *bodhipākṣikas,* the *tantra* also advocates the Bodhisattva *bhūmis* and the *yogic* practices involving the psychic channels. The text firmly asserts that Buddhahood abides in the *skandhas* and *indriyas*. There is no Buddhahood except through the body (*deha*); it is not born in the body but abides in the body. The thirty-seven

---

70. *dngos po med pa'i sems nyid.*
71. Vīryavajra, TTP, vol. 55, 255.4.3-7.
72. Vīryavajra, TTP, vol. 55, 255.4.8/5.2.
73. Vīryavajra, TTP, vol. 55, 255.5.5.
74. Vīryavajra, TTP, vol. 55, 255.5.8.
75. Vīryavajra, TTP, vol. 55, 256.1.7.
76. *rang lhag par gnas pa'i lam.* Vīryavajra, TTP, vol. 55, 256.1.8.

bodhipākṣikas, in addition to their conventional or exoteric significance, are also interpreted in esoteric or *tantric* terms. Indrabodhi interprets them in terms of various sets such as the *skandhas*, *dhātus*, and *indriyas,* and different *samādhis*.[77] According to him, the *tantric* perception of the *skandhas* and other categories relate to the *yoga tantras*, and the use of the psychic channels appertains to the *yoginī tantras*. Ultimately these two approaches epitomise the union of the conventional and absolute realities. The *bodhicitta* in this section denotes the penetration into the transcendent (*lokottara*) and absolute (*paramārtha*) reality.[78] Vīryavajra explains that on account of the one flavour of *samsāra* and *nirvāṇa,* the *maṇḍalas* are shown as having the nature of the non-dual *bodhicitta*. He interprets the thirty-seven *bodhipakṣikas* as a meditational process on the union of wisdom and means. The means stands for thirty-seven illusion-similarities (*māyopama*) and wisdom for thirty-seven kinds of emptiness (*śunyatā*), and the thirty-seven kinds of their *yuganaddha* epitomise the *mahāsukha*. When this has been realised by the mind, one relies on the four *mudrās* and perceives the objects (*viṣaya*) as the emptiness of wisdom, and the object-perceiver as the emptiness of the means.[79]

Section Three propounds the essence of the supreme and secret knowledge (*jñāna*). The text describes it as the supreme bliss and Vajrasattva epitomising all the Buddhas. It constitutes the one flavour of knowledge (*jñāna*) and the knowable (*jñeya*). According to Vīryavajra, this section basically outlines the approach of the *Śaṃvara* (*bDe mchog*) and *Samāyoga* (*mNyam sbyor*) *tantras*.[80] He also says that it explains the nature of transcendental knowledge and higher vision, and the means of gaining the transcendental essence.[81]

According to Indrabodhi, Section Four provides an expanded exposition of how the variety of living beings become Buddhas through virtuous activities.[82] Vīryavajra, however, says that it teaches in an expanded way the *nidāna* of the *Guhyasamāja* and other *tantras*.[83]

Chapter Two deals with the consecrations. Abhayākaragupta[84] says that since the process of generation and the process of realization do not exist without consecrations and *maṇḍalas*, Section Five outlines the procedures of consecrating the *bodhicitta*. He also explains that the consecrations are treated within the context of the process of generation and the process of realization.[85] Vīryavajra specifies

77. Indrabodhi, TTP, vol. 55, 19.5.2.
78. Indrabodhi, TTP. vol. 55, 26.5.5.
79. Vīryavajra, TTP, vol. 55, 256.3.4.
80. Vīryavajra, TTP, vol. 55, 253.2.6.
81. Vīryavajra, TTP, vol. 55, 257.2.4.
82. Indrabodhi, TTP, vol. 55, 29.4.1.
83. Vīryavajra, TTP, vol. 55, 253.2.7.
84. Abhayākaragupta, TTP, vol. 55, 132.5.6. Indrabodhi, TTP, vol. 55, 38.5.4.
85. Abhayākaragupta, TTP, vol. 55, 107, 3.2.

that here we have an exposition of the water, secret, and *prajñājñāna* consecrations.[86] The actual text explains the *abhiṣeka* of disciples, drawing the *maṇḍala* and summoning deities, the *yoga* involving female partners, dispensation of the *samaya*, and other relevant matters appertaining to the consecrations.

Since the consecrated *bodhicitta* does not become manifested without being meditated upon, Section Six explains the appropriate ways of contemplating it. This is basically done by meditating on the various configurations of wisdom and means.[87] Abhayākaragupta says that for those with sharp faculties who wish to gain both the conventional and transcendent consecrations, and to gain the state of Mahāvajradhara, there is here explained the *saṃpannakrama* meditation on the method of accomplishing the *mahāmudrā* which involves the *yoga* with a *mudrā*.[88] The actual text sketches different meditational approaches to the understanding of the nature of *upāya* and *prajñā*. Emptiness or non-emptiness should not be meditated upon, but rather keeping aloof and free from being engaged in thought processes, one's meditation should resemble the sky. *Prajñā* resembles the nature of *niṣprapañca*, and both *prajñā* and *upāya* are without subjects or supports. Things should not be considered in terms of grasping or abandoning. One should enter the *bhaga* and meditate on the Buddha. This is the non-dual state and the very best nature of the *bodhicitta*; *prajñāpāramitatā*, *samatā*, and the essence of all things. The mind, clad in impurities which are difficult to suppress, is said by Vajradhara to be *saṃsāra*. The mind free from impurities is the highest being free from the subject and object: this is said to be *nirvāṇa*. There is no gaining Buddhahood without means and wisdom. Therefore, one must practise the four *mudrās*: ignorance (*avidyā*) is *samayamudrā*, hatred (*dveṣa*) is *mahāmudrā*, envy (*irṣyā*) is *karmamudrā*, and passion (*rāga*) is *dharmamudrā*. The *yogi* should generate the *mudrās*, perceive their union as deities and perform different activities.

According to Abhayākaragupta[89] Sections Seven to Twelve (= section three of Chapter Two to section four of Chapter Three) are intended for those with average and weak faculties. They meditate on the process of realization by following the order of the process of generation. Section Seven sets out the various ritual models of visualisations of the deities and *maṇḍalas* of different *tantras*. While the previous section explained the meditational exercises according to the process of realisation, this section sets out the process of generation of the essential means

86. Vīryavajra, TTP, vol. 55, 253.2.7.
87. Abhayākaragupta, TTP, vol. 55, 139.28; Indrabodhi, TTP, vol. 55, 38.5.4. Vīryavajra says that after explaining the *prajñājñāna* consecration, now the four *abhiṣekas* are explained. Vīryavajra, TTP, vol. 5, 262.2.4. He also says that this section teaches the profound *saṃpannakrama* of the four inconceivables (*bzhi pa bsam gyis mi khyab pa'i zab pa'i rdzogs rim*). Vīryavajra, TTP, vol. 55, 253.2.8.
88. Abhayākaragupta, TTP, vol. 55, 107.3.3.
89. Abhayākaragupta, TTP, vol. 55, 107.3.4.

(*upāya*).[90] Vīryavajra[91] does not refer to people with average and dull faculties but does confirm that these six sections follow the process of generation. At the beginning of Section Seven, the text states that it will explain the manifestation of all the retinues. The *maṇḍala* of all the Tathāgatas is said to be the very knowledge (*jñānatā*) of *śūnyatā*. The text also sketches the *sādhana* of the wrathful ones and the peaceful deities; the rite of reciting *mantras*, and drawing images. As for meditational exercises, first one meditates on *maitrī*, then on *karuṇā* and *sukha*, and then on the *upekṣā* of them all or the empty *bodhicitta*. Then the *sādhana* of Heruka and eight goddesses is outlined with Vajravārāhī as a *prajñā*.

Abhayākaragupta says that Section Eight shows the method of meditating on different deities in order to achieve the appeasement (*kṣanti)*, prosperity (*puṣti*) and so forth by means of charms (*cakra*) and other devices.[92] According to Indrabodhi, this section briefly explains the pacifying and other rites in order to appease and control the living being of this degenerate age (*kaliyuga*) who are fond of fierce and other adverse activities. It also illustrates the *sādhanas* which are for the benefit of living beings.[93] Vīryavajra says that while the previous section explained the *sādhanas* of the male deities, this section explains the *sādhanas* of the female deities,[94] and again that while the previous section taught meditation on many Herukas, this section teaches meditation on many goddesses by means of the *tantras* derived from Tārā.[95] The text itself does indeed briefly mention the four rites, and instructs how one should arrange various potent devices on the outer part of the *maṇḍala*. One meditates on the *cakras*, recites the Tārā *mantra*, meditates on the protective circle, and one perfects all deities with the principal *mantra*. In addition to Tārā, the text also speaks of the *sādhana* meditation on Kurukullā visualisation and the five Buddha goddesses.

Although Chapter Three is named by Indrabodhi as "drawing the great *Vajradhātu-maṇḍala*", he explains in his commentary that this implies not just one particular *maṇḍala* but rather the basic structure of the most important *maṇḍalas*. Section Nine explains the *sādhana* of Heruka and Nairātmya. While the two previous sections dealt with male and female deities separately, this section explains the method of the eight headed Heruka (Hevajra) and his female partner surrounded by *ḍākinīs*.[96] Section Ten explains the *sādhana* of the knowledge

---

90. Abhayākaragupta, TTP, vol. 55, 143.2.7.
91. Vīryavajra, TTP, vol. 55, 253.3.5.
92. Abhayākaragupta, TTP, vol. 55, 147.1.2.
93. Indrabodhi, TTP, vol. 55, 53.1.6.
94. Vīryavajra, TTP, vol. 55, 266.1.6.
95. Vīryavajra, TTP, vol. 55, 253.3.1.
96. Vīryavajra, TTP, vol. 55, 266.4.6.

ḍākinīs (*jñānaḍākinī*),[97] and Section Eleven teaches the *sādhana* of *anātma* through the use of appropriate seed syllables.[98] This is basically done through visualising the union of the solar and lunar discs, and the union of the vowels and syllables. Section Twelve outlines the meditational and drawn *maṇḍala*[99] derived from the *Tattvasaṃgraha*.[100] The text itself explains the production of the *maṇḍala* referred to as the *vajradhātu*, and reiterates the stages of consecration as outlined in the first chapter of the *Sarvatathāgatatattvasaṃgraha*.

According to Vīryavajra, the four section of Chapter Four and two section of Chapter Five (= Section Thirteen to Eighteen) explain the matters relating to the entire *yogic* assembly (*ganacakra; tshogs kyi 'khor lo*) and show how it becomes absorbed.[101] While the preceding six sections explained the process of generation, the six sections that now follow show the *gaṇacakra* in its branches perfected according to both the process of generation and the process of realization. First the speech symbols are explained. This is done in Section Thirteen.[102] Indrabodhi says that here we have the inner *samayamudrās* of all the *ḍakinīs* abiding in the *maṇḍala*.[103] According to Abhayākaragupta, this section teaches the use of signs in order to assemble the *vajrayoginīs* of the *yogins* following the path of the process of realization and the process of generating.[104] The text itself basically consists of a chain of syllables which are said to represent the *mudrās* expressed through the *samayas* of the *ḍākinīs*. Section Fourteen, according to Vīryavajra, demonstrates the consecration goddesses (*dbang gi lha mo*).[105] Abhayākaragupta specifies that here we have the names and characteristics of the twenty-four *yoginīs* of the Śaṃvara *maṇḍala*,[106] and Indra-bodhi interprets this section as the symbols of the *mudrās* of the seven *yoginīs* derived from the six timely messengers (*dus kyi pho nya mo drug*).[107] In the *tantra's* text, this short section is named as "the signs and *mudrās* of the *kaṭapūtanīs*". The text itself does appear to provide grounds for the above interpretations. According to Indrabodhi, the next section, Section Fifteen, teaches the character of the *mudrās* and the characteristics of the thirteen *ḍākinīs* of the thirteen pure *bhūmis*,[108] and Abhayākaragupta says

97. Vīryavajra, TTP, vol. 55, 267.1.6. Abhayākaragupta, TTP, vol. 55, 150.2.2. Vīryavajra also says that it is the meditation on the *jñānaḍākinīs* of the *rdo rje gdan bzhi*; TTP, vol. 55, 253.3.2.
98. Vīryavajra, TTP, vol. 55, 267.4.1. Indrabodhi, TTP, vol. 55, 62.3.1.
99. Abhayākaragupta, TTP, vol. 55, 153.3.4.
100. Vīryavajra, TTP, vol. 55, 253.3.2.
101. Vīryavajra, TTP, vol. 55, 253.3.3.
102. Vīryavajra, TTP, vol. 55, 269.4.8.
103. Indrabodhi, TTP, vol. 55, 64.1.5.
104. Abhayākaragupta, TTP, vol. 55, 170.4.2.
105. Vīryavajra, TTP, vol. 55, 270.1.3.
106. Abhayākaragupta, TTP, vol. 55, 171.4.8.
107. Indrabodhi, TTP, vol. 55, 65.5.8.
108. Indrabodhi, TTP, vol. 55, 66.2.4.

that this section teaches the penetration into the character of women belonging to the Lāmā's family.[109] Finally Section Sixteen explains other *mudrās*,[110] which according to Indrabodhi are the bodily signs of the thirty six outer *yoginīs*.[111] The text itself indeed provides descriptions of communicating through various signs. The complex meditational exercises on the characteristics of the various categories of *yoginīs* and *ḍākinīs* are now followed by an explanation of the places where the *yogins* and *yoginīs* should gather. Thus, Section Seventeen (= the first section of Chapter Five) provides the names and explains the nature of the places of pilgrimage known as *pīṭhas* and *upapīṭhas*.[112] The next section, Section Eighteen, explains "the purity of the *skandhas* and the *āyatanas*" as a complex *samādhi* on the *gaṇacakra*.[113] Indrabodhi explains that this consists of adhering to the inner bliss of the *avadhūtī*,[114] and Abhayākaragupta says that it constitutes the attainment of the very essence of Vajradhara.[115] The text itself outlines an advanced and complex meditational process executed by highly perfected *yogins* who have perfected all the stages covered in the preceding sections. The meditation itself involves visualisation of the *maṇḍala* and adhering to the *mahāmudrā*. It is at this stage that the *skandhas*, *dhātus*, and *āyatanas* of embodied beings (*dehin*) are declared to be pure by nature.[116] The *rūpa skandha* is said to be Vairocana, the *vedanā skandha* Vajrasūrya (rDo rje nyi ma), the *saṃjñā skandha* Padma-narteśvara (Pad ma gar dbang phyug), the *saṃskāra skandha* Vajrarāja (rDo rje rgyal), the *vijñāna skandha* the essence of Vajrasattva, and the essence of them all Heruka.[117]

Section Nineteen further explains meditational exercises at a transcendental level which aim to perceive reality as *cittamātratā*. Without pursuing the practice, there can be no outer and inner attainments.[118] Although one is already entrenched in the order of generations and of realization, there can be no attainment of the

109. Abhayākaragupta, TTP, vol. 55, 172.2.4. According to Vīryavajra, Section Fifteen shows the characteristics of three kinds of goddesses: *dag byed kyi lha mo*, *dpa' bo'i lha mo*, and *rags gnag ba'i lha mo*. Vīryavajra, TTP, vol. 55, 270.1.8. And again in another place he says that this section shows the characteristics of the *dpa' bo* and *bka' nod pa*. Vīryavajra, TTP, vol. 55, 253.4.
110. Abhayākaragupta, TTP, vol. 55, 172.4.5.
111. Indrabodhi, TTP, vol. 55, 66.3.4.
112. Indrabodhi, TTP, vol. 55, 66.4.3. Abhayākaragupta, TTP, vol. 55, 172.5.2. Vīryavajra, TTP, vol. 55, 270.3.2.
113. Vīryavajra, TTP, vol. 55, 271.1.7.
114. Indrabodhi, TTP, vol. 55, 68, 1.3.
115. Abhayākara, TTP, vol. 55, 175.4.2.
116. Tibetan Version, TTP, vol. 2, 258.5.4.
117. Tibetan Version, TTP, vol. 2, 259.1.1.
118. Indrabodhi, TTP, vol. 55, 72.3.1 & 73.1.2.

mahāmudrā without the further practice.[119] A *yogin* who remains free from discursive thinking and detached from all things becomes a master of the threefold world. Section Twenty further elaborates on the same practice[120] and explains the character of the *yogins* who are proficient in it.[121]

According to Indrabodhi, the first three sections (= Sections 21-23) of Chapter Six provide an exposition of the *ubhaya tantras*, and section four (= Section 24) reiterates the teaching on the pattern of many treatises (*gzhung lugs*).[122] According to Vīryavajra the first section (21) of this chapter teaches the *nidāna* of Śaṃvara (bDe mchog) and how one should perceive the emergence of the blissful *vajra*-body (*dga' ba'i rdo rje'i lus*); the second section (22) explains the meditation on the *bindu*; the third (23), the meditation on the psychic channels; and the fourth (24), the meditation on heat (*drod*) and the *bodhicitta*.[123] To put it in a different way, these sections teach the way of perfecting the *yogic* body through identification of the various parts of the body with a set of secret syllables and the psychic channels with the twenty four places of pilgrimage. Section Twenty Two explains the arrangement of the psychic channels within the body.[124] Commenting on this section, Abhayākaragupta states that the body of individual living beings has the nature of a Tathāgata.[125] Section Twenty Three elaborates on the *maṇḍalas* and other things according to the process of realization of the highest wisdom.[126] It basically explains the body *maṇḍala* and how a *yogin* should execute within his body different kinds of ritual activities such as *homa* or recitation. Section Twenty Four explains the various *cakras* within the body which it identifies with the Buddha Bodies and *mahāsukha*. It also explains the emergence of pure deities, and the order of the *ḍākinīs*.

So far the *tantra* has explained the progressive stages leading to the highest attainments culminating in Chapter Six with gaining a perfected Buddha Body. Now, the *tantra* proceeds to teach how the *yogins* endowed with *nirmāṇa* bodies should gain the worldly attainments. This basically amounts to acting in an external manner in order to benefit living beings by performing various kinds of rituals.[127] The whole of Chapter Seven provides expositions regarding a whole

---

119. Abhayākaragupta, TTP, vol. 55, 184.3.7. According to Vīryavajra, this section explains a *yoga* of expanding the process of generation. Vīryavajra, TTP, vol. 55, 253.3.5.
120. Indrabodhi, TTP, vol. 55, 73.1.3. For Vīryavajra, this section teaches a yoga of expanding the process of realization; TTP, vol. 55, 253.3.5.
121. Abhayākaragupta, TTP, vol. 55, 188.2.7.
122. Indrabodhi, TTP, vol. 55, 74.5.1.
123. Vīryavajra, TTP, vol. 55, 253.3.6-7. Abhayākaragupta says that now the process of realization is elucidated in different ways. Abhayākaragupta, TTP, vol. 55, 190.3.2.
124. Indrabodhi, TTP, vol. 55, 78.4.8.
125. Abhayākaragupta, TTP, vol. 55, 196.1.7.
126. Abhayākaragupta, TTP, vol. 55, 198.5.5.
127. Indrabodhi, TTP, vol. 55, 84.1.3. Vryavajra, TTP, vol. 55, 273.3.7.

range of rituals such as the four kinds of *homa*, offerings of *bali*, recitations of *mantras*, consecrations (*ptatiṣṭhā*) of *maṇḍalas*, and a number of other rituals devised for various purposes. It should be added here that the ability to perform rituals effectively also implies the inner power of being able to control various events and adverse forces.

The sections of Chapters Eight and Nine teach the important branches[128] of the practice which further perfect the *yogin's* body, abilities, and powers.

Chapter Eight explains the manner of inner realisation of the four *tattvas*: *vajra*, bell, rosary, *jñāna*. Without understanding these four *tattvas* there is no quick attainment of *siddhis* by the *yogins*.[129] Section Twenty Nine explains the characteristic of the *vajra* and the bell.[130] The *vajra* is characterised in terms of a *maṇḍala* replete with male deities, and the bell epitomises wisdom in terms of a set of female deities, Māmaki and others. Wisdom is like a vase of *amṛta* with goddess Prajñāpāratā inside it. Then, the union of the *vajra* and the bell is described. Section Thirty explains the manner of meditating upon and reciting *mantras*, and the nature of rosaries (*bgrang phreng*) employed for counting the recitations of *mantras*. Section Thirty One provides a comprehensive exposition of the *tantric* treatment of the process of dying and other relevant matters which can help to gain a better rebirth.[131] The text explains how the various bodily apertures serve as passages leading to different types of rebirth, and teaches the use of *mantras* and a variety of meditational exercises on how to discharge one's life (*srog*) through the *brahmarandhra*. The proficiency in knowing and controlling the process of dying constitutes the fourth *tattva* generally described as ascertaining the characteristics by means of knowledge (*jñāna*).[132] This section is said to represent the rejection of the erroneous knowledge of non-believers and the manner of placing them in the Buddha knowledge.[133]

Section Thirty Two provides a set of *mantras* of various deities which are required to perform the rites of the previously explained *sādhanas*.[134] Since the process of generation has the nature of *mantras* and those endowed with the *mantra* body (*sngags kyi sku can*), and since the pacifying and other rites constitute branches of the process of generation, they are accomplished through *mantras*.[135]

---

128. Vīryavajra, TTP, vol. 55, 253.4.1.
129. Indrabodhi, TTP, vol. 55, 94.3.6.
130. Vīryavajra, TTP, vol. 55, 253.4.1.
131. Abhayākaragupta, TTP, vol. 55, 230.2.4.
132. Vīryavajra, TTP, vol. 55, 296.3.5.
133. Indrabodhi, TTP, vol. 55, 100.3.4.
134. Indrabodhi, TTP, vol. 55, 100.3.5. Vīryavajra says that this section refers to the four activities (*phrin las bzhi*).
135. Abhayākaragupta, TTP, vol. 55, 234.3.5.

The four sections of Chapter Nine explain various activities which make the world, as it were, a perfect place. Section Thirty Three poetically describes a meditational process of generating oneself as a Buddha from the nature of the Tathāgatas.[136] This particular activity is performed by accomplished *yogins* abiding in the *nirmāṇakāya,*[137] and being permeated by the blessings of the various manifestations of Vajradhara endowed with the nature of the perfected *maṇḍalas.*[138] Vīryavajra says that this section explains the activities of knowing the three worlds as gods.[139] In order to accomplish the rites of the worldly and transcendent attainments, and to eliminate the obstructive spirits (*bgegs*), the next section explains the *bali* rites, and the presentation of offerings with *mantras*.[140] Indrabodhi treats this section as explaining the presentation of the transcendent *bali*.[141] Sections Thirty Five and Six provide expositions on painting images and making books, and a set of *mantra* syllables of different kinds of music (*rol mo*) for upholding the bliss of the outer means and wisdom in meditation. The apparent intention of all such activities is to appease all adverse forces and to suffuse the whole existence with the Buddha Word.

Chapter Ten constitutes an explanation of the attainments and wonderful happenings that surround a fully perfected *vajra*-master. Section Thirty Seven explains the *sādhana* of the *vajra*-master. It is described as the attainment of the *mahāmudrā* and the great *maṇḍala* arranged inside the heart *maṇḍala* of an unparalleled master. Section Thirty Eight outlines the manner of offering veneration (*bsnyen kur*) to the *vajra*-master who has perfected the *mahāmudrā*.[142] The worship and veneration of accomplished and able *yogins* and their *mudrās* constitute the mundane fruit resulting from their inner attainments. The texts speaks of all kinds of wonderful happenings such as falling stars and meteors (*gnam rdo*), and various gods coming to voice or sing their acts of veneration. Having become perfected as a *yogin* in this very life, the next section speaks of the highest or transcendent attainments which are expressed as the activities of the Buddha nature.[143] Such *yogins* do not reside anywhere and yet they are everywhere, know everything, and abide in the mind of all beings, free from all evil and other worldly impediments. The last section further elaborates on the previous section, and provides a set of *samayas* of the body, speech and mind specifically designed for accomplished *yogins*.

---

136. Indrabodhi, TTP, vol. 55, 101.5.1.
137. Indrabodhi, TTP, vol. 55, 100.4.2.
138. Abhayākaragupta, TTP, vol. 55, 235.4.1.
139. Vīryavajra, TTP, vol. 55, 298.1.6.
140. Abhayākaragupta, TTP, vol. 55, 238.3.6.
141. Indrabodhi, TTP, vol. 55, 102.4.6.
142. Abhayākaragupta, TTP, vol. 55, 244.4.6.
143. Indrabodhi, TTP, vol. 55, 103.4.7. Vīryavajra, TTP, vol. 55, 253.4.3.

2. *Sanskrit and Tibetan Versions of Chapter I*

The Sanskrit and Tibetan versions of Chapter One are edited here on the basis of the sources listed in note one. Since the edition of the Sanskrit text relies on three manuscripts all of which appear to be rather late copies, it cannot be considered in the light of modern scholarship as being a critically edited text. There are lines or passages with doubtful and difficult readings, which cannot be easily improved, mainly because there is a risk of further distortions rather than improvements. Frequently, the passages which have difficult and corrupted readings are not readily comprehensible. On occasions the Sanskrit and Tibetan versions differ, and the interpretations suggested by the commentaries are not always helpful in establishing the precise reading or grammatical forms. In addition to this, whenever quoted in the Tibetan versions of the commentaries originally written in Sanskrit, the wording of such passages does not always correspond to the one given in the *tantra's* text, which clearly suggests that the commentators did not have before them the same text as is currently available to us. Furthermore, although the text is predominantly in proper Sanskrit, it does contain many characteristics of the so called "Buddhist hybrid Sanskrit". A number of nouns and verbs have unconventional forms some of which are attested as hybrid but others are not. In some passages the grammatical forms of nouns and verbs are dubious and unusual, and yet they seem to be deliberate because they fit the metre. Hence it is difficult to correct the text by merely introducing the classical grammatical forms. However, despite doubtful readings in various places, on the whole the Sanskrit text is fairly good, and I trust that it can be treated as a useful working text.

The Tibetan version is fairly free from errors and corruptions except for few passages which are not entirely satisfactory because, it seems, the original Sanskrit text employed by the translators was either corrupted or not clearly comprehensible. Most of such passages correspond to the same places in the Sanskrit text which are also doubtful or corrupted. There is also evidence in some places that the Sanskrit text employed by the Tibetan translators was different in some places from the text available to us.

I hope that the lay out of the Sanskrit and Tibetan texts is acceptable and not too difficult to understand. For practical reasons, mainly in order to have corresponding Sanskrit and Tibetan passages on the same pages, I have placed the Tibetan text in the foot section. However, I trust that the reader will easily distinguish the Tibetan text from the notes to the Sanskrit text.

* * *

*[1] oṃ nāmo vajraḍākāya[2] / evaṃ mayā śrutam ekasmin samaye bhagavān sarvatathāgatakāyavākcittavajrayoṣidbhageṣu vijahāra / tatra khalu bhagavān aśitikoṭiyogīśvaramadhye[3] vajragarbham avalokya smitaṃ akārṣit / samanantarasmite 'smin vajragarbha utthāyāsanād ekāṃsam uttarāsaṅgaṃ kṛtvā dakṣiṇaṃ jānumaṇḍalaṃ pṛthivyāṃ pratiṣṭhāpya[4] kṛtāñjalipuṭo bhūtvā bhagavantam etad avocat / śrotum icchāmi jñānendra sarvatantranidānam[5] rahasyaṃ sampuṭodbhavalakṣaṇam[6] /

*[7] bhagavān āha[8] / aho
vajragarbha sādhu sādhu mahākṛpa[9] sādhu sādhu //
mahābodhisattva[10] sādhu sādhu guṇākara[11] //
yad rahasyaṃ sarvatantreṣu tat sarvaṃ pṛcchyate tvayā[12] /

*[13] atha te vajragarbhapramukhā mahābodhisattvāḥ praharśot phullalocanāḥ / pṛcchantīha[14] svasaṃ-(1b)-dehāt praṇipatya muhur muhur / sarvatantraṃ kim ucyate nidānaṃ tu kathaṃ bhavet / rahasye 'tha[15] katham ucyate saṃpuṭodbhāvaḥ[16] kathaṃ nāma lakṣaṇaṃ tatra kathaṃ bhavet //

1.* rgya gar skad du sampuṭināmamahātantra / bod skad du yang dag par sbyor ba zhes bya ba rgyud chen po //

(244a) rdo rje mkha' 'gro la phyag 'tshal lo / 'di skad bdag gis thos pa'i dus gcig na / bcom ldan 'das de bzhin gshegs pa thams cad kyi sku dang gsung dang thugs kyi snying po rdo rje btsun ma'i bhaga rnams la bzhugs so / de nas yang bcom ldan 'das kyis rnal 'byor dbang phyug bye phrag brgya bcu'i nang nas rdo rje snying po la gzigs te 'dzum pa mdzad do / 'dzum pa mdzad ma thag tu de'i tshe rdo rje snying po stan las langs te / bla gos phrag pa'i gtu byas nas phus mo g.yas pa'i lha nga sa la btsugs te / thal mo sbyar ba byas nas bcom ldan 'das la 'di skad ces gsol to / ye shes kyi dbang po rgyud thams cad kyi gleng gzhi'i gsang ba yang dag par sbyor ba las byung ba'i mtshan nyid nyan par 'tshal lo //

2. 2. A oṃ vajraḍākāya namaḥ, B oṃ namaḥ śrīvajrasatvāya.
3. B reads tatra vajragarbhaprabhṛtibodhisattvasabhāmadhye
4. A&C pratisthāpya
5. A&C nidānakaṃ
6. A&C sampuṭodbhūtaṃ lakṣālakṣaṇasampuṭaṃ

7.* e ma'o
rdo rje snying po legs so legs so // snying rje chen po legs so legs so //
byang chub sems dpa' chen po yon tan gyi phung po legs so legs so //
gang zhig rgyud thams cad du gsang ba de thams cad 'dod pas zhus shig //

8. This phrase is not in B & Tib. but it is referred to by the commentaries.
9. B mahāsattva
10. A&C bodhisattva, B mahābodhisattvaḥ
11. B guṇākaraḥ, C guṇākarāḥ
12. B pṛcchatecchayā

13.* de nas rdo rje snying po la sogs pa'i byang chub sems dpa' chen po de rnams rab tu 'dzum zhing mig phye bas phyag 'tshal te / rang gi the tshom yang dang yang du zhus pa / rgyud ni thams cad ci zhes brjod / gleng gzhi yang ni ji ltar lags / 'di la gsang ba ci zhes gsungs / ji ltar yang dag sbyor byung ming / de la mtshan nyid ji ltar lags //

14. C cchantīha
15. B rahasyatyatra
16. A&C saṃpuṭodbhāva

*[1]bhagavān āha / sarve ca te tantrāś ca sarvatantrāḥ [2]/ sarvatantra-[3]-śabdena[4] samājādayaḥ teṣāṃ nidānaṃ bhūtaniścitam[5] ity arthaḥ / hariharahiranyagarbha-śrāvakapratyekabuddhānām agocaratvād rahasyaṃ / saṃpuṭaṃ[6] prajñopā-yātmakaṃ / tad evodbhavaṃ[7] saṃpuṭa-[8]-samāpattir[9] ity arthaḥ / udbhava utpattiḥ / evaṃ bhūtaṃ sthira- [10]-calātmaka- [11]-sarvabhāvasvabhāvātmakaṃ lakṣyate / ity anena lakṣaṇam / atha vā[12] sarvatantranidānasaṃpuṭaśabdena vajrasattvo 'bhidhīyate / rahasyety anena upadeśika-[13]-mantroddhāro maṇḍale[14] devatādy-[15]-abhiṣekalakṣaṇam[16] / prajñopāyātmakaṃ tatraṃ[17] tad me niga-(2a)-ditaṃ[18] śriṇu //

*[19]prathamaṃ śūnyatāṃ vicintya malaṃ[20] prakṣalya[21] dehināṃ //
rūpadhātv[22] iti śūnyānāṃ[23] śabdaṃ tasyaiva[24] kārayet //

1.* bcom ldan 'das kyis bka' stsal pa / (244b) rgyud thams cad de ni rgyud thams cad do / rgyud thams cad kyi sgras na 'dus pa la sogs pa'o / de rnams kyi gleng gzhi ni byung bar nges pa zhes bya ba'i don to / khyab 'jug dang dbang phyug chen po dang / tshangs pa dang nyan thos dang / rang sangs rgyas rnams kyi spyod yul ma yin pa'i phyir gsang ba'o / yang dag par 'sbyor ba ni thabs dang shes rab kyi bdag nyid can no / de las byung ba ni yang dag par sbyor ba'i ting nge 'dzin ces bya ba'i don no / 'byung ba ni skye ba ste / de ltar gnas pa dang g.yo ba'i dngos po'i rang bzhin gyis bdag nyid can du gyur pa'o / mtshan nyid ces bya ba ni 'das mtshon par byed pa'o / yang na rgyud thams cad kyi gleng gzhi yang dag par sbyor ba las byung pa'i sgras ni rdo rje sems dpar gsungs so / gsang ba zhes bya ba 'dis ni man ngag can gyi sngags btu ba dang / dkyil 'khor gyi lha la sogs pa'i mtshan nyid do / thabs dang shes rab bdag nyid rgyud / de ni de yis bshad kyis nyon //

2. A tantrā
3. B omits
4. B sarvaśabdena
5. B nidānabhūtaniścitam
6. B saṃpuṭāṃ
7. A&C tantrodbhavaḥ
8. A&C sampuṭaḥ
9. B samāpattur, C Samādhipattir
10. A sthila
11. B omits ātmaka
12. B omits
13. B jāpadeśiko
14. B maṇḍaleya, C māṇḍaleya
15. B āditya
16. A&C lakṣanaśca
17. B tatra
18. A&C nigaditaḥ

19.* dang por stong nyid bsams pas ni / lus can rnams kyi dri ma bkru //
gzugs kyi khams ni stong pa yi / sgra la yang ni de yis bya //
dri yi khams ni stong pa yi / ro la de nyid kyis ni bya //
reg bya'i khams ni stong pa yi / yid la de nyid kyis ni bya //

20. B omits
21. B prakṣālamala
22. B rūpavān
23. C śūnyāṃ
24. A&C tathaiva

gandha-[1]-dhātv iti śūnyānāṃ rasaṃ tasyaiva[2] kārayet [3]//
sparśadhātv iti śūnyānāṃ manas tasyaiva kārayet //
*[4]vajragarbha uvāca [5]/
cakṣurātmeti[6] śūnyānāṃ madhye vijñānaṃ kathaṃ bhavet //
śrotrātmeti [7] śūnyānāṃ madhye vijñānaṃ kathaṃ bhavet //
ghrāṇātmeti śūnyānāṃ madhye[8] vijñānaṃ kathaṃ bhavet //
jihvātmeti śūnyānāṃ madhye vijñānaṃ kathaṃ bhavet[9] //
kāyātmeti[10] śūnyānāṃ vijñānaṃ kathaṃ bhavet //
mano veti[11] śūnyānāṃ madhye vijñānaṃ kathaṃ bhavet //
*[12] tasmān nāsti rūpaṃ na draṣṭā ca na [13] śabdo [14] na śrotāro [15] //
na gandho nāpi ghrātā ca na raso nāpi rasakaḥ //
na sparśo nāpi spraṣṭā ca na cittaṃ nāpi caitikaṃ [16] // (2b)
*[17] bhagavān āha /
sṛṇu[18] tattvaṃ yathā mārgam advayaṃ dvayavarjitaṃ //
apratarkyam avijñeyaṃ durbodhyaṃ tārkikais tathā //

---

1. A gandhāṃ
2. A tathaiva, C taścaiva
3. B kāsyet

4.* rdo rje snying pos gsol pa /
mig gi rang bzhin stong pa yi / nang du rnam shes ji ltar lags //
rna ba'i rang bzhin stong pa yi / nang du rnam shes ji ltar lags //
sna yi rang bzhin stong pa yi / nang du rnam shes ji ltar lags //
lce yi rang bzhin stong pa yi / nang du rnam shes ji ltar lags //
lus kyi rang bzhin stong pa yi / nang du rnam shes ji ltar lags //
yid kyi rang bzhin stong pa yi / dbus su rnam shes ji ltar lags //

5. B vajragarbhovāca
6. B ātmani
7. A&C śrotāteti, B śrotrāyatti
8. B omits
9. B omits the whole line.
10. B kāya ātmani
11. A mano ca hiḥ, C mano vahiḥ

12.* de phyir gzugs (245a) med lta bu med / sgra med thos pa po yang med //
dri med snom pa po yang med / ro med myong ba po 'ang med //
reg med reg pa po yang med / sems med sems las byung ba 'ang med //

13. A drasṭhāraṇa
14. C śabdaḥ
15. B śrotāraḥ
16. A&C citrikāṃ

17.* bcom ldan 'das kyis bka' stsal pa /
gnyis med gnyis ni rnam spangs pa'i / de nyid lam ni ji bzhin nyon //
rtog ge med cing rnam shes med / de bzhin rtog ge bsam mi rtogs //
sangs rgyas kun gyi gsang ba ni / nam mkha' lta bur mnyam pa nyid //
nyon thos rnams kyis mi shes te / mi shes pa'i mun pas bsgribs //
bag chags sad pa'i ye shes gang / rang rgyal rnams kyi sprul ba'o //
gsang ba sangs rgyas spyod yul nyid / de rnams kun gyis mi shes so /

18. C śūnyatatvaṃ

rahasyaṃ sarvabuddhānām ākāśasama- [1]-sādṛśaṃ tathā //
śrāvakā na prajānanti ajñānatamasākṛtāḥ //
vāsanāntanayaṃ[2] jñānaṃ pratyekabuddhanirmitaṃ //
te 'pi sarve na jānanti rahasyaṃ buddhagocaraṃ //
*[3]samsārārṇavagorāṇām uttīrṇagatacetasāṃ //
madhye vartitadehānām uttīrṇalakṣa ucyate //
lakṣalakṣaṇalakṣyāṇām[4] vijñānaṃ[5] jñānacetasāṃ[6] //
jñānena jñeyam ālokya jñeyānāṃ gatim ikṣayed[7] //
gatīkṣaṇa- [8]-cetasya[9] tu yathā[10] svecchādigamyatāṃ[11] //
sahasrānekadhā yogī pūrvajanmagati- [12]-gatāḥ //
samatāṃ[13] śūnye[14] saṃcitya[15] pūrvalakṣaṇa uktitaḥ //
śūnyakṣetrādidehasya bījāropaṃ tu[16] buddhimān //
*[17] nādī- [18]-suṣirād[19] vinirgataṃ vira-(3a)-jaṃ tat prakīrtitaṃ //
bodhicittaṃ prabhāsvaraṃ suddhasphaṭikasaṃnibhaṃ[20] //

---

1. A&C omit sama
2. B vāsanacanayaṃ

3* 'khor ba'i rgya mtsho'i 'jigs pa las / rgal bar 'gro ba'i sems kyis ni /
lus kyi dbus su bskor ba yi / rgal ba mtshon par gsungs pa ste //
rnam shes ye shes sems kyis ni / mtshan nyid mtshan gzhi mtshon par byed //
ye shes kyis ni shes bya blta / shes bya rnams kyi 'gro ba brtag //
'gro ba brtag pa'i sems kyi ni / ji ltar rang 'dod la sogs 'gro //
'gro bar sngon ni skye ba ni / stong phrag du ma dag tu 'gro //
yo gis sngar gsungs mtshan nyid kyi / mtshan nyid stong par bsams nas ni //
lus kyi stong pa'i zhing sogs la / blo dang ldan pas sa bon gdab //

4. A&C lakṣālakṣaṇalakṣāṇāṃ, B lakṣalakṣaṇalakṣyāṇa
5. B vijñānā
6. B jñānacetasā
7. B gatir ikṣaṇaḥ
8. A gatikṣaṇa-, B gatir ikṣaṇa-
9. A&C -cetās
10. B yathat
11. B svacchādhigamyatāṃ
12. C gatiṃ
13. B samatā
14. B&C śūnya
15. B saṃsmitya
16. A bījāpayatu, C bījāpayet tu

17.* rtsa yi mdzes spyi las byung ba / de ni rdul bral rab tu grags //
dag pa'i shel gyi 'od dang mnyam / byang chub sems ni 'od gsal ba //
ye shes lnga yi dngos de nyid / yungs dkar gyis ni sbom phra tsam //
de yi nang du gnas pa'i lha / mi gsal gsal ba'i rang bzhin can //
ma mo phyed pa mchog tu phra / thig le'i gzugs kyi yid kyi dngos //
snying gi dbus su rtag gnas shing / 'od zer ldan zhing gzi brjid che //
sgo ni dgu po thams cad du / de ni rim pas 'pho bar 'gyur //

18. A nābhi, C nādiṃ
19. A śuṣirāt, B susirāt, C śūṣirad
20. B samaprabhaṃ

pañcajñānamayaṃ tattvaṃ sarṣapasthūla-[1]-mātrakaṃ //
tasya madhye sthitaṃ devam avyaktaṃ vyaktarūpiṇaṃ //
ardhamātraṃ paraṃ śūkṣmaṃ bindurūpaṃ[2] manomayaṃ //
hṛnmadhye vasate nityaṃ jyotirvarṇo[3] mahādyutiḥ //
*[4]dvādaśāntaṃ navāntaṃ ca āpādatalamastakaṃ //
tantur eko[5] vinirgatya nābhimadhye vyavasthitaḥ[6] //
pañcamīkalāmātras tu nāgendrākṛtivistaraḥ[7] //
sā[8] kalāpi bhitvā[9] tu vajramadhye vinirgatā[10] //
yonimadhye sthitaṃ bījaṃ dharmadhātudravīkṛtaṃ //
kramasaṃcaraṇaṃ[11] tasya navadvāreṣu[12] sarvadā //
*[13] agnibrahmam idaṃ tathā [14] //
pṛthivīdvayabījasya cakṣus [15] tasyaiva yojayet //
vāyuśūnyādibījasya nāsākarṇādicetasā //
amṛtāmbu-[16]-bījasya jihvendriyaprabhur īśvaraḥ //
grīvā-(3b)-mohabījānāṃ bāhubhyāṃ kleśakas [17] tathā //
calitahṛdaye [18] deśeṣu paśubhyāṃ[19] nābhimūlayoḥ //

---

1. A pnala
2. B rūpa
3. B jyotirvattaṃ
4. *bcu gnyis (245b) mtha' dang dgu yi mthar / rkang mthil mgo bo med bar ni //
thag pa gcig ni rnam phyung nas / lte ba'i dbus su rnam par gnas //
cha ni lnga pa tsam nyid ni / klung dbang dbyibs su rgyas pa la //
de yi cha yang phye nas ni / rdo rje'i dbus su rnam phyung ste //
skyes gnas dbus su sa bon gnas / chos dbyings khu bar byas nas ni //
5. B tanturekaṃ
6. B vyavasthitaṃ
7. B vistarā
8. B sa-
9. B bhinnaṃ
10. B vinirgataṃ
11. A&C saṃcalanaṃ
12. A&C -dvāleṣu
13. * de bzhin me ni tshangs pa'i dngos /
sa yi sa bon gnyis kyis ni / mig la de nyid sbyar bar bya //
rlung gyi stong sogs sa bon gyi / sems kyis sna dang rna ba sogs //
bdud rtsi chu yi sa bon lce / dbang por gtso bo dbang phyug nyid //
mgrin par gti mug sa bon te / lag par nyon mongs de bzhin no //
g.yo ba snying gi gnas rnams su / phyugs bdag lte ba'i rtsa bar ni //
yan lag brgyad kyi sa bon gyis / yan lag brgyad kyi cho gas 'dzin //
brtan sogs g.yo bar bcas pa yi / 'gro kun khyab par byed pas khyab //
14. A omits
15. A cakṣu
16. A ambusu
17. A&C kleśatas
18. B hṛda
19. A&C pāṇibhyāṃ

aṅgāṣṭakena[1] bījānām aṣṭāṅgaṃ[2] dhārayed vidhinā[3] //
vyāptivyāptaṃ jagat sarvaṃ sthāvarādyaṃ[4] sajaṅgamaṃ[5] //
*[6]ādhāraṃ bhavate tasya brahmādyāś ca[7] surāsuraiḥ //
bhavanaṃ bhagam ity āhur yatra saṃcarate prabhuḥ //
karmākarma bhavet tasya yāvat dehe vyavasthitaḥ //
kurute sarvaṃ kṛtakarmāṇi yat kiṃcit śubhāśubhaṃ[8] //
yogas[9] tu samatā proktā[10] pūjanaṃ bhāvanaṃ bhavet //
karmadehaṃ[11] yad ābhagnaṃ tādṛśo[12] devatā bhavet //
svaśaktis[13] tu tadā tasya yena vyāptaṃ sthiraṃ calaṃ //
varṇaṃ tasya vijānīyād ākāśa-[14]-samasādṛśaḥ[15] //
nirvāṇe tu sthito vīra[16] nirlepamalavarjita[17] // iti //
*[18] mātaraṃ bhaginīṃ caiva duhitraṃ[19] bāndhavīṃ tathā //
brahmānīṃ kṣatriṇīṃ caiva vaiśikāṃ[20] śūdriṇīṃ[21] tathā[22] //

---

1. B aṅgāstena.
2. A aṅgāṣṭaṃ
3. A vidhiḥ
4. B -dyā
5. B jaṅgamaḥ

6.* tshangs sogs lha dang lha min rnams / de yi gnad du gyur pa yin //
gang la gtso bo spyod gyur pa'i / khyim ni bhaga zhes su gsungs //
ji srid lus la rnam gnas pa / de yi las dang las min 'gyur //
dge dang mi dge gang chung zad / byas pa'i las ni thams cad byed //
rnal 'byor mnyam pa nyid du gsungs / rab tu sbyor ba bsgom pa yin //
gang tshe las kyi lus bcom pa / de ltar lha ru 'gyur ba yin //
gang gis brtan dang g.yo khyab pa / des ni de tshe rang gis nus //
nam mkha' lta bur mnyam nyid ni / de yi kha dog shes par bya //
mya ngan 'das nas dpa' bo ni / gos pa med cing dri ma spangs //

7. A&C brahmāsa
8. A kurute sarvakarmāṇi śubhāni cāśubhāni vā, C kurute sarvakarmāṇi śubhāny āśubhāni vā
9. B yogam
10. B proktaṃ
11. B dehe
12. B tādṛśaṃ
13. saśaktiṃ
14. B āgama-
15. A sadṛśaṃ mataṃ, C saśaṃ mataṃ
16. B vīran
17. B nirlepaṃ malaravriteti

18.* ma dang srid mo nyid dang yang / bu mo de bzhin gnyen mo dang //
bram ze mo dang rgyal rigs dang / rje'u mo de bzhin dmangs mo dang //
gar ma tshos ma g.yung mo (246a) dang / de bzhin du ni gdol pa mo //
thabs dang shes rab cho ga yis / de nyid rig pas mchod par bya //
ji ltar bye bar mi 'gyur bar / rab tu 'bad pas bsten par bya //
ma gsang sbrul dang chom rkun sogs / sa la spyod pa sdug bsngal byed //

19. A&C duhitāṃ, B duhitri
20. B vaisyā, C vaiśvikāṃ
21. B śūdrīṃ
22. B adds naṭī

rajakīṃ (4a) naṭikāṃ[1] caiva[2] ḍombīṃ caṇḍālinīṃ tathā //
prajñopāyavidhānena pūjayet tatvavatsalaḥ //
sevitavyāḥ[3] prayatnena[4] yathā bhedo na jāyate //
agupte kriyate duḥkhaṃ vyādacaurādi-[5]-bhūcaraiḥ //
*[6]mudrāḥ[7] pañcavidhāproktāḥ[8] kulabhedena bheditāḥ //
brahmāṇī dvijakulajā sā ca[9] tathāgatā- [10]-matā //
kṣatriṇī[11] rājagotrā[12] sā moricchandrādikulajā[13] // amṛtavajreti kathyate /
vaiśā[14] gopālikā caiva sā karmakulikā matā[15] //
śūdriṇī vṛṣaṇī caiva mahāvairocanī matā[16] //
naṭī padmakulī caiva rajakī karmakaulikā[17] //
ḍombī vajrakulī khyātā ratnacaṇḍālinī jñeyā[18] //
pañcamudrā tu viniścitā[19] //
tathāgatyaṃ kulaṃ[20] caitat saṃkṣepeṇābhidhīyate //
*[21] tathatāyāṃ gataḥ śrīmān āgataś ca tathaiva ca //

---

1. B omits
2. B ca
3. B sevitavyā, C seviṣyā
4. C prayalena
5. B caurāgni
6.* rigs kyi dbye bas phye nas ni / phyag brgya rnam pa lngar ni gsungs //
bram ze skyes gnyis rigs skyes ma / de bzhin gshegs pa nyid du gsungs //
rgyal rigs ma ni rgyal po'i rus / rma bya zla sogs rigs las skyes //
rdo rje bdud rtsi zhes byar grags /
rje'u mo ba glang skyong ba ste / las kyi rigs las skyes par gsungs //
dmangs mo yang ni bran mo ste / rnam par snang mdzad chen por gsungs //
gar ma padma'i rigs nyid de / chos ma de bzhin las kyi rigs //
g.yung mo rdo rje'i rigs su bshad / rin chen gdol pa mor shes bya //
phyag rgya lngar ni rnam par nges /
'di rnams de bzhin gshegs pa'i rigs / mdor bsdus pas ni brjod par bya //
7. A&B mudrā
8. B proktā
9. B omits sā ca
10. A tāthāgatā
11. A kṣetriṇī
12. B&C gotrī
13. A omits morī etc, B moricchaṃdādikulajā, C moricchidrādikulajā
14. B vaiśikā, C vaipikī
15. B instead of caiva etc reads mattā karmakulajā
16 B śūdrī vṛṣalī ca mahāvairocano mataḥ, C sūdrī vṛṣaṇī caiva mahāvairocanī matā
17. B&C -kulī tathā
18. A instead of ratna etc reads moricchidrādikaulajā ratnāvarṇalinījñeyā
19. A&C niścitā
20. B&C tathāgatānāṃ
21.* dpal ldan de bzhin nyid gshegs shing / de bzhin slar yang gshags pa nyid //
'dis ni shes rab rig pas ni / de bzhin gshegs par mngon par brjod //
rigs ni rnam pa lnga ru gsungs / rig ni brgya dang mtha' yas dang //
sku gsung thugs kyi dbye ba yis / phyi nas rnam pa gsum du 'gyur //
rigs dang 'byung ba lnga rnams dang / phung po lnga yi rang bzhin gyis //

anayā prajñayā yuktyā tathāgato 'bhidhīyate //
kulam pañcavidhaṃ (4b) proktam anantaṃ śatadhā-[1] -kulam //
paścāt trividhatāṃ yāti[2] kāyavākcittabhedanaiḥ //
kulānāṃ pañcabhūtānāṃ pañcaskandhasvarūpinām[3] //
vajraratnapadmamaṇi-[4]-dhārāṇāṃ prabhūtikulāni[5] //
nāsti bhāvako na bhāvyo 'sti nāsti mantro na ca devatā[6]//
tiṣṭhetau mantradevau ca niṣprapañcasvabhāvataḥ //
akśobhyavairocanāmogharatnāro-[7]-likasāttvikaiḥ //
*[8]brahmā viṣṇuḥ śivaḥ sarvo vibuddhas tattvam ucyate //
brahmā nirvṛtito[9] buddho viśanād[10] viṣṇur ucyate //
śivaḥ sadā sukalyāṇāt sarvaḥ sarvātmani[11] sthitaḥ //
satsukhatvena tattvaṃ ca[12] vibuddho bodhanād[13] rateḥ[14] //
dehe sambhavatīty[15] asmād devateti nigadyate //
*[16]bhago 'syāstīti yoyojāt[17] bhagavān iti kathyate[18] //
bhagāni[19] ṣadvidhāny āhur aiśvaryādi-[20]-guṇākhilāḥ[21] //

---

rdo rje rin chen pad nor bu / 'dzin pa'i rim pa'i rigs rnams so //
sgom pa po med sgom bya med / sngags med lha yang yod ma yin //
spros pa med pa'i rang bzhin nyid / sngags dang lhar ni yang dag gnas //
rnam snang mi bskyod don yod dang / rin chen dpag med sems dpa'o //

1. A&B satathā
2. B trividhaṃ yāṃti
3. B rūpiṇiṃ
4. B vajracakramaṇipadmakhaḍga
5. B prabhūtiḥ / kulāni ceti
6. B nāsti bhavaka na bhāvyo 'sti mantran nāsti na devatā
7. B vairocanākśobhyo moghaś ca ratnārolikasātvikaiḥ, C ratnolikasātyikaiḥ

8.* tshangs pa khyab 'jug zhi ba dang / thams cad sangs rgyas de nyid brjod //
tshangs pa sgrib bral sangs rgyas nyid / (246b) 'jug phyir khyab 'jug brjod par bya //
zhi ba rtag tu dge ba ste / thams cad kun gyi bdag nyid gnas //
dam pa'i bde bas de nyid de / dga' ba rtogs phyir rnam sangs rgyas //
gang phyir lus las byung ba nyid / lha zhes mngon par brjod par bya //

9. A nirvvattato, C nirvṛtto
10. A&C visanād
11. B sarvātmano
12. A tattvajo, C tattvajñā
13. B vibuddhanād for vibuddho bodhanād
14. A&C ataḥ
15. C sambhavantīty

16.* 'di la bhaga mnga' ba'i phyir / bcom ldan 'das zhes brjod par bya //
bhaga rnam pa drug tu brjod / dbang phyug la sogs yon tan kun //
yang na nyon mongs la sogs pa / 'joms pa'i phyir na bcom ldan 'das //
gang phyir skye 'gro skyed pa'i phyir / shes rab ma shes brjod par bya //
gang phyir skal pa ston pa'i phyir / shes rab de nyid srid mo nyid //

17. B omits yoyojāt, C bhago syāstīti buddhasya yojāt
18. B nikhatyate
19. A&C bhagāṃs tu
20. A omits ādi
21. A&C -ākhilān

atha vā kleśādikaṃ[1] bhagnavān iti bhagavān //
ja-(5a)-nanī bhaṇyate[2] prajñā janayati janaṃ jataḥ[3] //
bhaginīti tathā prajñā vibhāgaṃ darśayed yataḥ //
*[4]rajakī[5] bhaṇyate prajñā [6]sattvānāṃ rañjanād yataḥ[7] //
duhitā[8] bhaṇyate prajñā guṇanāṃ[9] duhanād yataḥ[10] //
nartakī bhaṇyate prajñā ca cala-[11]-tvād mahākṛpā //
asparśā bhagavatī[12] yasmād[13] ḍombī tasmāt prakathyate //
*[14]japaṃ jalpanam ākhyātam ālikāliprajalpanāt //
maṇḍalaṃ pādalekhaḥ[15] syāt malanād maṇḍalaṃ vadet[16] //
karas[17] sphoṭo bhaved mudrā aṅgulyā[18] moṭanaṃ tathā //
tad dhyeyaṃ cintitaṃ yac[19] ca dhyeyaṃ yasmād vicintanaṃ //
*[20]pitari prāptaṃ yathā saukhyaṃ tatsukhaṃ bhuñjyate svayaṃ[21] //
maraṇaṃ yena sukhe neha tat sukhaṃ dhyānam ucyate //
ity abhidhānābhidheyabodhicittotpādādibhāvanātattvaprakaraṇaṃ prathamam //
*[22]atha saptatriṃśadbodhipākṣikān dharmān khatayiṣyāmi [23] /

---

1. B -ādi
2. B bhanyate
3. B janayati yasmād jagag janaṃ, C janayantīti yasmād jagad janaṃ yataḥ

4.* shes rab tshos mar brjod pa ni /
sems can thams cad 'tshed pa'i phyir / btso bslag ma zhes de bzhin brjod //
yon tan 'jo bar gsungs pa'i phyir / shes rab bu mor brjod par bya //
snying rje chen pos g.yo ba'i phyir / shes rab gar mar brjod par bya //
gang phyir bcom ldan mi reg pa / de phyir g.yung mor brjod par bya //

5. B adds iti
6. B sarva-
7. B instead of rañjanād yataḥ reads rajakīti tathā smṛtā
8. B duhitrī
9. B gunasya
10. B instead of yataḥ reads duhiteti nigadyate
11. A&C cañca-
12. A bhavatī
13. C jasmād

14* ā li kā li rab smras pa / bzlas pa smra bar yang dag bshad //
rkang pa'i rjes ni dkyil 'khor yin / nyid phyir dkyil 'khor brjod par bya //
lag pa sgyur ba phyag rgya yin / sor mo nyed pa 'ang de bzhin no //
gang phyir rnam sems bsam gtan ni / gang sems de ni bsam gtan no //

15. A&B lekha
16. A&C ucyate
17. B uras
18. C aṅguñjalyā
19. B omits from here to pitari

20. pha las bde ba gang thob pa / de yi bde ba rang gis bza' //
bde ba gang gis mching ba 'dir / de yi bde ba bsam gtan brjod //
brjod par bya ba dang rjod par byed pa'i byang chub kyi sems bskyed pa la sogs pa'i bsgom pa'i de kho na'i rab tu byed pa ste dang po'o //

21. A svaraṃ

22.* de nas byang chub kyi chos sum bcu rtsa bdun brjod par bya'o /

adhyātmakāye (5b) bahirdhā-[1]-kāye adhyātmabahirdhā-[2]-kāye kāyānudarśī viharatīty api samprajānan[3] smṛtimān vinīyaloke avidyā-[4]-daur manasye[5] //

*[6]adhyātmavedanā bahirdhāvedanā adhyātmabahirdhāvedanānudarśī[7] viharatīty[8] api samprajānan[9] smṛtimān vinīyaloke avidyā-[10]-daur manasye //

*[11] adhyātmadharmeṣu bahirdhādharmeṣu adhyātmabahirdhādharmeṣu dharmānu-darśī vihara-tīty api saṃprajānan[12] smṛtimān vinīyaloke avidyādaur manasye //

*[13] adhyātmacitte bahirdhācitte adhyātmabahirdhācitte cittānudarśī viharatīty api saṃprajānan[14] smṛtimān vinīyaloke avidyādaur manasye //

imāni catvāri smṛtyupasthānāni //

*[15] anutpannānāṃ pāpakānām akuśalānāṃ dharmāṇām anutpādanāya[16] chandam ja-nayati vyāyacchati vīryam arabhate / cittaṃ pragṛhṇāti (6a) samyakpraṇidhiṃ[17] dadhāti //

*[18] utpannānāṃ pāpakānām akuśalānāṃ dharmāṇāṃ prahāṇāya chandaṃ janayati vyāyacchati vīryam ārabhate cittaṃ pragṛhṇāti samyakpraṇidhiṃ dadhāti //

---

nang gi lus dang / phyi'i lus dang / phyi nang gnyis ka'i lus la lus kyi rjes su blta zhing gnas pa'i phyir yang dag par rab tu (247a) shes te / ma rig pa la sogs pas yang gnyis su gyur pa'i 'jig rten la dran pa dang ldan pa'o//

23. A khatayayiṣyāmi

1. B bahir

2. B ātmabarddhā

3. B saṃprajanya

4. A&C abhidhyā-

5. C mamanasye

6.* nang gi tshor ba dang / phyi'i tshor ba dang / phyi nang gnyis ga'i tshor ba la tshor ba'i rjes su blta zhing gnas pa'i phyir yang dag par rab tu shes te / ma rig pa la sogs pas yid gnyis su gyur pa'i 'dul ba'i 'jig rten la dran pa dang ldan pa'o //

7. C dharmānudarśī

8. A vihatīty

9. B saṃprajanya

10. A&C abhidhyā

11.* nang gi chos rnams dang / phyi'i chos rnams dang / phyi nang gnyis ka'i chos rnams la chos kyi rjes su blta zhing gnas pa'i phyir yang dag par rab tu shes te / ma rig pa la sogs pas yid gnyis su gyur pa'i 'dul ba'i 'jig rten la dran pa dang ldan pa'o //

12. A saṃprajanya, C saṃprajānaṃ na

13.* nang gi sems dang / phyi'i sems dang / phyi nang gnyis ka'i sems la sems kyis rjes su blta zhing gnas pa'i phyir yang dag par rab tu shes te / ma rig pa la sogs pas yid gnyis su gyur pa'i 'dul ba'i 'jig rten la dran pa dang ldan pa'o //
'di rnams ni dran pa nye bar gzhag pa bzhi'o //

14. B samprajanya

15.* sdig pa mi dge ba'i chos ma skyes pa rnams mi bskyed pa'i phyir 'dun pa skyed do / brtson 'grus rtsom mo / sems rab tu 'jog go / smon lam yang dag par 'debs so //

16. A&C anutpannāya

17. A, B, C -praṇi

18. *sdig pa mi dge ba'i chos skyes pa rnams spang pa'i phyir 'dun pa skyed do / 'bad do / brtson 'grus rtsom mo / sems rab tu 'jog go / smon lam yang dag par 'debs so //

*[1]anutpannānāṃ kuśalāṇāṃ dharmāṇāṃ utpādanāya[2] chandaṃ janayati vyāyacchati[3] vīryam ārabhate cittaṃ pratigṛhṇāti samyakpraṇidhiṃ dadhāti //
*[4]evam utpannānāṃ kuśalāṇāṃ dharmāṇāṃ sthitaye[5] aprameyopāyabhāvanā-[6]-paripūraye / punar[7] bhāvanāvṛddhivaipulyachandaṃ janayati vyāyacchati vīryam āra-bhate cittaṃ pratigṛhṇāti samyakpraṇidhiṃ dadhāti // imāni catvāri samyakprahāṇāni //
*[8]chandasamādhiprahāṇasaṃskārasamanvāgataṃ ṛddhipādaṃ bhāvayati / viveka-niḥsṛtaṃ[9] virāganiḥsṛtaṃ[10] nirodhaniḥsṛtaṃ vyavasargapariṇataṃ / mā me chando 'tilīno[11] bhaviṣyati / nātipragṛhīta[12] iti //
*[13] vīrya-(6b)-samādhiprahāṇasaṃskārasamanvāgatam ṛddhipādaṃ bhāvayati / vi-vekaniḥsṛtaṃ virāganiḥsṛtaṃ nirodhanisṛtaṃ vyavasargapariṇataṃ / mā me vīryam atilīnaṃ bhaviṣyati / nāti-[14]-pragṛhītam iti //
*[15] mīmāṃsāsamādhiprahāṇa-[16]-saṃskārasamanvāgatam ṛddhipādaṃ bhāvayati / viveka-niḥsṛtaṃ virāganiḥsṛtaṃ nirodhaniḥsṛtaṃ vyavasargapariṇataṃ mā me mīmāṃsātilinā bhaviṣyati / nātipragṛhītā iti //

1.* dge ba'i chos ma skyes pa rnams bskyed pa'i phyir 'dun pa skyed do / 'bad do / brtson 'grus rtsom mo / sems rab tu 'jog go / smon lam yang dag par 'debs so //

2. B anutpādāya

3. B vīyacchati

4.* de ltar dge ba'i chos skyes pa rnams gnas par bya ba'i phyir thabs tshad med pa bsgom pas yongs su gang ba'i phyir yongs su gang bar gyur pas bsgom pa dam pa 'phel bar bya ba'i phyir 'dun pa skyed do / 'bad do / brtson 'grus (247b) rtsom mo / sems rab tu 'jog go / smon lam yang dag par 'debs so //
'di rnams ni yang dag par spong ba bzhi'o //

5. B sthitāyā-

6. B bhavanāyai

7. B instead of punar reads aparipūraye pariṇāmaya bhūyād.

8.* dun pa'i ting nge 'dzin spong ba'i 'du byed dang ldan pa'i rdzu phrul gyi rkang pa bsgom par bye ste / bye brag phyed pas nges par 'byung ba dang / 'dod chags dang bral bas nges par 'byung ba dang 'gog pas nges par 'byung ba dang / rnam par byang bar gyur pas bdag gi 'dun pa nub par 'gyur zhing shin tu rab tu 'jog pa ma yin pa'o //

9. B&C nisṛta in this section

10. A nisthānaṃ

11. A ativilīno

12. B -grahītā

13.* brtsom 'grus kyi ting nge 'dzin spong ba'i 'du byed dang ldan pa'i rdzu phrul gyi rkang pa bsgom par bya ste / bye brag phyed pas nges par 'byung ba dang / 'dod chags dang bral bas nges par 'byung ba dang / 'gog pas nges par 'byung ba dang / rnam par byed par gyur pas bdag gi brtson 'grus nub par 'gyur zhing shin tu 'jog pa ma yin pa'o //

14. B nāpi

15.* dpyod pa'i ting nge 'dzin spong ba'i 'du byed dang ldan pa'i rdzu phrul gyi rkang pa bsgom par bya ste / bye brag phyed pas nges par 'byung ba dang / 'dod chags dang bral bas nges par 'byung ba dang / 'gog pas nges par 'byung ba dang / rnam par byed par gyur pas bdag gi dpyod pa nub par 'gyur zhing shin tu rab tu 'jog pa ma yin pa'o //

16. B pramāhāṃ

*[1]cittasamādhiprahāṇasaṃskārasamanvāgatam ṛddhipādaṃ bhāvayati / viveka-niḥsṛtaṃ virāganiḥsṛtaṃ nirodhaniḥsṛtaṃ vyavasargapariṇataṃ / mā me cittaṃ[2] atilīnaṃ[3] bhaviṣyati / nātipragṛhītam[4] iti / ime catvāri[5] ṛddhipādāḥ //

*[6]sakāmāvararāṃ lokikīṃ[7] samyagdṛṣṭiṃ śraddadhāti[8] / svakarmavipāka-pratiśaraṇo bhavati / yad evaṃ[9] karma kariṣyāmi kalyāṇaṃ vā pāpakaṃ vā tasya karmaṇo vipākaṃ (7a) prativedayiṣyāmi[10] / sa jīvitahetor api pāpakaṃ karma nābhi-[11] -saṃskaroti / idam ucyate śraddhendriyaṃ //

*[12]yān dharmān śraddhendriyeṇa śraddddhāti tān dharmān vīryendriyeṇa samudānayati / idam ucyate vīryendriyaṃ //

*[13]yān dharmān vīryendriyeṇa samudānayati tān dharmān smṛtīndriyeṇa na[14] vipraṇā-śayati / idam ucyate smṛtīndriyaṃ //

*[15]yān dharmān smṛtīndriyeṇa na[16] vipraṇāśayati tān dharmān samādhīndriyeṇa ekā-grīkaroti / idam ucyate samādhīndriyaṃ //

*[17]yān dharmān samādhīndriyeṇa ekāgrīkaroti tān dharmān prajñendriyeṇa prativi-dhyati sa teṣu teṣu dharmeṣu pratyavekṣaṇajātīyo bhavati / idam ucyate prajñendriyaṃ //

1.* sems kyi ting nge 'dzin spongs pa'i 'du byed dan ldan pa'i rdzu phrul gyi rkang pa bsgom par bya ste / bye brag phyed pas nges par 'byung ba dang / 'dod chags dang bral bas nges par 'byung ba dang / 'gog pas nges par 'byung ba dang / rnam par byang bas nges par 'byung bas bdag gi sems nub par 'gyur zhing shin tu rab tu 'jog pa ma yin pa'o //
'di rnams ni rdzu 'phrul gyi rkang pa bzhi ste //

2. B citto

3. B 'tilīno

4. A pragṛhītaṃ, B -gṛhito

5. A catvāra, C catvā

6.* 'dod par dpyod pa dang bcas pa'o / jig rten pa'i yang dag pa'i lta ba la dad par byed de / rang gi las kyi rnam par smin pa la (248a) so sor yid ches par gyur pa gang zhig de ltar las byang bar 'gyur ba dge ba 'am sdig pa de dang de'i las kyi rnam par smin pa so sor nyams su myong par 'gyur pa'i phyir de ni 'tsho ba'i rgyur yang sdig pa'i las mngon par 'du mi byed pa'o / 'di ni dad pa'i dbang por gsungs so //

7. B sakāmācārīlaukikī-

8. C śruddadhāti

9. B yadyevaṃ

10. B adds iti

11. A karmaṇāṃ, B karmaṇāpti, C karmanā

12.* gang zhig chos rnams la dad pa'i dbang pos dad pa byed pa'i chos rnams la brtson 'grus kyi dbang pos shes par byed do / 'di ni brtson 'grus kyi dbang por gsungs so //

13.* gang zhig chos rnams la brtson 'grus kyi dbang pos shes pa de'i chos rnams ni dran pa'i dbang pos rab tu 'jig par mi byed pa'o / 'di ni dran pa'i dbang por gsungs so //

14. A&C omit

15.* gang zhig chos rnams la dran pas rab tu 'jig par mi byed pa de'i chos rnams ni ting nge 'dzin gyi dbang pos rtse gcig tu byed pa'o / 'di ni ting nge 'dzin gyi dbang por gsungs so //

16. A,B &C omit

17.* gang zhig chos rnams la ting nge 'dzin gyi dbang pos rtse gcig tu byed pa de'i chos rnams ni shes rab kyi dbang pos so sor rig pa ste / de ni chos de dang de rnams la so sor rtog pa skye bar 'gyur ro / 'di ni shes rab kyi dbang por gsungs so //

*[1]etāni pañcendriyāṇi pañcabalāni bhavanti / tadyathā / śraddhābalaṃ vīryabalaṃ smṛtibalaṃ samādhibalaṃ prajñābalaṃ / imāni (7b) pañcabalāni //

*[2]tatra katamāni saptabodhyaṅgāni / tadyathā / smṛtisaṃbodhyaṅgaṃ / dharmapravicayasaṃbodhyaṅgaṃ / vīryasaṃbodhyaṅgaṃ / prītisaṃbodhyaṅgaṃ / praśrabdhi-[3]-saṃbodhyaṅgaṃ / samādhisaṃbodhyaṅgaṃ / upekṣāsaṃbodhyaṅgaṃ / vivekaniḥsṛtaṃ virāganiḥsṛtaṃ nirodhaniḥsṛtaṃ vyavasarganiḥsṛtaṃ pariṇataṃ dharmapravicayādisaptabodhyaṅgāni bhāvayet[4]/

*[5]āryāṣṭāṅgo mārgaḥ tatra katamaḥ / samyagdṛṣṭir yā lokottarā nātmadṛṣṭisamutthitā[6] na jīvo na sattvo na pudgalo na poṣo na manujo na mānavo[7] na kārako na vedakadṛṣṭi-samutthitā[8] nocchedaṃ na śāśvatadṛṣṭisamutthitā[9] na bhavo na vibhavo na kulavyākṛta-dṛṣṭir[10] yāvan na samsāro na nirvāṇa-[11]-dṛṣṭisamutthito[12] / iyam ucyate samyagdṛṣṭiḥ //

1.* dbang po lnga po 'di rnams 'phel ba ni stobs lnga ru 'gyur te / dad pa'i stobs dang / brtson 'grus kyi stobs dang / dran pa'i stobs dang / ting nge 'dzin gyi stobs dang / shes rab kyi stobs te / 'di rnams ni stobs lnga'o //

2.* de la byang chub kyi yan lag bdun gang zhe na / 'di lta ste / dran pa yang dag byang chub kyi yan lag dang / chos rab tu rnam par 'byed pa yang dag byang chub kyi yan lag dang / brtson 'grus yang dag byang chub kyi yan lag dang / dga' ba yang dag byang chub kyi yan lag dang / shin tu sbyangs pa yang dag byang chub kyi yan lag dang / ting nge 'dzin yang dag (248b) byang chub kyi yan lag dang / btang snyoms yang dag byang chub kyi yan lag ste / bye brag phyed pas nges par 'byung ba dang / 'dod chags dang bral bas nges par 'byung ba dang / 'gog pas nges par 'byung ba dang / kun nas nyon mongs pa dang bral ba'i kun nas rnam par byang bar gyur pa dang / chos rab tu 'byed pa ni byang chub kyi yan lag bdun la sogs pa bsgom pa'o //

3. A&B prasrabdhi, C prasradhī

4. B bhāvayati

5.* de la 'phags pa'i lam yan lag brgyad pa gang zhe na / yang dag pa'i lta ba ni gang zhig 'jig rten las 'das pa ste / bdag tu lta bas kun nas bslang ba ma yin pa dang / sems can med pa dang / 'tsho ba med pa dang / gso ba med pa dang / skyes bu med pa dang / gang zag med pa dang / shed las skyes med pa dang / shed bu med pa dang / byed pa po med pa dang / tshor ba po med pa'i lta bas kun nas bslang ba chad pa ma yin pa dang / rtag par lta bas kun nas bslang ba ma yin pa dang / srid pa bral ba'i lta bas kun nas bslang ba dang / rigs su lung bstan pa'i lta bas kun nas bslang ba dang / ji srid 'khor ba ma yin zhing mya ngan las 'das pa'i yang ma yin pa'i lta bas kun nas bslang ba ste / 'di na yang dag pa'i lta bar gsungs so //

6. B dṛṣṭisamanvitā

7. B adds na māna

8. A&C na vedako

9. A&C na śāśvato nocchedo

10. B na kulavyāhadrāsamusthitādṛṣṭisamusthitā

11. A nirvāṇaṃ, B parinirvāṇa

12. A&C add yāvan na samsāro na parinirvāṇadṛṣṭisamuthitā

*[1]yaiḥ saṃkalpair rāgadveṣamoha-[2]-kleśāḥ samuttiṣṭhanti[3] tān (8a) saṃkalpān na saṃkalpayati / yaiḥ saṃkalpaiḥ śīlasamādhiprajñāvimuktivimuktijñāna-darśaṇaskandhāḥ samutthiṣṭhanti tān saṃkalpān saṃkalpayati / ayam ucyate samyaksaṃkalpaḥ //

*[4]yā vāg[5] ātmanaṃ parān vā na tāpayati nātmānaṃ na parān[6] kleśayati / nātmānaṃ na parān[7] upahasati[8] / tayā samāhitayuktayā vācā samanvāgo bhavati / yayā vācā samyaktāyām[9] avatārayati / iyam ucyate samyagvāk /

*[10]yat karma kṛṣṇaṃ kṛṣṇavipākaṃ tat karma nābhisaṃskaroti / yat karma śuklaṃ[11] śuklavipākaṃ tat karmābhisaṃskaroti / yat karma śuklakṛṣṇavipākaṃ tat karma nābhisaṃskaroti / yat[12] karma śuklakṛṣṇavipākaṃ śuklakṛṣṇavipāka-[13]-kṣayāya vartate[14] tat karmābhisaṃskaroti / satkarmapratisaraṇaṃ[15] samyakkarmāntaḥ / ayam ucyate samyak-karmāntaḥ /

1.* gang zhig yang dag pa'i rtog pa ni 'dod chags dang / zhe sdang dang / gti mug dang / nyon mongs pas kun nas bslang ba'i rtog pa de ni yang dag pa'i rtog par mi 'gyur ro / yang dag pa'i rtog pa gang zhig tshul 'khrims dang / ting nge 'dzin dang / shes rab dang / rnam par 'grol ba dang / rnam par 'grol ba'i ye shes mthong ba'i phung pos kun slong ba de'i yang dag pa'i rtog pa de ni yang dag pa'i rtog par 'gyur / 'di ni yang dag pa'i rtog par gsungs so //

2. B mohāḥ

3. B samuttiṣṭhante

4.* gang zhig tshig gis bdag la gdung bar mi bya zhing gzhan la gdung (249a) bar mi bya ba dang / bdag la mi bya zhing gzhan dag nyon mongs par mi bya ba dang / bdag la mi bya zhing gzhan dag la yang dbya bar mi bya ba ste / de mnyam par bshag pa dang ldan pas tshig dang ldan par 'gyur zhing / gang gi tshig gis yang dag pa'i 'phags par 'jug par 'gyur ba 'di ni yang dag pa'i ngag ces gsung so //

5. B yayā vācānā-

6. A&C omit ātmānaṃ na parān

7. A&C as in the previous note

8. B upahaṃti

9. A samyagāyām, B samāgāyāmā-, C samyagatāyām

10.* gang zhig las nag po dang / nag po'i rnam par smin pa de'i las mngon par 'du mi byed pa dang / gang zhig las dkar ba dang dkar po'i rnam par smin pa de'i las mngon par 'du mi byed pa dang / gang zhig las dkar po dang / nag po'i rnam par smin pa de'i las mngon par 'du mi byed pa dang / gang zhig las dkar po dang / nag po dang / dkar po'i rnam par smin pa dang / nag po zad pa'i bsam pas gnas pa de'i las mngon par 'du byed de / dam pa'i las lta bur 'gyur ba ni yang dag pa'i las kyi mtha'o //

11. C śukraṃ

12. A&C ye

13. A&C omit

14. B saṃvartata

15. B pratisaraṇaḥ

*[1]yad āryavaṃśa-[2]-dhūta-[3]-guṇasaṃleśānutsarjanatā[4] na kuhanatā[5] na lapa-natā[6] (8b) na kathāsuratā[7] svācāra-[8]-śīlatā paralokeśvarīyuktatā[9] ātmalā-bhātmasaṃtuṣṭi-[10]-niravadyatā[11] āryānujñātā[12] jīvanatā[13] / ayam ucyate sam-yagājīvaḥ //

*[14]yo vyāyāmo mithyāryair[15] ananujñāta[16] rāgadveśamohakleśān asevita-vyān[17] ic-chati[18] / so vyāyāmaḥ / samyagārya-[19]-mārgasatyāvatāro nirvāṇagā-mīpratipadam arpayati / taṃ vyāyāmaṃ samanugacchati[20] / ayam ucyate samyag-vyāyāmaḥ //

*[21]yā sūpasthitā-[22]-prakampyā[23] ṛjukāyākuṭilā saṃsāradoṣādīn avadarśikā[24] / nirvāṇapathapraṇetrī[25] smṛtiḥ / smaraṇaṃ[26] /[27] ayam āryamārgasamprayogaḥ / ayam ucyate samyaksmṛtiḥ /

1.* gang gi tshe 'phags pa lta bur dul ba dang / yon tan yang dag pa'i chos zhum zhing dul ba dang / kha gsag med pa dang / mang du smra ba ma yin pa dang / gtam la mi dga' ba dang / rang gi spyod pa'i khrims dang / 'jig rten pha rol gyi dbang phyug dang ldan pa dang / bdag gi rnyed pa kha na mtho ba med pas bdag chog par 'dzin pa dang / 'phags pa'i bka'i gnang bas 'tsho ba ste / 'di ni yang dag pa'i 'tsho bar gsungs so //

2. B vaṃśai
3. B vrata
4. A -ānusajjanatā, C -ān sarjjanatā
5. A kuhabhanatā
6. B&C layanatā
7. B surabhitā na vivekasūratā
8. A&C svācā
9. B -lokesvanayuktā
10. B ātmalābhasaṃtuṣṭir
11. B anavadyatā
12. A āryāḥ nujātā, B āryānujāta
13. B ājīvanatā

14.* rtsol ba ni gang zhig brdzun pa dang / 'phags pas ma gnang ba dang / 'dod chags dang / zhe sdang dang / gti mug dang / nyon mongs pa rjes su sten par mi 'dod pa ni rtsol ba ste / rtsol ba gang zhig yang dag pa'i 'phags pa'i lam gyi bden par 'jug cing mya ngan las 'das bar 'gro ba / dang so so'i gnas su skyed par byed pa de ni rtsol ba yang dag par rjes su 'brang ba ste / (249b) 'di ni yang dag pa'i rtsol bar gsungs so //

15. A mithyā āryar
16. A anantajāta, B anujāta, C anantajñāta
17. A sevitavyān
18. B -kleśānusevitaṃ vyācāmaṃnatseti
19. B saṃprasāryaṃ
20. A&C saṃsamanucchati

21.* gang la nye bar gnas pa de ni rab tu mi g.yo ba dang / lus drang pos kyog pa ma yin pa dang / 'khor ba'i skyon sna tshogs la sogs pa dbang du byed pa ston cing / mya ngan las 'das pa'i gnas 'dod pa'i dran pa ni mi brjed pa ste / 'di ni 'phags pa'i yang dag pa'i lam la sbyar ba'o / 'di ni yang dag pa'i dran par gsungs so //

22. B yāsūpasthitāṃ
23. A&C -prakampya
24. B -ādin vasaṃ darśakaḥ
25. A&C -praṇeti
26. A&C omit
27. B adds samyagābhya

*[1]samyaktvena samādhir yasmin samādhau sthitaḥ sarvasattvavimokṣāya[2] samyaksthiratvaṃ nirvāṇam avakrāmati[3] / ayam ucyate samyaksamādhiḥ //
*[4]etā eva samākhyātā muditādyās tu bhūmayaḥ //
āla-(9a)-yo bodhisattvānāṃ indriyādisvarūpiṇām[5] //
ālayaḥ sarvabuddhānāṃ skandhādīnāṃ viśeṣataḥ //
buddhānāṃ[6] bodhisattvānāṃ buddhatvāvāhikāparāḥ //
dvātriṃśadbodhicittānāṃ ya ihāyānti pūrṇatām[7] //
indriyaskandhabhūtānāṃ buddhatvaṃ tad anantaram //
*[8]svadehe caiva buddhatvaṃ sthitaṃ[9] nānyatra kutracit //
dehād anyatra buddhatvam ajñānenāvṛtam[10] matam //
svadehasthaṃ mahājñānaṃ sarvasaṃkalpa- [11] -varjitam //
vyāpakaḥ sarvavastūnāṃ dehastho 'pi na dehajaḥ //
*[12] vajragarbha uvāca[13] / dehe katamā[14] nāḍyaḥ / bhagavān āha /
śatam ekaṃ dvidaśādhikaṃ catuścakra- [15] -prabhedataḥ //
bodhicittasvarūpeṇa nāḍīdvātriṃśad uttamā matāḥ[16] // tadyathā /

1.* yang dag pa'i ting nge 'dzin ni ting nge 'dzin gang la gnas nas sems can thams cad rnam par thar par bya ba'i phyir yang dag par gnas te / mya ngan las 'das pa mnan pa'o / 'dis ni yang dag pa'i ting nge 'dzin zhes gsungs so //

2. A&C -vipramokṣāya

3. B avakrāmayati, C ati

4.* de nyid yang dag bshad pa ni / dga' ba la sogs pa rnams te //
dbang po la sogs rang bzhin gyi / byang chub sems dpa' rnams kyi gnas //
phung po la sogs khyad par gyi / sangs rgyas thams cad kyi ni gnas //
sangs rgyas byang chub sems dpa' yi / sangs rgyas nyid ni mchog tu 'bab //
byang sems sum cu rtsa gnyis kyis / gang tshe 'dir ni gang gyur pa //
dbang po phung po 'byung ba yi / sangs rgyas de yi de ma thag //

5. C -rūpiṇa

6. B buddhādīnāṃ

7. B yad āyāṃtiha purṇatāṃ

8.* rang lus nyid la sangs rgyas nyid / gzhan na gang gu 'ang mi gnas so //
lus las gshan du sangs rgyas nyid / mi shes pa yis bsgribs par brjod //
ye shes chen po rang lus gnas / rtog pa thams cad yang dag spangs //
dngos po kun la khyab pa po / lus gnas lus la ma skyes pa'o //

9. B sthitā

10. B avṛtar

11. C sarvakalpa

12*. rdo rje snying pos gsol ba / lus la rtsa du lags / bcom ldan 'das kyis bka' stsal pa /
'khor lo bzhi yi rab dbye bas / brgya phrag gcig dang nyi shu lhag //
byang chub sems kyi rang bzhin gyis / rtsa rnams sum bcu rtsa gnyis mchog //
gsungs pa / 'di lta ste / mi phyed ma zhes brjod pa dang / phra gzugs ma dang / brtse ba ma dang / g.yon pa ma dang / thung ngu ma dang / rus sbal skyes ma dang / bsgom pa ma dang / dbang ma dang / skyon pa ma dang / 'jug ma dang / ma mo dang /

13. B āha

14. B katame

15. A -cakraḥ

16. A triṃśattamāmatā, C -mata

abhedyā matā sūkṣmarūpā divyā vāmā tu vāmanī [1] //
kūrmajā bhāvakī sekā doṣā viṣṭā māturā[2] //
*[3]śavarī[4] śītadoṣmā [5] ca lalanā rasanāvadhūtī[6] //
pravaṇā [7] varṇā[8] ca sāmānyā[9] hetudāyikā //
viyogā [10] premaṇī siddhā pāvakī [11] sumanā[12] tathā //
tṛvṛtā [13] kāminī gehā caṇḍikā[14] māradāyikā[15] //
etā nādyo bhagavan kīdṛśāḥ //
tribhavapariṇatāḥ / sarva-[16]-grāhyagrāhakavarjitā / iti
*[17] pañcendriyapañcabalasaptabodhyaṅgāryāṣṭāṅgamārgaparyantādivivaraṇaṃ[18]
bodhicittāvatāro nāma dvitīyaprakaraṇam // (9b)
*[19] atha bhagavantaṃ sarvatathāgatāḥ pūjāṃ kṛtvā praṇipatyaivam āhuḥ /
bhāṣasva [20] bhagavan sāraṃ rahasyaṃ jñānam uttaram /

---

1. A&C dāmanī
2. B mātarā
3.* 250a) mtshan mo dang / gsil sbyin ma dang / tsha ba ma dang / brkyang ma dang / ro ma dang / kun dar ma dang / 'bab ma dang / mdog ma dang / gzugs can ma dang / rgyud sbyin ma dang / sbyor bral ma dang / sdug gu ma dang / grub ma dang / 'chod mi dang / de bzhin du yid bzang ma dang / sum skor ma dang / 'dod ma dang / khyim ma dang / bdud 'dral ma'o / bcom ldan 'das rtsa 'di dag ji lta bu lags / srid gsum yongs su gyur ba ste / gzung ba dang 'dzin pa thams cad yongs su spangs ba'o //
4. A, B & C sarvarī
5. B sītadā uṣmā
6. B adds ca
7. B pramāṇā
8. A&C hṛṣṭā ca varṇā, B kṛṣṇavarṇā
9. A sāmānaya
10. B adds ca
11. B ca pākkī
12. B sumanas
13. A&C tṛvartta
14. B caṇḍākā
15. B kāmadārikā
16. B sarvā
17.* dran pa nye bar gzhag pa gzhi dang / yang dag par spong ba bzhi dang / rdzu 'phrul gyi rkang pa bzhi dang / dbang po lnga dang / stobs lnga dang / byang chub kyi yan lag bdun dang / 'phags pa'i lam yan lag brgyad pa'i mthar thug pa la sogs pa'i rnam par 'grol ba / byang chub kyi sems 'jug pa zhes bya ba ste rab tu byed pa gnyis pa'o //
18. B vicaraṇam
19.* de nas bcom ldan 'das la de bzhin gshegs pa thams cad kyis mchod pa byas nas phyag 'tshal te 'di skad ces gsol to // gsang ba'i ye shes bla med pa / snying po bcom ldan bshad du gsol //
de nas bcom ldan 'das kyis de bzhin gshegs pa thams cad kyis gsol ba btab par mkhyen nas/ rgyud thams cad kyi snying po ye shes mar me rdo rje zhes bya ba'i ting nge 'dzin la snyoms par zhugs te / rgyud thams cad kyi gsang ba 'di bka' stsal pa /
gsang ba'i mchog gi dgyes pa na / thams cad bdag nyid rtag tu bzhugs //
sangs rgyas kun dngos sems dpa' ni / rdo rje sems dpa' bde ba'i mchog //
'di ni bcom ldan rnal 'byor te / brtan pa rtag pa mchog tu yang //
yid srub so sor skyes ba nyid / rtag tu rang bzhin gnan dka' ba //
20. C bhāṣayasva

atha bhagavān sarvatathāgatādhyeśaṇāṃ viditvā sarvatantrahṛdayajñāna-pradīpavajraṃ nāma samādhiṃ samāpadyedaṃ sarvatantrarahasyam udājahāra /
rahasya-[1]-parame ramye sarvātmani sadā sthitaḥ //
sarvabuddhamayaḥ sattvo vajrasattvaḥ paraṃ sukham //
asau hi bhagavān yogaḥ sthiraḥ[2] pa-(10a)-ramaśāśvataḥ[3] //
manmathaḥ[4] pratyutpannaṃ tu[5] svabhāvo duratikramaḥ //
*[6]vicitrakarmayogena vicitravidhikāṅkṣiṇām //
buddhavajradharādhyās tu kṛtakārinayāḥ[7] smṛtāḥ //
sarvabuddhādisthiracala[8] sarvabhāvo[9] bhavaty asau //
sarvabuddhasamāyogaḍākinījālasamvaraḥ[10] //[11]
anena māyāyogena sarvato[12] viśvam uttamam //
*[13]buddhādibhir vineyaiḥ siddhaṃ sarvasattvārtham uttamaṃ //
sarvaṃ[14] strīmāyāyā[15] siddhaṃ svarūpaparivartanaiḥ //[16]
vicitramāyāmudreyaṃ ḍākinīti ca[17] mlecchayā[18] //
dauvihāya-[19]-sagamane[20] dhātur atra vikalpitaḥ[21] //

---

1. A rahasye, B rahasyai
2. A&C sthitaḥ
3. A&C add paraḥ, B -śāśvatamanmathaḥ
4. A&C manmatha
5. B sadā caiva

6.* sna tshogs las kyi rnal 'byor gyis // (250b) sna tshogs cho ga 'dod pa yi //
sangs rgyas rdo rje 'dzin sogs rnams / sems can rnams ni 'dul bar brjod //
sangs rgyas kun sogs brtan dang g.yo / thams cad dngos po srid pa 'di //
sangs rgyas kun dang mnyam sbyor ba / mkha' 'gro ma yi dra ba'i sdom //
'dis ni sgyu ma'i rnal 'byor gyis / thams cad las ni sna tshogs mchog //

7. A -kāritatāḥ, C kāritayāḥ
8. B -calāṃ
9. A -māvo, B -bhāvā
10. B samvare
11. The next two and a part of the third line are missing in A
12. B sarvatā

13.* sangs rgyas sogs pas 'dul ba'i phyir / dngos grub sems can kun don mchog //
rang gi ngo pos yongs bsgyur bas / bud med sgyu ma thams cad 'grub //
sna tshogs sgyu ma'i phyag rgya 'di / mkha' 'gro ma zhes kla klo'i skad //
ṭaivaihāyasar 'gro bar / skad dbyings 'di ni rnam par brtag //
nam mkha' kun tu spyod 'grub pas / mkha' 'gro ma zhes rab tu grags //
kun nas sna tshogs phyag rgya ste / kun las sna tshogs sdom pa'o //
rdo rje rdo rje 'dzin pa nyid / padma de bzhin padma 'dzin //
nor bu nor bu 'dzin pa nyid / 'di rnams kyi ni rigs rnams yin //

14. A&B sarva-
15. C māya-
16. B adds duścāriṇāyo pi siddhyaṃti sarvalābhasukhotsavaiḥ
17. B&C omit
18. B milicchayā
19. B ḍaivaihāya
20. A sanamane
21. A vikampitaḥ, B vikalpikaḥ

sarvākāśacarā siddhir ḍākinīti prasidhyati //
sarvato viśvamudrā tu sarvato viśvasaṃvarair iti //
vajraṃ vajradharaś caiva padmaṃ padmadharas tathā //
maṇir maṇidharaś caiva bhavanty eṣāṃ kulāni ca //
*[1]atha sarvatathāgatābhibhavanavirajapadaṃ[2] nāma samādhiṃ samāpadyedaṃ[3] bodhicittam udājahāra /
na śūnyaṃ nāpi cāśūnyaṃ madhyamā nopalabhyate[4] // (10b)
prajñāpāramitāyogo[5] hy[6] upāyo[7] karuṇātmanāṃ //
tatas su-[8]-karuṇopāyaḥ prajñāpāramitāsphuṭaṃ //
avikalpeṣu dharmeṣu na bhāvo na ca bhāvanā //
avikalpādhimokṣe 'pi kalpayet sarvakalpanāṃ[9] //
avikalpeṣu dharmeṣu sattvārthaparikalpanā[10] //
tathāgatātmakaṃ dharmaṃ na dharmī na ca dharmatā //
pratiśrutkāravasamāt[11] tato 'sau dharmavāg abhūt[12] /
*[13]tato mahāyānasambhavabhāvanāguṇavistaraiḥ /
traiyadhvikā sarvatathāgatā anena stotrarājena saṃstuvanti[14] sma /
namo 'stu yogādhipa [15]sattvamocaka //

1.* de nas de bzhin gshegs pa thams cad zil gyis gnon pa rdul dang bral ba'i gnas zhes bya ba'i ting nge 'dzin la snyoms par zhugs te / byang chub kyi sems 'di bka' stsal pa /
stong min stong pa min pa 'ang min / dbu mar dmigs par mi 'gyur te //
shes rab pha rol phyin sbyor ba / thabs ni snying rje'i bdag nyid de //
de nas mdzes pa'i snying rje thabs / shes rab pha rol phyin gsal ba //
rnam rtog med pa'i chos rnams la / dngos po med cing bsgom pa 'ang med //
rnam rtog med pas rtag mos pas / brtag pa kun gyis brtag par bya //
rnam rtog med pa'i chos rnams la / sems can don ni yongs su brtag //
de bzhin gshegs pa kun bdag chos / chos can med cing chos nyid med //
sgra brnyan lta bur mnyam pa nyid / de nas 'di ni chos dga' byung //

2. B -pan
3. B samāpantedaṃ
4. C madhyamānyepalabhyate
5. A&C -yogā
6. C yośaṣṭū-
7. A&C upāyaṃ
8. A tu, B sva-
9. C -kalpanaṃ
10. A&C -parikalpanāṃ
11. A pratiśrutkāravasanāt, B pratiśrutkārasamās
12. A&C bhavet

13.* de nas (251a) theg pa chen po las byung ba'i bsgom pas yon tan rgyas pa rnams kyis dus gsum gyi de bzhin gshegs pa thams cad kyis bstod pa'i rgyal po 'dis yang dag par bstod pa /
rnal 'byor gyi bdag po sems can grol bar mdzad pa la bstod cing phyag 'tshal lo //
sems can bdag nyid skyes pa gcig par mdzad pa la bstod cing phyag 'tshal lo //
'khor ba'i rgya mtsho'i gti mug gcod par mdzad pa la bstod cing phyag 'tshal lo //
de kho na thams cad kyi ye shes gcig tu ston par mdzad pa la bstod cing phyag 'tshal lo //

14. A sastuvanti, B stuvanti
15. C sapa-

namo 'stu sattvātmaja[1] ekabhāvaka[2] //
namo 'stu saṃsārārṇavamohachedaka[3] //
nam 'stu sarvatattva-[4]-jñānaikadarśaka //
namāmy ahaṃ sadā //
*[5]punar api pūjāṃ kṛtvā praṇipatya evam[6] āhūḥ //
bhāṣasva bhagavan sāraṃ sarvadharmaikavigrahaṃ[7] //
bhagavān āha /
yad yad[8] indriyamārgatvaṃ yāyāt tat tat[9] (11a) svabhāvataḥ //
asamāhitayogena nityam eva samāhitaḥ //
yasmāt sarvātmanātmani[10] vijñānaṃ[11] skandham āśritaṃ[12] //
na kecit pratibudhyante mūḍhacittā[13] narā dhamāḥ //
*[14] cittā cittaṃ ca cidrūpaṃ vijñānaṃ jñeyasvarūpakaṃ //[15]
kāryeṣu[16] kāraṇatvaṃ ca dharmāṇāṃ dharmabhāvanā //
yasmāt dharmabahutvena[17] nadīsrotar[18] ivodadhiḥ //
mokṣo hi[19] eka eva syād bahutvaṃ[20] nopalabhyate //

---

1. C sarvātmaja
2. C omits bhāvaka
3. A chedeka, C chedamaṃ
4. A satva

5.* yang mchod pa byas nas phyag 'tshal te 'di skad ces gsol to /
chos rnams thams cad gcig pa'i sku'i / snying po bcom ldan bshad du gsol //
bcom ldan 'das kyis bka' stsal pa /
dbang po gang dang gang lam nyid / de dang de yi rang bzhin 'gyur //
mnyam par ma bzhag rnal 'byor gyis / rtag par shin tu mnyam bzhag nyid //
gang phyir thams cad bdag nyid kyi / rnam shes phung por gnas pa ni //
skyes bu tha mal sems rmongs pa / la las so sor rtog mi nus //

6. A&C praṇipatyevam
7. B -dharmaikāvagrahaṃ
8. B yadyapi-
9. A&C tatva for tat tat
10. B sarvātmanā ātmanaṃ
11. A vijñānaṃ
12. A -taḥ, C -ta
13. B cetā

14.* sems dang sems byung sems kyis dngos / ye shes shes bya rang bzhin can //
'bras bu rnams la byed pa nyid / chos dang chos can bsgom pa nyid //
gang phyir chos ni du mas ni / chu po'i rgyun ni rgya mtsho ltar //
thar pa nyid ni gcig pu yin / mang po dmigs par mi 'gyur ro //
ji ltar nang gu rnam gnas pa / bla ma'i zhal las rnyed par 'gyur //
de kho na nyid mdor bstan pa ste rab tu byed pa gsum pa'o //

15. B cittācittaṃ ca vijñeyaṃ vijñānaṃ jñānasampadā
16. A&C kāyeṣu
17. A&C -bahūtvena
18. B&C śrotam
19. B di, C sti
20. A bahūtvaṃ

guruvaktrāt tal labhyate yathādhyātmaṃ[1] vyavasthitaḥ[2]//
iti tattvoddeśaprakaraṇaṃ tṛtīyam //
*[3]athātaḥ sampravakṣāmi sarvatantreṣu[4] nirṇayam[5] //
samatvāt[6] sarvasattvānāṃ tryaśram[7] udārarūpiṇaḥ[8] //
ādhāras tu bhavet teṣāṃ[9] brahmādyāḥ[10] sasurāsurāḥ[11] //
saiva prajñapāramitā saṃvṛttākārarūpiṇī //
sa eva viṣayātītaḥ sarvaprāṇihṛdi sthitaḥ //
*[12]kiṃ te vistarato mānaḥ[13] saṃkṣepāt (11b) tad eva buddhatvaṃ[14] //
buddhatvaṃ[15] yat prāptaṃ[16] kalpāsaṃkhyeyakoṭibhir yāvat //
asmin api janmani tvaṃ prāpnoti sat sukhenaiva //[17]
atha vajradharatvam atha vānenaiva cakravartitvam //
aṣṭamahāsiddhiṃ vā anyāṃ manasīpsitāṃ[18] vāpi //
*[19]moho rāgo dveṣo mānas tv irṣyā ca pañcasaṃkleśāḥ //
sattvās tu pratibaddhā vai yena jayanti[20] svāṅgena[21] //[22]

---

1. B -ātma
2. B vyavasthitaṃ

3.* de nas rgyud rnams thams cad du / gtan la phab pa rab bshad bya //
sems can kun la mnyam pa'i phyir / sku gsum rgya cha'i gzugs can nyid //
tshangs sogs lha dang lha min bcas / de rnams kyi ni gnas su (251b) 'gyur //
de nyid shes rab pha rol phyin / kun rdzob rnam pa'i gzugs can ma //
de nyid yul rnam par 'das / srog chags kun gyi snying la gnas //

4. A&C -tantraika
5. A&C nirṇayāṃ
6. B samat
7. A tisram, C tryasram
8. B -rūpiṇaṃ, C rūpiṇa
9. B ādhāraṃ bhevaty eṣāṃ
10. B buddhādhyāḥ
11. A&C brahmādīnāṃ ca sarvataḥ

12.* de phyir nga rgyal ci zhig bya / mdor bsdus pas ni sangs rgyas nyid //
bskal pa bye ba grangs med pas / ji ltar sangs rgyas gang thob pa //
gang gis dam pa'i bde bas khyod / skye ba 'dir ni thob par 'gyur //
yang na rdo rje 'dzin pa nyid / yang na 'khor los sgyur ba 'am //
'dis ni dngos grub chen po brgyad / gzhan yang 'di la 'dod pa 'ang //

13. A&C 'taḥ, B manaḥ
14. B omits tad eva and reads vibuddhatvaṃ instead of buddhatvaṃ
15. A nānyair instead of buddhatvaṃ
16. B yadaṃ prāpya, C yad aprāpaṃ nānyair yatprāptaṃ
17. B from -koṭibhiḥ // yāvat prāpnoty asmin janmani // yena tvaṃ svasukhenaiva //
18. B anya mansepsitaṃ

19.* gti mug chags sdang nga rgyal dang / phrag dog dang ni nyon mongs lngas //
sems can so sor bcings pa gang / rang gi yan lag nyid kyis 'joms //
'dis ni 'gro drug sems can bcings / 'khor bar 'khor zhing skye ba nyid //
nyon mongs pas ni mongs gyur pas / sdig pa du ma byed par 'gyur //
de phyir 'di bcom cing mkhyen nyid / sangs rgyas kyis sbrul rigs pas ni //

20. A&C jāyanti
21. C svāṅgenaiva
22. B omits this line and reads saṃtānapratibaddhāḥ // yedyūttisvārthakaṃ caiva //

ebhir baddhāḥ sattvāḥ ṣaḍgatisaṃsāravarttito jātāḥ //
kurvanty anekapāpaṃ kleśair vimohitāḥ[1] santaḥ /
atha caitān vihantuṃ vidagdhabuddhena nirmitāḥ[2] //
*[3]dṛṣṭvā duḥkhaviyogaṃ[4] saṃsārārṇavapatitānām //
pratyayabhūtāḥ kleśāḥ prajñopāyas tu[5] nirmita-[6]-hetuḥ //
phalabhūto asau[7] lakṣyas[8] tridhātuṣu nirmala-[9]-lokaḥ //
ye yena vidhināsthāpyā[10] bhūtās te tasya rūpiṇaḥ / /
*[11] indhanavahninyāyena ramyaṃ jinanāṭakaṃ (12a) divyam //[12]
ayaṃ eva[13] śuddhalakṣo [14]skandhāyatanadhātavaḥ //
taṃ hanti samartho[15] bhūtvā [16] śatrusamo yathā śatruḥ[17] //
mohaṃ mohaviśuddhyā dveṣaviśuddhyā tathā[18] dveṣam //
rāgaṃ rāgaviśuddhyā mānaviśuddhyā mahāmānam //
īrṣyām īrṣyāviśuddhyā sarvaviśuddhas[19] tu vajradhṛg nāthaḥ[20] //
*[21] tad rūpaviśudhyā pañcakleśāḥ samaṃ yānti //

---

1. B vyāmohitān
2. A&C yuktiḥ

3.* 'khor ba'i rgya mtshor lhung ba yi / sbyor bral sdug bsngal mthong nas ni //
thabs dang shes rab sbrul pa'i rgyus / nyon mongs rnams ni yid ches 'gyur //
mtshon pa 'di ni 'bras bur gyur / khams gsum du ni dri med snang //
gang dang gang gis gnas gyur pa / de ni de yi ngo bo can //

4. A -viyoga
5. B prajñopāyasva
6. A&C nirmitā
7. A phalabhūtokvasau
8. B phalabhūtāsaulakṣa
9. A&B nirmalā
10. B yena yenanantānāśritā

11.* bud cing bsreg pa'i rags pas ni / dgyes pa'i rgyal ba gar mkhan mchog //
phung po khams dang skye mched rnams / 'di nyid rnam dag mtshon pa 'di //
ji ltar dgra po nus pa la / dgra po nus pas de bsnun pa //
gti mug dag pas gti mug ste / zhe sdang dag pas zhe sdang nyid //
'dod chags dag pas 'dod chags te / nga rgyal rnam dag nga rgyal che //
phrag dog dag pas phrag dog nyid / thams cad rnam dag rdor 'dzin mgon //

12. B nāṭakaṃ // divyam
13. A ayeva
14. A&C pañca-, B yaṃ
15. B taṃ taṃ hasti samarthaḥ
16. B omits
17. A instead of śatrusamo etc reads sasantu samārthā yathā śaṃtum, and C samārthā yathā śatruṃ
18. B omits
19. B omits
20. A&C bhāvaḥ

21.* de yi ngo bo rnam dag pa / nyon mongs lnga ni mnyam par 'gyur //
de ltar rigs ni lnga rnams dang / ye shes lnga dang sangs rgyas lnga //
'di las rdo rje snying po dang / (252a) khro bo khams gsum sems can skye //
nang gi dbye ba 'di nyid ni / bla ma'i zhal las rnyed par 'gyur //

etāni[1] pañcakulāni pañcajñānāni pañcabuddhāḥ //
ebhyo jātāḥ[2] sattvā vajragarbhaḥ krodhāḥ tridhātuś[3] ca //
ayam evādhyātmabhedo guruvaktrāl labhyate 'tispaṣṭena //
*[4]ye guruhīnāḥ sattvā na labhante[5] te mantramudrām api //
jambudvīpe tato 'smin buddhādhyuṣite trikoṇake śuddhe //
ekārākṛtimadhye rasasyaivaṃ[6] yathā bhavati //
trikoṇe maṇḍale ramye vajrāralivinismṛtam //
dharmodayeti vikhyātam yoṣitāṃ[7] bhaga ity api //
*[8]tasya (12b) madhye[9] gataṃ padmam aṣṭapatraṃ sakarṇikam[10] //
tatrālikālisammiśrā aṣṭau varṇavyavasthitāḥ //
kurvanti karmasaṃghātaṃ mantrarūpeṇa dehinām //
pañcāśadakṣarāṇy eva vedās tu saṃsthitā ime[11] //
tantrāṇāṃ caiva mantrāṇāṃ śāstrāṇāṃ bāhyarūpiṇām //
etāni vajragarbhasva-[12]-rūpāṇi nānyad ebhyo 'sti kiṃcit //
*[13] akacaṭatapayaśavargaratāni[14] pañcāśad[15] api //

---

1. B ete
2. B yātāḥ
3. A&C tridhātukaś
4.* bla ma dman pa'i sems can rnams / sngags dang phyag rgya rnyed mi 'gyur //
gang zhig shin tu gsal bas ni / mdzam gling de 'dir sangs rgyas bsngags //
gru gsum dag pa e yi dbyibs / dbus su dgyes pa'i evaṃ yin //
gru gsum dkyil 'khor nyams dga' bar / rdo rje ra li rnam par byung //
btsun mo'i bhaga zhes kyang bya / chos kyi 'byung gnas zhes byar bshad //
5. B labhanti
6. A&C vaṃyasyaivaṃ
7. A&C yoṣitaṃ
8.* de yi nang song padma'i na / 'dab ma brgyad pa snying por bcas //
de la ā li kā li 'dres / sde tshan brgyad ni rnam par gnas //
sngags kyi gzugs kyi lus can gyi / las kyi tshogs ni byed par 'gyur //
yi ge rnams ni lnga bcu nyid / rig byed rnams la nye bar gnas //
sngags rnams nyid dang rgyud rnams dang / phyi rol tshul gyi bstan bcos kyi //
rdo rje snying po'i rang bzhin 'di / gzhan du a las cung zad med //
9. B madhya
10. B sakeśara
11. B vedāni saṃsthitāni vai
12. A&C sarva-
13. *akacaṭatapayaśa / sde tshan dga' ba lnga bcu yang //
mnyam pa dag tu sprul ba rnams / rdo rje ra li padmar song //
'dab ma brgyad po phyogs rnams dang / mtshams rnams su ni 'di rnams rigs //
de rnams dbus su ze 'bru la / dam pa'i dbang phyug ma yod do //
sde tshan brgyad po rnams kyis ni / yi ge dam pa yongs su bskor //
a ni yig 'bru kun gyi mchog / don chen sde tshan gtso bo ni //
lus can rnams kyi sngags kun ni / 'di nyid las ni yang dag 'byung //
14. A vargaṃ ca tāni
15. B pañcadaśa

samāni nirmitāni [1] vajrāralau [8] padmagatāni //
pratidalam [2] aṣṭa dikṣu viditāni //
eṣaṃ madhye tu kiñjalke vidyate parameśvaraḥ //
aṣṭabhir vargakaiś [3] caiva veṣṭitaḥ paramākṣaraḥ //
akāraḥ sarvavarṇagro [4] mahārtho [5] varganāyakaḥ //
tatra [6] eva samudbhūtāḥ sarvamantrās tu dehiṇām //
*[7]yaḥ khaḍgāñjanapādalepagulikāpātālayakṣāṅganāḥ //
trailokyodaravartisutakagati-[8]-(13a)-karmānugāḥ siddhayaḥ //
yāḥ sarvās tu maharddhayaḥ svābhavane satpañcakāmānvitāḥ //
tā vargāṣṭakamadhyagāt svaravarād niryānti vargātmakāḥ [9] //
yaḥ kaścit prasaro vācā janānāṃ pratipadyate //
sa sarvo mantrarūpo hi tasmād eva prajāyate //
*[10] nādo hi mantra [11] ity uktaṃ sarveṣāṃ tu śāririṇām //
viśvagraṃthimahāsthānād dharmāraler [12] viniścaret //
na kaścin niyato mantraḥ siddhyṛddhyās [13] tu vyavasthitaḥ [14] //
anutpannasvabhāvo hi mantro vargeśvaraḥ paraḥ //
*[15] ataḥ paraṃ pravakṣyāmi saṃputodbhavalakṣaṇam //

---

1. A&C samānimitāni
8 . A vajrāralo, B vajrāvalī-
2. B pratidale
3. B vargaiś
4. A&C -agrau
5 A&C mahāthau
6. B tata

7.* gang zhig ral gri mig sman dang / rkang byug ri lu rkang 'og dang //
gnod sbyin mo'i yan lag ma / 'jig rten gsum gyi khongs su rgyu //
dngul chu'i 'gro bas rjes su 'brang / gang zhig thams cad mthu che ba //
rang gi khyim du lnga bcu 'dod pa dang ldan par 'grub po /
de ni sde tshan brgyad nang son / dbyangs mchog sde tshan bdag (252b) nyid 'byin//
skye bo rnams kyi tshig rgyas pa / gang zhig cung zad rtogs bya ba //
de kun sngags kyi gzugs kyis ni / de phyir rab tu skye bar 'gyur //

8. B varttisutakagatiḥ, C varttisthutagati
9. B tās tā vargāṣṭakamadhyagā aravarāṃ niryānti vargāṣṭakāḥ

10.* lus can rnams ni thams cad kyi / sgra ni sngags zhes brjod par bya //
sna tshogs mdud pa'i gnas chen las / chos kyi ra li rnam par 'byung //
dngos grub rdzu phrul rnam gnas pa'i / sngags dang nges pa gang yang med //
rang bzhin gyis ni ma skyes pa'i / sngags kyi yig 'bru dbang phyug mchog //

11. A&C mantram
12. B dharmārali
13. B siddhi ṛddhyau and omits tu
14. B vyavasthitāḥ

15.* yang dag sbyor 'byung mtshan nyid ni / de nas mchog tu rab bshad bya //
e yi sa ru shes par bya / las kyi phyag rgya spyan ma nyid //
snying rje chen mo thabs chen mo / rang bzhin sna tshogs spyod yul ma //
lte bar sna tshogs 'dam skyes la / sprul pa'i 'khor lor rnam par gnas //
vaṃ ni chu ru shes par bya // chos kyi phyag rgya māmakī //
byams pa dang ni smon lam tshul / lha mo rdo rje'i rigs gtso mo //

ekāraḥ pṛthivījñeyā [1] karmamudrā tu locanā //
mahākṛpā [2] mahopāyaviśvarūpā [3] viśvagocarā [4] //
sthitā nirmāṇacakre vai nābhau catuḥṣaṣṭāmbuje [5] //
vaṃkāras tu jalaṃ jñeyaṃ dharmamudrā tu māmakī //
maitrī- (13b)-praṇidhirūpā tu devī vajrakulā mukhyā [6] //
sthitā sā [7] dharmacakre tu hṛdaye svaṣṭa-[8]-dalāmbuje //
*[9]makāro vahnir uddiṣṭā [10] mahāmudrā tu pāṇḍarā //
muditā- [11] -balayogena devī padmakulodbhavā //
sthitā saṃbhogacakre tu kaṇṭhe dvyaṣṭa-[12]-dalāmbuje //
yākāro vāyurūpas tu sarvakleśaprabhaṃjakaḥ //
mahāsamayamudrā vai devī karmakulā mukhyā [13] //
upekṣājñānayogena tārā saṃsāratāriṇī //
sthitā mahāsukhacakre [14] dvātriṃśadalapaṅkaje //
*[15]ekāreṇa smṛtā prajñā vaṃkāraś cāpy upāyakaḥ [16] //
vaṃkārabhūṣitaś [17] cāsav [8]ekāraḥ śobhate dhruvam //
adho ūrdhvaṃ [18] samāpattyā [19] prajñopāyasvabhāvataḥ //
ekāro vaṃkāraś caiva dvayaṃ dvayam udāhṛtam //[20]

---

snying khar chu skyes 'dab brgyad la / chos kyi 'khor lor yang dag gnas //

1. B ekārapṛthivījñeyaṃ
2. B -kṛpo
3. B -rūpo
4. C -goca
5. B viśvapaṃkaje
6. A&C -kulodbhavā
7. B omits
8. B hṛdaye aṣṭa-

9.* ma ni me ru brjod pa ste / phyag rgya chen mo gos dkar mo //
dga' dang stobs kyi rnal 'byor gyis / lha mo padma'i rigs byung ma //
lkog mar chu skyes 'dab brgyad gnyis / longs spyod 'khor lor yang dag gnas //
ya ni rlung gi rang bzhin te / nyon mongs thams cad rab 'joms byed //
dam tshig phyag rgya chen po nges / lha mo las kyi rigs gtso mo //
btang snyoms ye shes rnal 'byor gyis / sgrol ma 'khor ba sgrol ma'o //
'dab skyes 'dam ma sum bcu gnyis / bde chen 'khor lo chen por gnas //

10. A uddhiṣṭā, C dviṣṭā
11. A&C mudritā
12. B dveṣta
13. A&C -kulodbhavā
14. A mahāsukhe śiraścakra, B mahāsukhā mahācakre tu, C mahāsukhe śiraścakre

15.* e ni shes rab brjod par bya / vaṃ ni thabs dang ldan pa nyid //
vaṃ gyis rnam par brgyan pa nyid / e ni nges par mdzes par 'gyur //
thabs dang shes rab rang bzhin gyis / steng dang 'og tu snyoms par 'jug //
e nyid dang ni vaṃ nyid dag / (253a) gnyis gnis su ni brjod pa nyid //

16. B upāyakaṃ
17. A bhūṣitāś
18. A&B adhordhva, C adhordhvaṃ
19. A samāpannā
20. A&C omit this line

*[1]evam iti nipātena[2] avocat paryantaṃ tantrasamudāyaḥ sūcyate vā[3] / vakṣyati[4] mayā śrutam evaṃ hi mahārāgo[5] 'tra sadā sthitaḥ[6] (14a) / śruśravanaṃ nirdiṣṭaṃ ta[7] yaś ca mahāsukho nāthaḥ / mayaiva śrutam mayā śrutam[8] iti śrotreṇa jñānena śrutaṃ na tv adhigatam / adhigate[9] tu bhagavan ko doṣaḥ /

*[10]bhagavān āha / saṃgītikārakadeśakayor abhedaḥ syāt / atha vādhigatam eva vaineyajanavaśāt / deśaka eva saṃgītikārakaḥ syāt / deśako 'ham ahaṃ dharmaḥ śroto 'haṃ[11] svaguṇair yutaḥ / tat kathaṃ jāyate[12] nṛtyati yatra mahā-sukhanātho[13] nṛtyaty ekam anekaraseneti vacanāt[14] / yat kiṃcid ākhyātaṃ bhagavatā[15] kulaputrāḥ tan mayā ekasmin eva kāle[16] ekasmin eva kṣaṇe śrutaṃ ity adhigatam / anenācintya-vimokṣasamādhilābhitvaṃ tac cittam[17] / samayaḥ kāla ity uktaḥ /

*[18]kālo hi trividho[19] mataḥ sukālaś caiva duḥkālo //
acintyaḥ kāla eva ca /

1.* 'di skad ces bya ba'i tshig gi phrad ni de skad ces gsungs nas zhes bya ba'i mthar thug pa'i rgyud kyi tshogs la bsnyegs so zhes brjod do / bdag gis thos pa zhes bya ba ni de skad du 'dod chags chen po 'di la rtag tu gnas pa'o / śru zhes bya ba ni 'dzag par gsungs so / ta zhes bya ba ni g ang yang bde ba chen po'i mgon po'o / bdag gis thos pa zhes bya ba ni bdag nyid kyis thos pa'i phyir rna ba'i ye shes kyis thos pa yin gyi / rtogs pa ni ma yin no / bcom ldan 'das mi rtogs pa'i skyon gang lags //

2. B niryāta
3. B sūcakaḥ for sūcyate vā
4. B vacmi
5. A&C -rājo
6. B sthitāḥ
7. A&C omit
8. A&C omit mayā śrutam
9. C adhiyate

10.* bcom ldan 'das kyis bka' stsal pa / sdud par byed pa dang 'chad pa po dag dbyer med par 'gyur ro / yang na rtogs pa nyid ni gdul bya'i skye bo'i dbang du byas nas 'chad pa po nyid dang sdud par byed pa yin te / 'chad pa po nga chos kyang nga / rang gi tshogs ldan nyan pa nga / de dag ji ltar 'tshal bar bgyi / gang du bde ba chen po'i mgon po gar mdzad pa'i tshe / gcig nyid gcig dang du ma'i ro zhes bya ba'i tshig gis rol par mdzad pa'o / rigs kyi bu bcom ldan 'das kyis gang cung zad gsungs pa de bdag gis gcig na zhes bya ba ni dus gcig nyid la'o / gcig na zhes bya ba ni skad cig la'o / thos pa zhes bya ba ni lhag par son pa ste / 'dis bsam gyis mi khyab pa'i ting nge 'dzin rnyed do zhes bya bar bsnyegs so / dus zhes bya ba ni dus tshod ces gsungs so //

11. A&B śrotāham
12. C jñāyate
13. B mahāsuhanāmā
14. C ekam aneti vacanāt
15. B bhagavan
16. A omits from -nātho till here
17. B sūcayati for tac cittam

18.* dus ni rnam pa gsum du brjod / bde ba'i dus dang sdug bsngal dus //
bsam gyis mi khyab dus nyid do /
'o ma'i rgyun ltar sna bug tu / 'ong ba bde ba'i dus su gsungs //
me'i gzugs kyis 'gro ba nyid / sdug bsngal dus dang de gcig grags //
gcig ni lhan cig med pa yin / dus na bsam gyis mi khyab 'gyur //

19. B tridho

kṣiradhārāvan[1] nāsāpuṭarandhreṇāgataḥ sukāla ucyate //
gataś caiva bahnirūpena duḥkālas tayor ekaḥ prakīrtitaḥ // (14b)
asahāyo bhaved ekaḥ kālas tv acintyatāṃ gataḥ //
*[2]na rāgo na virāgaś ca madhyamā nopalabhyate //
tatra rāga āśaktilakṣaṇaḥ / virāgo nirodho mataḥ[3]//
ābhyāṃ rahitā madhyamā na pratīyate / etat[4] trayan nopalabhyate[5] //
rāgaś caiva virāgaś ca miśrībhūtam anāvilam //
tathā rāgavirāgābhyām ekaḥ samarasaḥ kṣaṇaḥ //
samarasaḥ[6] sarvabhāvānāṃ bhāvanāsamayas tv eka[7] //
tadyathā aiśvaryasya samagrasya rūpasya yaśasaḥ śrīyaḥ / jñānasyārtha-prayatnasya ṣaṇṇāṃ[8] bhaga iti smṛtaḥ[9]/ so 'syā 'stīti[10] bhagavān //
*[11] atha vā ye[12] vaipākṣikā dharmās tān bhagnavān iti bhagavān / sarvatathāgata-kāyavākcittāni tāny[13] eva hṛdayaṃ tad eva vajraṃ saiva yoṣit tasyā bhagas[14] tatra vijahāra / he bhagavan vijahāreti kim uktaṃ bhavati //

---

1. A&C vata

2.* 'dod chags med cing chags bral med / dbu mar dmigs par mi 'gyur ro // (253b)
de la 'dod chags nus mtshan nyid / 'dod chags bral ba 'gog par gsungs //
'di bral dbu mar mi rtog pas / 'di gsum dmigs par mi 'gyur ro //
'dod chags nyid dang chags bral nyid / 'dres par gyur pa rnyo ba med //
de bzhin 'dod chags chags bral las / ro mnyam gcig bu'i skad cig ma //
dngos po kun gyi ro mnyam pa / bsgom pa'i dus ni gcig tu gsungs //
'di lta ste / dbang phyug dang / gzugs dang / grags pa dang / dpal dang / ye shes dang / brtson 'grus phun sum tshogs pa ste / bhaga drug ces gsungs so / de 'di la mnga' ba'i phyir bcom ldan 'das so //

3. B nirodhasatyaṃ

4. C etatat

5. B etad ūpanopalabhyate

6. A&C samarasaṃ

7. A&C bhagavān sa ucyate, B bhagavān samayas tv eka

8. A&C ṣarṇṇāṃ

9. B śrutiḥ

10. B so syāstīti, C so 'syostīti

11.* yang na gang zhig mi mthun pa'i phyogs kyis chos de rnams bcom pa'i phyir bcom ldan 'das so / de bzhin gshegs pa thams cad kyi sku dang / gsung dang / thugs rnams dang / de rnams nyid kyi snying po dang / de nyid kyi rdo rje dang / de nyid kyi btsun mo dang / de'i bhaga de la bzhugs so / kye bcom ldan 'das bzhugs so zhes bya bas ci gsungs lags /

12. B ya ca vai

13. A&C omit tāny

14. B bhagavaṃ

*[1]bhagavān āha / samarasarva-(15a)-tathāgatavicitropāyena vineyajana-[2]-manāṃsi hṛtavān ity arthaḥ / sarvatathāgata-[3]-kāyavākcittahṛdayavajra-svabhāvāyāṃ[4] dharmo-dayāyāṃ yadā bhagavān vijahāra tadā mayā śrutam iti / tad-[5]-yathā / yena[6] kleśo 'pi nihanyate prajñādhīnāś ca te kleśās tasmāt prajñā bhaga[7] ucyate / tasmin bhage[8] sakalatathāgatayoṣit-[9]-sahitaḥ sthitaḥ[10] /

*[11] aho hi sarvabuddhānāṃ[12] sarvajñajñānam uttamam[13] //
yat tathāgatasaukhyārthaṃ bhāryatvam api svīkṛtam[14] iti //

kulaputrā evaṃ mayā śrutaṃ varṇā dharmādau nityasaṃsthitāḥ / śuddhāḥ saṃbuddhasiddhijanakā[15] ye kathyā vajrapāṇe[16] te[17] mayā kathitāḥ / varṇair ebhiḥ[18] sattvāḥ[19] prayānti[20] saṃsārapāram atidūram[21] / lakṣyaṃ kṛtvā sākṣād asakṛt[22] tal līnacittena prāpnoty asmin janmani buddhatvaṃ vajrasattvatvaṃ[23] vā //

1.* bcom ldan 'das kyi bka' stsal pa / de bzhin gshegs pa thams cad kyi ro cig pa thabs sna tshogs kyis 'dul ba'i skye bo'i yid 'phrog pa dang ldan pa zhes bya ba'i don to / de bzhin gshegs pa thams cad kyi sku dang / gsung dang / thugs kyi snying po rdo rje'i rang bzhin gang gi chos kyi 'byung gnas la / gang gi tshe bcom ldan 'das bzhugs pa de'i tshe bdag gis thos pa / 'di lta ste / shes rab gang gis nyon mongs pa dang / nye ba'i nyon mongs pa 'joms pa de'i phyir shes rab bhagar gsungs te / bhaga der de bzhin gshegs pa thams cad btsun mo lhan cig du bzhugs so //

2. A&C vineyamata
3. B omits sarvatathāgata
4. B -vajrayoṣisvabhāvopāya
5. A&C omit
6. A&C omit
7. B bhagar
8. B yasmin bhagate
9. A yoṣi B yoṣitaḥ
10. C sahitasthitaḥ

11.* e ma sangs rgyas thams cad kyi / kun mkhyen ye shes bla na med //
de bzhin gshegs pa'i de don gang / btsun mo nye bar mdzad pa'o //
rigs kyi bu 'di skad bdag gis (254a) thos pa zhes bya ba'i yig 'bru ni / chos kyi thog mar rtag tu yang dag par gnas pa ste / dag pa dang yang dag par rdzogs pa'i sangs rgyas kyi dngos grub skyed par byed pa'o / lag na rdo rje ma bshad pa de nges khyod la bshad do / tshig 'bru 'di rnams kyis sems can rnams 'khor ba las pha rol du shin tu ring bar 'gro ba mngon du mtshon par mdzad pa dang / mngon du mdzad pa de nub pa'i sems kyis skye ba 'dir sangs rgyas nyid dam / rdo rje sems dpa' thob par 'gyur te /

12. C -buddhānyaṃ
13. B anuttaraṃ
14. A apīsvītaṃ, B upakalpata
15. B saṃbuddham iti janakāḥ
16. B vajrapaṇai
17. A&C omit
18. A varoribhi, B vaṇair iti
19. B sattvaḥ
20. A&C prayāntu
21. A&C saṃsāram atidūram, B saṃsāraḥ pāram iti dūraṃ
22. B asakyaṃ
23. B vajrasattvaṃ

*[1]yad eva padam[2] (15b) acintyaṃ na prāptaṃ yac ca[3] sugataiś ca buddhā [4]bhavanti sattvāḥ samyag uktās tu lakṣite / lakṣyasevita-[5]-mātreṇa avīcau prayāti saṃkliṣṭacittena saṃtyajyātaḥ saṃkliṣṭaṃ bhavabhayabhītas tu sādhakaḥ / śrīman bhāvayati śuddhacittaḥ / prajñopāyaprayogena tena yathā saṃprāptaṃ[6] śuddhaṃ saṃvedanātmakaṃ[7]akṣyaṃ prajñopāyavikāraṃ gaganasamaṃ tribhuvanālokam / tal lakṣyaṃ dūrlakṣyaṃ sarvagataṃ hetupratyayādhīnam / cintāmaṇir iva loke[8] svaparārthakaraṃ siddhyagram //
iti sarvatantranidānarahasyāt śrīsaṃpuṭodbhavaḥ kalparājaḥ prathamaḥ samāptaḥ //

1.* gang dag bsam gyis mi khyab pa'i gnas ma thob pa de ni bde bar gshegs pa ste sangs rgyas yin no / mtshan gzhi mtshon par byed pa ni sems dpar yang dag par gsungs te / sdang bas bsten pa can gyis mnar med par rab tu ltung bar 'gyur bas na / kun nas nyon mongs pa can gyi sems kyis ro spang bar bya'o / kun nas nyon mongs pa can gyi srid pa'i 'jigs pa las 'das pa'i sgrub pa po dpal dang ldan pas dag pa'i sems sgom par byed de / thabs dang shes rab kyi sbyor ba 'dis ji ltar yang dag pa thob pa dag pa'i yang dag par rig pa'i bdag nyid can gyi mtshan gzhi thabs dang shes rab kyis nus pas nam mkha' dang mnyam zhing gnas gsum du snang ba ste / de'i mtshan gzhi ni mtshon par dka' ba dang / thams cad du song zhing rgyu dang rkyen spangs pas yid bzhin gyi nor bu lta bur 'jig rten gyi rang dang gzhan gyi don byed de / dngos grub thams cad kyi mchog go //
rgyud thams cad kyi gleng gzhi gsang ba dpal yang dag par sbyor ba las byung ba'i brtag pa'i rgyal po ste dang po rdzogs so //

2. B yāty eva padavinim
3. B yadvat
4. A buddho
5. A lakṣyasecitta, B lakṣiḥ lakṣasevita
6. B saṃprāpta-
7. B satyaṃ vedanātmakaṃ
8. A&C lokeṣv and omit svapara

A Buddhist Inspiration for a Contemporary Psychotherapy

Gay Watson

Introduction

The Buddhist world view is an holistic one; philosophy, psychology, religion, morality and even medicine are seamlessly interwoven into one cloth. In Western history all these disciplines have become increasingly independent and isolated. As an American psychologist wrote recently: "we have lost sight of the deeper roots of our discipline in philosophy, and, in turn, of philosophy in religion."[1] Such separation is a loss as the independent Western disciplines have themselves come to realise, creating such hybrid discourses as Systems Theory and Cognitive Science, for as psychologist Jerome Bruner has declared: "a psychology of mind can never be free of a philosophy of mind."[2] It is my contention that good psychotherapeutic practice has much to learn from such an holistic approach and that only such an approach can heal the alienation and reactionary narcissism that comes from our increasing feeling that we are distinct and separate from our world. I will argue that Buddhism offers not only a long tradition of integrated view, a view that is coming to seem evermore compatible with the contemporary world view of the West, but also methods of practice for instantiating that view that are particularly helpful and relevant today. For, as D.T. Suzuki said: "personal experience is...the foundation of Buddhist philosophy"[3], and it can thus reunite theory with lived experience.

According to traditional Buddhist method, I shall divide this exploration into Ground, Path and Goal. Ground will attempt to provide the context, first taking a brief look at the historical development of Western psychotherapies, and then focusing on Buddhism and the philosophical and psychological teachings which I consider particularly fit it as a source of meaning and psychotherapeutic techniques in the contemporary world.[4] Following this necessarily brief

---

1. D. Goleman in Goleman & Thurman, eds., *Mind Science*, Boston, Wisdom, 1991, 3.
2. J. Bruner, *In Search of Mind*, New York, Harper & Row, 1983, 129.
3. D.T. Suzuki, *On Indian Mahayana Buddhism*, ed. E. Conze, New York, Harper & Row, 1968, 237.
4. When speaking of Buddhism, I am attempting as far as possible, to give an overall view, explicating those doctrines which are central to Buddhism in general, rather

introduction to the two subjects I will endeavour to put together some suggestions about the specific value and relevance of this Buddhist outlook in relation to various problematics.

Path will look at those aspects of Buddhist practice which may be of particular value on the psychotherapeutic journey.

Goal will attempt to compare and contrast the goals of these two paths, the Buddhist and the therapeutic. Hopefully then, in the light of what has gone before, we may perhaps gather a few ideas as to what might be some features of a contemporary Buddhist-inspired psychotherapy.

GROUND

Western Psychology

First I should like to distinguish between my use of the terms psychology and psychotherapy.[5] In this paper I shall generally use psychology to denote the theory of mind, and psychotherapy as praxis relating to the healing of disease or to the healthful expansion of the potential of the mind, but I am aware that at times there is some overlap.

In terms of its therapies, Western psychology is often divided into four major schools—Behaviourist, Analytic, Humanistic, and most recently, Transpersonal. I will first attempt to compare them briefly in terms of their philosophies, key concepts, goals, therapeutic relationship and techniques. Behaviourism as its name implies is concerned with visible behaviour and the physical body and believes that humans are shaped by socio-cultural conditions. Its outlook is deterministic; behaviour is the result of learning and conditioning and stimulus-response mechanisms. It is not concerned with hypothetical and invisible consciousness, memory and interior processes of mind.

As behaviour is learned through imitation and reinforcement, abnormal behaviour is seen as a result of faulty learning, and therapy is based upon learning theory, focusing on overt behaviour, precise goals, treatment plans and objective evaluation. The emphasis is on present behaviour, with little concern for past history. The goals of therapy are to eliminate maladaptive behaviour patterns and to replace them with constructive ones. Within the therapeutic relationship, the therapist is active and directive, functioning as a teacher, and clients are also expected to be active in the process. The personal relationship is

---

than restricted to any particular school or outlook. However, I acknowledge that the balance is weighted towards the view of Mahāyāna in general, and Tibetan Buddhism in particular.

5. According to the Oxford Dictionary, psychology is "(a) the science of the nature, function, and phenomenon of the human soul or mind. (b) A treatise on, or system of psychology." Psychotherapeutic is given as "of or pertaining to the treatment of mental or psychic disease."

not emphasized. The main therapeutic techniques are operant conditioning, systematic desensitization and assertiveness training, all of which are based on principles of learning theory, and intended to effect behavioural change.

Behaviourism, with its scientific outlook and refusal to acknowledge introspection and personal experience had a stranglehold on academic psychology until recently, but has given way to Cognitive Psychology, allowing mind and consciousness back into consideration, and giving rise to Cognitive Behaviour therapies which pay more attention to cognitive factors in determing behaviour and effecting behavioural change. Yet the influence of the physical sciences and Behaviourism is still strong, with the result that much of Cognitive Science, a contemporary hybrid discipline drawing on psychology, philosophy, linguistics, neurosciences, evolutionary biology and computer science, is concerned with artificial intelligence, and betrays a continuing reluctance to engage with specifically human intelligence. Yet there are exceptions and there is now some extremely exciting work going on in this field.[6]

The classical Analytic school arises from the works of Sigmund Freud. Its basic philosophy is that human beings are driven by sexual and aggressive impulses, and that behaviour is largely determined by unconscious motives and conflicts. It stresses the importance of early development, suggesting that later personality problems come from repressed conflicts usually occurring in childhood. Normal personality development depends on the successful resolution and integration of stages of psychosexual development. Unsuccessful resolution of one or more stages results in faulty personal development. Key concepts include the theory of unconscious motivations, division of the structure of the personality into id, ego and super-ego, the arousal of anxiety as the result of repression of basic conflicts between impulses and socialisation, and the development of ego defences to control this anxiety.

The goals of therapy are to bring the unconscious elements into consciousness, so the client can relive early experiences and work through the repressed conflict. To this end the therapeutic relationship is relatively distant, the analyst remaining anonymous allowing the analysand to develop projections towards the analyst, and the focus is on working through this transference. Therapy is usually frequent and long-term. Key techniques are dream analysis, free association, analysis of resistance, transference and interpretation. Therapy is verbal and not concerned with the body.

---

6. See particularly J. Bruner, *Acts of Meaning*, Cambridge, Mass., Harvard, 1990; J. Searle, *The Rediscovery of Mind,* Cambridge, Mass, M.I.T., 1992; F.J.Varela, E. Rosch, E. Thompson, *The Embodied Mind,* Cambridge, Mass, M.I.T., 1991; G. Edelman, *Bright Air, Brilliant Fire, On the Matter of the Mind,* London, Allen Lane, 1992.

Since the time of Freud there have been many developments in Analytic Psychology. Developmental and interpersonal issues have been particularly stressed by the Object Relations school in England, and Ego Psychology in America, which have taken Analytic Psychology away from its narrow focus on drive issues, as also has Heinz Kohut's Self Psychology. Most lively have been recent French developments centring around the work of Jacques Lacan who has allied Psychoanalysis to linguistic studies, believing the unconscious is structured like a language.

Humanistic Psychology is based upon a phenomenological rather than theoretical approach, and maintains that humans have an inclination towards health and full-functioning. It is concerned with what one of its founders, Abraham Maslow called "Being needs", the higher needs of value and meaning which arise from the sphere of culture and are superimposed upon basic biological survival needs. It upholds the increase of awareness of previously ignored or repressed feelings to actualize potential and increase trust, self-awareness and self-direction. Normal personal development results in and from congruence between the self experience and self concept, and faulty development from discrepancy between them. The emphasis is on the present moment, on the experience and on the expression of feelings. The goal of therapy is to provide a safe space for self exploration so that blocks to awareness and growth may be recognised and aspects of self formerly denied or distorted can be experienced. Clients are helped to move towards openness to all experience, greater trust in self, greater awareness of ongoing experience and increased spontaneity. The therapeutic relationship is of prime importance, and is a real and direct relationship rather than one based upon transference or projection. The emphasis is on the therapist's warmth, empathy, genuineness, congruance and communication of these qualities to the client. Techniques are considered less important than the therapist's attitude. Main techniques are active listening, reflection, clarification and presence. All the above relates directly to Carl Rogers' Person Centred approach as the prime exemplar of this school, which includes many different therapies such as Gestalt, Body centred therapies and existential therapies which may also combine the humanistic approach with analytic techniques.

Building on Humanistic psychology, Transpersonal Psychology is the fourth and most recent school. Towards the end of his life, Abraham Maslow wrote:

> "I consider Humanistic, Third Force Psychology, to be transitional, a preparation for a still 'higher' Fourth Psychology, transpersonal, trans-human, centered in the cosmos rather than in human needs and interest, going beyond humanness, identity, self-actualization, and the like."[7]

7. A. Maslow, *Towards a Psychology of Being*, Princetown, Van Nostrand, 1962, iii.

Transpersonal psychology considers that impulses toward the spiritual are basic for full humanness, and attempts to

> "integrate spiritual experience with a larger understanding of the human psyche... it is a project that attempts a true synthesis of spiritual and psychological approaches to the psyche."[8]

To this end, traditional therapeutic techniques are allied with meditation and other awareness exercises derived often from Eastern disciplines, and what may be termed 'altered states of consciousness' are explored. The view of the school is of the necessary integration of man and cosmos rather than a pure emphasis on the individual subject. "What truly defines the transpersonal dimension is a model of the human psyche that recognizes the importance of the spiritual or cosmic dimension and the potential for consciousness evolution."[9] The therapeutic relationship is again of prime importance, the power structure between therapist and client is not highly defined, the therapist is a guide and companion in 'joint practice'. Techniques are also of less importance than the relationship and the presence of the therapist, and may include awareness practices, particularly in the training of the therapist.

Ken Wilber's Spectrum of Consciousness (Fig. 1) is a useful comparative model which sees different therapies as addressing different dualities arising from a unified base of consciousness which he terms Mind, and sees as identical to the reality of the universe. (Capital M to distinguish it from the plurality of individual minds.) The first level from the ground is that of the Transpersonal Bands, where man is no longer conscious of his identity with the whole, but neither is he confined within the boundaries of the individual organism. It is on this level that Jung's collective unconscious, and mystical experiences of unity would be located. Above this is the Existential level, the level of the total organism separated from its environment. The upper limits of this level contain what Wilber calls the Biosocial Bands, "the internalised matrix of cultural premises, familial relationships and social glosses, as well as the all pervading social institutions of language, logic, ethics and law."[10] Above this again is the Ego Level where rather than being associated with his total psychosomatic organism, man identifies with his ego or mental representation or self image.

---

8. M. Washburn, *The Ego and the Dynamic Grand*, Albany, New York, SUNY Press, 1988, 1.
9. S. Grof, *Beyond the Brain*, Albany, New York, SUNY Press, 1985, 197. There are also perhaps echoes here of Heidegger's later writings concerning "The Fourfold" of earth, sky, divinities and mortals. (*Poetry, Language, Thought,* tr., A, Hofstadter, New York, Harper, 1971, 173). Compare also "Psyche was for the Greeks an unbreakable relationship between men, gods and nature which even encompassed death." C. Hampden Turner, *Maps of the Mind,* New York, Collier, 1982, 14.
10. K.Wilber in Vaughan & Walsh, *Beyond Ego,* Los Angeles, Tarcher Inc, 1980, 76.

The Spectrum of Consciousness

FIGURE 1

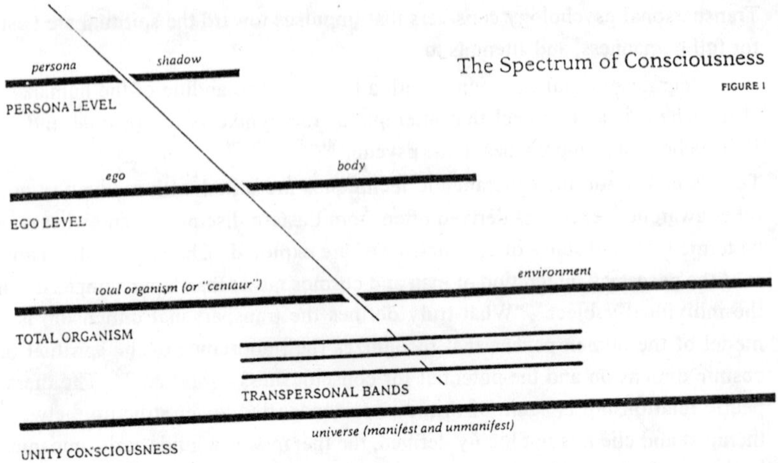

Therapies and the Levels of the Spectrum

FIGURE 2

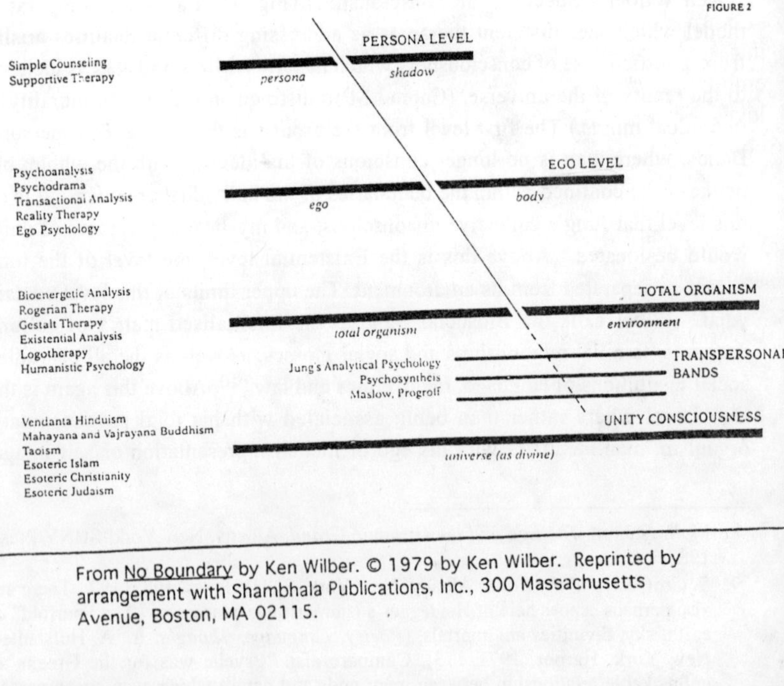

Finally this identity is divided yet again at the Shadow Level, into persona versus shadow, those aspects of personality with which one identifies and those which one cannot or will not own. Each level of the spectrum evolves from a perceived division or duality, which is accompanied by repression of the preceding unity, projection of that into two divided parts accompanied by identification with one part rather than whole, and rejection of the unidentified portion. In the Primary Dualism, Mind is divided, its non-duality is repressed and it is then projected as organism versus environment, with concomitant duality of subject and object, and the simultaneous creation of space. This first separation of organism and environment by the Primary Dualism creates the Existential Level where the Second major Dualism occurs, severing the unity of life and death, simultaneously creating time. In an attempt to flee death, the Ego Level is created with the occurence of the Tertiary Dualism repressing the unity of the whole psychosomatic organism, projecting as the divided parts an idealized stable psychic image versus soma, and identifying solely with that mental representation, the ego or self image. Finally above the Ego Level is the Shadow level. Here is further division, the Quaternary Dualism, wherein the unity of ego is repressed and projected into persona versus shadow, the opposition of those aspects of personality with which one identifies, and those which one rejects.

In opposite order, the different schools primarily address different levels, and attempt to heal different dualities (Fig. 2). Analytic schools have addressed the intra-personal area, conflict between id and ego, conscious and unconscious, the embraced persona and the rejected shadow. Behaviourism dealing only on the level of overt behaviour fits less easily with this model as it is unconcerned with consciousness or Mind, but does deal with the inter-personal level. Humanistic Psychology is concerned with the total psychophysical organism in its interface with self and other, self and environment in the Biosocial Bands. It addresses the dualisms of body and mind, attempting to redress the modern Western imbalance in favour of mind, and of life and death, existence and non-existence. In terms of Existentialism, the prime repressed is not sexual impulse as with Psychoanalysis, but death. Finally, Transpersonal Psychology extends the territory still further to include levels of consciousness that are supraindividual, addressing the primary dualism of self and other, organism and environment. In the Transpersonal Bands, there is a way of looking *at* emotional and ideational complexes without being totally identified with them and thus looking *through* them. This is the state of witnessing, which is found in Buddhist meditation, and which is addressed by the disidentification exercises of Psychosynthesis. Recently David Loy has re-interpreted the Freudian Oedipal process yet again, suggesting that the prime repressed is neither sexual drive nor death but 'lack of being', in Buddhist terms '*anatta*'. Interpreted thus, the Oedipal project is the attempt of the developing self to

> "attain closure on itself, foreclosing its dependence on others by becoming autonomous. *To be one's own father is to be one's own origin.*

> Rather than just a way to conquer death, this makes even more sense as the quest to deny one's own groundlessness by becoming one's own ground: the ground (socially sanctioned but nonetheless illusory) of being an independent person."[11]

This is the attempt to heal the split of self from other, self from world, the repression of non-duality. In the Buddhist view the sense of self is considered a mental construct rather than a self existing reality. This constructed sense of self wants to make itself real, to ground itself:

> "the ego self is this *attempt* of awareness to objectify itself, by grasping itself—which I can no more do than a hand can grasp itself... The consequence of this is that the sense-of-self always has, as its inescapable shadow, a sense-of-*lack*."[12]

In Buddhist terms, the answer to this lack is to see that both the feeling of self and the feeling of lack are unnecessary and illusory, since the Prime Duality of self and other is itself illusory, and there neither is nor ever has been a self-existing self apart from the world. Here, already, we have a Buddhist interpretation of a psychological presentation. Let us look at the Buddhist teachings themselves.

Buddhism

The Buddhist view has a very long history of investigation into the mind and perception. It also has an ancient tradition of methods of practice designed to instantiate experientially the views which it presents. It offers a psychology of transformation, a definition of health and the possibilities of the human mind that goes far beyond anything available to a western psychotherapy, still struggling to liberate itself from a psychology of sickness, the deficiency model from which it arose. For both these reasons Buddhism presents a rich resource for western psychotherapy, a discipline which also attempts to be transformative and not merely descriptive.

After such a broad yet fundamental statement, I would like to look at some specific aspects of Buddhist philosophy which may underwrite such contention. One of the theories I consider to be of particular value to those living within the context of the contemporary Western world is that of dependent origination (*pratītyasamutpāda*). In its simplest form it is stated thus:

> "When that is present, this comes to be; on the arising of that, this arises.
> When that is absent, this does not come to be; on the cessation of that,

---

11. D. Loy, "The Nonduality of Life & Death, A Buddhist View of Repression", in *PEW,* 40.2, 1990, 157.
12. *ibid.*

this ceases."[13]

In the longer form of the twelve links,[14] dependent origination is presented in terms of human life, of the unceasing wheel of saṁsāra or bound existence. This circular chain of dependent origination provides a theory of causality, which in direct contradistinction to most Western ways of thought, is not linear and substantive, but circular, reciprocal and interdependent, wherein the emphasis is shifted from things and events to process and relationship. Mind and body, belief and action, object and environment are seen to be in a reciprocal relationship, all constitutive parts of a dynamic mutually causative whole. The pivotal link, although the process is circular, is ignorance—ignorance of realisation that all is impermanent, unsatisfactory and without self or fixed essence. In the Mahāyāna, and in particular the Madhyamaka school, this lack of self or essence is expanded into the central doctrine of emptiness (*śūnyatā*). Emptiness is grounded on, and indeed *is,* this very interdependence; the emptiness of inherent existence or self-sufficient essence of the mutually dependent parts. As Nāgārjuna wrote:

> "We declare that whatever is relational origination is *śūnyatā* . It is a provisional name (*i.e.* thought construction) for the mutuality (of being) and, indeed, it is the middle path."[15]

I suggest that it is this concept of the 'Middle Path' or 'Middle Way' between absolutism and nihilism that is of such value in the context of contemporary Western discourse[16] since it not only provides a view but equally importantly a 'way' of realising or instantiating such a view. It is also a view which upholds a transcendent function while not denying the actuality of everyday existence. This is explained in the doctrine of the Two Truths; the fundamental Buddhist view that there are two levels of reality or truth, the relative and conventional reality of phenomena, and the absolute reality of their ultimate emptiness of own-being or essence.

---

13. *Majjhima-nikāya* I, 262; *Samyutta-nikāya* II, 28, in D.J. Kalupahana, *A History of Buddhist Philosophy,* Honolulu, University of Hawai Press, 1992, 56.
14. Ignorance, dispositions, consciousness, psychophysical personality, six senses, contact, feeling, craving, grasping, becoming, birth, old age and death, grief, lamentation, suffering, dejection and despair. *Samyutta-nikāya* II, 16-17. D.J. Kalupahana, *op. cit.*, 58.
15. Nāgārjuna, *Mūlamadhyamakakārikā*, XXIV, 18; tr., K. Inada, Tokyo, Hokuseido Press, 1970.
16. For a discussion of the Middle, Way see M. Sprung, "Being and the Middle Way", in M. Sprung, ed., *The Question of Being*, University Park, Pensylvania State University Press, 1978. He describes a 'way' as "not composed of a subject and a world. There is no dichotomy of subject and object, inner and outer." The Middle Way is "the practice of wisdom, not a means to it. It embodies knowledge but is not a knowing.", 136.

Here, ontology and epistemology are united; two levels of reality are, in fact, two ways of understanding. This is an important factor in the Buddhist psychology of perception. "From the common Buddhist outlook, we cannot really distinguish between an 'objective' and a 'subjective' world, we cannot really isolate 'facts' from 'judgements'."[17] In the Mahāyāna, these beliefs underlie all Buddhist theories of perception, wherein all mind states are seen to arise from the interaction of various interdependent causes and conditions, and pure non-conceptual clear mind comes to be veiled with obscurations, chief of which is ignorance of emptiness. Each moment of pure perception is obscured by accretions of ignorance, volitional dispositions and feelings. The aim in Buddhist practice is to train the mind in a gradual progression from false view to valid perception using different logical tools (consequence, syllogism, conclusive reasoning), and finally to achieve direct perception of reality as a result of meditative training. Through understanding emptiness and the processes of perception, the mind is trained to avoid the seemingly inbuilt commitment to hypostatization and substance ontology that Paul Feyerabend has called "the natural interpretation."

These Buddhist doctrines, I contend, can uphold value in an impermanent world, for the interdependence expressed by the apophatic negations of Nāgārjuna, the eight negative marks of all phenomena:

> "non-origination, non-extinction,
> non-destruction, non-permanence,
> non-identity, non-differentiation,
> non-coming (into being), non-going (out of being)",[18]

is also cataphatically expressed in the doctrine of the non-obstruction and interpenetration of the six characteristics of Fa Tsang's Hua Yen Buddhism, which observes the interdependency of three pairs of antitheses: universality and particularity, identity and difference, integration and disintegration.[19] Emptiness may be viewed not merely as negation, but also as possibility, indeed as that without which nothing is possible.

> "Any factor of experience which does not participate in
> relational origination cannot exist. Therefore any factor of
> experience not in the nature of *sunya* cannot exist."[20]

---

17. C. Lindtner, *Nagarjuniana,* Delhi, Motilal Banarsidas, 1987, 270. A note appended to the above quotation refers to the ambiguity found in such key terms as *artha* = object or meaning, *upalabdhi* = exist or perceive, *prapanca* = universe or language, *satya* = reality or truth, *sad* = real or good.
18. Nāgājuna, *Mūlamadhyamikākarikā,* dedicatory verse, tr., Inada, *op. cit,* 1970, 39.
19. see F. Cook, *Hua Yen Buddhism*, University Park, Pensylvania State University Press, 1977, 48, 76ff.
20. Nāgārjuna as note 16, XXIV, 19.

When emptiness is realised, what is seen is suchness, *tathatā*, the suchness of things as they are, freshly presented rather than represented through the veils of conceptuality and emotion. As described by David Loy:

> "If each link of *pratitya samutpada* is conditioned by all the others, then to become completely groundless is also to become completely grounded, not in some particular, but in the whole network of interdependent relations that constitutes the world."[21]

Experience and Meaning

These theories, I suggest, may be of great value in the West where the tremendous changes in recent science and philosophy have swept the ground from beneath traditional beliefs and led to a climate of nihilism and emotional vacuum, which must influence the approach of any contemporary psychotherapy. For the presenting symptoms of psychotherapeutic patients have changed considerably since Freud's time. As a contemporary philospher has described:

> "It has frequently been remarked by psycho-analysts that the period in which hysterics and patients with phobias and fixations formed the bulk of their clientele, starting in their classical period with Freud, has recently given way to a time when the main complaints centre around 'ego loss,' or a sense of emptiness, flatness, futility, lack of purpose or loss of self-esteem... it seems overwhelmingly plausible... that the comparatively recent shift in style of pathology reflects the generalization and popularization in our culture of that 'loss of horizon', which a few alert spirits were foretelling for a century or more".[22]

Each of the schools of psychotherapy described earlier presents an attempt to find a field of meaning which will encompass and contain the dualities it addresses. A search for meaningful models for our lives is central to psychotherapy. Carl Jung believed that "psychoneurosis must be understood, ultimately, as the suffering of a soul which has not discovered its meaning"[23] and that "it is only meaning which liberates."[24] Victor Frankl, the creator of Logotherapy, also considered that man is "primarily motivated by the search for meaning to his existence, by the striving to fulfill this meaning and thereby to actualize as many value potentialities as possible. In short man is motivated by

21. D. Loy, "Avoiding the Void: The Lack of Self in Psychotherapy & Buddhism", *JTP,* 24, 2, 1992, 174.
22. C.Taylor, *Sources of the Self, The Making of the Modern Identity*, Cambridge, Mass, Harvard University Press, 1989, 19. He describes "loss of horizon" as a "dissipation of our sense of cosmos as a meaningful order."
23. C.G.Jung, 1959, "Psychotherapists or the Clergy", in his *Collected Works*, vol. 11: *Psychology and Religion East and West*, trans. R.F.C. Hull, London, Routledge, 334
24. *ibid.*, 330.

the will to meaning."[25] Such meanings are no longer found objects but must be created:

> "A large part of self-understanding is the search for appropriate personal metaphors that make sense of our lives. Self-understanding requires unending negotiation and re-negotiation of the meaning of your experience to yourself. In therapy, for example, much of self-understanding involves consciously recognizing previously unconscious metaphors and how we live by them. It involves the constant construction of new coherences in your life, coherences that give meaning to old experiences. The process of self-understanding is the continual development of new life stories for yourself."[26]

T.S. Eliot wrote: "We had the experience but missed the meaning."[27] There is, however, another way of looking at this—from the other pole. We have so many theoretical meanings which have lost their grounding in experience that we have in fact lost the experience itself. As the historian of mythology Joseph Cambell has said: "we let the concept swallow up the percept... thus defending ourselves from experience."[28] When previous sources of meaning and certainty are threatened, we tend to cling to the forms, in defense against the uncertainty of experience. It is my contention in this paper that Buddhism can help to provide views which can uphold meanings acceptable to the contemporary world, and methods of experiential praxis which instantiate these views; can, in short, unite meaning and experience. This is certainly the field of psychotherapy, for I would say of psychotherapy what Campbell states of art: "The function of art is to render a *sense of existence,* not an *assurance of some meaning.*" [29]

Heidegger defined the modern period "by the fact that man becomes the centre and measure of all being...."[30] Today, far from such certainty decentred man is now in the postmodern world, defined by Lyotard by its "incredulity towards metanarratives",[31] those metanarratives upon which, in the past, we have founded our theories of meaning and value. I would like to look at five particular themes which reoccur in the contemporary Western discourse as

---

25. V. Frankl, *Psychotherapy & Existentialism,* London, Pelican, 1967, 74.
26. G. Lakoff & M. Johnson, *Metaphors We Live By*, Chicago, Chicago University Press, 1980, 233.
27. T.S. Eliot , "The Dry Salvages", *Collected Poems 1909-1963,* London, Faber & Faber, 1963.
28. J. Campbell, *The Flight of the Wild Gander,* New York, Harper, 1990, 186.
29. *ibid.*, 188.
30. M. Heidegger, *Nietzsche,* Vol. IV, New York, Harper & Row, 1982, 28.
31. J.F. Lyotard, *The Postmodern Condition*, trans. G. Bennington & B. Massumi, Manchester, Manchester University Press, 1984, xxiv.

exemplars for our present purposes of both lost certainties and new views. It is my view that there is a great deal of commensurability between these new views in the West and traditional Buddhist views, and that Buddhism has much to offer because of the length and strength of its tradition, and most especially in its methods of cultivation, whereby such views are not merely descriptive, but realised experientially and embodied as Sprung has described in a 'way'. Indeed, the Buddhist 'Middle Way' may offer a middle path of movement and transformation between now unacceptable alternatives.

Interdependence

First, Buddhism offers an holistic world view of interdependence of man and the world. A viewpoint that can not only live with, but also be grounded in change and impermanence. In this century the sense of scientific certainty in the West, the Newtonian universe of space, time, matter and linear causation has been turned upside down, and even the ability of science to find the truth about an objectively existing real world has been challenged. In the astrophysics of vast distances and the micro world within the atom, discoveries have been made with implications for our intermediate human world that have still not become part of our experience, and which call into question the very possibility of pure, objective perception. A recent definition of perception as "a process in which meaning, motivation and emotional response all enter in at deeply subconscious levels... The 'outer world' and the 'inner world' are mutually fabricated in an active reciprocal process"[32] fits well with the Buddhist view. Such a view may provide a middle way of interdependence between the traditional Western dualities, a non-dual alternative to either/or, for "...in the Western tradition, when you doubt the existence of a real objective world, the only alternative you have is subjectivity. Everything is thrown back on the individual mind."[33]

This interdependence calls for an interdisciplinary approach, and is currently the field of exploration of various hybrid disciplines such as the Cognitive Science and General Systems Theory, on the fringes of which some very interesting dialogues have taken place with Buddhist thought.[34] Systems Theory

---

32. J. Hayward, *Shifting Worlds, Changing Minds*, Boston, Shambhala, 1987, 35.
33. J. Hayward, in J. Hayward & Varela, eds., *Gentle Bridges, Conversations with the Dalai Lama on the Sciences of Mind*, Boston, Shambhala, 1992, 13.
34. See J. Macy, *Mutual Causality in Buddhist and General Systems Theory*, Albany, New York, SUNY Press, 1991, and F.J. Varela, E. Thompson & E. Rosch, *The Embodied Mind*, Cambridge, Mass., M.I.T., 1991. Also, two volumes of discussion between the Dalai Lama and Westerners concerning Mind Sciences; D. Goleman & R. Thurman eds., *Mind Science*, Boston, Wisdom, 1991, and J. Hayward & F. Varela, eds., *op. cit.;* also G.Watson, S. Batchelor & G. Claxton, eds., *The Fly & the Flybottle*, Sharpham, Devon, Sharpham Trust, 1992.

is perhaps the Western model which comes closest to the Buddhist world view.[35] Both are grounded in interrelationship. According to the Buddhist model perception arises from convergence of sense organ, sense object and consciousness, the last of which is, as we have discussed, causally affected by conditionings and tendencies of past perception, feeling and action. In the Systems Theory model input from environment arrives in terms of percepts which are interpreted in terms of the system's constructs which screen and order the data registered by the senses. As these constructs too are formed by past experience, perception here also is seen to be 'theory-laden'. Similarly in a reciprocal interplay of structure and process, body and mind, doer and deed, self and society are seen as mutually co-dependent. Each system or subsystem is embedded in a larger whole.

One result of such a view is an end to ego-centricity. When we can see that our normal understanding of self is an incorrectly separated and reified part of a larger process, a construct of the mind's grasping for identity to fulfil its perceived lack, we can give up this self, and the sense of lack too, will disappear, since neither lack nor separate self really existed. When we give up clinging to this constricted separated self, this template or label which we have superimposed on the flow of experience, we see that it has obscured our awareness of our own identity with that flow. Abandoning clinging to self, "only process remains and we are that process in its totality."[36]

Self

This Cognitive Science and Systems Theory view of the self as a small part of a larger system, a false reification of part of a process, is at least comparable to the Buddhist view of non-self. As the certainty of an objectively existent world has faded, so has that of a single unified self. Many works of literature, science and the discoveries of Freud all deconstructed this view, and though current theories are multifarious and come from many different angles, they all seem agreed that the self is, in fact, a construct of one sort or another, dependent on many things.

Out of the various disciplines I would like to give some examples. Philosopher Charles Taylor believes that the self is based on "an orientation to the good, that we essentially are (i.e. define ourselves at least inter alia by), where we stand on this."[37] Physicist Danah Zohar seeks the sense of self in quantum physics.[38] Ethologist John Crook sees a sense of self as developmentally dependent upon:

35. For a detailed comparison see J. Macy, *op. cit.*.
36. L.E. Olds, *Metaphors of Relatedness*, Albany, SUNY, 1992, 65.
37. C.Taylor, *Sources of the Self, The Making of the Modern Identity*, Cambridge, Mass, Harvard University Press, 1989, 33.
38 .D. Zohar, *The Quantum Self*, London, Flamingo, 1991.

> "the growth of its (the child's) cognitive abilities in categorization, its experience of contingency and agency in interaction with care-givers, and its experience of the emotional quality of its own conscious states...'Identity' is not some immutable property of the species but an often painfully constructed set of conceptualizations and attendant feelings that relate the individual to his transient experience of the world."[39]

George Lakoff and Mark Johnson also see the self as a conceptualization, for them the separation of the subject of experience is a product of language, of the coherent sturucture of metaphors, the cultural presuppositions in which our experience is embedded. They believe, as quoted earlier, that "a large part of self understanding is the search for appropriate metaphors that make sense of our lives."[40]

Language

There is a central concern with language in contemporary Western thought. Here again the picture is one of the ending of old certainties. As we saw that according to Buddhist psychology perception is not viewed as representation of an independently-existing world, so in contemporary discourse language is no longer seen as merely taking its meaning from being a faithful representation of an objective external reality, but rather as helping to create the very ways in which we experience the world. "Our concept of reality is a matter of our linguistic categories."[41] Wittgenstein's philosophy outlined the idea of language 'games' in which words take their meaning from their context, their relationship to other words rather than by virtue of their representative character. We can no longer uphold a referential view of language or a correspondence theory of truth, which is indeed the view found in Madhyamaka. Current Buddhist scholars have indeed reinterpreted Madhyamaka works in the light of recent linguistic philosophy.[42]

---

39. J. Crook, *The Evolution of Human Consciousness*, Oxford, Clarendon Press, 1980, 254 & 276, (parentheses mine).
40. G. Lakoff & M. Johnson, *op. cit.*, 233.
41. J. Searle in B. Magee, ed., *Men of Ideas*, London, BBC, 1978, 184.
42. see R. Thurman, *Tsong Khapa's Speech of Gold in the Essence of the Eloquence*, Princetown, Princetown University Press, 1984, 92. "These subtleties could not even be tranlated intelligibly into Euro-American philosophical discource, were it not for the consummation of the enterprise of critical philosophy reached by Wittgenstein. The overthrow of dogmaticist privacy in his mature works provides for the first time in Western philosophy a texture of inquiry suitable to parallel that of Tsong Kha pa." See also C. Gudmunsen, *Wittgenstein and Buddhism*, London, Macmillan, 1977; C.W. Huntingdon, *The Emptiness of Emptiness,* Honolulu, University of Hawaii, 1989; F. Streng, *Emptiness, A Study in Religious Meaning*, Nashville, Abingdon Press, 1967. For a study of Western philosophical interpretations of Nāgārjuna, see

"From the Mādhyamika's perspective, the meaning of a word or concept invariably derives from its applications within a context of sociolinguistic relations and not through reference to any self-sufficient and independently real object."[43]

Embodiment

Professor of Linguistics George Lakoff and philosopher Mark Johnson believe that our language is based on metaphor and that the ground of many of our most basic metaphors come from embodiment, and propose embodiment as the origin of meaning.[44] Johnson suggests that our embodiment is essential to who we are, and to what meaning is, and in another view of interdependence, that our very "consciousness and our rationality are tied to our bodily orientations and interactions in and with our environment."[45] Neurobiologist Gerald Edelman agrees with this theory but feels that it fails to show *how* this comes to pass, and how symbolic idealized cognitive models of language arise as the result of the mechanisms of perceptual and conceptual categorization. For this he believes a biological theory of brain function and consciousness based on facts of evolution and development is necessary, and is supplied by his own theory of Neuronal Group Selection. Such a theory places mind and consciousness in brain function without reductionism, attempting to avoid the strict dualism of mind and matter. Edelman believes his theory "aims to provide a biological basis for the construction of meaning...With this foundation, we can see how consciousness based on evolved value systems and driven by language, leads to the extension and modification of those systems in a culture."[46] This provides a biological foundation for the view of a Cultural Psychology advocated by Jerome Bruner in his book *Acts of Meaning*.[47] Another philosopher John Searle, has a similar view:

"Mental phenomena are caused by neurophysiological processes in the brain, and are themselves features of the brain....Both consciousness and

---

A.Tuck, *Comparative Philosophy and the Philosophy of Scholarship*, New York, OUP, 1990.

43. C.W. Huntingdon, *op. cit.*, 113.
44. G. Lakoff & M. Johnson, *op. cit.*; M. Johnson, *The Body in the Mind,* Chicago, University of Chicago Press, 1987, xxxviii.
45. M. Johnson, *op. cit.*, xxxviii.
46. G. Edelman, *Bright Air, Brilliant Fire, On the Matter of the Mind*, London, Allen Lane, 1992, 175.
47. J. Bruner, *Acts of Meaning,* Cambridge, Mass., 1990. If the Cognitive Revolution was an overthrow of Behaviourism in favour of establishing meaning as the central concept of psychology, Cultural Psychology takes the view that the construction and usage of meanings are culturally influenced, and that no human nature is thus independent of culture.

> intentionality are biological processes caused by lower-level neuronal processes in the brain, and neither is reducible to something else".[48]

Western thought, caught again between the choice of Mind/Body dualism or monism of one alternative, finds itself in an impasse. As Searle states:

> "It is essential to show that both dualism and monism are false because it is generally supposed that these exhaust the field, leaving no other options."[49]

Again the middle way of emptiness and the two truths may offer a different hermeneutic.

Varela, Thompson and Rosch propose a dialogue between Buddhism and Cognitive Science, to bring about a change in the nature of reflection from

> "abstract disembodied activity to an embodied (mindful), open-ended reflection. By *embodied*, we mean reflection in which body and mind have been brought together. What this formulation intends to convey is that reflection is not just *on* experience, but reflection *is* a form of experience itself—and that reflective form of experience can be performed with mindfulness/awareness. When reflection is done in that way, it can cut the chain of habitual thought patterns and preconceptions such that it can be an open-ended reflection, open to possibilities other than those contained in one's current representation of the life space."[50]

The authors look to Buddhist traditions of mindfulness/awareness to act as a bridge between the descriptions of Cognitive Science and human experience, believing that these can provide the grounding in embodied experience, and the transformative power to enable us to live healthily and happily in a world without fixed foundation, for "the intimation of egolessness...opens up the lived world as path, as the locus for realization."[51]

Alternative to Nihilism

These foregoing topics arise mainly from the current scientific point of view but alongside, and sometimes as a result of the loss of scientific certainty, has gone a similar loss of the certainties of philosophy and religion. Starting with Nietzsche, through Heidegger, the Existentialists and Derrida, philosophies of presence and transcendence, 'ontotheologies' and 'logocentrism' have been attacked and deconstructed, and their underlying grounds of validity devalued. When meaning is seen to be merely a function of use within a particular discourse, philosophy can hardly be foundational or systematic, for any

---

48. J.Searle, *The Rediscovery of Mind*, Cambridge, Mass, M.I.T., 1992, 1 and xii.
49. *ibid.*, 3.
50. F. Varela, E. Thompson, E. Rosch, *op. cit.*, 27.
51. *ibid.*, 234.

ahistorical, transcendent or extra-linguistic foundations upon which to build have been deconstructed and delegitimised. In the words of contemporary philosopher Richard Rorty, philosophy today can only be therapeutic or edifying. Rather than weaving an endless series of arguments in a futile attempt to establish some new absolute or justification for a presupposition of some metaphysical reality behind appearances, we should accept everyday pragmatic considerations as sufficient in themselves and find meanings in the very changefulness which lacks foundation. According to Rorty "the point of edifying philosophy is to keep the conversation going rather than to find truth."[52] That would seem to accord with Buddhist conventional truth but leaves out of account any possibly different truth. I believe that the Buddhist absolute truth—of emptiness—can offer both a different sort of truth and one which does not, as Rorty fears, attempt "to close off conversation by proposals for universal commensuration through the hypostatization of some priviledged set of descriptions" resulting in "the dehumanization of human beings."[53]

Wittgenstein wrote that the aim of philosophy is "to show the fly the way out of the fly bottle",[54] and this idea of libeıation is, of course, central to Buddhism, whose philosphy is pre-eminently at the service of soteriology. I would like to suggest that not only did Nāgārjuna's Madhyamaka view of emptiness and dependent origination carry out the deconstruction of unjustifiable absolutism nearly two thousand years ago but that it also leaves an opening for value and for meaning which the contemporary West seems to find difficult or impossible in the absence of transcendental absolutes. The goal offered by Buddhism is transformation and liberation. The ground is seen not as an absolute nor a private object, or any reified concept or unfounded being outside of any system, but rather the totality of the dependently originated system itself. Questions of representation and correspondence, subject and object are dissolved into an inactive presentation,

> "leaving behind nothing other than a dramatic awareness of the living present - an epiphany of one's entire form of life. No form of conceptual diffusion remains, and no questions begging for answers that re-inforce a deep-seated resistance to acceptance that this life, as it is now lived, is the only arbiter of truth and reality."[55]

The Japanese philosopher Keiji Nishitani saw in emptiness the sole concept which could lead beyond the nihilism which he saw as 'relative nothingness':

---

52. R. Rorty, *Philosophy and the Mirror of Nature*, Oxford, Blackwell, 1980, 377.
53. *ibid.*
54. L. Wittgenstein, *Philosophical Investigations,* tr. G.E.M Anscombe, Oxford, Blackwell, 1967, 103.
55. C.W. Huntingdon, *op. cit.*, 136.

> "the representation of nothingness in nihilism still shows traces of the bias of objectification, of taking nothingness as some 'thing' called nothingness."[56]

In contrast *sūnyāta*, having emptied itself of even this representation of emptiness is "to be realized as something united to and self-identical with being."[57] This field of *sūnyāta* becomes a third possibility, a non-duality beyond the many dualities that have constricted so many Western views. Beyond the field of reason and on the far side of nihilism which is to Nishitani a transitional state, one can reach absolute emptiness where in contrast to the nihilistic view one sees "not that the self is empty, but emptiness is the self: not that things are empty, but that emptiness is things."[58] Or, as in the *Heart Sūtra*, "Form is Emptiness, Emptiness is Form", and meaning and value can re-enter upon the very field of emptiness.

These necessarily brief notes may, I hope, illuminate the contention of this paper that dependent origination and emptiness may allow for a middle way between the eternalism of the old certainties and the nihilism which in the West has often resulted from their overthrow. It provides a path grounded in groundlessness and openness, a meaning which comes from the very freedom from fixed meaning, a dynamic holistic, ever-shifting meaning which creates itself as it evolves. Moreover, most importantly, within the Buddhist framework this view or ground is united with the experience of the practice of the path.

PATH

Buddhism, unlike other philosophies used as foundational for psychotherapy *e.g.* Existentialism, also provides a repertoire of practical methods. For psychotherapy is itself a discipline concerned with praxis, seeking methods both to access experience, to understand it and to transform it. The Buddhist path is generally grouped into three aspects: Discipline, Meditation and Wisdom. They are, of course, interdependent, but in so far as they are separable I believe the Wisdom aspect has been spoken of in the earlier part of this paper, and is most important in the training and in the understanding of therapists. I would like to quote here a statement from Medard Boss, the author of *Existential Foundations of Medicine and Psychiatry*:

> "It is not necessary that the patient himself learn to recognize theoretically the ontological existential structure of being-in-the-world. His insight need not extend beyond the limits of his individual, directly perceptible, ontic ways of relating to the therapist. But it is the duty of

---

56. Keiji Nishitani, *Religion and Nothingness*, tr., J. van Bragt, Berkeley, University of California, 1982, 95.
57. *ibid.*, 97.
58. *ibid.*, 138.

> the latter to become thoroughly acquainted with, and clearly aware of, the ontological nature of being together in order to give his treatment a scientific foundation."[59]

I believe this holds good equally for a Buddhist approach.

Discipline or Morality, I suggest, is important to a Buddhist therapy. The tendency in Western psychotherapy is to ignore moral issues except insofar as they relate specifically to the therapeutic relationship itself, and while shying away from the more culturally specific and overtly disciplinarian approaches of some Japanese Zen-based therapies such as Morita, and upholding the importance of the non-directive stance of most Western therapy, I feel that this is an area which should, at the very least, inform the attitude of the therapist. However, discussion of this issue is outside the scope of this paper. Yet a way of life based on an understanding of dependent origination and emptiness must imply a compassion, a 'feeling-with' and non-separation from others, a striving to turn away from a totally selfish and self-centred existence. Such a view will support a sense of morality based on mutuality, responsibility and response-ability, the ability to respond to others. As Joanna Macy points out, in the mutually causal view the liberation of the individual and the health of society are inseparable.[60]

However it is with the path of awareness, with right mindfulness and meditation that Buddhism offers the greatest tools for psychotherapy, in particular insight meditation, watching the mind (*Vīpaśyanā*). Indeed most people expect any discussion about Buddhism and therapy to centre primarily on meditation. Varela, Rosch, and Thompson point to the Buddhist mindfulness/awareness tradition as a bridge between Cognitive Science and experience. And indeed, perhaps it is in meditation that we can take the step Heidegger called for: "the step back from the thinking that merely represents ... to the thinking that responds and recalls."[61] However, while in no way denying the value of meditation as a therapeutic tool, I want to approach it in perhaps a rather different way, and to differentiate clearly between the use of meditation in a Buddhist context and in a therapeutic one. I see meditation as a formal practice in psychotherapy pre-eminently for the therapist, rather than for the client; for the therapist as a personal practice, as an aid in the exploration of, and familiarisation with, their own mind states. As training, it is a method for becoming aware of and understanding the number, quality, impermanence and change of mental states, and of building up the necessary 'balance' to enable one

---

59. M. Boss, *The Existential Foundations of Medicine and Psychiatry*, New York, Jason Aronson, 1980, 280.
60. J. Macy, *op. cit.*, Chapter 11.
61. M. Heidegger, *Poetry, Language, Thought*, tr., A. Hofstadter, New York, Harper, 1971, 181.

to ride one's experience without being imprisoned in reaction. Having become comfortable and relatively unshockable in their own mental world therapists can extend that same ease to their clients. Meditation is also the path to the experience and embodied realisation of the view of emptiness and interdependence.

It can also be a vehicle for transformation. "Some form of contemplative or meditative practice that is able to bring awareness of non-duality and the inherent compassion that is inseparable from it, would provide the practical basis for the change of our belief context and our world."[62] Specific meditational practices such as *maitrī* and meditation on the Four Immeasurable States obviously help to foster and generate healthy mind states, conducive to healing. They may be ways to teach the generation of the 'unconditioned positive regard' put forward by Humanistic Psychologist Carl Rogers as one of the four pillars of his person-centred approach which is so influential in contemporary counselling and psychotherapy. Such meditative practices as 'exchange of self and others' are most useful in the generation of altruism, in the fostering of positive attitudes and in the combatting of negative attitudes. The present Dalai Lama speaks often of such uses, all of which are of inestimable value for a therapist, which is not to say that they are not so for everyone. What I would say is that I do not believe therapy should be confused with Buddhist teaching. If a client has an existent formal practice, so much the better and more helpful, but if, during therapy they wish to learn one, I believe it is better they should seek out a Buddhist or meditation teacher, rather than learning from their therapist, and confusing the two roles of teacher and therapist.

Perhaps the most important aspect of the meditative state lies in the extension of this to a way of being for the therapist with a client. In view of what has been discussed above relating to the interdependence of self and other, knower and known, it should make sense that a meditative state, or a state of open and unfixed attention, as far as possible from the normal focused state of reification is a state best able to penetrate into the intermediate state of relationship. One of the few Buddhist psychotherapy trainings refers to this as Joint Practice. Its founder Maura Sills has written:

> "Core Process psychotherapy is simply a joint enquiry into relationship. It seems that if one can abide in the imminent experiential moment, no suffering arises. Our reactive relationship to experience is the vehicle for confusion and ignorance with its concomitant suffering."[63]

---

62. J. Hayward, *Shifting Worlds, Changing Minds*, Boston, Shambhala, 1987, 282.
63. M. Sills, "Veils and Seals: A Reflection on Buddhism and Cognitive Science", unpublished paper.

John Welwood, an American clinical psychologist and one of the best writers about Buddhist psychotherapy has also described this, and I consider his description is worth quoting at length:

> "In the therapy situation, the client's problems or emotions are like the thoughts that arise when you are sitting. You, the listener, provide the space which coming back to the breath allows in meditation. You have to fully respect and bow to the form—the client's real problem—listen to it and take it in. If you don't do that, there isn't a connection between the two of you that can effect healing....The process of transformation that happens between two people in therapy is similar to what may take place inside a single person in meditation. In mindfulness practice, as painful thoughts and emotions arise, we note them, bow to them, acknowledge them, then let them go and come back to the break, which is a concrete manifestation of open space. This process of going into and out of form in meditation is what allows transformation to take place....the great challenge of working on oneself is in bringing our larger open awareness to bear on our frozen karmic structures...Our large awareness usually gets buried or stuck in problems, emotion, reactions, or else it may try to detach and fly away into the sky. But a third alternative is to stay with our frozen structures and transform them. That is the core of practice, I believe, in both psychotherapy and meditation."[64]

Indeed such a meditative non-focused state is close to the "evenly hovering attention" which was the state recommended for analysts by Freud. It is a state commonly recommended, though differently described by many different schools of psychotherapy.[65]

Similarly in an interview, a teacher of meditation speaks of his experience of teaching a meditation class for therapists from three perspectives. The first was the general human one,

> "the second was the advantage for the therapist of being in a meditative state while they conduct therapy. Such a state creates the attentional focus and emotional dispassion that is a good therapeutic milieu... The third thing I taught them was that *some* clients, but of course not all, could be guided by the therapist into a meditative state, talking about their issues and doing their therapy *within* the 'witness state'."[66]

---

64. J. Welwood, "Principles of Inner Work, Psychological and Spiritual", *JTP*, 16, 1, 1984, 71-2.
65. see M. Lefebure, *Human Experience & The Art of Counselling*, Edinburgh, T.& T. Clark, 1985, 12; and J. Welwood, "Meditation and the Unconscious, A New Perspective", *JTP*, 1.1, 1977.
66. C. Tart, "Adapting Eastern Spiritual Techniques to Western Culture, A Discussion with Shinzen Young", *JTP*, 22.2, 1990, 163.

All this emphasis on awareness and presence is of particular importance when one takes into account that as Jung wrote "the attitude of the psychotherapist is infinitely more important than the theories and methods of psychotherapy."[67] Recent research has corroborated this opinion.[68] Medard Boss also wrote

> "of the certainty that what our psychotherapy needs above all is a change in the psychotherapists. If our science of mental health is to become more effective psychotherapists will have to balance their knowledge of psychological concepts and techniques with a contemplative awareness...This will have to be an awareness that exercises itself day after day in quiet openness; it must address the inexplicable origin of all that is, of the healthy and the sick and also of all psychotherapeutic interventions. Then psychiatrists, in their own way, will be able to help people who are becoming increasingly alienated from their own roots."[69]

If formal meditation practice is primarily for the therapist, mindfulness is surely primary for the client. The aim of therapy is to bring awareness, and in its wake, space and choice, to the conditioned reactive responses with which we greet new experience. Such awareness allows us to experience the reality of the Buddhist models of perception.

Today Thich Nhat Hanh is perhaps the finest teacher of the benefits of mindfulness, and current interpreter of the basic practice of the Fourfold Mindfulness of breathing and body, feelings, mind and the objects of mind. Mindfulness encourages us to ground our experience in awareness rather than in accustomed forgetfulness through which we lose touch with ourselves and our environment. It serves to bring us into the present moment "the only moment we can touch life."[70] This can help to heal alienation from ourselves, our experience and our world, and can re-introduce lived meaning. He too emphasizes the transformative power of mindfulness.

> "Our mindfulness has the same function as the light of the sun. If we shine the light of full awareness steadily on our state of mind, that state of mind will transform into something better. The point of meditation is to look deeply into things in order to be able to see their nature. The nature of things is interdependent origination, the true source of everything that

---

67. C.G. Jung, "Psychotherapists or the Clergy" in *Collected Works.* Vol. 11: *Psychology and Religion East and West,* tr., R.F.C. Hull, London, Routledge, 1958, 346.
68. See R. Russell, *Report on Effective Therapy and Legislative Testimony,* New York, RR Latin Associates, 1981; and George Mora, *Recent American Psychiatric Developments,* in American Handbook of Psychiatry, New York, Basic Books, 1960.
69. M. Boss, "Eastern Wisdom and Western Therapy", in J. Welwood, ed., *The Meeting of the Ways,* New York, Schocken, 1978, 191.
70. Thich Nhat Hanh, *Transformation and Healing,* Berkeley, Parallax Press, 1990, 40.

is. If we look into our anger, we can see its roots, such as misunderstanding (and ignorance), clumsiness (or lack or skill), the surrounding society, hidden resentment, habit (or our conditioning). These roots can be present both in ourselves and in the person who played the principal role in allowing the anger to arise. We observe mindfully in order to be able to see and to understand. Seeing and understanding are the elements of iiberation which allow us to be free of the suffering which always acompanies anger. Seeing and understanding bring about love and compassion. ... our anger is a field of energy. Thanks to our mindful observation and insight into its roots, we can change this energy into the energy of love and compassion a constructive and healing energy."[71]

For the purposes of this paper the meditation spoken of in this passage would be instantiated in the transaction between therapist and client.

A comparable approach in Western terms is that of Eugene Gendlin who contends that practising mindfulness can open us up to non-ego experience that is not purely unconscious, and occurs in awareness, but of which, without practice, we remain unaware. He refers to this as "intricacy" or "felt sense"[72] and it is the object of his technique of "Focusing." Not only does "focusing", awareness of experiential intricacy, help us to extend openness and retrieve experience for consciousness, but in so doing it can actually change us. It is another example of embodied enactive experience.

So a therapist will first foster mindfulness and awareness, which allows emotions, feeling and thoughts to arise into consciousness, bringing the client into touch with their inner life, offering therapy as joint practice, a meditation shared with the therapist as guide and protector, to explore in a protected space issues which might be overwhelming if faced alone, or in an unprotected space.

GOAL

I should like to suggest that the goals of Buddhism and psychotherapy are similar in quality though very different in quantity. The quality in question is that of liberation through clear perception and experience, liberation from constriction, grasping and ignorance. In the case of Buddhism it is an unconditional liberation from *saṃsāra* itself and all its ills; in therapy the goal is far less. It is a more or less conditional freedom, ranging from liberation from specific ills which cause particular suffering, to an open-ended attempt to push back the limitations of our potential.

---

71. *ibid.*, 86.
72. E. Gendlin, *Focusing*, New York, Bantam Books, 1978, 251; and "A Philosophical Critique of Narcissism", in D.M. Levin, ed., *Pathologies of the Modern Self*, New York University Press, 1987, throughout.

The incumbent Dalai Lama has been the most consistent advocate for the use and possibilities of Buddhist mind training in lesser contexts than that of the Buddhist path. In his address to the Oxford Union in 1991 he said:

> "Just as I believe it myself I often mention to others that it is possible for people to adopt various Buddhist meditative techniques or mental trainings without being a Buddhist. After all, adoption of a specific religion is the business of the individual whereas the techniques of training the mind can remain universally applicable."[73]

Elsewhere he has said of mind training: "The primary aim...is the attainment of enlightenment, but it is possible to experience even mundane benefits, such as good health by practising them." He states two reasons for the importance of understanding the nature of mind: "firstly for its intimate connection with *karma*; the other is that our state of mind plays a crucial role in our experience of happiness and suffering."[74]

Having stated that I advocate the claim that the goals of psychotherapy and Buddhism to be compatible, perhaps it is appropriate here to address briefly the topic which is often taken to show their crucial differences in both approach and end—the self. How can psychotherapy which is believed to be a work of strengthening and propping up the ego be compatible with a philosophy that declares as a major tenet the non-existence of the ego? As with emptiness, I suggest that such apparent contradictions melt in the light of a true understanding, and definition of terms, of non-self. The Buddha displayed a pragmatic ego, a distinct personality, operating conventionally within the *saṃsāric* world. This is necessary and acceptable. What is to be abandoned is the belief in this conventional and functional ego as being intrinsic, partless or permanent, and the egocentric self-cherishing that results from such a view.

Jack Engler, an American psychologist and *vipassanā* meditation teacher has written most convincingly on this subject :

> "Though they value ego-development differently, both Buddhist psychology and psycho-analytic object relations theory *define the essence of the ego in a similar way* as a process of synthesis and adaptation between the inner life and outer reality which provides a sense of personal continuity and sameness in the felt experience of being a 'self', a feeling of being and ongoingness in existence ...In both psychologies then, the sense of 'I', of personal unity and continuity ...is conceived as something which is not innate in personality, not inherent in our psychological or spiritual makeup, but as *evolving developmentally out of*

---

73. H.H. The Dalai Lama, "Tibet's Contribution to the Future", Oxford Union Address, 2/12/1991, London, Office of Tibet.
74. H.H. The Dalai Lama, in D. Goleman, R. Thurman, eds., *op. cit.*, 16.

> *our experience of objects and the kinds of interactions we have with them*....In fact, the self is viewed in both psychologies as a representation which is *actually being constructed anew from moment to moment.*"[75]

The developmental task is to acquire a coherent functioning sense of self, and then to see through the illusion or construct. In fact "you have to be somebody before you can be nobody",[76]and the issue is not, self or no-self but self *and* no-self. There are dangers here too from a Western psychological perspective. Ken Wilber has delineated what he calls the pre/trans fallacy, the danger of mistaking an early state of undeveloped and undifferentiated ego, with a later state of transcended or 'seen-through-ego'. There are many cases of those with borderline personality problems or problems of ego-stability being drawn to meditative experience, which is unhelpful to their prior need to strengthen their conventional ego boundaries. John Welwood has called this the problem of "spiritual bypassing" However, through all of this a clear distinction between ego as functioning sense of self, and ego-clinging or self-cherishing must be maintained. Interestingly, from the Western approach it is only Jacques Lacan who underlines the negative aspects of ego.

CONCLUSION

Bearing in mind the above discussion are there any constructive suggestions we can make about a Buddhist-inspired psychotherapy? I suggest there are. The first thing is that the Buddhist philosophy of dependent origination and emptiness allows for a way of being that without relying on any hypostatized transcendent outside our experience, can yet provide meaning and value in a groundless, impermanent world. In 1960 Abraham Maslow, the founding father of both Humanistic and Transpersonal Psychologies, wrote that what our fast-changing world needed was a new type of human being, that he called

> "'Heraclitian'—people who don't need to staticize the world, who don't need to freeze it and to make it stable...who are able confidently to face tomorrow not knowing what's going to come,...with confidence enough in ourselves that we will be able to improvise in that situation which has never existed before."[77]

Jeremy Hayward points out that only such

> "a profound examination of the dynamic creative perceptual process, by which worlds and selves are made and re-made every moment, will provide the clarity and confidence *within* uncertainty that is needed".[78]

---

75. J. Engler, "Therapeutic Aims in Psychotherapy and Meditation Developmental Stages in the Representation of the Self", *JTP*, 16.1, 1984, 28.
76. *ibid.*, 51.
77. A. Maslow, *The Farther Reaches of Human Nature*, London, Pelican, 1973, 61.
78. J. Hayward, *op. cit.*, 2.

This examination will not give us certainty or permanent foundation, that is not the point, but a balance that will allow us to ride the wave.

> "We must turn the conversation from talk of resolution...to discussion of an insight or attention—a refined purified love of *this world* that never ceases to illuminate, destablize and simultaneously affirm differences which are themselves supported by other, suppressed forms of illusory differences."[79]

The Buddhist view allows us to go beyond a limited version of self, soul, ego and even no-self. It is an open-ended search, a non-clinging to any ultimately deceptive and empty structure. Each new model may be more or less meaningful, more or less useful, but in time will be outgrown and transcended. Only a belief in the ultimate emptiness of all models allows for continuing growth and a paradoxical kind of balance in a world or impermanence and change.

Thus a Buddhist psychotherapy will be primarily open-ended exploration, without specific expectations and goals, attempting and daring to work with whatever comes up within a field of unknowing. The role of the therapist is to hold open this space of unknowing, this emptiness for the client, and to stay with and in it with her.

Secondly, Buddhist therapy is based on a profound belief in 'basic sanity' of each person, in the clear light mind or Buddha nature, unhindered by the adventitious veils and obstructions imposed upon it. Expression of this basic sanity are the four immeasurable states of friendliness, compassion, joy and equanimity. In turn both of the above characteristics will lead to a different way of being with the client, a 'joint practice' in which there is no highly defined power structure, or rigid parameters of theory, and, if the therapist has done her own work successfully, little therapist contamination. At the same time the relationship is seen as being of central importance to the healing process, and should be warm and nurturing though not collusive.

Thirdly, Buddhist therapy is based on perception and awareness practices of mindfulness and meditation, and from this basis I would suggest that a Buddhist psychotherapy may well be less cathartic than some others, a middle way between repression and continual expression—

> "rather than suppressing emotions or induging in them, here it is important to view them, and your thoughts, and whatever arises, with an acceptance and generosity that are as open and spacious as possible."[80]

---

79. C.W.Huntingdon, *op. cit.*, 142.
80. Sogyal Rinpoche, *The Tibetan Book of Living and Dying*, London, Rider, 1992, 61.

Thich Nhat Hanh too believes that over-expression of negative emotions will only water the *karmic* seeds for a similar future. He places great emphasis, as does the Dalai Lama on the cultivation of healthy mind states of appreciation and joy in the daily events of life mindfully engaged in for their own sake, rather than unremitting concern with the suffering of the past.

Fourthly, the path of mindulness and meditation will underline the fact that there is no ultimate undivided self or world apart from our experience, and that healing and value both lie in the present, in being as open as possible to our embodied experience in a way that is clear, without defence or hindrances of grasping either in the positive form of desire, or its negative form of aversion and fear. This is the arena of the Buddhist psychotherapist; what is going on in the very present moment of therapeutic encounter. For in being entirely present in the present moment, value unfolds, and meaning is created. They will never be present elsewhere.

Finally, one last possibility. As Buddhism changed in each new country and culture, I question whether it is not from the psychological field that Buddhism will take its Western form. Certainly there might seem to have been more fruitful meetings between Buddhism and the sciences of mind than with philosophy or religion. From the early days of popular Buddhist diffusion in the West there has been conversation between Buddhism and psychologists, particularly since the spread of Tibetan knowledge after 1959, and in the recent discussions with the Dalai Lama already mentioned. In one of these he stated recently:

> "There are two general areas for which dialogue or cross-communication between Buddhism and psychology could be very valuable. One is the investigation of the nature of mind itself, of the thought processes, conceptualization—simply straight investigation into the nature of mind. The second one is investigation of the nature of mind specifically in relation to therapeutic purposes, dealing with people who are subject to some mental imbalance or dysfunction—how to bring them to better health."

The main purpose or objective of Buddhist theory and practice of psychology is to utterly dispel the mental distortions, or *kleśas*, most importantly, attachment or anger. Mental imbalance, dysfunction, and so forth arise principally as a result of the mental distortions of attachment and/or anger. So, while on the one hand the major project in Buddhism is to utterly eradicate the *kleśas*, "there is a kind of secondary therapeutic side project. I feel that a lot from Buddhism could be of use in therapy."[81]

81. J. Hayward, F. Varela, eds., *op. cit.*, 115.

Perhaps this mutual interest of psychology and Buddhism comes about because "If one allows that philosophy's concern is with being, one must also recognise that the concern of psychoanalysis is with lack-of-being"[82] which might bring us back to *sūnyatā* and dependent origination.

82. M. Sarup, *Jacques Lacan*, London, Harvester Press, 1992, 43.

Bibliography

Becchetti, C., *Le mystère dans les lettres*, Éditions des Cahiers de France, Bangkok, 1991.

Adikaram, E.W., *Early History of Buddhism in Ceylon*, Colombo, 1946.

Aguilar, H., *The Sacrifice in the Ṛgveda (Doctrinal Aspects)*, Delhi, 1976.

Altieri, C., *Enlarging the Temple: New Directions in American Poetry during the 1960*s, Lewisburg, Bucknell University Press, 1979.

Altizer, T.J.J., "The Buddhist Ground of the Whiteheadian God", *Process Studies*, 5.4, 1975, 227-236.

Ankar, P. & P. O. Leijon, *Chinese Sculpture and Painting in General J. W. N. Munthe's Collection in the West Norway Museum of Applied Art*, Bergen, 1980.

Anonymous [Samanera Bodhesako], ed., *Clearing the Path: Writings of Nanavira Thera (1960-1965)*, Colombo, Path Press, 1987.

Aung, S.Z. & C.A.F. Rhys Davids, trs., *Points of Controversy or Subjects of Discourse, Being a Translation of the Kathāvatthu from the Abhidhamma-Piṭaka*, London, 1915.

Banerjee, A.C., *Sarvāstvāda Literature*, Calcutta, 1979.

Bapat, P. & A. Hirakawa, trs., *Shan-Chien-P'i-P'o-Sha, A Chinese Version by Saṅghabhadra of Samantapāsādikā*, Poona, Bhandarkar Oriental Research Institute, 1970.

Barratt, D.B., ed., *World Christian Encyclopedia: A Comparative Survey of Churches and Religions in the Modern World AD 1900-2000*, Nairobi, OUP, 1982.

Basham, J.A.L., *The Wonder That Was India*, 3rd, rev. ed., London, Sidgwick & Jackson, 1967.

Beal, S., *The Romantic Legend of Sâkya Buddha*, London, Trübner & Co., 1875.

Becchetti, C., "Une ancienne tradition de manuscrits au Cambodge," in *Recherches nouvelles sur le Cambodge*, ed. by F Bizot, EFEO, Paris, 1994, 47-62.

Bernon, O de & F. Bizot, *Le Rāmaker du vieux Chak*, Textes bouddhiques du Cambodge, 3, EFEO, Paris, 1995.

Beurdeley, C.M., *Guiseppe Castiglione, A Jesuit Painter at the Court of the Chinese Emperors*, London, 1972.

Beyer, S., *The Cult of Tārā. Magic and Ritual in Tibet,* Berkeley, Los Angeles & London, University of California Press, 1978.

Bhagvat, D., *Early Buddhist Jurisprudence,* Poona, Oriental Book Agency, 1939.

Bhattacharji, S., *The Indian Theogony, A Comparative Study of Indian Mythology from the Vedas to the Purāṇas,* Cambridge, 1970.

Bhavana-kosolthera, Venerable Pra, (Veera Ganuttamo), *Basic Meditation Practice by Vijja Dhammakaya Approach*, Bangkok, 1984.

Birch, C. & J. B. Cobb, Jr., *The Liberation of Life: From the Cell to the Community*, Cambridge, CUP, 1981.

Bizot, F. & O von Hinüber, *La guirlande de Joyaux*, Textes bouddhiques du Cambodge, 2, Paris, 1994.

Bizot, F., "La consécration des statues et le culte des morts," in *Recherches nouvelles sur le Cambodge*, ed. by F Bizot, Paris, 1994, 101–39.

Bizot, F., "La Grotte de la Naissance, Recherches sur le bouddhisme khmer, II," *BEFEO* , LXVII, 1980, 221–273.

Bizot, F., "Notes sur les *yantra* bouddhiques d'Indochine," in *Tantric and Taoist Studies in honour of R.A. Stein*, ed. by Michel Strickmann, Institut Belge des Hautes Etudes Chinoises, Vol. I, Brussels, 1981, 155–191.

Bizot, F., *Le bouddhisme des Thaïs*, Éditions des Cahiers de France, Bangkok, 1993.

Bizot, F., *Le Chemin de Laṅkā*, Textes bouddhiques du Cambodge, Paris, 1992.

Bizot, F., *Le Don de Soi-même. Recherches sur le bouddhisme khmer III*, PEFEO, Vol. CXXX, Paris, 1981.

Bizot, F., *Le Figuier à Cinq Branches, Recherche sur le bouddhisme khmer*, PEFEO, Vol. CVII, Paris, 1976.

Bizot, F., *Les traditions de la pabbajjā en Asie du Sud-Est, Recherches sur le bouddhisme khmer IV*, Abhandlungen der Akademie der

Wissenschaften in Göttingen, Philologisch-Historische Klasse, Folge 3, Nr. 169, Göttingen, Vandenhoeck und Ruprecht, 1988.

Bizot, F., *Rāmaker, L'Amour symbolique de Rām et Setā, Recherches sur le bouddhisme Khmer V*, PEFEO, Vol. CLV, Paris, 1989.

Bond, G.D., *The Buddhist Revival in Sri Lanka, Religious Tradition, Reinterpretation and Response*, Studies in Comparative Religion, ed. by F.M. Denny, Columbia, University of South Carolina Press, 1988.

Boss, M., "Eastern Wisdom and Western Therapy", in J. Welwood, ed., *The Meeting of the Ways*, New York, Schocken, 1978.

Boss, M., *The Existential Foundations of Medicine and Psychiatry*, New York, Jason Aronson, 1980.

Boyce, M., *A History of Zoroastrianism*, Leiden & Koln, 1975.

Boyers, R., "A Mixed Bag", *PR*, 36, 1969.

Bronkhorst, J., *The Two Traditions of Meditation in Ancient India*, Stuttgart, F. Steiner Verlag Wiesbaden, 1986.

Bruner, J., *Acts of Meaning*, Cambridge, Mass., Harvard University Press, 1990.

Bruner, J., *In Search of Mind*, New York, Harper & Row, 1983.

Buddhadāsa, Bhikkhu, *Toward the Truth*, ed. by D.K. Swearer, Philadelphia, The Westminster Press, 1971.

Buswell, R.E, ed., *Chinese Buddhist Apocrypha*, Honolulu, University of Hawaii Press, 1990.

Buswell, R.E. "The Path to Perdition: The Wholesome Roots and Their Eradication," in R.E. Buswell & R.M. Gimello, eds., *Paths to Liberation, The Mārga and Its Transformations in Buddhist Thought*, Honolulu, University of Hawaii Press, 1992, 107–34.

Buswell, R.E. & R.M. Gimello, eds., *Paths to Liberation: The Mārga and Its Transformations in Buddhist Thought*, Honolulu, University of Hawaii Press, 1992.

Byles, M., *Journey into Burmese Silence*, London, Allen & Unwin, 1962.

Caillat, C., *Atonements in the Ancient Rituals of the Jaina Monks*, Ahmedabad, LD Institute of Indology, 1975.

Campbell, J., *The Flight of the Wild Gander*, New York, Harper, 1990.

Carrithers, M.B., *The Forest Monks of Sri Lanka: An Anthropological and Historical Study*, Delhi, OUP (India), 1983.

Cattālayo, Phra Wai, *Brightness of Dhamma*, Bangkok, Mr Chuan Sornsongkram, 1986.

Chandra, Lokesh, "Oḍḍiyāna: A New Interpretation", in M. Aris and A.S.S. Kyi, eds., *Tibetan Studies in Honour of Hugh Richardson*, Warminster, Aris & Phillips, 1980.

Chapin, H., *A Long Roll of Buddhist Images*, revised by Alexander C. Soper, Ascona, 1972.

Chattopadyaya, D., ed. & tr., *Tāranātha's History of Buddhism in India*, Calcutta, 1980.

Ching, H., tr., *Sutra of the Past Vows of the Earth Store Bodhisattva*, New York, 1974.

Christiensen, A., *Les types du premier homme et du premier roi dans l'histoire legendaire des Iraniens*, vols. I-II, Stockholm, 1917.

Coleman, J.E., *The Quiet Mind*, New York, Harper and Row, 1971.

Conze, E., *The Large Sutra on Perfect Wisdom, with the Divisions of the Abhisamāyālaṅkāra*, Berkeley & London, University of California Press, 1975.

Conze, Edward, *Buddhist Meditation*, London, Allen and Unwin, 1956.

Cook, F., *Hua Yen Buddhism*, University Park, Pennsylvania State University Press, 1977.

Cousins, L.S., "*Samatha-yāna* and *Vipassanā-yāna*", in G. Dhammapāla, R. Gombrich & K.R. Norman, eds., *Buddhist Studies in Honour of Hammalava Saddhātissa*, Nugegoda, Sri Lanka, 1984, 55–68.

Cousins, L.S., "The 'Five Points' and the Origins of the Buddhist Schools", in *The Buddhist Forum*, Vol. II, ed. by T. Skorupski, London, SOAS, 1991, 27–60.

Cousins, L.S., "The Stages of Christian Mysticism and Buddhist Purification: the Interior Castle of St. Teresa of Avila and the Path of Purification of Buddhaghosa", in K.Werner, ed., *The Yogi and the Mystic — Studies in Indian and Comparative Mysticism*, London, 1989, 103–120.

Cowell, E.B. *et al.*, trs., *Buddhist Mahāyāna Texts*, SBE, XLIX, Oxford, 1894.

Cox, C., "Attainment through Abandonment: The Sarvāstivādin Path of Removing Defilements," in R.E. Buswell & R.M. Gimello, *Paths to Liberation, The Mārga and Its Transformations in Buddhist Thought*, Honolulu, University of Hawaii Press, 1992, 107–34.

Crook, J., *The Evolution of Human Consciousness*, Oxford, Clarendon Press, 1980.

Dalia, A., "The 'Political Career' of the Buddhist Historian Tsan-ning", in D.W. Chappell, ed, *Buddhist and Taoist Practice in Medieval Chinese Society* Honolulu, University of Hawaii Press, 1987, 146-180.

Day, C.B., *Chinese Peasant Cults, Being a Study of Chinese Paper Gods,* Taipei, 2nd ed., 1974.

Dhirasekera, J., "The Rebels against the Codified Law in Buddhist Monastic Discipline", *BS(BK),* 1, 1970, 90-77.

Dhiravamsa, V.R., *A New Approach to Buddhism*, London, 1972.

Dhiravamsa, V.R., *Insight Meditation*, London, 2508 (Buddhist date).

Dhiravamsa, V.R., *The Dynamic Way of Meditation, The Release and Cure of Pain and Suffering through Vipassanā Meditative Techniques*, Wellingborough, Northants, Turnstone Press, 1982.

Dhiravamsa, V.R., *The Middle Path of Life, Being Talks on the Practice of Insight Meditation*, London, 1974.

Dhiravamsa, V.R., *The Real Way to Awakening*, London, The Buddhapadipa Temple, 1969.

Dhiravamsa, V.R., *The Way of Non-attachment*, Wellingborough, Northants, Turnstone Press, 1975.

Doré, F.H., *Researches into Chinese Superstitions*, Shanghai, 1911.

Dowson, J., *A Classical Dictionary of Hindu Mythology*, London, 1957.

Dumézil, G., *The Destiny of a King,* Chicago and London, 1973.

Dworkin, R., *Law's Empire,* Oxford, OUP, 1988.

Edelman, G., *Bright Air, Brilliant Fire, On the Matter of the Mind,* London, Allen Lane, 1992.

Ehara, N.R.M., Soma Thera & Kheminda Thera, *The Path of Freedom by the Arahant Upatissa*, Colombo, Dr D. Roland D. Weerasuria, 1961.

Eimer, H., "Some Results of Recent Kanjur Research", *Archiv für Zentralasiatische Geschichtsforschung, VGH Wissenschaftsverlag*, Sankt Augustin, 1983.

Eliot , T.S., *Collected Poems 1909-1963,* London, Faber & Faber, 1963.

Ellis Davidson, H.R., *Gods and Myths of Northern Europe*, Harmondsworth, 1964.

Engler, J., "Therapeutic Aims in Psychotherapy and Meditation Developmental Stages in the Representation of the Self", *JTP*, 16.1, 1984, 28.

Evans-Wentz, W.Y., *The Tibetan Book of the Dead,* Oxford, OUP, 1927.

Evola, J., tr. by H. Musson, *The Doctrine of Awakening: A Study on the Buddhist Ascesiss,* London, Luzac, 1951.

Fairservis, W.A., *The Roots of Ancient India*, London, 1971.

Fielding, H., *The Soul of a People*, London, Macmillan, 1898.

Fields, R., *How the Swans Came to the Lake: A Narrative History of Buddhism in America*, Boston & London, Shambhala, 1992, 64.

Fox, W., *Toward a Transpersonal Ecology: Developing New Foundations for Environmentalism*, Boston, Shambhala, 1990.

Franke, H., *From Tribal Chieftain to Universal Emperor and God,* Münich, Verlag der Bayerischen Akademie der Wissenschaften, 1978.

Frankl, V., *Psychotherapy & Existentialism,* London, Pelican, 1967.

Frauwallner, E., "Abhidharma-Studien III", *WZKS*, 1971, 69–121.

Frauwallner, E., *The Earliest Vinaya and the Beginnings of Buddhist Literature*, Rome, 1956.

Gabaude, L., *Une herméneutique bouddhique contemporaine de Thaïlande: Buddhadāsa Bhikkhu*, PEFEO, Vol. CL, Paris, 1988.

Gehman, H.S. & J. Kennedy, trs., *The Minor Anthologies of the Pali Canon, Pt.IV.: Vimāna-vatthu: Stories of the Mansions; Peta-vatthu: Stories of the Departed*, London, PTS, 1942.

Geiger, W., *Pāli Literature and Language,* New Delhi, Oriental Books Reprint Corporation, 1978.

Gendlin, E., *Focusing*, New York, Bantam Books, 1978.

Gethin, R.M.L., *The Buddhist Path to Awakening, A Study of the Bodhi-Pakkhiyā Dhammā*, Leiden, E.J. Brill, 1992.

Giles, H., *The Travels of Fa-hsien*, Cambridge, CUP, 1923.

Gillman, D., "Chinese Buddhist Art", *Apollo*, 122 (285), 1985, 328–331.

Goldstein, J. & J. Kornfield, *Seeking the Heart of Wisdom, The Path of Insight Meditation*, Boston & London, Shambhala, 1987.

Goldstein, Joseph, *The Experience of Insight: A Simple and Direct Guide to Buddhist Meditation*, New York, Shambhala, 1983 [1976].

Goleman, D., in D. Goleman & R. Thurman, eds., *Mind Science*, Boston, Wisdom, 1991.

Gombrich, R. & G. Obeyesekere, *Buddhism Transformed: Religious Change in Sri Lanka*, Dehli, Motilal Banarsidass, 1990.

Gombrich, R., "From Monastery to Meditation Centre: Lay Meditation in Modern Sri Lanka," in P. Denwood & T. Piatigorsky, eds., *Buddhist Studies — Ancient and Modern*, London, 1983, 20–34.

Gombrich, R., "The Buddha's Book of Genesis?", *IIJ*, 35, 1992, 159-178.

Gombrich, R., "The Significance of Former Buddhas in the Theravādin Tradition", in S. Balasooriya *et al.*, eds., in *Buddhist Studies in Honour of Walpola Rahula*, London, Gordon Press, 1980.

Gombrich, R., *Precept and Practice, Traditional Buddhism in the Rural Highlands of Ceylon*, Oxford, Clarendon Press, 1971.

Gombrich, R., *Theravāda Buddhism: A Social History from Ancient Benares to Modern Colombo*, London, Routledge & Kegan Paul, 1988.

Grice, J.W.H., "Faking and Selling Chinese Antiques", *Country Life*, July 29, 1954.

Gridley, H., *Chinese Buddhist Sculpture under the Liao, Free Standing Works in Situ and Selected Examples from Public Collections*, Ann Arbor, 1988.

Griffin, D., "Contributions to a Theology of Nature", *BR*, 20, 1972, 3-24.

Grof, S., *Beyond the Brain*, Albany, SUNY Press, 1985

Gudmunsen, C., *Wittgenstein and Buddhism*, London, Macmillan, 1977.

Guenther, H.V., *Philosophy and Psychology in the Abhidharma*, Shambhala, Berkeley, 1974.

Gunaratana, Henepola, Mahāthera, *Mindfulness in Plain English*, repr. ed., Taipei, 1991.

Hamilton-Merritt, J., *A Meditator's Diary, A Western Woman's Unique Experiences in Thailand Monasteries*, Penguin, 1979 [1976].

Hartshorne, C., "Toward a Buddhistico-Christian Religion", in K. K. Inada & N. P. Jacobson, eds., *Buddhism and American Thinkers*, Albany, SUNY Press, 1984, 2-13.

Hartshorne, C., "Whitehead's Differences from Buddhism", *PEW*, 25.4, 1975, 407-413.

Harvey, P., "'Signless' Meditations in Pāli Buddhism," *JIABS*, 9.1, 1986, 25–52.

Hayward, J. & F.J. Varela, eds., *Gentle Bridges, Conversations with the Dalai Lama on the Sciences of Mind*, Boston, Shambhala, 1992.

Hayward, J., *Shifting Worlds, Changing Minds*, Boston, Shambhala, 1987.

Hazra, O.K.L., *Pali Language and Literature*, Emerging Perceptions in Buddhist Studies, no. 5, New Delhi, D.K. Printworld, 1994.

Heidegger, M., *Poetry, Language, Thought*, tr. by A. Hofstadter, New York, Harper, 1971.

Heissig, W., *The Religions of Mongolia*, London & Henley, 1980.

Hiltebeitel, A., "Rāma and Gilgamesh: the Sacrifices of the Water Buffalo and the Bull of Heaven", *HR*, 1980, 187-223.

Hirakawa, A., *A History of Indian Buddhism*, Honolulu, 1990.

Hoang-sy-Quy, H., "Le mythe indien de l'homme cosmique dans son contexte culturel et dans son évolution", *RHR*, 175, 1969, 133-54.

Holt, J., *Discipline: The Canonical Buddhism of the Vinayapiṭaka*, Delhi, Motilal Banarsidass, 1981.

Horner, I.B., *Ten Jātaka Stories*, Bangkok, 1974.

Horner, I.B., tr., *The Book of Discipline*, 6 vols., London, PTS, 1938-1952.

Houtman, G., "Traditions of Buddhist Practice in Burma," PhD thesis, University of London, London, SOAS, 1990.

Howard, A.F., "Buddhist Sculptures of the Liao Dynasty, A Reassessment of Osvald Sirén's Study", *BMFEA*, 56, 1984, 1–95.

Hsu, I.C. Y., "Late Ch'ing Foreign Relations 1866–1905", in J.K. Fairbank & Liu Kwang-Ching, eds., *Cambridge History of China*, Vol. 11: *Late Ch'ing, 1800–1911*, Cambridge, 1980.

Huber, E., *Açvaghosa Sûtrâlamkâra*, Paris, E. Leroux, 1908.

Hunt-Badiner, A., ed., *Dharma Gaia: A Harvest of Essays in Buddhism and Ecology*, Berkeley, 1990.

Huntingdon, C.W., *The Emptiness of Emptiness*, Honolulu, University of Hawaii Press, 1989,

Hurvitz, L., "'Render unto Caesar' in Early Chinese Buddhism", *SIS*, 5.3/4, 1957, 80-114.

Hurvitz, L., "The Abhidharma on the 'Four Aids to Penetration'", in *Buddhist Thought and Asian Civilization*, (Guenther volume), ed. by L.S. Kawamura, Emeryville, Dharma Publishing, 1977.

Śāstrī, Śānti Bhikṣu, *Jñānaprasthāna-śāstra of Kātyāyanīputra Retranslated into Sanskrit from the Chinese Version of Hiuan Tsang*, Śāntiniketan, 1955.

Inada, K., tr., *Mūlamadhyamakakārikā*, Tokyo, Hokuseido Press, 1970.

Jackson, N.P., *Buddhism and the Contemporary World: Change and Self-Correction*, Carbondale, S. Illinois University Press, 1983.

Jacobson, N.P., "A Buddhist-Christian Probe of the Endangered Future", *EB*, 15, 1982, 38-55.

James, A. & J., *A Meditation Retreat*, Box, Wiltshire, Aukana Publishing, 1986.

James, A., *The Unfolding of Wisdom, The Buddha's Path to Enlightenment*, Aukana, Bradford on Avon, 1993.

James, A.J., *Modern Buddhism*, Box, Wiltshire, Aukana Publishing, 1987.

Jantrupon, Chua, *Vipassanā Bhāvanā, Theory, Practice and Result*, tr. by F. Tullius, Chonburi, Boonkanjaram Meditation Centre, 1988.

Jayatilaka, D.B., ed., *Saddharmaratnāvaliya*, Columbo, Svadesha Mitraya Press, 1930.

Jettmar, K., *The Religions of the Hindukush*, Vol.I: *The Religion of the Kafirs*, New Delhi, Bombay & Calcutta, 1986.

Johnson, M., *The Body in the Mind*, Chicago, University of Chicago Press, 1987.

Jung, C.G., *Collected Works*, Vol. 11: *Psychology and Religion East and West*, tr. by R.F.C. Hull, London, Routledge, 334

Kákosy, L., *Egyiptomi és antik csillaghit*, Budapest, 1978.

Kalupahana, D.J., *A History of Buddhist Philosophy*, Honolulu, University of Hawaii Press, 1992.

Karunadasa, Y., *Buddhist Analysis of Matter*, Columbo, Department of Cultural Affairs, 1967.

Keown, D., *The Nature of Buddhist Ethics*, London, Macmillan, 1992.

Kern, H. 1884: *The Saddharma-puṇḍarika, or the Lotus of the True Law*, SBE, XXI, Oxford, 1965.

Khantipalo, Bhikkhu, *Calm and Insight, A Buddhist Manual for Meditators*, London, Curzon Press, 1981.

Kheminda, Thera, *Path, Fruit and Nibbāna*, Colombo, 1965.

King, M., "The Truth about Autopoiesis", *JLS*, 20, 1993, 218-236.

King, W.L., *A Thousand Lives Away*, Cambridge, Mass., Harvard University Press, 1965.

King, W.L., *Theravāda Meditation: The Buddhist Transformation of Yoga*, University Park & London, The Pennsylvania State University Press, 1980.

Kornfield, J., *Living Buddhist Masters*, Santa Cruz, Unity Press, 1977.

Lakoff, G. & M. Johnson, *Metaphors We Live By*, Chicago, Chicago University Press, 1980.

Lamotte, E., *History of Indian Buddhism, From the Origins to the Śaka Era*, tr. by S. Webb-Boin, Louvain, Institut Orientaliste, 1988.

La Vallée Poussin, Louis de, *Abhidharmakośabhāṣyam*, tr. by L. Pruden, Berkeley, Asian Humanities Press, 1988–1990.

Leach, E.R., *Pul Eliya: A Village in Ceylon*, Cambridge, CUP, 1971.

Leca, A-P., *The Cult of the Immortal: Mummies and the Ancient Way of Death*, London & Toronto, 1980.

Lefebure, M., *Human Experience & The Art of Counselling*, Edinburgh, T. & T. Clark, 1985.

Legge, J., *A Record of Buddhistic Kingdoms*, New York, Dover Publications, 1965.

Lessing, F.D., "The Topographical Identification of Peking with Yamāntaka", *CAJ*, 2, 1956.

Lessing, F.D., *Ritual and Symbol: Collected Essays on Lamaism and Chinese Symbolism*, Asian Folklore and Social Life Monographs, 91, Taipei, 1976.

Lessing, F.D., *Yung-ho-kung: An Iconography of the Lamaist Cathedral in Peking*, Stockholm, 1942.

Lincoln, B., *Priests, Warriors and Cattle: A Study in the Ecology of Religions*, Berkeley & London, University of California Press, 1981.

Lindtner, C., *Nagarjuniana*, Delhi, Motilal Banarsidass, 1987.

Lopez, D., ed., *Buddhism in Practice*, Princeton, Princeton University Press, 1995.

Lõrincz, L., ed., *Molon Toyin's Journey into the Hell*, Altan Gerel's Translation, Monumenta Linguae Mongolicae Collecta, VIII, Budapest, 1982.

Loy, D., "Avoiding the Void: The Lack of Self in Psychotherapy and Buddhism", *JTP*, 24, 2, 1992.

Loy, D., "The Nonduality of Life & Death, A Buddhist View of Repression", in *PEW*, 40.2, 1990.

Luk, C., tr., *The Śūraṅgama Sūtra*, London, 1966.

Lyotard, J.F., *The Postmodern Condition*, tr. by G. Bennington & B. Massumi, Manchester, Manchester University Press, 1984.

Macy, J., "The Greening of the Self", in A. Hunt-Badiner, ed., *Dharma Gaia: A Harvest of Eddays in Buddhism and Ecology*, Berkeley, Parallax, 1990, 53-63.

Macy, J., *Dharma and Development: Religion as a Resource in the Sarvodaya Self-Help Movement*, West Hartford, Conn., Kumarian Press, 1983.

Macy, J., *Mutual Causality in Buddhism and General Systems Theory: The Dharma of Natural Systems*, Albany, SUNY Press, 1991.

Magee, B., ed., *Men of Ideas*, London, BBC, 1978.

Magness, T., *Sammā Samādhi (Part Two) , Being an Exposition of Attainments Derived from Samatha-vipassanā*, Bangkok, c. 1961.

Magness, T., *Sammā Samādhi, Being an Exposition of the Method of Samatha-vipassanā as Discovered and Attained by all Buddhas*, Bangkok, c. 1960.

Magness, T., *The Life and Teachings of the Ven. Chao Khun Mongkol-thepmuni*, Bangkok, c. 1970.

Mahāsi, Sayadaw, *Satipaṭṭhāna Vipassanā*, Bangkok, 1975.

Mahāsi, Sayadaw, *The Progress of Insight*, Kandy, 1965.

Maquet, J., "Expressive Space and Theravada Values: A Meditation Monastery in Sri Lanka," *Ethos* , 3.1, 1975, 1–23.

Maquet, J., "Meditation in Contemporary Sri Lanka: Idea and Practice," *JTP*, 7.2, 1975, 182–96.

Marasinghe, G., *Gods in Early Buddhism*, Kelaniya, 1974.

Mascaró, J., *The Upanishads*, Harmondsworth, 1965.

Maslow, A., *The Farther Reaches of Human Nature*, London, Pelican, 1973.

Maslow, A., *Towards a Psychology of Being*, Princetown, Van Nostrand, 1962.

Matsunaga, A., *The Buddhist Philosophy of Assimilation*, Tokyo, 1969.

Maugham, R., *Search for Nirvana,* London, W.H. Allen, 1975.

Meisig, K., *Das Sûtra von der vier Ständen: Das Aggañña-Sutta im Licht sein chinesischen Parallelen,* Wiesbaden, Otto Harrassowitz, 1988.

Mendelson, E., *Sangha and State in Burma*, ed. by J. Ferguson, Ithaca, Cornell University Press, 1975.

Mettānando, Bhikkhu, "The Dhammakāya Movement — An Aspect from Within," in *IABS Tenth International Conference in Paris*, ed. by Ananda W.P. Guruge, The Permanent Delegation of Sri Lanka to Unesco, 1991.

Mookerji, R., *Men and Thought in Ancient India*, London, Macmillan, 1924.

Naess, A., *Freedom, Emotion and Self-Subsistence: The Structure of a Central Part of Spinoza's Ethics*, Oslo, University of Oslo Press, 1975.

Namto, A.S.S., *Moment to Moment Mindfulness, A Pictorial Manual for Meditators*, ed. by Martha Dharmapali, Fawnskin, California, Vipassana Dhura Meditation Society, 1989.

Nanamoli, Bhikku, *The Life of the Buddha*, Kandy, Buddhist Publications Society, 1978.

Nanavira, Thera, *The Tragic, the Comic and the Personal,* The Wheel Publication, No. 339-341, Kandy, Buddhist Publication Society, 1987.

Narada, Ven., *The Mirror of the Dhamma,* Singapore, Singapore Buddhist Meditation Centre, 1991.

Narāsabho, Phra Mahā Singhathon, *Buddhism: A Guide to a Happy Life*, Bangkok, Mahachulalongkorn Buddhist University, 1971.

Nash, R., *Wilderness and the American Mind*, New Haven, Yale University Press, 1982.

Nebesky-Wojkowitz, R., *Oracles and Demons of Tibet*, Graz, Akademische Druk-u. Verlagsanstalt, 1975.

Neville, R.C., "Buddhism and Process Philosophy", in K. K. Inada & N. P. Jacobson, eds., *Buddhism and American Thinkers*, Albany, SUNY Press, 1984, 121-142.

Nhat Han, Thich, *The Miracle of Mindfulness, A Manual on Meditation*, tr. by Mobi Ho, Boston, Beacon Press, 1987.

Nhat Han, Thich, *The Sun my Heart: From Mindfulness to Insight Contemplation*, Berkeley, Parallax Press, c. 1988.

Nhat Han, Thich, *Transformation and Healing*, Berkeley, Parallax Press, 1990.

Nishitani, K., *Religion and Nothingness*, tr. by J. van Bragt, Berkeley, University of California Press, 1982.

Norman, K.R., "Pāli Language and Scriptures", in *The Buddhist Heritage*, ed. by T. Skorupski, Tring, Institute of Buddhist Studies, 1989.

Norman, K.R., *Collected Papers,* 4 vols., Oxford, PTS, 1992.

Norman, K.R., *Pāli Literature,*Wiesbaden, Otto Harrassowitz, 1983.

Nyanaponika, Thera, *The Heart of Buddhist Meditation*, London, Rider, 1962 [1953].

O'Flaherty, W.D., *Hindu Myths, A Sourcebook Translated from the Sanskrit*, Harmondsworth, 1975.

O'Rahilly, C., ed & tr., *Táin Bó Cúalnge from the Book of Leinster,* Dublin, 1967.

Obeyesekere, G., *Land Tenure in Village Ceylon*, Cambridge, CUP, 1967.

Odin, S., "A Metaphysics of Cumulative Penetration: Process Theory and Hua Yen Buddhism", *PS,* 11.2, 1981, 65-82.

Olds, L.E., *Metaphors of Relatedness*, Albany, SUNY Press, 1992.

Olerud, A., *L'idée de macrocosmos et de microcosmos dans le Timée de Platon*, Uppsala, 1951.

Olschak, B.C. & T. Wangyal, *Mystic Art of Ancient Tibet,* London, George Allen & Unwin Ltd., 1973.

Pagels, E., *The Origin of Satan*, New York, Random House, 1995.

Parpola, A., "The Sky-Garment, A Study of the Harappan Religion and its Relation to the Mesopotamian and Later Indian Religions", *SO,* 57, Helsinki, 1985.

Piatigorsky, A., *The Buddhist Philosophy of Thought: Essays in Interpretation*, London & Dublin, 1984.

Pieris, R., *Sinhalese Social Organization: The Kandyan Period*, Columbo, Ceylon University Press, 1956.

Powell, R.L., *The Rise of Chinese Military Power 1895–1912*, Princeton, 1955.

Randall, R., *Life as a Siamese Monk*, Bradford on Avon, Aukana Publishing, 1990.

Rhie, M.M., *The Fo-kuang ssu, Literary Evidences and Buddhist Images*, New York & London, 1977.

Rinchen, *Les matériaux pour l'étude du chamanisme mongol I: Sources littéraires*, Asiatische Forschungen, Bd. 3, Wiesbaden, 1959.

Robertson, G.S., *The Kafirs of the Hindu-Kush,* London, 1896.

Robinson, R., *Early Mādhyamika in India and China,* Madison, Wisconsin, Wisconsin University Press, 1968.

Rorty, R., *Philosophy and the Mirror of Nature*, Oxford, B.H. Blackwell, 1980.

Ruegg, D. Seyfort, *Buddha-nature, Mind and the Problem of Gradualism in a Comparative Perspective, On the Transmission and Reception of Buddhism in India and Tibet*, Jordan Lectures in Comparative Religion XIII, London, SOAS, 1989.

Ruegg, D. Seyfort, *The Life of Bu-sTon Rin-po-che*, Rome Oriental Series, 34, Rome, 1966.

Russell, R., *Report on Effective Therapy and Legislative Testimony*, New York, RR Latin Associates, 1981.

Saddhātissa, H., *The Buddha's Way*, London & New York, Allen & Unwin, 1971/1972.

Sakaki, R., *Mahāvyutpatti*, Tokyo, Kokusho Kankōkai, 1925.

Sangharakshita, Bhikkhu, *The Eternal Legacy*, London, Tharpa Publications, 1985.

Sarathchandra, E.R., *The Sinhalese Folk Play and the Modern Stage*, Columbo, The Ceylon University Press Board, 1983.

Sarup, M., *Jacques Lacan*, London, Harvester Press, 1992.

Schayer, S., "A Note on the Old Russian Variant of the Purushasukta", *AO*, 7, 1935, 319-23.

Schmithausen, L., *Buddhism and Nature: The Lecture Delivered on the Occasion of the EXPO 1990*, An Enlarged Version with Notes, Studia Philologica Buddhica, Occasional Paper Series, VII, Tokyo, The International Institute for Buddhist Studies, 1991.

Schneider, U., "Yama und Yamī (ṚV X 10)", *IIJ*, 10, 1967, 1-32.

Schopen, G., "Death, Funerals and the Division of Property in the *Mūlasarvāstivāda Vinaya*", in D. Lopez, ed., *Buddhism in Practice*, Princeton, Princeton University Press, 1995.

Searle, J., *The Rediscovery of Mind*, Cambridge, Mass, M.I.T., 1992.

Selvanayagam, I., "Asoka and Arjuna as Counterfigures on the Field of Dharma", *HR*, 32, 1992, 59-75.

Shattock, E.H, *An Experiment in Mindfulness*, London, Rider, 1970 [1958].

Sickman, L. & A. Soper, *The Art and Architecture of China*, Harmondsworth, 1971.

Sirén, O., "Chinese Sculptures of the Sung, Liao and Chin Dynasties", *BMFEA*, 14, 1942, 45-64.

Sirén, O., *Chinese Sculpture from the Fifth to the Fourteenth Century*, 4 vols, London, 1925.

Skilling, P., "Theravādin Literature in Tibetan Translation", *JPTS*, 19, 1993, 69 183.

Skorupski, T., ed. & tr., *The Sarvadurgatīpariśodhana-tantra*, Delhi, Motilal Banarsidass, 1983.

Snellgrove, D.L., ed. & tr., *The Hevajra Tantra: A Critical Study*, Parts I & II, London Oriental Series, 6, London, OUP, 1959.

Snyder, G., "Buddhism and the Possibilities of a Planetary Culture", in B. Devall & G. Sessions, *Deep Ecology*, Layton, Utah, Gibbs M. Smith, 1985.

Snyder, G., *The Real Work: Interviews and Talks 1964-1979*, New York, New Directions, 1980.

Sogyal Rinpoche, *The Tibetan Book of Living and Dying*, London, Rider, 1992.

Soma Thera, "Contemplation in the Dhamma," in N.R.M. Ehara, Soma Thera & Kheminda Thera, eds., *The Path of Freedom by the Arahant Upatissa*, Colombo, 1961, 353–362.

Sprung, M., "Being and the Middle Way", in M. Sprung, ed., *The Question of Being*, University Park, Pennsylvania State University Press, 1978.

Stein, R.A., *Tibetan Civilization*, Stanford, Stanford University Press, 1972.

Streng, F., *Emptiness, A Study in Religious Meaning*, Nashville, Abingdon Press, 1967.

Strong, J.S., *The Legend of King Asoka*, Princeton, Princeton University Press, 1983.

Suzuki, D.T., *On Indian Mahayana Buddhism*; ed. by E. Conze, New York, Harper & Row, 1968.

Swearer, D.K., *Secrets of the Lotus, An Introduction to Buddhist Meditation, Contemporary Classical Interpretations of the Zen and Theravāda Traditions*, New York & London, Macmillan, 1971.

Tambiah, S.J., *The Buddhist Saints of the Forest and the Cult of Amulets, A Study in Charisma, Hagiography, Sectarianism and Millennial Buddhism*, Cambridge Studies in Social Anthropology 49, Cambridge, CUP, 1984.

Tambiah, S.J., *World Conqueror and World Renouncer, A Study of Buddhism and Polity in Thailand against a Historical Background*, Cambridge Studies in Social Anthropology 15. Cambridge, CUP, 1976.

Tao, J.S., *The Jurchen in Twelfth-Century China, a Study of Sinicisation*, Seattle & London, 1976.

Tart, C., "Adapting Eastern Spiritual Techniques to Western Culture, A Discussion with Shinzen Young", *JTP*, 22.2, 1990.

Taylor, C., *Sources of the Self, The Making of the Modern Identity*, Cambridge, Mass, Harvard University Press, 1989.

Taylor, C., *Sources of the Self, The Making of the Modern Identity*, Cambridge, Mass, Harvard University Press, 1989.

Taylor, J.L., *Forest Monks and the Nation-State, An Anthropological and Historical Study in Northeastern Thailand*, Singapore, Institute of Southeast Asian Studies, 1993.

Thomas, E.J., *History of Buddhist Thought*, London, Kegan Paul, 1933.

Thomas, E.J., *The Life of Buddha*, London, Routledge & Kegan Paul, 1975 [1927].

Thompson, H.C., *China and the Powers, A Narrative of the Outbreak of 1900*, London, 1902.

Thompson, W.I., "Pacific Shift", in J.B. Callicott & R.T. Ames, eds., *Nature in Asian Traditions of Thought: Essays in Environmental Philosophy,* Albany, SUNY Press, 1989.

Thompson, W.I., *At The Edge of History*, New York, Harper Colophon, 1971.

Thoreau, M.D., "The Preaching of the Buddha", *The Dial,* 4, Jan. 1844, 391-401.

Thurman, R., *Tsong Khapa's Speech of Gold in the Essence of the Eloquence*, Princetown, Princetown University Press, 1984

Tomomatsu, E., "Sūtrālamkāra et Kalpanāmandiṭikā", *JA,* 1931, 135-74.

Tregear, M., *Song Ceramics*, London, 1982.

Tuck, A., *Comparative Philosophy and the Philosophy of Scholarship*, New York, OUP, 1990.

Turville-Petre, E.O.G., *Myth and Religion of the North*, London, 1964.

Tweed, T.A., *The American Encounter with Buddhism 1844-1912: The Victorian Culture and the Limits of Dissent,* Bloomington, Indiana University Press, 1992.

Vajirañāṇa, Paravahera, *Buddhist Meditation in Theory and Practice, A General Exposition According to the Pāli Canon of the Theravāda School*, Colombo, M.D. Gunasena & Co. Ltd, 1962.

Van Den Broeck, J., *La Saveur de L'Immortel (A-p'i-t'an Kan Lu Wei Lun), La version chinoise de l'Amṛtarasa de Ghoṣaka (T. 1553)*, Publications de l'Institut Orientaliste de Louvain 15, Louvain-la-Neuve, Institut Orientaliste, 1977.

Varela, F.J., E. Rosch & E. Thompson, *The Embodied Mind,* Cambridge, Mass, 1991.

Varkonyi, N., *Sziriat Oszlopai,* Budapest, 1942.

Vetter, T., *The Ideas and Meditative Practices of Early Buddhism*, Leiden, E.J. Brill, 1988.

Von Gabain, A., "The Purgatory of the Buddhist Uighurs", in *Colloquies on Art and Archaeology in Asia,* 2, ed. by W. Watson, London, 1972.

Voyce, M., "The Legal Aspects of Early Buddhist *Vinaya*", PhD thesis, University of London, London, SOAS, 1982.

Walters, J., *Mind Unshaken*, London, Rider, 1961.

Washburn, M., *The Ego and the Dynamic Grand*, Albany, New York, SUNY Press, 1988.

Waterfield, R. "Baron Julius Evola and the Hermetic Tradition", *Gnosis*, 14, 1989-90.

Watson, G., S. Batchelor, & G. Claxton, eds., *The Fly & the Flybottle*, Sharpham, Devon, Sharpham Trust, 1992.

Watson, L., *The Romeo Error: A Matter of Life and Death,* Falmouth, 1976.

Wayman, A., "Studies in Yama and Māra", *IIJ,* 3, 1959, 44-73, 112-31.

Welch, H., *The Practice of Chinese Buddhism,* Cambridge, Mass., Harvard University Press, 1967.

Welwood, J., "Meditation and the Unconscious, A New Perspective", *JTP*, 1.1, 1977.

Welwood, J., "Principles of Inner Work, Psychological and Spiritual", *JTP*, 16.1, 1984.

Wetlesen, J., "Body Awareness as a Gateway to Eternity: a Note on the Mysticism of Spinoza and its Affinity to Buddhist Meditation", in S. Hessig, ed., *Speculum Spinozanum 1677-1977*, London, RKP, 1977, 479-494.

Wetlesen, J., ed., *Spinoza's Philosophy of Man: Proceedings of the Scandinavian Spinoza Symposium 1977*, Oslo, University of Oslo Press, 1978.

Wetlesen, J., *The Stage and the Way: Spinoza's Ethics of Freedom*, Assen, van Gorcum, 1973.

Wienpahl, P., *The Radical Spinoza*, New York, 1979.

Willemen, C., *The Essence of Metaphysics*, Études et Textes 4, Publication de L'Institut Belge des Hautes Études Bouddhiques, Brussels, 1975.

Windisch, W.O.E., *Māra und Buddha*, Leipzig, 1895.

Winston, D., "The Iranian Component in the Bible, Apocrypha and Qumran: A Review of the Evidence, *HR,* 5, 1966, 183-216.

Winternitz, M., *History of Indian Literature, 2* vols., New York, Russell & Russell, 1933.

Wittgenstein, L., *Philosophical Investigations,* tr. by G.E.M Anscombe, Oxford, B.H. Blackwell, 1967.

Yalman, N., *Under the Bo Tree*, Berkeley, University of California Press, 1967.

Zohar, D., *The Quantum Self,* London, Flamingo, 1991.

Zolla, E., "The Evolution of Julius Evola's Thought", *Gnosis*, 14, 1989-90.

Zürcher, E., *The Buddhist Conquest of China,* Leiden, E. J. Brill, 1959.